W9-BYY-455

DISCARDED

My Other Loneliness

Letters of Thomas Wolfe and Aline Bernstein

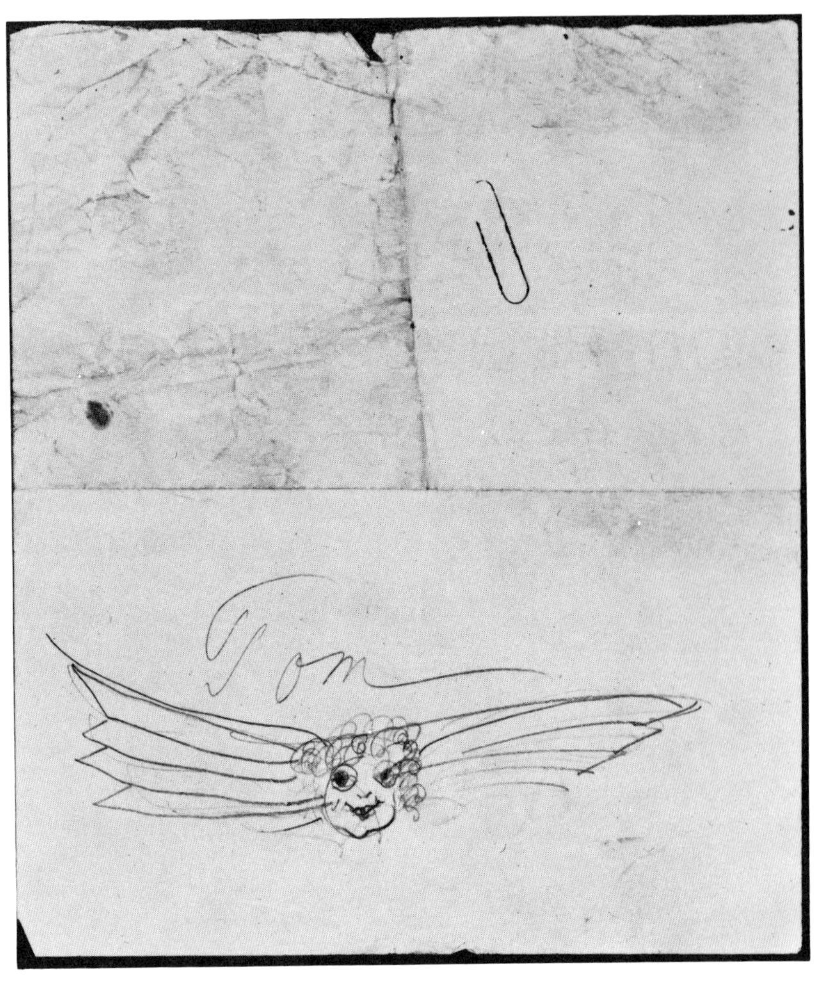

Undated drawing by Aline Bernstein
(By permission of the Houghton Library, Harvard University)

"My tender and golden love,
you were my other loneliness,
the only clasp of hand and heart that I had.
I was a stranger, alone and lost
in the wilderness, and I found you"
THOMAS WOLFE, 1928

"If you will listen, to me some day,
you will hear the voice of your friend
and your angel"
ALINE BERNSTEIN, October 1931

My Other Loneliness

Letters of Thomas Wolfe and Aline Bernstein

Edited by Suzanne Stutman

The University of North Carolina Press

Chapel Hill and London

Manufactured in the United States of America

Library of Congress Cataloging in Publication Data

Wolfe, Thomas, 1900–1938.
My other loneliness.

Bibliography: p.
Includes index.
1. Wolfe, Thomas, 1900–1938—Correspondence.
2. Bernstein, Aline, 1881–1955—Correspondence.
3. Novelists, American—20th century—Correspondence.
I. Bernstein, Aline, 1881–1955. II. Stutman, Suzanne.
III. Title.
PS3545.0337Z483 1983 813'.52 82-20102
ISBN 0-8078-1543-8
ISBN 0-8078-4117-x pbk.

To Fred,
Robert, Rhonda, and Craig

Contents

Illustrations

Chronological List of Letters

Number	Date*	Writer	Place of Composition
1.	[Fall, 1925]	A. B.	[New York City]
2.	[December, 1925]	A. B.	Westport, Conn.
3.	[December, 1925]	T. W.	Asheville, N.C.
4.	[May, 1926]	A. B.	[New York City]
5.	[June 3, 1926]	A. B.	[New York City]
6.	[June 3, 1926]	T. W.	Baltimore, Md.
7.	[June 4, 1926]	A. B.	New York City
8.	[June 4, 1926]	T. W.	Norfolk, Va.
9.	[June 5, 1926]	A. B.	New York City
10.	June 5, 1926	T. W.	Richmond, Va.
11.	[June 7, 1926]	A. B.	[New York City]
12.	[August 22, 1926]	A. B.	*S.S. Majestic*
13.	August 22, 1926	T. W.	Chelsea
14.	August 26 [1926]	T. W.	[London]
15.	September 2, 1926	A. B.	New York City
16.	September 5 [1926]	A. B.	[New York City]
17.	September 11, 1926	T. W.	Chelsea
18.	September 15, 1926	A. B.	New York City
19.	September 20 [1926]	A. B.	[New York City]
20.	September 21, 1926	T. W.	Brussels
21.	September 22, 1926	A. B.	[New York City]
22.	September 22, 1926	T. W.	Brussels
23.	September 23 [1926]	A. B.	[New York City]
24.	September 25, 1926	T. W.	Antwerp
25	[Late September, 1926]	A. B.	[New York City]
26.	September 27 [1926]	T. W.	Antwerp
27.	[October 2, 1926]	A. B.	[New York City]
28.	October 3 [1926]	A. B.	[New York City]
29.	October 6 [1926]	A. B.	[New York City]
30.	[October 9, 1926]	A. B.	Massachusetts
31.	October 10 [1926]	A. B.	[New York City]
32.	[October, 1926]	A. B.	[New York City]
33.	October 14, 1926	T. W.	London
34.	October 21 [1926]	A. B.	[New York City]
35.	October 28, 1926	T. W.	[Oxford]
36.	November 3, 1926	A. B.	[New York City]

*Brackets indicate that tentative dates and places were supplied by editor

Number	Date*	Writer	Place of Composition
37.	November 4, 1926	A. B.	[New York City]
38.	November 8 [1926]	A. B.	[New York City]
39.	November 9 [1926]	T. W.	[Oxford]
40.	[November, 1926]	T. W.	[Oxford]
41.	November 19 [1926]	A. B.	[New York City]
42.	November 22 [1926]	A. B.	[New York City]
43.	November 24 [1926]	A. B.	[New York City]
44.	December 1 [1926]	A. B.	[New York City]
45.	[December 10, 1926]	T. W.	Stuttgart
46.	[June, 1927]	A. B.	[New York City]
47.	[June 29, 1927]	A. B.	[New York City]
48.	[May, 1928]	A. B.	[New York City]
49.	June 7, 1928	T. W.	[New York City]
50.	[June 14, 1928]	A. B.	Paris
51.	[June 22, 1928]	A. B.	Rapallo
52.	[June 26, 1928]	A. B.	Rapallo
53.	[June 28, 1928]	T. W.	[New York City]
54.	[July 5, 1928]	A. B.	Karlsbad
55.	[July 17, 1928]	A. B.	Karlsbad
56.	July 19, 1928	T. W.	Paris
57.	[July 22, 1928]	A. B.	Karlsbad
58.	[July 24, 1928]	A. B.	Karlsbad
59.	[July 24, 1928]	T. W.	Paris
60.	[July 25, 1928]	T. W.	[Paris]
61.	[July 27, 1928]	T. W.	Brussels
62.	July 29, 1928	A. B.	[Munich]
63.	July 31, 1928	T. W.	Brussels
64.	August 4, 1928	A. B.	Vienna
65.	August 6 or 5, 1928	A. B.	Vienna
66.	[August 9, 1928]	T. W.	Brussels
67.	August 10, 1928	A. B.	Prague
68.	[August 11, 1928]	A. B.	Berlin
69.	August 11, 1928	T. W.	Cologne
70.	[August 12, 1928]	T. W.	Cologne
71.	August 13, 1928	A. B.	Hamburg
72.	August 14, 1928	A. B.	Shipboard
73.	August 22, 1928	A. B.	Shipboard
74.	August 27, 1928	T. W.	Wiesbaden
75.	September 7 [1928]	T. W.	Frankfurt
76.	[Early September, 1928]	A. B.	[New York City]
77.	[September 10, 1928]	T. W.	Munich
78.	[Early October, 1928]	A. B.	[New York City]

Number	Date*	Writer	Place of Composition
79.	October 4 [1928]	T. W.	Munich
80.	October 16, 1928	A. B.	[New York City]
81.	[October 18, 1928]	T. W.	Salzburg
82.	October 18, 1928	A. B.	New York City
83.	October 18, 1928	A. B.	[New York City]
84.	October 20, 1928	A. B.	New York City
85.	October 21, 1928	T. W.	Vienna
86.	October 23, 1928	T. W.	Vienna
87.	Late October, 1928	A. B.	[New York City]
88.	October 25, 1928	T. W.	Vienna
89.	October 29, 1928	T. W.	[Vienna]
90.	October 29, 1928	T. W.	[Vienna]
91.	October 30, 1928	T. W.	Vienna
92.	November 1, 1928	T. W.	[Vienna]
93.	November 8, 1928	A. B.	[New York City]
94.	November 10, 1928	T. W.	Budapest
95.	November 10, 1928	A. B.	[New York City]
96.	November 15, 1928	T. W.	Budapest
97.	November 17, 1928	T. W.	[Italy]
98.	November 17, 1928	T. W.	Vienna
99.	November 18, 1928	T. W.	[Vienna]
100.	[November 21, 1928]	A. B.	[New York City]
101.	November 22 [1928]	A. B.	[New York City]
102.	November 29, 1928	T. W.	[Vienna]
103.	July 9, 1929	T. W.	New York City
104.	August 4, 1929	T. W.	Quebec
105.	[Spring, 1930]	A. B.	Armonk [N.Y.]
106.	April 27, 1930	T. W.	New York City
107.	May 17, 1930	T. W.	*S.S. Volendam*
108.	May 20, 1930	T. W.	Paris
109.	May 23, 1930	A. B.	Armonk
110.	May 24, 1930	T. W.	Paris
111.	June 2, 1930	A. B.	Armonk
112.	June 16, 1930	A. B.	Armonk
113.	July 5, 1930	A. B.	Armonk
114.	[July, 1930]	A. B.	Armonk
115.	[July 25, 1930]	A. B.	Armonk
116.	August 12, 1930	T. W.	Geneva
117.	[Late Summer, 1930]	A. B.	[New York City]
118.	[August, 1930]	A. B.	Armonk
119.	August 18, 1930	A. B.	Armonk
120.	August 26, 1930	A. B.	Armonk

Number	Date*	Writer	Place of Composition
121.	[Late September, 1930]	A. B.	Armonk
122.	December 22, 1930	T. W.	London
123.	[January, 1931]	A. B.	[New York City]
124.	[January, 1931]	T. W.	[London]
125.	[March, 1931]	A. B.	New York City
126.	March, 1931	T. W.	New York City
127.	[March, 1931]	A. B.	New York City
128.	March 29, 1931	T. W.	Brooklyn
129.	[April, 1931]	A. B.	[New York City]
130.	[April, 1931]	A. B.	[Armonk, N.Y.]
131.	April 9, 1931	T. W.	Brooklyn
132.	May, 1931	A. B.	Armonk
133.	May 30, 1931	A. B.	Armonk
134.	[June, 1931]	A. B.	Armonk
135.	[June, 1931]	A. B..	Armonk
136.	[June, 1931]	A. B.	Armonk
137.	[August, 1931]	A. B.	New York City
138.	[August, 1931]	A. B.	[New York City]
139.	September 5, 1931	A. B.	Armonk
140.	[November, 1931]	A. B.	New York City
141.	[December, 1931]	A. B.	New York City
142.	[December, 1931]	A. B.	New York City
143.	[December, 1931]	A. B.	New York City
144.	[January, 1932]	A. B.	[New York City]
145.	January 14, 1932	A. B.	[New York City]
146.	[Winter, 1932]	T. W.	[New York City]
147.	[Winter, 1932]	T. W.	[New York City]
148.	March 22, 1932	A. B.	New York City
149.	[April, 1932]	A. B.	Armonk
150.	[June, 1932]	A. B.	New York City
151.	[June, 1932]	T. W.	[New York City]
152.	November 16, 1932	A. B.	[New York City]
153.	September 28, 1933	A. B.	Armonk
154.	October, 1933	T. W.	[New York City]
155.	[November, 1933]	A. B.	[New York City]
156.	December 11, 1933	T. W.	New York City
157.	December 12, 1933	A. B.	[New York City]
158.	February 19, 1934	A. B.	[New York City]
159.	[October, 1934]	A. B.	New York City
160.	January 21, 1936	A. B.	[New York City]
161.	April 3, 1936	A. B.	New York City
162.	[May, 1936]	A. B.	Armonk

Foreword
by Richard S. Kennedy

For us to be able to read this fascinating exchange of letters between one of America's most gifted writers and the extraordinary woman who risked love with a youthful, unpredictable genius and helped launch his career seems almost a miracle. But upon reflection I realize that it is principally the outcome of the patience, persistence, and tact of Suzanne Stutman.

For forty years, these letters have remained locked in the vaults of the Houghton Library at Harvard University under restriction both by the estate of Thomas Wolfe and by Aline Bernstein or her heirs. They were not restricted because they contained any dark secrets: indeed, the love affair had served as the fictional subject of both Wolfe's *The Web and the Rock* and Bernstein's *The Journey Down.* The reasons were other and various.

Mrs. Bernstein had always harbored an ambivalent attitude toward public knowledge of her affair with Wolfe. She made it quite clear to me when I interviewed her in 1950 that she was very proud of her relationship with Wolfe and that this liaison, in spite of its agonizing moments, provided the most important experience of her life. Yet it is also true that years earlier she had threatened to bring a lawsuit against Charles Scribner's Sons if they published a Wolfe novel in which she appeared as a recognizable character, and she hinted something similar to Edward Aswell, Wolfe's editor at Harper's, if Wolfe's posthumous novel, *The Web and the Rock*, were to present any unfavorable treatment of her as a fictional character. But her apprehension evaporated when the book was published; she was secretly pleased at her presence in it.

Thus it came about that when Edward Aswell became the administrator of the estate of Thomas Wolfe he restricted access to Wolfe's letters because he nurtured a plan that someday Mrs. Bernstein could be persuaded to edit them herself. Mrs. Bernstein, however, imposed her own restriction on publication for quite a different reason: she felt that making the letters public would cause too much pain for members of her family, although she did allow Elizabeth Nowell to print four of Wolfe's travel letters in her edition of *The Letters of Thomas Wolfe.* As a consequence, all during the period of research for my critical biography of Wolfe, *The Window of Memory*, I was not allowed to consult the Wolfe-Bernstein correspondence, and other applicants for access met the same refusal.

In the 1960s when Paul Gitlin became administrator of the Wolfe estate, he was more liberal in his attitude toward researchers than Aswell had been. He permitted Andrew Turnbull to consult the letters for his biography of Wolfe. When Paschal Reeves and I were editing *The Notebooks of Thomas Wolfe*, Gitlin made both sides of the correspondence open to us for information and allowed several quotations from Wolfe's letters to Mrs. Bernstein to be used in our commentary. But limitations still remained. Although Mrs. Bernstein was dead now, her daughter, Edla Cusick, refused us permission to quote from her mother's letters because, as she told me, it might upset her aunt, Ethel Frankau.

As time ran on in the 1970s, a fortunate set of circumstances developed. One of the graduate students in my seminar in Fiction of the Modern American South, Mrs. Suzanne Stutman, developed a strong interest in Aline Bernstein, her relationship with Wolfe, and her fiction. I began to realize that Mrs. Stutman, who seemed to me in personality and temperament very much like the Aline Bernstein I had met years previously, was the ideal person to edit the correspondence and suggested that she try to undertake the task as a Ph.D. dissertation. Paul Gitlin was amiable about the whole idea and gave his usual permission—OK for a dissertation but no guarantee of freedom to publish.

The job was long and difficult—even more so for a woman who had a full and complicated life as a college teacher with a husband and three children. The task of transcribing Wolfe's sprawling script was bad enough but the chronology of Mrs. Bernstein's letters proved another formidable problem. Years ago when the Wolfe papers had been under the supervision of Maxwell Perkins, he had unfortunately chosen as Wolfe's biographer John Terry, a former classmate of Wolfe's from college days and later his colleague in the English Department at New York University in the 1920s. Terry had no scholarly ability at all, and during the fifteen years that he held the title "official biographer," he wrote nothing and only succeeded in messing up the Wolfe papers, including his removal of all the Bernstein letters from their postmarked envelopes and generally confusing their order.

It took Mrs. Stutman two years to transcribe and annotate the letters and to establish their sequence. I can guarantee the accuracy of her work because she came to my office every Monday afternoon for a year so that I could check her typescript, and we could puzzle out together difficult passages of Wolfe's scrawl. When her job was done, she had a publishable book.

Yet in order to get one's work into print, a person sometimes has to be not just a scholar but a combination of Henry Kissinger and

Professor Harold Hill, the Music Man—as Mrs. Stutman discovered. After about a year of Philadelphia-to-New York shuttle diplomacy, she finally succeeded where everyone else had failed. This book is the result.

Scholars now have available in its fullest form the story that underlies *The Web and the Rock* and *The Journey Down.* What is more, all of us as readers have before us, in the complete texts of these letters, a human drama played out in all its intensity, a story of joy in love and of undeniable anguish. This oddly matched couple had months of happiness during which Wolfe produced his best and most fully controlled writing. Since Aline Bernstein became a mother substitute for him, it was inevitable that he would eventually wrench himself away from her in a desperate struggle to break the Oedipal tie. Yet as the nourisher of genius, she had the pleasure and pride of knowing that there had been a time when she had not been a mother figure but had been loved passionately and played the role of muse to a great writer. And there were times, even after their break-up, when Wolfe knew that she had taught him the meaning of love, as when he told her, "I shall love you all the days of my life, and when I die, if they cut me open they will find one name written on my brain and on my heart. It will be yours."

Acknowledgments

I wish to thank the many friends and colleagues who have helped to make this edition of letters a reality. I am grateful to Mr. Paul Gitlin, administrator of the estate of Thomas Wolfe, for permission to publish the Wolfe letters and for his kind and generous assistance. I would like to express my special gratitude to Edla Bernstein Cusick, the executor of the Bernstein estate, for her courtesy and assistance throughout this project. Professor Richard S. Kennedy, Temple University, played a very special role in the preparation of these letters for publication. It was he who first suggested this topic to me and he who consistently encouraged me to persevere during the many times when the project seemed hopelessly threatened. A truly outstanding advisor, teacher, and friend, he gave of his time and energy unstintingly. Without his efforts, this publication would not have been possible. Professor William Rossky has been my mentor, teacher, and friend for over twenty years. The example he has set for me, his assistance throughout this project, and his kindness during so many other important periods in my life have been invaluable. Thanks to Dr. Miles D. Orvell, who also spent countless hours poring over the Wolfe-Bernstein manuscript and who offered me valuable advice.

Thanks to W. H. Bond, director of the Houghton Library at Harvard, where the Wisdom Collection is housed, and to those of his staff who assisted me; to Myra Champion of the Pack Memorial Library, Asheville, North Carolina, for her kind assistance in tracking down information about the Wolfe family; to Edith Hampel, senior reference librarian of the Temple University Library, and her staff; a special thanks to my dear friend Hazel McCutcheon, head librarian of the Pennsylvania State University Library, Ogontz Campus, and to her capable staff, Elizabeth Meehan-Black, assistant librarian, Margaret Hindley, Lillian Marcy, Dita Schmidt, Joann Cliggett, and Rita Ware.

Several people have assisted me in my search for the photographs for this edition. Thanks to Mrs. Edla Cusick, who generously supplied pictures of Aline Bernstein. Mrs. Aline MacMahon Stein graciously shared pictures of herself and Aline Bernstein for use in this edition. Rodney Dennis, curator of manuscripts, Houghton Library, Harvard University, Suzanne N. H. Currier, associate curator of manuscripts, and Bridget Carr, of the manuscript department, and their staff were most helpful. Jerry W. Cotten, curator of photography, Wilson Library, University of North Carolina, placed his extensive collection of Wolfe photographs at my disposal. Thanks are also due to Aldo Magi, assistant editor of *The Thomas Wolfe Review*, for the photographs that he made available to me. Finally, thanks to Richard S. Kennedy, who supplied the negative for one of the Wolfe photographs found in these pages.

In preparing the manuscript, a special thanks is due to my close friend and colleague, Barbara Brown Hillje, who spent countless hours proofreading the material and who has offered me helpful advice and encouragement throughout this project. I appreciate the skill and efficiency with which Grace Stewert, my typist, prepared the original manuscript. Helene Cohan, from the foreign language department of Beaver College, and Lynn Christy, assistant professor of Russian at Pennsylvania State, graciously assisted with the German translations. Laurence G. Avery made many excellent suggestions concerning editorial policy. Sandra Eisdorfer and Gwen Duffey, my editors at the University of North Carolina Press, have offered me both sound professional advice and friendly encouragement throughout the period between the submission of the manuscript and its final publication.

Finally, I would like to offer thanks to my family and friends for their tolerance and encouragement; Edna Turock, for her love and support; George and Irene Stutman, for their love and encouragement; my wonderful children, Robert, Rhonda, and Craig, who never had as much homework as I did, for their patience. I offer special thanks to my dear father, Samuel Turock, who was always so proud of me. Most importantly, I thank my husband, Fred, who did everything from marketing to reading the text; without him, this project would never have been completed.

Editorial Policy

My primary goal when editing these letters was to maintain the integrity of the text so that the reader could read the correspondence in a form as close to the original as possible. I have kept editorial intrusions at a minimum and have interfered only for the following reasons:

1. When I felt that the reader needed assurance that an omission or mistake was indeed in the original
2. When it was absolutely necessary to clarify an otherwise confusing passage

Most of the silent corrections that I have made throughout the text were to change three idiosyncratic elements of Aline Bernstein's style that I felt would be needlessly annoying to the reader.

1. Instead of "th" at the ends of dates, Mrs. Bernstein used a symbol that looked like quotation marks. I have eliminated this symbol and have substituted "th" and "nd" when necessary.
2. Mrs. Bernstein used a period instead of a colon to separate the hours from minutes in time. I have substituted the standard form.
3. When quoting prices, Mrs. Bernstein was in the habit of using a decimal point but eliminating the following zeroes. I have eliminated the decimal point.

In addition, I have silently standardized paragraph indentation and have capitalized words at the beginnings of sentences in the rare cases when Wolfe or Bernstein neglected to do so. I have also regularized standard letter spacing and form.

Words that were illegible or were omitted from the text were indicated with brackets as follows:

1. An empty bracket indicates that words, salutations, or signatures were missing in the original
2. Dates and addresses supplied by the editor are bracketed
3. Words in brackets followed by a question mark were illegible or indecipherable in the original and represent the editor's educated guess
4. Words in brackets were missing in the text and were subsequently supplied by the editor
5. An ellipsis in a bracket indicates that the letter ended abruptly
6. When punctuation was omitted at crucial points within the material, such as ends of sentences, I have supplied the necessary punctuation in brackets

All brackets in this edition are the editor's; Wolfe and Bernstein used only parentheses.

To avoid an endless intrusion of brackets, I have corrected only those errors within the text which otherwise would prove particularly confusing to the reader. I added punctuation to the many run-on sentences only when absolutely necessary for clarity. Both Wolfe and Bernstein capitalized for emphasis. All such idiosyncratic capitalizations have been preserved without comment: e.g. "Her Majesty The Queen," "Young Man," "Be-Guilded Leviathan," and such simple words as "Food" and "Season." British and variant spellings and ampersands have been preserved without comment. Only misspellings that might be confusing to the reader have been marked with [sic]. Misspellings of proper names, such as Helen Hayes and Gerhard Hauptmann, and of foreign words and phrases have been left in their original form, as the frequent use of [sic] throughout the text would have proved an annoyance to the reader.

In the interest of authenticity, I have left certain stylistic idiosyncrasies in their original form. Both writers continuously separate compound words such as "my self," "every thing," "some one" and "straight forward"; "today" occurs as both "to day" and "to-day" in the original letters. Understandable personal abbreviations such as NP for Neighborhood Playhouse have not been expanded. Also left untouched are the following: periods at the ends of Bernstein's questions; both writers' omissions of commas in large numbers; missing hyphens; comma-spliced run-ons; dashes used to indicate various punctuation marks; inconsistent capitalization of words and punctuation in salutations; titles that are neither underlined nor quoted.

Approximately one half of the entire Wolfe-Bernstein correspondence was undated. I have tentatively dated them all, on the basis of context, and, during periods of European travel, of location. The numerous envelopes that were included with the letters were of virtually no help in dating, because many of them had been separated from the letters. I have added within brackets the location and date in the upper right-hand corner, when omitted in the text but determined by my research. Finally, of the nineteen hundred sheets that I transcribed and annotated, I located the chronological position of all but two postscripts to Bernstein letters.

Since Wolfe's handwriting is often incredibly difficult to read, it is important to explain to the reader the process of transcription. He accurately describes his handwriting as a "wild scrawl" (23 October 1928), and the reader will note many complaints by Mrs. Bernstein about the difficulty of deciphering it. For a period of over two years, the accurate transcription and dating of this material was my primary occupation. Magnifying glass in hand, I became familiar with the many idiosyncrasies of Wolfe's handwriting. Throughout his writing, various letters of the alphabet disappeared from his words, as he tried to keep pace with the speed of his thoughts. I was fortunate to have as advisor Richard S. Kennedy, who has certainly spent more years deciphering Wolfe's handwriting than any other Wolfe scholar. We would pore over the difficult passages like two archaeologists trying to decipher an ancient language. On the rare occasions that we failed to "translate" these passages, they were placed in brackets, as explained above. Mrs. Bernstein's writing, in sharp contrast to Wolfe's, was, to my great relief and gratitude, extremely legible. The resulting accuracy of the transcription of her letters gives me great satisfaction.

When cutting the material for this edition of selected letters, I desired above all to keep intact the "personality" of the correspondence. My major cuts came from the final portion of the correspondence, after the major Wolfe-Bernstein break in 1932. Most of these letters were Mrs. Bernstein's, and, as Wolfe had virtually stopped writing, tended to be repetitious. In addition, most of the numerous cables and postcards were eliminated. After these major cuts were made, I pulled as inconspicuously as possible those letters of lesser importance in the earlier period. In 1928, when both Wolfe and Bernstein were writing from Europe and the letters maintain a consistently high level of significance, very few letters have been omitted. Unless indicated by the notes, all letters are printed in their entirety.

Thomas Wolfe is a writer who has always appealed to a wide audience. When annotating this correspondence, I was conscious of this varied readership. Therefore, I have explained in the notes some material that is generally known to the expert, making the correspondence accessible to the largest number of people. Foreign words and phrases were translated only if the editor felt that a reader unfamiliar with the language could not deduce the general meaning of the material from the context. All of Mrs. Bernstein's theatrical references have been identified, as have the numerous productions of which she was so important a part.

It is the editor's hope that this policy will aid the reader in his appreciation and understanding of this fascinating material.

My Other Loneliness

Letters of Thomas Wolfe and Aline Bernstein

Introduction

The correspondence between Thomas Wolfe and Aline Bernstein constitutes the record of a love affair between two great twentieth-century figures. Written over an eleven-year period, from the inception of their relationship in 1925 until 1936, two years before Wolfe's untimely death, these letters tell the story of two talented and complex human beings who were desperately in love and yet struggling against a myriad of obstacles to keep that love alive. As the letters indicate, Aline Bernstein offered Wolfe love and faithfulness, in addition to the financial assistance and the belief and discipline that led to the creation of *Look Homeward, Angel.* Without doubt, much of Wolfe's best writing lies within these letters. A valuable companion to the notebooks, they reveal the vast, kaleidoscopic spectrum of his thoughts and a rich body of creative writing. They reflect the suffering of a man tortured by the agonies of his past and flawed by the distrust of women that caused him perpetually to flee a permanent relationship. Like his fiction, these letters portray the struggle of an artist, who, in striving to encompass the timeless verities of life, cut himself off from those he loved and remained forever alone.

The correspondence is part of the huge collection of Thomas Wolfe material housed in Harvard University's Houghton Library. At the time of Thomas Wolfe's death, his close friend and former editor Maxwell Perkins was named executor of the Wolfe estate. Shortly after, William B. Wisdom, a New Orleans lawyer who had known Wolfe and had admired his writings for years, purchased from Perkins this vast bulk of papers that consisted of letters, bills, documents, notebooks, and manuscripts. The only stipulation, to which Wisdom readily agreed, was that he keep this collection together by willing it to a single institution. Because of Wolfe's former attachment to Harvard and the many happy hours he had spent in the Harvard library, it seemed a natural choice. The letters in the Wisdom purchase were those of Aline Bernstein, and it was only after many years of negotiation that Mrs. Bernstein agreed to sell to Perkins the Thomas Wolfe portion of the correspondence, donating the money to the Federation of Jewish Philanthropies. Finally the correspondence, some 1,900 pages and ranging over the eleven-year period 1925–36, was complete.

"The most beautiful woman who ever lived"

When Wolfe met Mrs. Bernstein aboard the *Olympic* returning from Europe in August 1925, it was shortly before his twenty-fifth birthday, and she, at forty-four, was literally old enough to be his mother. For both, love was almost instantaneous and became the overriding passion of a lifetime. On the surface, the relationship between the lovers seemed a series of contradictions. She was a Jew, he, a Christian; she was a successful stage and costume designer for the Neighborhood Playhouse, at the pinnacle of her career, while he was unsuccessful in the theater; she was a northerner, from the sophisticated city, while he was from the provincial South; she stood firmly rooted in reality, while Wolfe consistently fought against losing himself within the violent landscapes of his imagination.

Each was to record the experience of the love affair in fiction: Wolfe in three of his major novels, *Of Time and the River*, *The Web and the Rock*, and *You Can't Go Home Again*; and Mrs. Bernstein in *Three Blue Suits* and *The Journey Down*. In addition, his 1926 letters to Mrs. Bernstein offer a privileged view into Wolfe's creative processes as he wrote his masterpiece, *Look Homeward, Angel*. The notes that Aline Bernstein recorded for Wolfe later in their relationship about her beloved actor father, Joseph Frankau, and her eccentric, emotional family, particularly her Aunt Nana, found their way into both Wolfe's fictional work and Mrs. Bernstein's autobiographical account of her early years, *An Actor's Daughter*. The letters, then, serve as a vital guide to the writing technique of both writers.

The correspondence can be read and appreciated on several levels. As a record of a love affair between two passionate human beings caught in the conflicting web of circumstance and their individual natures, it is unparalleled. Psychologically, the letters serve as an exploration into the mind of a gifted and tortured man who strives to come to grips with himself and his art. From a historical point of view, they were written against a setting of Europe and America in the mid-twenties and thirties, from the boom years of American optimism, the glitter of Prohibition, and such mass spectacles as the Dempsey-Tunney fight, to the demoralizing defeat of Al Smith, and the lean and harried years of the Depression.

Wolfe's descriptions of European life, culture, and landscape are the best among his collected writings. With his writer's eye, he records the characteristics of "the hated and hating French,"[1] the Germans who live to eat and drink and appear like "one enormous

1. *Letters*, 14 October 1926, #33.

belly,"[2] the defeated and dreamy Hungarians who "are sitting in their coffeehouses, reading incessantly their newspapers."[3] From Brussels he writes of the parade of Socialist and Communist parties and of "a forest of great banners of red silk," waving for miles "like a new Crusade, richer and vaster than any of the old ones."[4] He describes his trip up the Rhine and past the rocks where the enchanting Lorelei is said to dwell, the great hills "huge masses of rock that rise almost sheer into the air,"[5] and the river itself winding through the countryside "like a magic thread."[6]

Mrs. Bernstein's letters offer a glimpse into the customs and habits of the cultural elite in New York's glittering twenties. The theatrical world is realistically recreated with mention of such people as the Lewisohn sisters, Theresa Helburn, Eva Le Gallienne, the Lunts, and Aline MacMahon. After a party given by Lawrence Langner, director of the Theatre Guild, at which she had seen such notables as Ernest and Madeleine Boyd, Thomas Beer, and Horace Liveright, she wrote to Wolfe, "The guests were like a book list in a periodical."[7]

The forms these letters take are a reflection of the personalities of both Thomas Wolfe and Aline Bernstein. For Wolfe, it was almost as impossible to write a short letter as it was to write a short novel. Totally irresponsible, except to his writing, he would write Mrs. Bernstein sixty-page diaries but forget to mail them: "Thus I think of you all the time, begin a letter, sleep, write, add to the letter, and finally, wondering in horror how it shall ever get to you, I remember suddenly that there are postage stamps, and strange things called ships, in which I don't believe."[8] All that he saw and felt, the wide spectrum of his experience and emotion, he presented to her in his letters. For weeks, as he traveled abroad, she was the only human being with whom he communicated. His trust of her soft acceptance was infinite, and he recorded for her in characteristic encyclopedic form a diary of his observations and reflections.

Thomas Wolfe at twenty-four was bursting with youth and vitality; dark, brooding, huge in stature, he had about him the air of an extraordinary child. He had come to New York the year before after successfully completing a master's degree at Harvard University, during which time he had studied in Professor George Baker's play-

2. *Letters*, 4 October 1928, #79.
3. *Letters*, 15 November 1928, #96.
4. *Letters*, 9 August 1928, #66.
5. *Letters*, 27 August 1928, #74.
6. Ibid.
7. *Letters*, 1 December 1926, #44.
8. *Letters*, 27 September 1926, #26.

writing seminar, the prestigious "47 Workshop." Unsuccessful with his dramas in New York, primarily because of his characteristic long-windedness and his inability to edit his material, Wolfe had failed to achieve the recognition he so desperately craved.

Aline Bernstein was in 1925 at the apex of her career. She was soon to become the first woman to be granted acceptance into the influential United Scenic Artists Union, which would make her eligible to design for Broadway productions. Married to the prominent New York stockbroker Theodore Bernstein, she had raised two children and was devoted to her family. She possessed a fine control of both herself and her work, a balance that was to prove invaluable for the erratic, excessive Wolfe. Yet she radiated an exuberance and a love of life at once innocent and childlike. Totally feminine, she was capable and at ease in both worlds. An excellent cook, she was to create for Wolfe the sense of home and order for which his tormented spirit was constantly searching.

Some time in the winter of 1926, the two moved to the top floor of a house at 13 East Eighth Street which Mrs. Bernstein had rented as a studio, and during the spring, they made plans for a brief summer tour of Europe. After their European sojourn, Mrs. Bernstein left Wolfe in England to work alone on his autobiographical manuscript while she returned home for the fall theatrical season, but she continued to support him so that he could devote himself solely to his writing. The first major portion of the correspondence dates from August to December 1926, during the time that the solitary Wolfe was reentering his past life to create the splendid imaginative world of *Look Homeward, Angel.*

Throughout the course of his turbulent life and writings, Thomas Wolfe considered himself and his heroes to be exiles, wanderers in search of a door into experience that would illuminate man's purpose and destiny. Travel always carried for Wolfe the ability to begin anew, to encircle the great world that lay before him. Faustian in his appetites, he thirsted to understand the cultures of the many lands to which he journeyed, to drink their beer and wine, taste their food, engulf their precious art. Yet his travel always had about it a quality of isolation and remoteness. He seemed to be viewing life like a man at a window of a speeding train—an image that he loved and used frequently in his writing. When he traveled, he was able to flee the "real" world about him and to live silently within the world of his imagination. "My life has begun to acquire again the remote and lonely quality it had when I was wandering about before,"[9] he wrote to Mrs. Bernstein in September 1926 from England. "I seem to be

9. *Letters*, 25 September 1926, #24.

the phantom in a world of people; or the only person in a world of phantoms—it's all the same."[10]

It was Mrs. Bernstein's letters, written to him almost daily in 1926 as he worked to get down the body of writing that was to become *Look Homeward, Angel*, that were to hold him to the world of reality. For he lived great portions of his life as if they were a dream, and the dream was that of his own past experience. His fantastic imagination encapsulated all that he had read so that he became, in fact, the hero of a great tale or legend, and that legend was his own quest through life. "The only loyalty that can endure . . . is loyalty to a myth or to a phantom,"[11] he wrote, "And the reality of a dream may not be re-visited."[12]

Thus Wolfe became in his own mind like the hero Faust, and Aline Bernstein evolved in his letters into the various earth goodesses: Helen, Demeter, Solveig, and Penelope. As he wrote of her in *The Web and the Rock*, he was never able to view her realistically. After their first encounter, his romantic imagination reshaped her into a composite of all the goddesses of his dreams and of all the fictional princesses about whom he had read. Wolfe's quest, throughout his life as well as his fiction, was for the eternal, the ideal, the absolute. "Is it not strange," he wrote in November 1926, "how this small earth is built in pieces, but all eternity is one."[13] For Wolfe, reality was the dream; what was real to him was the timeless world of his own all-encompassing imagination.

In 1926, during this period of intense self-exploration, Mrs. Bernstein's letters were Wolfe's lifeline. She urged him to eat well, dress warmly, and not drink too much. She kept him informed of the happenings of the theatrical world: which plays she was working on, gossip about celebrities and actors, reflections on the social and intellectual climate of New York. She wrote about the garment workers' strike, the New York heat, to which Wolfe was particularly sensitive, and the craze of redevelopment that was hitting the city. Most of all, however, she offered him the needed words of love and encouragement that enabled him to concentrate on his work, the transcribing from mind to paper of what was to become *Look Homeward, Angel*, the record of his secret life.

It was not long before she found that the erratic and uncontrollable elements within Wolfe's volcanic personality could erupt in his letters without warning. Thus, if she mentioned her theater friends Irene and Alice Lewisohn, he would rail against their mistreatment

10. Ibid.
11. *Letters*, 5 June 1926, #10.
12. Ibid.
13. *Letters*, 9 November 1926, #39.

of his plays. Other mention of the theater would bring attacks against a range of villains who were in his mind trying to destroy him and his art, ranging from "Them," to the *Dial* subscribers, to the Phi Beta Kappa Jews.[14] An innocent remark could cause Wolfe to fall into a frenzy of bitterness and abuse. He masked his irrational behavior in emotional, highly symbolic language, at times reverting to Renaissance imagery to describe her imaginary betrayals and complaining that he had been "cuckolded" by Mrs. Bernstein's duplicity. Shortly after she had left him in England to return home in August 1926, he wrote to the astonished and anguished Mrs. Bernstein: "I suppose I may look forward with some fortitude to being gulled on that side of the Atlantic while I am asleep in my bed on this side, and to realize my translation only when I wake to find myself antlered like a mountain goat."[15] Soon after this, he wrote again of his fear of betrayal and duplicity, "and women, fatal, false, silken, soft breasted cushion-bellied women awake to lust."[16]

Wolfe associated woman with inconstancy and betrayal, a view he could never rise above and one that tortures his autobiographical heroes Eugene Gant and George Webber. In *Look Homeward, Angel*, the father came to symbolize abundance and creativity while the mother, who has broken up the warm center of the child's life for a cold, sterile boardinghouse, symbolized betrayal. Wolfe's ambivalent behavior toward women was something he was unable to understand or analyze. It appears to have stemmed from a deep-seated resentment and, at times, hatred of his mother, which he would not admit even to himself. As a youth, he could worship his teacher in preparatory school, Mrs. Roberts, because she was inaccessible to him; later in life when he had conquered others, he became repelled by the specter of maternal domination that haunted him. Significantly, then, it was only because Mrs. Bernstein had begun to cease to exist in reality as a love object that he was able, in the 1928 letters, to maintain an unprecedented outpouring of love and affection.

Early in their relationship Mrs. Bernstein was bemused by Wolfe's ravings: "You love me and you miss me and you get these dreadful thoughts about me,"[17] she wrote in 1926. By 1928, after months of

14. In June, Wolfe had written to Mrs. Bernstein, "Let's leave false laughter as the final dishonesty of the Dial circulation, and all other Phi Beta Kappa Jews." Realizing his foolishness, he added, "This is only my gentle raillery" (5 June 1926, #10). In October, after a particularly beautiful passage, he suddenly digressed: "We are forever beaten, but before we die we have the power to rise up and curse *Them*" (27 September 1926, #27).

15. *Letters*, 26 August 1926, #14.

16. *Letters*, 14 October 1926, #33.

17. *Letters*, 22 August 1926, #12.

bitter fighting and accusations when he left her to tour Europe alone, she became more painfully aware of his irrational behavior: "I wish that there could be some way you could be spared the other pain caused by the dreadful black clouds of fantasy that have embittered you towards me. . . . I vow that . . . I have been a true and good person to you in every respect."[18]

Throughout his lifetime, his ability to love deeply, to make a full commitment to another human being, was undercut by this dark side of his soul, which he frequently referred to as his "madness." Complex and erratic yet capable of great discipline regarding work habits at Harvard and teaching responsibilities at New York University, Wolfe was often so emotionally immature that his letters frequently resemble the outpouring of a painfully egocentric adolescent. Throughout the correspondence, his sane and rational reflections would be almost inexplicably interrupted by grotesque ravings and accusations. In September 1926, when he feared that Mrs. Bernstein had gone to the Dempsey-Tunney fight, which symbolized for him his own potential defeat and humiliation, he raved on hysterically for pages. Yet he refused to erase his black outpourings: "They are part of the evil texture of my soul, and you shall know me for the half-monster I am."[19]

Wolfe indeed had a Jekyll-and-Hyde personality. In his view of women, he was so entrapped within the virgin-whore dichotomy that plagued writers like Joyce and Lawrence that it seems at times as though he could not forgive Mrs. Bernstein for being his own mistress. By 1928, yearning for her love and yet terrified by what it implied for him, he wrote once more of his confusion, unable to translate the implications of this nightmare vision:

> The terrible mystery of living has laid its hands upon my heart and I can find no answer. All about me I see the jungle rut and ramp—the little furtive eyes all wet with lust, and the brutes heavy of jowl and gut, and ropy with their sperm. I see the flower face, the compassionate eyes of love and beauty, the pure untainted loveliness—I see it under the overwhelming shade of darkness: the hairy stench, the thick blunt fingers fumbling at the heart, the foul wet belly. . . . My heart is smothering in its love for you. You are the most precious thing in my life, but you are imprisoned in a jungle of thorns, and I cannot come near you without bleeding.[20]

18. *Letters*, May 1928, #48.
19. *Letters*, 14 October 1926, #33.
20. *Letters*, 11 August 1928, #69.

The relationship was threatened not only by Wolfe's ambivalent and inexplicable behavior toward women but by the vast age difference between the lovers. Wolfe's proclivity toward an affair with an older woman is in keeping with his nature. He had had an unnaturally dependent relationship with his mother, and she was quite possessive of him. While he rebelled bitterly against her throughout his lifetime, he was violently drawn to her. The bond was financial as well as psychological, for his mother continued to support him until in 1925 Aline took over the role of the emotional and financial mother figure. As he had found a mother substitute in his teacher, Mrs. Roberts, while a young boy, so he now unconsciously transferred his affections to Mrs. Bernstein. Early in their relationship he wrote to her from Europe concerning his timeless vision of her, in words reminiscent of those he later used in *Look Homeward, Angel*:

> It seems to me that this great pageant of my life, beginning in cheap legendry, in which all was victory, faultless perfection, has led my dark soul across perilous seas, scarring me here, taking a tooth or an ear, putting its splendid blemish on until now I come to my autumn home, the streaked hairs, the rich widehipped body, the brief repose which lasts forever for it is founded on sorrow and the skirts of winter—beyond youth, beyond life, beyond death. You live timelessly like Helen, like deep-breasted Demeter, like Holvig.[21]

Within the same letter he referred to Mrs. Bernstein as "my grey haired widehipped timeless mother."[22]

Wolfe was never able to come to terms with the vast age difference between himself and Mrs. Bernstein, and for this reason, he avoided the issue completely, transforming her into an ageless, timeless, mythological figure. Wolfe makes virtually no mention, throughout the letters or the fiction, of Mrs. Bernstein's age. She was painfully aware, however, of the great discrepancy in their ages. Throughout the letters she exhibits an interest in keeping herself youthful looking for Wolfe. Prone to heaviness, she would constantly diet to keep from acquiring a more matronly figure. In 1928, when she feared that their love affair was over, she blamed the break primarily on this age difference: "This much I know that the irrevocable difference in our ages is the only thing that has kept me from you."[23]

Yet it was not so much age as the strong, unnatural dependence and the expectation that Wolfe placed upon those few figures he loved and exalted which eventually caused the deterioration of these

21. *Letters*, 9 November 1926, #39.
22. Ibid.
23. *Letters*, 22 July 1928, #57.

relationships. He idolized both Aline Bernstein and his editor, Maxwell Perkins of Scribner's, with a burning desperation, and it was in part this great need that caused him ultimately to bolt in terror.

By the summer of 1928, when Wolfe traveled to Europe without Mrs. Bernstein, the relationship had changed dramatically. Although he still loved her and could not yet break away, her smothering love and constancy were more than he could bear. For months he roamed through Europe seeking to avoid a meeting with Aline, who was touring with friends through Italy and Germany. Their letters are filled with fascinating details of the countries that they visited, the art, the architecture, and the characteristics of the people. Indeed, some of Wolfe's best descriptive writing is found in these letters, as he strove to make her see clearly, as if she were with him, each detail that passed before his eyes.

These letters contain an intricate and fascinating account of Wolfe's experiences in Germany during the Oktoberfest: his participation in a bloody brawl, his hospitalization, and his trip to Oberammergau with a half-crazed old woman scholar to see the Passion Play. In late October 1928, Maxwell Perkins of Scribner's showed interest in the huge manuscript of what was to become *Look Homeward, Angel*. Mrs. Bernstein tried frantically to communicate this information to Wolfe by letter and telegram, but to no avail. When he finally learned, on 29 October, that a "Mr. Peters" had shown an interest in his manuscript, he was too far removed within his own world of loneliness and unreality to react.

For the next month, Wolfe roamed through Europe like a man in a dream, making virtually no mention of his writing. He left for home late in December, arriving in New York on New Year's Eve. On 2 January, he had his first interview with Perkins; it was not until the following interview, however, on 7 January, that Perkins agreed to publish "O Lost." On 9 January, Wolfe recorded in his notebook "On this day I got a letter from Scribner's confirming their acceptance of my book." Under this notation were two signatures, those of Aline Bernstein and Thomas Wolfe.

Throughout his lifetime, Wolfe was to be afraid of those for whom he felt great emotion, afraid of those toward whom he felt the urge to yield. He had the great good fortune to be loved by two exceptional human beings, Maxwell Perkins and Aline Bernstein. Although he could not accept them as they truly were, both had the maturity to recognize the genius of the man, and both were to love him with an unwavering constancy despite all that he did to dissuade them.

From the inception of their relationship, Wolfe did not see Mrs. Bernstein as she really was; she became for him almost instantly the composite of all his fantasies. Years later, in *The Web and the Rock*, which is based upon their love affair, he described George Webber's initial idealization of Esther Jack: "He was never able thereafter to see her as a matronly figure of middle age, a creature with a warm and jolly little face, a wholesome and indomitable energy for every day. . . . She became the most beautiful woman who ever lived—and not in any symbolic or idealistic sense—but with all the blazing, literal and mad concreteness of his imagination" (*W&R*, p. 296). For the duration of their relationship, this central image of Mrs. Bernstein remained for Wolfe fixed and inviolate. Although he was to hurt her deeply with his fantastic fears and accusations, she remained throughout these years the person to whom he knew he could exhibit the full range of his complex and tormented spirit. In the summer of 1928, shortly before the Oktoberfest brawl, he had written her from Europe: "It has been almost three years since we met. . . . Everything I have said or seen or felt during those three years, have been radiated from you, or have streamed in toward you. You are past any reckoning my great vision. To see you as others see you, to see you as you really may be, I cannot. . . . You were my other loneliness."[24]

Yet for the duration of the relationship, he resented his total dependence upon Mrs. Bernstein, and her ability to function well within a variety of roles. She was wife, mother, successful stage designer, friend of the famous—and his lover. Intensely practical and strong of will, she was able when working to come to grips with her problems immediately and to work diligently until they were resolved. As romantic as she was concerning her relationship with Wolfe, she possessed a core of firm objectivity and judgment about his work which she exhibited in the letters. Throughout the course of their relationship, she expressed a profound interest in his writing, exhorting him to edit his material and not to fall victim to his proclivity toward the flowery and musical phrase.

Increasingly throughout the letters, however, she expressed doubts about her ability as a costume designer and her genuine desperation and despair concerning the deterioration of their relationship. These were aspects of her life which, apparently, she did not allow others to see. Wolfe became angry and resentful when, during their 1930 separation, she threatened suicide in several letters to him during a time when she was receiving rave reviews for her work. He, who was accustomed to exhibiting the full intensity of his emotions even to a complete stranger, could not understand her need or her ability to appear in control of all other aspects of her life. He concluded that this purported inconsistency must be one more expression of her duplicity and inconstancy.

24. *Letters*, 12 August 1928, #70.

Despite her personal success, however, Aline Bernstein desired most to be the beloved of Thomas Wolfe. Early in their relationship she had written to him: "I think, to tell you the truth, that the very best I can do in life is to cook for a certain Tom Wolfe, to mend his clothes and make him generally comfortable. And to put on a gold dress in the evening and sparkle for him, so he will not think the romance of life is all gone. I feel the very center of romance now, a princess in a castle, in duress, and some day maybe a rescue and tight tight loving arms."[25] Like Thomas Wolfe, Aline Bernstein was intrinsically a romantic. The correspondence is punctuated throughout with their telegrams, which, by their concentrated form, add an air of intensity to the language. Each treated this love with the utmost seriousness and awed devotion.

The lovers shared, in addition to this appreciation of the romance of life, the artist's appreciation of the senses. The letters abound in keen physical detail, as the correspondents sketched with words each aspect of the scene surrounding them. Like Wolfe, Mrs. Bernstein had had an opulent childhood surrounded by emotional and eccentric family members, most notably her actor father, Joseph Frankau, and her sensuous and shockingly outrageous Aunt Nana. Both had spent portions of their youth in boardinghouses and shared the love of abundant, well-cooked meals and the tastes of varieties of well-prepared foods.

At Mrs. Bernstein's urging, Wolfe became increasingly interested in art and music. Throughout the letters, he chronicled for her what he favored of the art treasures of Europe. As opinionated in this as in everything else, he was partial to a relatively small group of artists. From each country he visited in 1928 came descriptions of his favorites: the nudes of Rubens and Cranach, the Picassos and Van Goghs, and, most particularly, their mutual favorite, Breughel. Mrs. Bernstein shared with Wolfe a sense of inner music, as well, which was important in both of their lives. In *The Journey Down*, the heroine refers to this quality as her "music box," a silent melody that comes to her in moments of intense emotion. Mrs. Bernstein's musical sense carried over into her imagery, as is evidenced in September 1926 when she wrote to Wolfe of seeing things "like organ notes and deep chords."[26]

It was Mrs. Bernstein's slight deafness that drew Wolfe to Beethoven's house in August 1928. With characteristic idealization and overstatement he wrote to her, "Beethoven, and Helen Keller, and you, my darling. Because of their deafness they get a kind of magnifi-

25. *Letters*, 15 September 1926, #18.
26. Letters, 22 September 1926. This letter has been edited from the text.

cent strength and freedom."[27] Soon after he wrote this, he stuffed his ears with cotton and walked about for a day in silence so that he could better identify with these deaf heroes.

Ultimately, they came to share a love of writing that would lead Mrs. Bernstein to write three novels within an eight-year period. During the years of their declining relationship, she wrote endless sketches for Wolfe about her childhood which he eventually used in part as the material for "The Good Child's River" and *The Web and the Rock*. Her appetite for writing stimulated, she was to concentrate for several years on expressing her particular vision of the world about her. Her later letters are punctuated throughout with this desire to write, and one sketch about her visit to the dentist with her subsequent awareness, through pain, of her own spiritual inviolability, can be found virtually unchanged in her book, *An Actor's Daughter*.

In the 1928 letters in particular, the European letters of each are rich in detailed, textured descriptions. Artists and soulmates, they shared a keen delight in all aspects of the world about them. They discussed art, literature, music, architecture, and the beauty of the natural world. Wherever he went, Wolfe listed the great variety of books and experiences upon which he had gorged himself.[28]

Mrs. Bernstein's vision served as a valuable lens for Wolfe. With his Faustian desire to encompass the entirety of experience, he too often missed the subtleties of life and character. Mrs. Bernstein's vision was at once profound and innocent. She possessed an air of wonder, humanity, and compassion. In 1931, as she was recording her thoughts and experiences for Wolfe, she wrote to him of an old copper jar whose beauty she had intuitively recognized under the superficial dirt and grime. "This is what I think," she had written characteristically, "there is nothing that cannot be made beautiful."[29]

It was, perhaps, her inner dignity and firm sense of self that armed Aline Bernstein against Wolfe's increasingly frequent tirades against her. Early in the relationship Wolfe had used the term "Jew" as one of endearment,[30] but as the relationship cooled, her Jewishness became the source of vituperation and abuse. In the beginning,

27. *Letters*, 27 August 1928, #74.

28. An inveterate maker of lists, Wolfe made lists of his varied readings throughout his letters and notebooks. An example of one such list can be found in the *Letters*, 9 November 1926, #39.

29. *Letters*, August 1931, #137.

30. Wolfe was in the habit of beginning his letters "My Dear Jew," early in the relationship. He referred to Jewish girls as "Rebeccas." In his notebook, he called Mrs. Bernstein "Grey Rebecca."

Mrs. Bernstein, only too aware of Wolfe's inherent prejudice, had written, "I should like to be the great and lovely mistress of your dreams. I wish I had a quiet beautiful retreat and 10000 books. But I am only a Jew."[31] She was intensely proud, however, of her heritage and of her value as a human being. No one could have defended her as eloquently as she defended herself after Wolfe and his mother had unceremoniously booted her out:

> I maintain that neither you nor your mother have any understanding of my self, of the freedom I demand for my mind and my life. I will not be bound in thought nor behavior by any thing I do not choose my self. I have lived a fine life, I have held to the performance of my duties at home, and if I have not lived sexually with the man I married, it is no bodies business but ours, certainly not your mother's. I have retained purity in the practice of my work, I have been an uncompromising artist in a world that is full of compromise and ugliness. When we met and loved each other, I gave you the whole strength and beauty of my free soul and free mind.[32]

At the end of the letter, she wrote, "I love you forever, and now we drop into a great unknown pool, seperate [sic]."[33]

"Ten years, ten rooms, ten thousand sheets of paper"

A study of Wolfe's letters offers the reader a privileged view into the writer's mind and into the way he transformed experience into fiction. The 1925–26 letters are saturated with the language, symbols, and people who were to populate the pages of *Look Homeward, Angel.* Since all of Wolfe's fiction was basically autobiographical, these encyclopedic letters serve as an important aid in the study of his mind and art. They enable the reader to understand better the fluctuation between fantasy and reality, fact and fiction, within the dynamic chronicle of Wolfe's work.

As early as 1925, he was writing of his family in terms that foreshadowed his fictional portrayal: "I came home to a Christmas of death, doom, desolation, sadness, disease, and despair: my family is showing its customary and magnificent Russian genius for futility and tragedy."[34] In the late spring of 1926, before he left for Europe

31. *Letters*, 23 September 1926, #23.
32. *Letters*, 14 January 1932, #145.
33. Ibid.
34. *Letters*, December 1925, #3.

to work on his manuscript, as the letters indicate, Wolfe was in the process of actively attempting to reenter his past. He wrote to Mrs. Bernstein from Norfolk and Richmond that he had traveled there in the hope of evoking old memories. In his letter of 4 June 1926 from Richmond, he reminisces about the episodes he was later to describe more explicitly in chapter 33 of *Look Homeward, Angel*. In the same letter, he evokes the ghost of his childhood, the lost youth who roams the pages of his autobiographical Bildungsroman: "Come back, bright boy, as thou wert in the dayspring of my memory, before thy life had yet turned the dark column, and the wind and the rain were musical; and flowers grew."[35]

On 23 June 1926, Wolfe sailed for Europe aboard the *Berengaria*. Mrs. Bernstein had left shortly before on business, and the two were reunited in Paris. There he began working on an autobiographical outline for his novel. On 19 August, after touring together through France and England, Mrs. Bernstein tearfully left for home, while Wolfe settled in Chelsea and began working feverishly on his manuscript. On 22 August, he wrote to her of the lodgings he had found. "I have two rooms (the whole first floor) of a house in Wellington Square. The place is very clean, and well furnished: I pay 45 shillings a week, which includes service. Breakfast is extra."[36] He wrote to her also of his fears of the recurrence of a nightmare concerning past voyages. His dream sounds uncannily like the enchanted and supernatural realm of Wolfe's imagination—and is an astonishing prediction of the basic themes of much of his future writing:

> Then I dreamed most frequently of voyages; in a dark but visible universe, under a light that never fell on land or ocean, I crossed haunted and desolate seas, the solitary passenger of spectral ships; and there was always the far sound of horns blowing under water, and on the American shore, no matter how far, the plain but ghostly voices of the friends I had had, and the foes; rising forever, with its whole spectral and noiseless carnival of sound and movement, was New York, like a bodiless phantom, and my unknown home, which I had never had, but whose outlines were perfectly familiar to me; and thus I passed without lapse of time through all the horrible vitality of this strange world, all tumult . . . but the ghost of people, near enough to touch, but illimitably remote, until, returning in my agony from the place I had sought, voyaging again upon the haunted sea, under the unearthly light, I awoke with my hand

35. *Letters*, 4 June 1926, #8.
36. *Letters*, 22 August 1926, #13.

> upon my throat, to cry "I have voyaged enough. I will go no more."[37]

The sea was a double symbol for Wolfe, the world of his unconscious and the timeless universe of preexistence. Greatly influenced by Wordsworth, he believed that the child was closer to innocence and awareness than the man. Throughout *Look Homeward, Angel* "horns blowing under water" symbolize some echo of the lost world of preexistence, and the "bright boy" and "lost youth" of childhood is the possessor of that fragile truth that Wolfe so desperately sought in his voyages. His language is characteristically musical and otherworldly, like much of *Look Homeward, Angel*, as he skirts the borderline between the worlds of fantasy and reality. As the previous passage suggests, there is much that is mystical in Wolfe's writing, as there was in Coleridge, one of his favorites.

On 26 August 1926, Wolfe wrote of the regularity that his life was beginning to assume. In September, shortly before he left for Belgium on a ten-day holiday, he wrote, "I do from 2000–2500 words a day—almost a book in a month, you see, but mine will be much longer."[38] Soon after, he made reference to the "secret life" to which he was so often to refer in his novel, the world of his imagination: "I get tremendously excited over my book—at times in an unnatural drunken ecstasy, it seems to me to be working into one of the most extraordinary things ever done. . . . This book finishes it—it is a record of my secret life."[39] From Brussels he wrote one week later that he had done more writing in the past month than at any other period in his life.

It has already been noted that Wolfe rarely forgot any detail from his reading or his personal experience. He would file these facts or incidents away until he could find some chance to use them. The letters abound in such examples. In the postscript to his 26 August 1926 letter, Wolfe referred to the *Carmina* of Catullus and transcribed lines in Latin for Mrs. Bernstein to translate. The meaning was certainly pertinent for the two lovers, as the first line reads, "My Lesbia, let us live and love / And not care tuppence for old men / Who sermonize and disapprove."[40] In chapter 17 of *LHA* Wolfe makes reference to this poem as Eugene challenges his dull Latin teacher, Mr. Leonard, with comments on Catullus. "'He wrote about being in love,' Eugene said with sudden passion. 'He wrote about being in love with a lady named Lesbia. . . . She was a man's wife!' he said

37. Ibid.
38. *Letters*, 11 September 1926, #17.
39. Ibid.
40. For a translation of the entire poem, see *Letters*, 26 August 1926, #14.

loudly, 'That's what she was. . . . She was a bad woman,' said Eugene. Then most desperately, he added: 'She was a Little Chippie.' " Interestingly, it appears that Wolfe had unconsciously made a subtle association between Lesbia and Aline Bernstein.

Wolfe often referred to Mrs. Bernstein in terms of legendary and mythological figures, and some of these references carried directly to the pages of his manuscript. While roaming through the museum at Antwerp, he became fascinated by the "broad deep bellied goddesses of Rubens" and was prompted to write: "I want eternal life, eternal renewal, eternal love—the vitality of these immortal figures: I see myself sunk, a valiant wisp, between the mighty legs of Demeter, the earth Goddess, being wasted and filled eternally. I want life to ebb and flow in me in a mighty rhythm of oblivion and ecstasy. Upon a field in Thrace Queen Helen lay, her amber belly spotted by the sun."[41] Wolfe was so taken with this final sentence that he recorded it in his notebook and it later appeared almost verbatim in chapter 15 of *LHA*, following one of his innumerable fantasies about wealth and sensuous goddesses: "Upon a field in Thrace Queen Helen lay, her lovely body dappled in the sun" (*LHA*, p. 161).

Wolfe makes use of this type of association in creating one of the most fantastic letters of the correspondence. In his 27 September 1926 letter from Antwerp, he wrote to Mrs. Bernstein, "If you went to the great prize fight [the Dempsey-Tunney championship] I curse and loathe you forever. . . . The defeat and humiliation of that brute Dempsey I share in: the news of the defeat of a champion has always saddened me."[42] An incredible tirade follows, one that displays dramatically his stereotyped attitudes toward "well-bred" men and women. In chapter 8 of *LHA*, Wolfe was to use the "loathing of physical humiliation, not based on fear, from which he never recovered" in reference to the episode in which the young Eugene Gant was punished by his principal, Mr. Armstrong, for having written bawdy poetry. Upon re-reading the letter, he noted to Mrs. Bernstein that his reaction was a throwback to his Cambridge days when he saw himself "beaten and battered to the earth time after time by a rival, in front of my mistress. . . . I came at such a time into complete absolution of the world, the web, all women."[43] It is fascinating that Wolfe had made this symbolic association so early. In *The Web and the Rock*, written several years later, the web came to symbolize, among other things, all that is false and illusory, all that ensnares.

41. *Letters*, 25 September 1926, #24.
42. *Letters*, 27 September 1926, #26.
43. Ibid.

Primarily, it symbolizes entrapment by the black widow herself: woman.

Wolfe had moved from Chelsea to Bloomsbury upon his return from Europe. On 14 October 1926, he wrote that he was working well. "Since you left," he wrote, "I have written over 60000 words of a book that may be almost 200000."[44] On 20 October, he moved to Oxford. "England," he wrote, "is a sad, cold, desperate country" and the students not the "flaming faces of future Shellys and Coleridges" but "much like the people at Harvard and Yale, only younger, fresher and more innocent."[45] On 28 October, he wrote to Mrs. Bernstein concerning the book's progression: "The book stands thus: I work five or six hours every day on it now—I see my way through the first three books as straight as a string. I brood constantly over the fourth and last—the book lifts into a soaring fantasy of a Voyage, and I want to put my utmost, my most passionate in it. The prefatory action to these four books I can write down in ten days. . . . The book is swarming with life, peopled by communities, and governed by a developing and inexorable unity."[46] By 8 November, he was able to write of his experience: "I have somehow recovered innocency—I have written it almost with a child's heart: the thing has come from me with a child's wonder, and my pages are engraved not only with what is simple and plain but with monstrous evil, as if the devil were speaking with a child's tongue. The great fish, those sealed with evil, horribly incandescent, hoary with elvish light, have swum upwards."[47]

Wolfe was, however, becoming tired, drained, and depressed. England, with its dreary climate, his excruciating schedule, and the dulling regularity of his life had begun to take its toll. He would not be able to work much longer without a break. From New York, Mrs. Bernstein had written him that her collection of his letters and cables had grown so bulky that it had been necessary to transfer them from her handbag to "a nice wooden box" on her bedside table.[48] His quest into the past and its subsequent transferal to paper he viewed as a great adventure.

This phase of the adventure was over, it seemed. On 13 November, Wolfe wrote that he had been in Oxford for exactly four weeks. "During the last two months and a half I have written 100,000

44. *Letters*, 14 October 1926, #33.
45. Ibid.
46. *Letters*, 28 October 1926, #35.
47. Ibid.
48. *Letters*, 8 November 1926, #38.

words. . . . The first book is finished the third almost finished. I must do what I can on the second before I come back."[49] "I am beerfat and heavy," he wrote at the end of this letter, "the wild thing is drugged, the cry does not break from my throat now. But it will again."[50]

Wolfe did not work further on his novel after he left Oxford. He traveled to Europe, as planned, and crossed the Rhine into Germany in "a typhoon of excitement." He carried the manuscript with him in Mrs. Bernstein's green suitcase, which was filled to bursting with "the twelve great ledgers." From Munich he wrote in December 1926 that the people of Germany were "simple, more honest, and a great deal more friendly than the French."[51] Tired and homesick, the bulk of his mission accomplished, Thomas Wolfe was ready to come home.

The 1928 letters, some 350 pages in length, constitute the largest segment of the correspondence. Although Wolfe labeled his European trip "The Grand Tour of Renunciation," he was, in fact, unable to sever his deep emotional and psychological ties to Mrs. Bernstein. Shortly before he left for Paris in July 1928, he wrote to her with characteristic ideality:

> Love to me is still the fantastic and absolute thing that it is in the books, and never is in life. And the way I should like to be, the way I should like to act is not meanly or badly as I often do, but in the grand and heroic manner of people in books. . . .
>
> Now that you have gone away I see you as if you were in a book—if you have any blemishes I don't remember them, if you wore a different suit every day, I don't remember them all. . . . I love you more than anyone in the world.[52]

It was to this "ideal woman" that he directed his outpourings during the next several months in Europe. As he was not actively working on a novel during the summer of 1928, the force of his creative energies overflowed into his correspondence, and it contains examples of the best of Wolfe's writing.

Throughout the summer, Wolfe carefully avoided Mrs. Bernstein, who was touring Italy and Germany with friends. By late July, he had begun to acquire again the sense of freedom and release characteristic of his European travels. When he was alone and not taxed by the actual demands of the relationship, he was able to communicate

49. *Letters*, 13 November 1926, #40.
50. Ibid.
51. *Letters*, 10 December 1926, #45.
52. *Letters*, 7 June 1928, #49.

with her lovingly and rationally. Over the summer, perhaps because he sensed that he had escaped a confrontation with her, his letters expressed a more tranquil mood: "I am wandering alone like a phantom in strange cities; my heart is full of loneliness—in loneliness of soul I walk along the streets, but I think and dream great things, my eyes and face are calm and good; I am beginning again to be the person I can be."[53]

Although Wolfe wrote quite lovingly to Mrs. Bernstein during this period, she could not believe that he was sincere. From aboard the *Reliance* on 14 August, she dryly wrote: "One thing you seem to be clear about, and that is that at present you are swept with a tremendous feeling for me. But I cannot see what goes with it. You surely have no sense of responsibility towards me. I hardly think that ever enters your mind."[54]

On 1 September 1928, Wolfe wrote from Frankfurt of his second meeting with Joyce, whom he had encountered on a bus tour of the city. The two men sat and walked together, each smiling nervously and gesturing silently to one another. Characteristically, Wolfe was too shy to speak to his idol: "I must wait now for the third time we meet—The Magic Third!—which will be in Dresden or in Heaven."[55] He had not communicated with anyone for seven weeks. For him this period of isolation had served as a time of spiritual recuperation. "I look wild and crazy and ragged," he wrote, "but I believe I am almost as sane as I can hope to be."[56]

He did not write to Mrs. Bernstein again until 4 October. For sixty pages, Wolfe chronicles for her a series of fantastic events, beginning with his description of the injuries incurred during the Oktoberfest drunken brawl: "I had a mild concussion of the brain, four scalp wounds and a broken nose. . . . I am shaven as bald as a priest."[57] His absorbing description of the Oktoberfest, the injuries he sustained in a rowdy beer hall, and his journey to Oberammergau were subsequently to surface in the later fiction

In the interim, as was noted earlier, Aline Bernstein had written frantically on 16 October to tell Wolfe that Madeleine Boyd had called to say that Scribner's was greatly interested in his book. On 18 and 20 October, she tried to contact him by telegram but to no avail. Depressed and drained, Wolfe wandered aimlessly throughout Vienna, unaware of her efforts. On 25 October he wrote: "It has

53. *Letters*, 27 July 1928, #61.
54. *Letters*, 14 August 1928, #72.
55. *Letters*, 1–7 September 1928, #75.
56. Ibid.
57. *Letters*, 4 October 1928, #79.

been a matter of 3½ months since I landed this time upon this land of Europe—and what have I got to show for it? Some 30000 or 40000 words actually written. . . . Impulse is killed in me, life is dead."[58] On 29 October, he wrote to tell her that a "Mr. Peters" from Scribner's had contacted him about his manuscript. "In my present state Scribners does not make even a dull echo in me."[59]

In November 1928, Wolfe included in his correspondence with Mrs. Bernstein vivid descriptions of his trips to art museums and the theater and of his wanderings through Hungary, including a marvelous account of the villagers of Mezö-Kövsd. After he had seen *Faust*, he wrote: "Faust's own problem touches me more than Hamlet's—his problem is mine, it is the problem of modern life. He wants to know everything, to be a God—and he is caught in the terrible net of human incapacity."[60]

On 29 November 1928, he wrote Mrs. Bernstein his final letter from Europe. Included is a poem that he had created for her on the theme of man's limited capacity, a reflection of the frustration he was experiencing. He also expounded on the complexity of American life, a theme that would play a major part in his later fiction:

> All I see now is the magical towers of New York, made by money and power. I even have a sense of power and pride because my country is so young and strong. I want to become part of it, to make use of it in my life.—I wonder if we do see things better when we are away from them—from here I see only the glorious elements in America, the great towers, the wealth, the hope, the opportunity, the possibility of everything happening. But deeper in my Soul is the remembrance of other things, the horrible, fatal things that sicken me when I'm there—the bigotry, the hypocrisy, the intolerance, the Ku Kluxers, the politicians—the cruelty and evil cynicism of the men in power.[61]

The year 1929 was exciting for Wolfe, culminating in the October publication of *Look Homeward, Angel* and the resulting instantaneous success and notoriety. In December 1929, at Maxwell Perkins's urging, he applied for, and subsequently received, a Guggenheim fellowship that would enable him to travel and work independently on his projected novel, "October Fair." On 27 April 1930, Wolfe departed for Europe on the *Volendam*, leaving behind a distraught Aline Bernstein. In one of his few communications with her that

58. *Letters*, 25 October 1928, #87.
59. *Letters*, 29 October 1928, #90.
60. *Letters*, 18 November 1928, #99.
61. Ibid.

year, he wrote from Paris on 20 May, "Pray for me to do a good and beautiful piece of work: that is the only way to find any sort of peace."[62]

In the meantime, Mrs. Bernstein was writing about her past life for him, material that both would later use, he in *The Web and the Rock* and she in *An Actor's Daughter*. Prophetically, she wrote: "I have been writing the events of my life for you, but find it very hard to make it simple. I keep putting down all kinds of extraneous things, first thing you know it will turn into a novel and then I'll have to use it myself."[63]

On 24 May 1930, Wolfe wrote from Paris of his frustrating experience with Emily Davis Vanderbilt Thayer, who was to become the model for the character Amy Carlton in "The Party at Jack's" section of *You Can't Go Home Again*. He complained bitterly to Mrs. Bernstein that Emily had compared her lover Raymonde to him: "Emily said he was 'a genius' and that we both had much in common, and that we were both to be brothers. This was during luncheon: I got violently sick, and could eat no more, and had to rush into the restaurant to vomit."[64]

By the summer of 1930, Wolfe had decided that he must no longer write to Mrs. Bernstein in order to avoid what he considered to be her smothering and inhibiting influence. Throughout the fall and winter of 1930, she frantically besieged him with letters and cables, sending in October a birthday note punctuated dramatically with a drop of her own blood. Aside from two telegrams in December, pleading with her to desist from such harassment, Wolfe did not write to her again until after he returned home in March 1931.

In the early months of 1931, Wolfe continued to work furiously upon the characterizations of Esther Jack and her family, most notably her actor father. On 4 March he arrived home, settling at 40 Veranda Place in Brooklyn. Mrs. Bernstein, who had been suffering the past year from attacks of vertigo due to a circulatory disorder, read in the paper of his arrival and subsequently became so ill that she required hospitalization. When Wolfe heard the news, he sent her a letter in which he spoke of establishing in his fiction a fitting tribute to her: "I could never write a word about you or about my love for you in print that was not full of that love I bear you—no matter what bitter things we have said, I remember what was glorious magnificent and lovely, and I remember all that was beautiful and grand in you: all of my hope now and for the future is that I can

62. *Letters*, 20 May 1930, #108.
63. *Letters*, New York, 23 May 1930, #109.
64. *Letters*, 24 May 1930, #110.

wreak out of pain, hunger, and love a living memorial for you."[65] A total split, however, was imminent. When Wolfe's mother came to visit him in January 1932, she provided the impetus he needed. His two "mothers" had fought over possession of Thomas Wolfe—and Julia Wolfe had won.

During the next several years, Wolfe wrote a number of unmailed fragments to Mrs. Bernstein in which he confided his innermost thoughts. Some time in the winter of 1932, shortly after their bitter argument, he confided in an unsent letter that he had written 40,000 or 50,000 words, making a character called Esther Jacobs "talk magnificently." Within the same fragment is a questionnaire, in which he posed a series of the most personal sexual questions.[66] He also wrote of his work on "K19" and added a description of his short story "The Web of Earth," which was based on his mother's recollections to him during her January visit. "Max says I'm having the biggest wave of creative activity he ever saw," he wrote, "and I hope to God nothing is done now to destroy it. From now on I shall put nothing on paper but what I have seen or known—my vision of life."[67]

It was not until December 1933 that Thomas Wolfe finally broke his long silence with Aline Bernstein. Although the actual letter apparently has been lost, he kept three lengthy drafts, in which he wavered characteristically between words of love and bitterness. Of his nomadic existence in Brooklyn he wrote: "What is life and what is it for? Ten rooms, ten different places in ten years, in each of them all of the life, hunger, joy, magic, fury, pain and sorrow that the world can know. Ten years, ten rooms, ten thousand sheets of paper in each of them covered with ten million words that I have written."[68]

Mrs. Bernstein's novel, *Three Blue Suits*, was published in November 1933. Wolfe, in a formal, typewritten letter—the only letter he ever sent her not in his own hand, praised her work, although he mistakenly assumed that "Mr. Froelich" was patterned after Theodore Bernstein. He also chafed bitterly at her portrayal of the character Eugene in the story of the same title. Most alarming to him was her suggestion that he had deserted her by accepting the Guggenheim fellowship.

Throughout 1934, Wolfe maintained his silence. During that year, he was working feverishly with Maxwell Perkins to assemble and edit the manuscript of *Of Time and the River*. When he left for Europe on 2 March 1935, shortly before *Of Time and the River* was published, he sent Aline a prepublication copy and marked the pas-

65. *Letters*, March 1931, #126.
66. *Letters*, Winter 1932, #146.
67. *Letters*, Winter 1932, #147.
68. *Letters*, October 1933, #154.

sage at the end of the book in which Eugene first sees Esther aboard ship: "He turned, and saw her then, and so finding her, was lost, and so losing self, was found, and so seeing her, saw for a fading moment only the pleasant image of the woman that perhaps she was, and that life saw. He never knew. He only knew that from that moment his spirit was impaled upon the knife of love . . ." (*OT&R*, p. 911). Next to this passage he had inscribed the words: "My dear."

In May 1935, upon the occasion of Emily Davis Vanderbilt Thayer's suicide, he wrote a postcard to Mrs. Bernstein which remained unmailed. In language and theme, it is strikingly similar to material from *The Web and the Rock* and *You Can't Go Home Again*:

> I think about you a great deal and all the people I met through you and your group ten years ago. . . . It was a lie of life, false, cynical, scornful, drunk with unimagined power, and rotten to the core. And through that rottenness, through that huge mistaken falseness and corruption, there will run forever the memory of your loveliness—your flower face and your jolly dynamic little figure on my step at noon—the food, the cooking, and the love. . . . [69]

"The artist's point of view"

Since Wolfe and Mrs. Bernstein wrote primarily from their own experience, many of the people, places, and events described in the correspondence are recreated in their fiction. A close comparison of the letters with the later novels reveals some fascinating insights into how Wolfe and Bernstein molded the events of their lives into fictional form. A major portion of Wolfe's two posthumous novels, *The Web and the Rock* and *You Can't Go Home Again*, deal with the story of the love affair and with his fictional recreations of himself and Aline Bernstein as George Webber and Esther Jack. In 1933, Mrs. Bernstein published *Three Blue Suits*; the third story, "Eugene," deals fictionally with Wolfe's decision to apply for a Guggenheim fellowship and the heroine's reaction to this news. In *The Journey Down*, published in 1928, Mrs. Bernstein presents her version of the love affair, during the nine-year period from 1925 until 1934.

Wolfe's letters to Mrs. Bernstein came to a virtual halt after 1930. It was only then that he began his eight-year struggle to come to grips with the fictional account of the love story.[70] He would write

69. Letters, June 1935. This letter has been edited from the text.

70. For a detailed account of Wolfe's development of this material, see Richard Kennedy's *The Window of Memory*.

sketches about the love affair many times between 1930 and 1938, and these fragments would eventually become the basis for his two posthumous novels. According to his agent, Elizabeth Nowell, he struggled with this unmanageable mass of material for years and was never satisfied with its tentative final form. Most probably, he would have revised it further had he lived to do so.

Originally, he had decided to entitle the story of the love affair "Faust and Helen." Throughout the later correspondence, as was noted earlier, he had complained of his Faustian desire to gorge himself on the whole of experience. As was noted earlier, Wolfe was in the habit of constantly idealizing and mythologizing Mrs. Bernstein, comparing her to such legendary figures as Demeter, Solveig, and Helen. In her version of the love affair, *The Journey Down*, she was to write of a fantasy the heroine had experienced in a similar mythological fashion. "I believed that I was spread across the earth, the front of my body pressed the ground, my arms flung wide and my hands resting on a green hill. My face was crushed down against moist and fragrant grass; the sun warmed my back, the air touched me lightly and blew through my hair. Beneath my body ran a river; and the water in that river in its flow washed the sadness from my middle."[71]

In June 1931, Wolfe decided to write about his European experiences; he decided to call this material "Oktoberfest" or "The October Fair." In addition, he began working on a story dealing with much of what Mrs. Bernstein had told him of her early life and of her actor father, Joseph Frankau. As the letters indicate, she had written many of these sketches for him during the summers of 1930 and 1931, and she was eventually to use one episode in particular from the 1930 letters in her own fiction. The sketch about her visit to the dentist is reproduced almost verbatim in chapter 4 of *The Journey Down*:

> The pain of the drilling was terrible, and the sensation was worse than anything I had ever imagined. I squirmed and wriggled and a moustache of sweat formed on my lip. . . . Suddenly I knew that the pain was hurting nobody but myself. Here was a man so close that I could feel the human warmth exuding from him, and he did not feel my pain; the tissues of his hand touched the stuff of my tooth, touched the very pain itself, yet he could not feel it. I was an entity, a body so completely and so perfectly made that no one need know what I felt or thought, if I did not choose to show it. I felt Godhead in me, and at once the tenseness of my muscles relaxed.[72]

71. *The Journey Down*, p. 197.
72. Ibid., pp. 126–27.

Because Wolfe worked on a myriad of themes and experiences simultaneously, he developed a technique of writing in fragments. He would work on his sketches until he tired of them and put them away for revision or completion at a later date. Many of the segments that later became sections of *The Web and the Rock* were written in this manner. Several of these sketches were so complete that he was able to extract them from the large manuscript and use them as short stories. "The Quarrel" and "Penelope's Web," among others, have their own set of characters, their own progression and conclusion. In 1931, he wrote both the "October: 1931" and the "Late April 1928" segments of the love affair. In 1932, he worked on the quarrel scene, entitling it "A Vision of Death in April." Much of the material that he wrote at this time later became book 6 of *The Web and the Rock*. Not until 1933, however, did he consider the entire framework for his material, starting with the Old Catawba scene that would later open *The Web and the Rock*, continuing through the love affair and ending with the hospital scene and his subsequent realization that "you can't go home again."

In 1935, after *Of Time and the River* was published, Wolfe returned to "The October Fair," which he envisioned as part of a six-part plan:

Look Homeward, Angel	(1884–1920)
Of Time and the River	(1920–1925)
The October Fair	(1925–1928)
The Hills Beyond Pentland	(1838–1884)
The Death of the Enemy	(1928–1933)
Pacific End	(1791–1884)

A study of Wolfe's outline, which can be found in the appendix of Richard Kennedy's *A Window of Memory*, indicates that Wolfe later decided to extend "The October Fair" segment of the manuscript dealing with the love affair from 1928 to 1930. *The Web and the Rock* was later to follow the 1925–30 chronology. His chronology was fixed, for the most part, by the order of his experience.

Wolfe was still unable to come to terms with the material, however, because of the emotional turmoil that made it difficult to establish the distance and objectivity he needed, so once more he set it aside. After changing names and backgrounds and evolving material for his larger-than-life hero who would fit into the epic scheme, by the fall of 1936 he was ready to draw upon his entire experience for the whole book. He decided to make it mythic, with his central character reenacting the classic search for identity, beginning as an orphan boy and growing up to continue the search for his place in the world as his experience expanded ever outward.

Since 1935, Wolfe had been following a new method that allowed him greater control over his material than before. He had begun dictating to a secretary, often reworking the dictated material at a later date. In the latter part of 1936, Wolfe wrote the bulk of the material that was to become his final manuscript of *The Web and the Rock* and *You Can't Go Home Again.* Much of what later became the first nine chapters of *The Web and the Rock* was written during this period. In the spring of 1937, he wrote what would later become chapters 32 to 35 of *The Web and the Rock.*

In 1937, he also completed "The Party at Jack's," the most complex and ambitious unit of his later writings. By the summer of 1938, he had finished his third draft of this material and thought about incorporating it with the love story material. It was not until this time that he decided on a name for his heroine. Earlier he had changed her name from Esther Jacobs to Rebecca Feitlebaum (one is reminded of Mrs. Bernstein's early reference in the letters to the name "Rebecca" and of Wolfe's allusions to his Jewish "Grey Rebecca" in the notebooks). Finally, he settled on the name of Esther Jack.

In March 1938, Wolfe decided to make his book a completely autobiographical chronicle, pulling together all of the projects he had been previously working on, including "The October Fair" material that contained the love story. He worked for two months on revisions before he gave the huge manuscript to Edward Aswell of Harper and Brothers, his new editor, as of December 1937, after he had officially split with Scribner's and Maxwell Perkins. His hero was to have a new name and his book a new title. He evolved its name and purpose in his notebook:

The Weft That the Weaver Hath Woven
The Weft That the Weaver Hath Wrought
The Web That the Weaver Has (Hath) Woven
The Web That the Weaver Has (Hath) Wrought
The Years That the Locust Has Eaten

The City: The Rock

The Web and the Rock
The Web in the Rock

Let His Name be Webber

THE WEB AND THE ROCK

A story of the voyage of Everyman:
His Going To and Fro Upon the Earth
His Walking Up and Down In it:

And His desire for Home;
His Vision of the Lost, the Found,
The Ever-Real, the Never-Here America
by Thomas Wolfe[73]

Because the first 170 pages of *The Web and the Rock* are considered by most critics to be the best portion of the book, the second section, the love story, has been grossly underrated. Obviously, the two portions do not fit together smoothly, and it must be remembered that the book was arranged and published posthumously—although Aswell was following Wolfe's outline. While "The Hound of Darkness" section in particular represents the writing of a much more mature and socially conscious writer, the second and longest section of the novel, concerning the hero's journey to the Golden City of New York and his love affair with Mrs. Jack, follows a scheme and pattern larger and more universal than the superficial story line suggests.

One of the most significant changes that Wolfe made in his new material concerned the character of George Webber. His complete defense of Eugene Gant in his earlier fiction was altered so that George Webber was satirized and took quite a beating from the author. According to Aswell, this is what Wolfe meant when he said that there was "no longer a trace of Eugene Gantiness left in his mind and spirit." It is a fact that is often overlooked in the reading of this book. The writer was a mature artist, standing at a distance from his material, able (but for occasional lapses) to see his young hero with the detachment of an artist who had a greater purpose in mind than the mere recital of events. Beneath the surface story of a young provincial's journey to New York, his ensuing love affair, and the ultimate disillusionment with and rejection of both the woman and the city lies a complex pattern of undercurrents and themes. His story deals with the loss of illusion through change, the loss of innocence through experience, and the eventual loneliness that the hero must face. Like Don Quixote, the young idealistic hero is blinded by the deceptions of his own imagination. The love affair represents but one road on the journey of Everyman through life and the hero's stumbling search for equilibrium within a web of illusion. Wolfe strove to lift the veil, to observe life closely, and to see it as it really is, not merely the surface, but the inner reality as well. He attempted to find the truth behind many conflicting and illusory forces: good versus evil, real versus ideal, fixity versus change, simplicity versus multiplicity.

73. Richard Kennedy and Paschel Reeves, *Notebooks*, 2:954.

Into this web of illusion comes Mrs. Esther Jack. Though not a member of the aristocracy, she is an intellectual Jew in New York who is a member of the literary elite. Older, wealthy, passionate, yielding, she is indeed an answer to George Webber's dreams. Initially, he sees her as she really is, a middle-aged woman, small and energetic, with a fresh and healthy look—nice looking, but she would have caused few people to look at her a second time. But for the hero reality quickly shifts to illusion as he comes to envision Esther Jack as "the most beautiful woman who ever lived."[74]

George Webber may not be able to view Esther realistically, but, for the most part, Thomas Wolfe can. Carefully and methodically he develops a character both rich and totally believable. She is complex, yet constant in her love. She is emotional yet she possesses a sense of balance that allows her to view people, situations, and attitudes rationally and with understanding. She becomes, in fact, the filter through which all of the violent opposites of George's distorted vision flows, the rose-colored fantasy, the black and mad nightmare. It is her view juxtaposed against his that enables the reader to judge which is the true reality.

Wolfe's fictional creation, Esther Jack, is consistent with the attitude he presents in the letters toward Mrs. Bernstein. Sometime later, in 1933, Wolfe broke a long silence to tell her: ". . . no matter what else you did, or what anguish, madness and despair I knew, that . . . woman who came to my room day after day for years was beyond every standard of comparison, the greatest, loveliest, and most beautiful woman I have ever known. And I also want to tell you that I now know I loved that woman with my life, that she is mixed into my blood and that I shall love her forever. . . ."[75]

There were two Aline Bernsteins for Thomas Wolfe—the woman who actually existed and the timeless ideal who seemed to be the greater reality within the realm of his imagination. This dichotomy is typical of Wolfe. Perhaps he tried to turn Aline Bernstein and her fictional counterpart into mythological figures because he was unable to come to grips with the fact that she was old enough to be his mother and, in fact, had in many ways become a surrogate mother to him. Throughout the correspondence, Mrs. Bernstein is either saint or sinner, for Wolfe's vision was so inflexible at this time that no compromise was possible. In the fiction, however, the author was able to view her with somewhat greater detachment—although during his lifetime he was never able to present her in other than a timeless fashion.

74. *The Web and the Rock*, p. 296.
75. *Letters*, October 1933, #154.

Throughout both *The Web and the Rock* and *You Can't Go Home Again*, there is no doubt that Wolfe's finest fictional creation is Esther Jack. In both chapter 26, "Penelope's Web," and chapter 49, "Dark October," he gives his heroine pages of monologue through which she can express her rich and enchanting personality. Her reflections of her childhood years echo passages of Mrs. Bernstein's letters, especially her reflections on the old and dirty copper jar she had found hidden in an antique shop:

> I cannot sleep, this is what I think, there is nothing in life that cannot be made beautiful. Years ago I bought a jar on Allen street, because it had a good shape. I paid 65 cents for it. I scraped and polished it, and found it was made of copper with circles worked all round the bowl. It comes from somewhere in the east. I had it made into a lamp and every night when I put on the lights, its surface gives me back fires. It gives me this because I knew and recognized its beauty under the grime of its wandering.[76]

Quite possibly, some of this material has its roots in the sketches that Mrs. Bernstein wrote for Wolfe during the summer of 1931 about her childhood.

A year before, during their estrangement in the summer of 1930, Mrs. Bernstein had written to Wolfe in Europe of the long hours spent in working on the sketches: "Long long into the night I lay awake trying to think how best to tell my story."[77] Wolfe was taken with this sentence and copied it in his notebook for later use. In chapter 26 of *The Web and the Rock*, he was to use this material as a part of Esther's monologue, but not before he had changed the language, the date, and the circumstances:

> "Long, long into the night I lay—"
> (One!)
> "Long, long into the night I lay awake—"
> (Two!)
> "Long, long into the night I lay awake, thinking how I should tell my story."
>
> Oh how lovely those words are! They make music in me just like bells.[78]

By establishing this poetic melody, he develops these lines as one of the thematic references for Esther Jack. In addition, he ties the words

76. *Letters*, August 1931, #137.
77. *Letters*, 23 May 1930, #109.
78. *The Web and the Rock*, pp. 378–79.

to Mrs. Jack's love of language and music and imparts to her the childlike quality that permeates the character throughout the book. By placing the material in 1926, during a more idyllic time in the relationship of his characters, Wolfe is able to avoid any reference to their later estrangement—particularly from the heroine's point of view.

There are other indications that Wolfe took similar incidents from actual experience and used them for his own artistic purposes. In 1931, Mrs. Bernstein wrote to him of an incident in which she had lost her way and a policeman had assisted her in getting home. In "Dark October," a policeman questions the distraught Esther Jack concerning her reasons for sitting alone on a park bench in the dead of night. The language with which she responds is suggestive of Aline Bernstein as Mrs. Jack explains for whom she is waiting: "He has the face of a demented angel, his head is wild and beautiful, and there is madness and darkness and evil in his brain. He is more cruel than death and more lovely than a flower."[79] In 1930, after reflecting upon why she remained faithful to Wolfe despite the pain and heartache he had caused her, Mrs. Bernstein wrote: "Why I cling to you so, God only knows, but you are made of stuff so glorious, so terrible, and if I let you go you will be lost."[80]

Throughout their association, Wolfe could never understand why Mrs. Bernstein surrounded herself with people whom he considered to be both corrupt and decadent. In a 1928 letter from Cologne, he characteristically compared her incorruptibility with that of the flock who surrounded her:

> When I think of you—a rich and rare substance, so beautiful and so single among all the people I have known, I wish for this for you as well. You are unhappily situated among the most prominent and prosperous Geese or Geese Drivers: I have been mad so many times to see you in the procession, obediently mouthing the season's jargon, eating the goulosh that began in Moscow and ends in Harlem. Yet I know it cannot hurt you very much, for you were born glorious and exempt from all the weary toil and struggle that marks my effort towards some little wisdom.[81]

Some time later, when Wolfe wrote his pivotal chapter "The Party at Jack's" for *You Can't Go Home Again*, he established his heroine, Mrs. Jack, as a timeless beauty, untarnished by the glitter of the false

79. Ibid., p. 629.
80. *Letters*, Late Summer 1930, #117.
81. *Letters*, 12 August 1928, #70.

people who surround her. One of the decadent figures from real life about whom he wrote in the letters and later fictionalized in this chapter was Emily Davis Vanderbilt Thayer, a friend of Mrs. Bernstein's whom she had met on a 1938 European trip. Mrs. Thayer came to represent for Wolfe all the corrupt and tragic elements of a particular segment of American society, for although Mrs. Thayer was beautiful on the surface, he considered her to be inwardly decadent and potentially evil. In 1930, he wrote to Mrs. Bernstein of having been contacted by Mrs. Thayer in Europe and subsequently having been dragged to a series of exhausting and humiliating tête-à-têtes with her literary acquaintances. She had compared Wolfe to her lover of the moment, which had caused the volatile and temperamental Wolfe to become physically ill. He reflected on the emptiness of Emily's personality in a letter to Mrs. Bernstein:

> The people who are good invariably have something in them on which they can rely—when they have nothing in them on which to rely, and go hanging about from place to place relying on things and people, they are no good. That is the trouble with Emily. . . . [She thinks] she is a terrible "destructer-ess" who wrecks men's lives . . . she'll be hanging around this way 20 years from now, trying to fill up her own emptiness with other folks' richness. . . .[82]

Wolfe was abstracting the qualities that he attributed to Mrs. Thayer and using them as the basis for the character of Amy Carlton in "The Party at Jack's." Amy Carlton is notable for her selfishness, superficiality, and "doll faced beauty." Like the others at the party, with the exception of Mrs. Jack, she lives a sterile and meaningless existence and is as lifeless as the puppets in Piggy Logan's circus. In this chapter Wolfe develops a stunning satire of the decadent American upper class.

A close comparison between the correspondence and the fictional works offers many other examples of how Wolfe used actual events and people as a basis for his fictional creations. On the basis of such comparison, it is also possible to explore those key events that Wolfe chose to exclude from his fictional re-creation. In both later novels, Wolfe chose not to include huge segments of his experience, and the letters serve as a valuable tool to "fill in" several of these great gaps in time. In *The Web and the Rock* there are no details of his 1926 trip, and his four-year stay in Brooklyn is merely noted in a single sentence although stories in *From Death to Morning* draw upon this period. Wolfe organized much of his material around the pivotal

82. *Letters*, 24 May 1930, #110.

months of April and October, both of which were symbolically important in his work. He passes quickly from chapter 28, "April, late April," which concentrates on the love affair in April 1926, to chapter 29, which takes place in April 1927, virtually omitting the fascinating details of the creative process involved in *LHA*. By writing nothing in his fiction of his emotional and financial dependence upon Mrs. Bernstein during these crucial months, he negates her key role in the creation of *Look Homeward, Angel.*

Of the many variations between fact and fiction that can be extracted from a close study of the correspondence and the text, the most significant differences deal with Wolfe's treatment of the Oktoberfest. He recognized the potential importance of this material immediately, and in October 1928 he wrote to Mrs. Bernstein concerning its possible later use: "My dear, will you save these letters that I have written you. They have been poor jumbled letters, but outside of my notes, they give the only fairly consecutive account of my life for the last four months. Please save the last one about the Oktoberfest—it is a broken mumbling sort of nightmare, but I put down without any literary varnish some of the things that were happening at the time."[83] Fully fifty pages are devoted in the letters to a description of these bizarre happenings, whereas Wolfe devoted relatively few pages in his book to a sketchily presented version of one of the most fascinating episodes in his life. The greatest difference, in both intensity and scope of the accounts, is reflected in the comparison between Wolfe's portrayal of the fight scene in chapter 48 and his recital of the events in his letters to Mrs. Bernstein. In chapter 48, "The Hospital," he wrote: "What happened then he did not know. In that quick instant of his drunken fear, had he swung out and smashed his great stone mug into the swinelike face, the red pig's eyes, of the hulking fellow next to him? He did not know, but there had been a fight, a murderous swinging of great mugs, a flash of knives, the sudden blinding fury of red, beer-drunk rage."[84] The four-page version of the fight that Wolfe recounted for Mrs. Bernstein in the letters was full of exact and dramatic detail. After he had knocked a man over a table and had run exultantly out of the hall "feeling like a child who has thrown a stone through a window," he finds himself trapped by an angry mob in an alley:

> I stopped and turned and in that horrible slippery mudhole I had a bloody fight with these people. I remember the thing now with horror as a kind of hell of slippery mud, and blood,

83. *Letters*, 21 October 1928, #88.
84. *The Web and the Rock*, p. 623.

> and darkness, with the rain falling upon us several maniacs who were trying to kill. At that time I was too wild, too insane to be afraid, but I seemed to be drowning in mud—it was really the blood that came pouring from my head into my eyes—and there was *always*, *always* alive in me one bright living spark of sanity and consciousness.[85]

Although Herr Doctor remains basically the same in both book and letters, and Johann, the assistant, even retains the same name throughout both versions of the story, such details are missing from the novel as the minister who visited Wolfe's hospital room intending to save his soul: "He came in, all dressed up in a frock coat, with a bible under his arm—a little ninny man with a mustache, looking as Lutheran as God."[86] Interesting to note also is the varied treatment of the nuns in the book and the letters and Wolfe's dramatically altered description of the hospital room in *The Web and the Rock*. In order to portray it as a much more somber and torturous place, he added the crucifix above the door "nailed with tormented gaunt ribs, and the twisted thighs, the starved face, and the broken agony of Christ."[87] Wolfe has drawn conclusions from his fictional portrayal of the Oktoberfest events which are much more profound than the observations that he presented in the letters. Together the two sources provide a fascinating perspective on his creative use of actual experience.

Wolfe had come, in his novels as well as in his life, full circle. Once more he stood alone, but this time it was with the realization that neither fame nor love could be enough in man's search for truth and creativity. His life had been a series of opposites and contradictions. While striving always to be free, he yearned for the dependence and security that comfort the human soul. By 1937 he had conquered the overdependence on emotional supports, a tremendous ordeal, causing him to cast aside his two most beloved friends, Aline Bernstein and Maxwell Perkins. He had arrived, in his last years, on the other side of loneliness, a loneliness not of youth but of maturity, not of hope but of acceptance of the common human condition of isolation. Though he yearned for fixity, he became the prophet of change. As he stated in his famous Purdue speech: "I had not realized yet that the world changes, that the world is changing all the time, that the world, indeed, is in a constant and perpetual state of revolution—

85. *Letters*, 4 October 1928, #79.
86. *Letters*, 23 October 1928, #88.
87. *The Web and the Rock*, p. 623.

and that a man, a creative man most of all, if he is going to live and grow, must change with the world."[88]

Wolfe's battle was the human battle, his quest to find that which endures in the face of change was the quest of Everyman; inevitably his vulnerability is our own. Like Whitman, he embraced diversity, the diversity of his own divisions, psychoses, and antagonisms. His journey exemplified a passage from innocence to knowledge, from hate to love, from the isolated eccentric to the voice of the common man. What he learned is that there is no one door, no simple entrance to knowledge and that to conquer the labyrinth of life by setting out on any narrow path is to lose the battle. Man must abandon his dreams and face the chaos of reality. Wolfe wrote:

> I have found out that the man who hopes to create anything in this world of any enduring value, or beauty, must be willing to wreak it out of his spirit at the cost of unbelievable pain and labor; I know of no other way it can be done, he must work in the solitude and loneliness of art, no one can do it for him, and all of his childish dreams of a various and golden life, in which he has time to do everything and triumph in all of them, are out of the question.[89]

Since Mrs. Bernstein also wrote various works of fiction based upon sketches, episodes, and people mentioned in the letters, a comparison between the correspondence and her fictional works is also of especial interest. In the previous critical studies concerning the Wolfe-Bernstein relationship, little if anything has been said about Aline Bernstein's ability as an author. As early as 1926, Wolfe had commented in the letters on her writing ability:

> I find when I write you the greatest difficulty in coming to an end—and usually somewhere I spin a part of my entrails into it. Your letters have a beginning, a middle, and an ending—they do not sprawl—they work up swiftly to a note of passion, and decline accurately to one of hope or despair. . . . And yet while I grope darkly about in these letters, you obtain a sense of form, proportion, perfection of your woe into two and a half pages and all according to the most approved laws of dramatic and fictional technique.[90]

Although she began writing sketches of her childhood for Wolfe as early as 1930, she did not begin working on material for her own

88. *Thomas Wolfe's Purdue Speech, Writing and Living*, ed. William Braswell and Leslie A. Field (Lafayette, Indiana, 1964).

89. Thomas Wolfe, *Letters*, ed. Elizabeth Nowell.

90. *Letters*, 13 November 1926, #40.

fiction until somewhat later. In November 1933, she wrote to tell Wolfe of the publication of *Three Blue Suits*, a collection of three short stories: "Mr. Froelich," "Herbert Wilson," and "Eugene." The work is a sensitive and delicately written portrayal of three men, tied loosely together by each man's ownership of a blue suit and its significance on a pivotal day in the life of each. The first story, "Mr. Froelich," deals with a day in the life of a prosperous New York businessman. The focus on this particular day is upon the women in his life, each of whom he has in some way "purchased" with his vast wealth: the secretary, who hates him and knows "that her plain face had been deliberately hired";[91] the beautiful golden mistress who "always fulfilled his dream of her";[92] and the useless wife, who possesses "too much fat . . . too much lace, too many ribbon rosebuds."[93] Mr. Froelich, while totally in control of his world, displays an emptiness similar to those characters presented in "The Party at Jack's" sections of Wolfe's later fiction.

"Herbert Wilson," the second story, deals with the day after the funeral of Bert Wilson's wife, Hattie, after a marriage of twenty-four years. Bert Wilson is a fabric salesman, one of those people whom others can see countless times over the years and never remember. On the day before Hattie's funeral, Bert has traded the ineffectual gray suit he has habitually worn for the new blue serge that he has always wanted. He had not had the courage to wear it to Hattie's funeral, however, for "when he saw Hattie's bleak face resting so quiet on the white satin, he dared not put it on. She might open her eyes and think he was a stranger."[94] The day after the funeral Bert anticipates doing all of the things he has always wanted to do. He eats in a restaurant and is served by a lovely young waitress, he window shops, he comes to work elegantly dressed. He finds, however, that nothing is any different. His customers treat him no differently than they ever have. When he gets home, he is forced to face the reality of being alone:

> He closed his door with a little bang. The sitting room smelt of crushed leaves and lilies, there was a piece of fern and the wilted head of a white carnation on the floor. He stopped at the door of the bedroom, a sudden pang darting through his body. The bed was unmade, as he had left it, his slippers and pajamas on the floor, yesterday's collar and tie on the bureau, the old grey suit folded on the arm chair. He sat on the bed, on the

91. *Three Blue Suits*, p. 14.
92. Ibid., p. 20.
93. Ibid., p. 12.
94. Ibid., p. 30.

> rumpled sheets and blanket, his shoulders stooped forward, his head bent, his coat hanging like a rag, the collar up and out beyond his neck. Two great tears fell down his cheeks. He buried his head in the pillow, put out his hand and patted the other pillow beside it. "Poor Hattie," he sobbed, "poor Hattie."[95]

"Eugene" is the only autobiographical story of the three, and it deals with the day on which a young writer puts on his blue suit for a meeting uptown with his publisher. "Eugene" is the only story of the three written primarily in dialogue; it bears a striking resemblance stylistically to *The Journey Down*, which was published some five years later. Thomas Wolfe had shown his ability to climb into his heroine's mind; Aline Bernstein did no less in expressing her awareness of Thomas-Eugene's thoughts:

> . . . he wished with all his heart that things could be always just the way he wanted them. He wanted a world where he could wander at his own sweet will, he wished that he could write in thought, he wished that his books would spring full printed from his brain, without the drudgery of pencil guided by his hand on paper, typing, cutting, revising. He wished that he could tell her of his deep love, and still make her see the necessity of his going. . . . He wished that he was far away in space and time, far enough so that he could write the book about her. . . .[96]

Wolfe commented upon the "Mr. Froelich" and "Eugene" sections of the book in his December 1933 letter. He mistakenly assumed that Mrs. Bernstein had used her husband, Theodore Bernstein, as a model for the first story. Of "Eugene," he bitterly chaffed at such a realistic portrayal and took issue with her indirect accusation that he had "sold her out" for the Guggenheim money. She should be much more careful, he noted, when dealing with the fictionalized account of real people:

> I don't believe that anything that is good and shows the integrity of the artist's spirit can do anyone any damage in the end, and of course, as I have found out in the last four years, the trouble and confusion comes from the difference between the artist's point of view, which is concerned with the general truth drawn from his personal experience, and the point of view of people which is, particularly if they are in your book, con-

95. Ibid., pp. 45–46.
96. Ibid., pp. 73–74.

> cerned with making personal identifications from something which is intended as a general truth. . . . It is right to have a passionate bias in everything you create. It is right to feel the indignation, the conviction, the certitude, the sense of conflict, with which it seems to me everyone who creates something must have, but I don't think you can stack the cards against someone in order to justify yourself without being yourself the loser for it. The temptation to do this carries with it its own punishment and if you try to set up dummy figures of your own instead of real people just for the satisfaction it gives you to knock the dummy figures down, your work will suffer for it in the end.[97]

Mrs. Bernstein defended what she had written and repudiated his accusations. She also explained to him her purpose in writing: "I am going on writing, but I will never be a professional, I will write only just what I want to get out of the fullness of my experience and understanding."[98]

True to her word, Mrs. Bernstein published *The Journey Down* in 1938 and *An Actor's Daughter* in 1941. The first novel presented her version of the relationship with Wolfe from its inception, her downward journey after their separation until her suicide attempt and her subsequent reaffirmation of her own intrinsic value and love of life. *An Actor's Daughter* presents Mrs. Bernstein's autobiographical account of her early years, until shortly after her parents' death, and her arrival at the threshold of womanhood. It is an enchanting book that deals with many of the marvelous people from Mrs. Bernstein's past. It is no wonder, after reading about her actor father, her captivating Aunt Nana, and the others in her early life, all described in her rich and musical style of writing, that Wolfe listened with rapt attention as she spent countless hours reciting these tales to him.

Through both the Wolfe and Bernstein versions of the love affair, the common element is the timelessness of the enduring love each had for the other, despite the events that caused them to separate. Like Wolfe, in his fictional portrayal of her, Mrs. Bernstein also presents a description of the hero's blinding power over her: "She looked at him across the tea-table, his face was unmistakably kindled by the divine fire. She wondered if all who saw that face could see all that she could see there. . . . In that one quiet scene, over the peaceful tea-table, she looked at him and was blinded."[99]

It becomes increasingly apparent that this correspondence is to be appreciated as a valuable addition to the Wolfe archives for many

97. *Letters*, 11 December 1933, #156.
98. Letters, 16 December 1933. This letter has been edited from the text.
99. *The Journey Down*, pp. 61–63.

reasons, but the most compelling is that it stands as an invaluable primary source for the study of the fictional writings of both authors. Theirs is a story of courage: on Wolfe's part to reveal the full scope of his mercurial personality; on Aline Bernstein's part to continue to love such a man devotedly, despite the outward show of scorn and the abuse he heaped upon her. Together, they dared always to be exceptional. Their letters are a fitting tribute to them both.

1925–1926: Idyllic Years

Thomas Wolfe first met Aline Bernstein aboard the Olympic *in August 1925 on his return trip from Europe. Their love for one another was deep and almost instantaneous, and by October they had become constant companions. The following year and a half was near-perfect for the two lovers. It culminated with their trip to England, during which time, after Mrs. Bernstein's departure for New York, he wrote the major part of the book that was to become* Look Homeward, Angel. *Yet the turbulence that lay ahead was foreshadowed in many of the letters that Wolfe wrote during this period. His bitter and unjustified accusations concerning Mrs. Bernstein's fidelity were to become increasingly strident as the relationship continued.*

1. [New York, Fall 1925]
My dear—

I came down but couldn't get in—will you call me up at dinner time? The flowers are lovely. They were the only ones I got. I tried to get you on the telephone about 1:30 after I came up from meeting my sister[1] but no answer.

My love, Aline

1. Ethel Frankau. Miss Frankau, who lived with the Bernstein family, was an executive at Bergdorf-Goodman's. Throughout its duration, Miss Frankau remained violently opposed to her sister's relationship with Wolfe.

2. Westport, Conn.[1] [December 1925]
My dear—

We are going home this afternoon, and I wonder if I will have some word from you. I have been going along on your telegram since you left. Did you ever get a place to sleep on the way home? If I had only had the time, I am sure that I could have made them put an extra car on for you.—It has been bitter cold ever since you went away, but clear and sunny. We have been out of doors all the time, skating or walking, and yesterday we motored up to New Haven to do a little light antique-ing. I have never given Lillian a wedding present, and we found some lovely old silver. This place is a dream[,] so beautiful and so comfortable. I am not much of a skater, but Edla[2] is and she takes me around a good bit. I have been in my bed before ten every night, and then a nice quiet read.—I wish you could have been down for my stage debut.[3] It was grand, you never in the world would have known me. I wore a black wig and a tight fitting long dress, and stood very straight and quiet like a lady. Mr. Baker[4] was very enthusiastic about the production. I had a talk with him during the second intermission and all the time I wanted to speak of you but I didn't. I wonder whether you are working on the other play.[5] And have you had glorious meals at home? And have you been to lots of parties? At any rate, you have had a rest from your teaching and other worries and dissatisfaction. I have been thinking of you pretty constantly (most inelegant expression)[. . . .]

1. Mrs. Bernstein's friend, Lillian Wadsworth, had a home in Westport, Connecticut.

2. Mrs. Bernstein's daughter. Wolfe's fictionalized character based upon Edla was referred to as Alma throughout the *W&R* and *YCGHA*.

3. In December 1925, the Neighborhood Playhouse performed the Chassidic play, *The Dybbuk*, one of its finest performances. It is possible that Mrs. Bernstein performed in this play as one of the townspeople.

4. Professor George Pierce Baker. Wolfe had been a member of his 47 Theatre Workshop at Harvard.

5. Most probably *Mannerhouse*, because Mrs. Bernstein would call it "the other play" since it was *Welcome to Our City* that was in her suitcase on board ship when she met Wolfe for the first time.

3. [Asheville, North Carolina] Monday [December 1925]

This is the only paper handy at the moment—it must serve, for my desire to write you a word is stronger than my need to wait.[1]

Your letters and your cablegrams came:—they have been almost committed to memory—red Embers in them ashes of my heart and hope[.] I came home to a Christmas of death, doom, desolation, sadness, disease, and despair: my family is showing its customary and magnificent Russian genius for futility and tragedy.

A cousin of the Wolfe family died a few hours before my arrival;[2] pneumonia—He was a good hearted, good natured and uninspired drunkard, was taken ill on a weekend spree, and lived four days. The infinite capacity of my people to pile it on strains belief. My brother[3] met me at the station with the news that another member of my damned and stricken family had been lost; that he was troubled by his appendix, my mother by a severe bronchial cold which might develop into pneumonia, and that my sister,[4] just returned from an interrupted rest cure at the hospital, had hysteria and had broken down under the nervous strain of Christmas preparation. He then wished me a merry Christmas.

Today my mother, thanks to good medical attention, and her own sturdiness, seems practically well; my brother is robust and damnably nervous, as usual, and my sister, able to talk coherently for the first time without tears, has been carted away to the hospital for a rest. She has exhausted herself by her own nervous generosity—

The Wolfe family, circa 1914. (In left group, left to right, standing) *Thomas Wolfe; Julia Wolfe; W. C. Wolfe; Fred Gambrell (?), husband of Effie Wolfe;* (seated) *two Gambrell children (?).* (In right group) *Effie Wolfe Gambrell; Fred Wolfe; Mabel Wolfe; Ben Wolfe; and four Gambrell children (?) (From a copy in North Carolina Collection, UNC Library, Chapel Hill)*

which is a kind of obsession—by brooding over her failure to have children, and by frequent and stealthy potations of corn whiskey, a jug of which is always on tap in the cupboard. This last none of us will admit, and all of us know it is true. To finish it, under concerted amount of family funerals in the company of long faced relatives, listening to uneasing post mortems at home and abroad on the causes of my kinsman's demise—how he was hale and well Sunday, what he had said, done, eaten, how old man Weaver or old lady Campbell or young Jack Rogers had been taken under similar circumstances (we are here today and gone tomorrow; itsallforthebest, heshappierwhereheis; wereallputhereforapurpose; itwastheLord'swill; and various other philosophical profundities tending to prove that the demise of a toper from exposure and whiskey is really the result of beneficent machinations of Godalmighty); advice as to the people I should visit, the food I should eat, the times I should do it—I have blown up, moved to a hotel, and saturated the leaden waste that coats my soul with quantities of white raw burning devastating corn whiskey!

What the upshot will be I know not—whether I stay here a week, a month, a year, or the rest of my life. I have passed the greater part of my life very pleasantly in hell, and I may spend the remainder of it very pleasantly in a large, comfortable, convenient and well equipped mad house, which beckons to me invitingly forty miles down the mountain.

My people—my mother, sister, brother-in-law[5]—had planned to go to Florida this week[6]—that, apparently, is off. My own crown obsession at present is that I must go to Richmond—for I know not what—but go to Richmond I will, by God, if I have to walk, freeze, starve, beg and murder.

The weather is stabbing cold: the Janus-headed Perversity who rules my crazy destiny presented me with ordeal by ice the moment I came South. If I go North it will be to find the roses out.

If I wonder at what you have written concerning the purification of soul association with me has brought you[,] it is because of its implication to me: if you feel cleansed, it is purification by flame, torture, hell-fire—at your exceeding great cost. Whoever touches me is damned to burning. You are a good great beautiful person—as faithful here as this hot life has let you be—but eternally true and faithful to yourself and all others in the enchanted islands where, unknown to these phantoms, our real lives, our real ages tick out their beautiful logic.

The suggestion that I can do anything for you—that, miserable as I am, I have power to cleanse purify or judge such a person, almost dehumors me by its extravagance.

Write me when you can. Tom

The same address[.]

1. Wolfe wrote this letter on paper torn from a small tablet.

2. According to Myra Champion, former head librarian at Pack Memorial Public Library in Asheville, this cousin was Jacob Harry Wolfe, son of Wesley E. and Mary Wolfe of Asheville. He died at the age of thirty-seven, a single man, on 25 December 1925. Wesley E. Wolfe, William Oliver's brother, had also left Pennsylvania to settle eventually in Asheville.

3. Fred Wolfe, who was portrayed as Luke Gant in *LHA*.

4. Mabel Wolfe Wheaton, Helen Gant Barton in *LHA*.

5. Ralph H. Wheaton, Hugh Barton in *LHA*.

6. The Wolfe family had substantial land holdings in Florida.

Sometime during the winter of 1925–26, Wolfe moved into the loft apartment at 13 East Eighth Street, which Mrs. Bernstein shared as a studio. They spent hours together here, recounting childhood memories and recreating scenes and personalities from the past. During the spring, Wolfe resolved to begin working upon an autobiographical novel. Aware that he could not begin so important a task under the present circumstances, Mrs. Bernstein offered to finance a trip to Europe as soon as his teaching duties were over. She would continue to support him so that he could give up his job at the university and work without interruption until he was ready to come home.

Late in May, Wolfe traveled to Boston. After briefly returning to New York, he continued on to New Jersey, Maryland, and Virginia.

4. [New York] Neighborhood Playhouse/Monday [May 1926]
My dear—

The Grand St. Follies[1] have to hold off a moment while I write to you. It was nice to get your letter and know where you are. You can't imagine what a queer feeling it was to have you gone, and not sure where[.] I sent you a telegram and I trust you received it.—I also have had a little taste of spring, I went to see Lillian at Westport Saturday evening and came home Sunday at about 4 P.M.—Every thing was so lovely. We had a long walk Sunday morning early, I wanted to share every tree and flower with you. You will be back soon I know but it doesn't seem likely, I cannot get used to not having you near. Your attitude toward the Boston leg[2] is reassuring, but I do not like what you say about your being domesticated. Darling you must never be not wild, but naturally I like to be wild along with you.—I should like to go like lightning somewhere. Not to Boston though. I took your books back to the Library Saturday and tomorrow expect to go about the ticket. You cannot imagine how it is to work at 8th St without you. I looked at your blue suit[3] so hard today I was convinced it would get up and walk around. But it didn't, but it will some day soon, with someone inside it. Maybe though you will not wear it again, as you have two others now. I know you must be resting yourself, I only hope the naughty small instructor hasn't crossed your path.—Please dear keep well and do some writing each day.—I long to see you and talk to you. We are almost snowed under with work but I am getting on famously and hope to have some time free for you when you come. I have been getting home to bed early, by 11:30 or 12. The night at Westport I turned in at 9:30, and really have had a lot of sleep, more than usual. —God bless you my dear, my love to you[.] Aline

1. A yearly satirical revue, created for the Neighborhood Playhouse by Agnes Morgan and Helen Arthur, two of its directors, *The Follies* consisted of several sketches that parodied various theatrical presentations of the previous season. It was enormously popular. Each spring, Mrs. Bernstein designed the numerous costumes and sets for the revue.

2. Some time after 27 May, Wolfe went to Boston to get books that he had left with his uncle, Henry Westall. He returned to New York to give a final examination at

Aline Bernstein at 333 West 77th Street, New York City, circa 1925–26 (Courtesy of Edla Cusick)

N.Y.U. On 6 June, he left for Asheville, stopping first in New Jersey, Maryland, and Virginia.

3. In 1933, Mrs. Bernstein was to write of a character, Eugene, based upon Thomas Wolfe, in her short novel, *Three Blue Suits.*

5. [New York, 3 June 1926][1]
My dear:

I want to tell you that I put your money etc, in an envelope with my name upon the outside, and put the envelope in the safe at the Neighborhood playhouse. There is also an inner envelope with your name upon it. The receipt for your ticket from the Frank Tours Co. I forgot to include,[2] I still have it in my purse. But it is a relief to me to have the money in a safe place for you[.] God forbid that any thing will happen, but if it should, Helen Arthur knows where the envelope is.—It seems so much longer ago than yesterday that you left, and added to the fact that it is horrid without you. I have a constant little worry about your being in a wild motor ride. You have told me such tales about the carelessness of your companion. Also you have no overcoat and it is very cold here.

We are getting on with our work, but more stuff is being written and put into the show all the time,[3] and tonight it seemed as though we were never going to finish. I tried several times to write you today down there but no place was quiet. I went in to the studio a couple of times and looked at your old goloshes and Derby hat right up on the same shelf with Irene's new hat.[4] I haven't been in at 8th St. today, but I must go soon and clean it up.—Today has been heavenly weather[,] clear and very cool. But every one tells me I go round with a glum face. This is an old pad of paper that I bought in Paris last year, and in among the leaves I found a play that I had written some time ago. I thought it was good, but I just read it again and it is awful. Parts of it are quite nice, and there are some good ideas in it[.] But I had better stick to designing and cooking. I thought I had lost this play. You would laugh at me if you ever read it, and yet [for] some reason or other I wish [you could] read it now tonight. I [have taken] my big poetry book in bed to[night] I [am] reading up so that I can [better pass the] next test. I certainly flunked the last one, what a shame too after all the work you put in on me this year. Darling, please be an angel and don't get drunk, or if so not too drunk too often. You are attached to me some where by a string and it keeps pulling at me.—My love to you[.] Aline

This is one Helen Arthur told me today—[G]entlemen prefer blondes, but blondes [are] not so particular.

1. The corner of this letter has been torn away.

2. Wolfe was planning to sail to Europe aboard the *Berengaria* on 23 June. Mrs. Bernstein purchased his ticket. This reference is probably to the money that she set aside for his European stay.

3. *The Grand Street Follies.*

4. Irene Lewisohn. The Lewisohn sisters, Alice and Irene, had sponsored the Neighborhood Playhouse and were on its Board of Directors. Coincidentally, Wolfe had submitted his play, *Welcome to Our City*, to the Neighborhood Playhouse in January 1925. Irene Lewisohn had approved it, and Mrs. Bernstein carried the manuscript with her to Europe to gain Alice Lewisohn's approval. Hence, when she first met Wolfe aboard ship, she had with her the copy of his play, which the Playhouse later rejected.

6. Baltimore, Maryland / The Emerson Hotel / Thursday [3 June 1926]

My Dear:—

I have just escaped from my wild friend,[1] sending him on, despite protests, to Washington. We put up last night at Havre de Grace after lunch at Princeton and supper at Philadelphia. Town filled with Shriners and American flags. Havre de Grace pleasant. Drive over this morning beautiful. The trees of Maryland opulent—always were[.]

Arrived here, my friend hunted up old classmate at Yale, atty' at law, who took us to his apartment, gave us cocktails, and had his nigger fix us lunch. Soup, peas, potatoes, veal cutlets, tomatoes, strawberry shortcake, coffee. Most good![2]

I'm going down the bay to Norfolk on to-night's boat. Friend wanted reason—I had none, which he couldn't understand. Thank God, I'm alone. Back to the same of that summer's misery and enchantment when I was seventeen.[3] By Bacchus, how the rubble gleams when touched by the lights of the carnival!

I may meet the Demon Drink Saturday in Richmond—he, afraid desperately [of] being alone, but understanding it in me[.]

My dear, I have been gone a day, and I still love thee. Be thou ever—and ye will! Semper ⟨in⟩fidelis![4] Tom

Wire me Saturday to the Jefferson Hotel, Richmond, Va.

1. Henry Stevens was a friend of Wolfe's from Asheville, who had come north to attend Yale Law School, from which he graduated. Stevens's behavior was often erratic and he drank excessively. He committed suicide in 1933. Wolfe used him as the model for the character of Robert Weaver, in *OT&R* and "K 19."

2. Wolfe and Mrs. Bernstein shared a constant, sensual delight in food, and often described sumptuous meals to one another.

3. For Wolfe's fictional representation of his Norfolk trip, see *LHA*, chapter 33.

4. Wolfe crossed out the first part of this word, but not enough so that Mrs. Bernstein could not read it.

7. New York / Neighborhood Playhouse [4 June 1926]
My dear,

I had your letter with my morning coffee, and I will take a chance that this may reach you at Richmond. The letter made me so happy, I have been walking on air all day. It made me happy all but the Latin Tag, with the prefix crossed out. But I know what I know, and that is how dearly I love you and how I am yours within myself. I wrote to you yesterday, to Asheville and will telegraph tomorrow. We are loading up with more and more to do. It was a relief to know you are no longer with your wild companion.—You are my wild companion, and I hope you will always be so. The way I care for you is like a cube root. It just multiplies in every direction. God bless you[.]

Aline

I am trying to write this with every one coming in to ask questions. I wish I was a better writer—

8. Norfolk, Virginia / Hotel Southland / Friday night [4 June 1926]
My Dear:—

I am sleeping, you observe, "where life is safe,"[1] and have spent part of the day in a series of parleys, debates and refusals with one of the negro bell-boys, who wants to sell me a pint of corn whiskey, a quart of gin, and a girl, "who's jest beginnin' at it"—all reasonably priced.

I came in on the boat this morning at an ungodly hour—seven o'clock, which means six because Virginia is not on daylight savings. (Though God knows why she should be!) My song is "hollow, hollow, hollow"[2] ("Did you ever yearn?") I am the fabulous Saint, Thomas the Doubter, who at best has never doubted, and who is always fooled. Someday I shall return somewhere and find not only doors and windows bigger, but the roses blooming as I knew I left them.

Here, in this dying town, the drear abomination of desolation, I spent a summer of my youth eight years ago, gaunt from hunger, and wasted for love, and I saw the ship and the men go out, the buttons, the tinsel, and the braid. But my heart has ticked out madder time; the dogs have howled too long for the men who will come no more; and a great deal of blood has gone under the bridge. (Are you moved, girl?)

"Come back, bright boy, as thou wert in the dayspring of my memory, before thy life had yet turned the dark column, and the wind and the rain were musical; and flowers grew."[3]

I found some professional ball players that I knew, and spent part of the day talking to them. Once in the night, my daemon spoke to me about you, once there was the thrust of the knife through my bowels—but what's night for, anyway? I am going to Richmond tomorrow—then, perhaps, home.

But Norfolk I am leaving forever—the singing and the gold[4] is gone. Tom

1. Reference to a picture of the Hotel Southland, under which is printed, "Sleep where life is safe."

2. Tennyson, *Idylls of the King*, "The Passing of Arthur," 1.33: "And hollow, hollow, hollow all delight."

3. This is an unpublished poetic passage of Wolfe's.

4. Wolfe's symbolic phrase for ecstatic happiness was "the apple tree, the singing and the gold." In Mrs. Bernstein's fictionalized account of their relationship, *The Journey Down*, she uses this phrase as the title for the second chapter, in which she recounts their idyllic stay in England.

9. New York / Saturday, 10:15 P.M. [5 June 1926]
My dear—

I hope it is not so cold in Richmond, or wherever it is that you are[.] We all have ear laps on, and red flannel under wear, so to speak. I had a nine o'clock appointment with the dentist today, he is taking the nerve out of my bad tooth, it is most unpleasant, but will be alright when finished, and no more aches.[1] I have not stopped working since, but will go home in about ten minutes. Lish[2] and I just ate a pound of cherries and we both have the belly ache. I do not like Saturdays without you, [some] how Saturday is your day more than any other. Do you realize that for months we have spent it together? Lillian asked me to come to Westport this week end, but I have too much to do.—Tom dear, you must learn to write more legibly. There are still words in your letter that I do not understand. I am going to give you a copy book this summer[3]—I telephoned about your cousin, but she was not there, so I did not send the flowers.[4]—Milt Gross[5] has written us a fine sketch for the Follies, about the Dybbuk. I think it is one of his best, and I hope that the girl who is doing it will be able to carry it. We are all in a state of worry now, every thing seems dull and nothing will ever be finished. But it will be finished, I know, and you will come back here, and I will get on a boat and go to Europe *and not have to design another thing for a long time.* My head is going stale and needs a rest. I have to design 22 more costumes, they will be very bad I'm sure.—Good night darling, I will write again, soon, if the 22 things are ever designed or not. I shall try to stay in bed tomorrow morning. My family are all out of town again but the maids are in and I shall not be afraid tonight, as I was last week. I hope to find a letter when I get home. Please try to remember that I am nice and have a lot of love for you. I am no sort of a writer at all, but your loving and devoted friend[.] Aline

1. Both Wolfe and Mrs. Bernstein had severe and recurrent dental problems.

2. Alice Beer, one of the Playhouse Workshop assistants. She is the sister of Thomas Beer, the biographer of Stephen Crane.

3. In England, Mrs. Bernstein bought him the copybook in which he began writing notes for *LHA*.

4. Probably either Elaine Westall Gould or Hilda Westall Bottomley, Wolfe's Boston cousins.

5. A minor playwright and humorist. His book, *Nize Baby*, was a bestseller of the 1920s.

10. Richmond, Virginia / The Jefferson / Saturday June 5, 1926

My Dear:—

I came up from Norfolk this afternoon and I found here your telegram and your letter, all of which made me very happy—particularly what you said about being lonely. If you want to cheer me up, please write to me often, telling me that you are unhappy.

Let me assure you that I have found yet neither the pot of gold, nor the rainbow—those parts of Virginia I have seen these last days have been sopping wet: Richmond, to which my heart has turned with much affection, is reeking drearily with mist and rain. The Jefferson is a good hotel, though—rare enough in the South (Florida and Asheville to the contrary). I have a spacious room, a gleaming bath, and after more food such as I had at lunch—fried chicken, succotash, fried tomatoes, coffee, and pie, I hope I shall begin to recover my shattered health. My appetite, I am happy to believe, is perking up already.

My dear, believe me—the thought that I am loved by such a person as you are gives me the most enormous pleasure of my life. My fierce, vain, egotistic nature, always athirst, has been laid in a repose it has never known before, and what is best in me, my great capacity for fidelity—if you'll pardon me for speaking the truth, that bottom and permanent steadfastness (the unity in the midst of my everlasting change) has been awakened. You protest justly against my occasional taunts of infidelity, but would you have me suddenly turn believer, who have been a sceptic so long. As a matter of fact, the reason I disbelieve so vocally, is because I have always believed silently in everything; and knowing now that nothing is worth such belief as I have given, which seeks out the essences of things, making them not false, but as they ought to be before they got dirtied, so that flowers are flowerlike, music great, Norfolk one of the high places of the earth, and a slut the melted smear which deforms, but cannot conceal, the outlines of the original princess. What is there left for me to do, who know these things and sometimes hate myself in my heart for learning nothing, except to continue in this mighty secret faith, but protect myself outwardly by my mockery? Then, I am prepared for anything

—either to be exalted by love, or to be sanctified by treachery: it is necessary to get nourishment both from honey and bile. Or again, if I am deceived, it is always possible to shake the head, smiling whimsically, and pass on to someone else, thus creating a belief in others, as well as in myself, that the thing was a manner valiantly adhered to and believed in while it lasted, but now easily to be supplanted by another—equally real for the time. [Yet] who should say if it turn heads, my ecstasy will make a poem, if it come tails, out of my pain (after a period of maturing recollection and growth) I shall write a book?

I am finishing this on Sunday. I go home to-night. Richmond, of course, is a flat failure. The only loyalty in this world that matters, because it is the only loyalty that can endure (if you examine this you will see that it is true) is loyalty to a myth or to a phantom. And the reality of a dream may not be re-visited. I ate too much dinner, and every time I make an epigram, I belch in the middle of it—this should be funny in an English play: "My dear Hilery (belch)."

I have spent the afternoon reading the bible and Froissart's *Chronicles*[1] how Sir Oliver de Clisson, the Constable of France, was finally set upon by assassins at midnight in Paris; how he was struck in the head and plunged from his horse against a baker's door, bursting it, rolling in, and thereby saving his life; and how Ruth wiggled her tits against the soles of Boaz' feet, while the old man slept; and how he waked and married her;[2] and of a man by the name of Bakbakkar.[3]

I suppose you are working hard on those perfectly killing *Grand Street Follies*; it is a curious thing, which I am sure you have not often noticed, how a bad joke by a poor comedian about his wife, or a piece of cheese, or Prohibition, is received as a bad joke, but how a bad joke about a bad play, or a bad book by Michael Arlen,[4] or a bad production by the Theatre Guild goes over with the literate Yanks as not only explosively comic, but barbed with subtle and penetrating satire. How the critics will yodel! Woolcott[5] with his pouting harlot's language "prankful," "fulsome," "your correspondent's old bones" etc—and six of them will call it "excellent fooling." Well, God bless you in it, and may the suckers thrive and multiply—but don't, my dear snigger over your own bad clowning. Let's leave false laughter as the final dishonesty of the Dial[6] circulation, and all other Phi Beta Kappa Jews.

I'm not in a bad temper—this is only my gentle raillery.

I have written at length, because tonight the expedition pushes off into the wilderness, and it may be months before you hear again.

Good bye, my dear—God bless you[.] I hope to have news of you when I go home. Home?—Hah: Tom

1. Froissart's chivalric *Chronicles of England, France, and Spain.*

2. Ruth 2:7.

3. Levite, I Chron. 9:15.

4. A popular writer of the period. With the publication of his first novel, *The Green Hat*, in 1924, Arlen achieved instant fame. His novels were representative of the mannered world of society.

5. Alexander Woolcott (1887–1943) was drama critic for the *New York World* from 1925 to 1928 and a close friend of Mrs. Bernstein's. He was famous for his biting wit.

6. The most distinguished literary magazine of the 1920s, *The Dial* favored formalism in art and literature, to which Wolfe was opposed.

11. [New York] 333 West Seventy-Seventh Street[1] / Monday 9 A.M. [7 June 1926]

My dear—

Once you told me that when you went away you would be like a dream. That is not so, you are real, all around me. I had one of my wakeful nights last night, and held long lovely conversations with you. You were tender and your hair curled like the angels, the way I like it. I thought it best to write you this morning before I go down town. It is growing difficult to have any time or privacy at the playhouse[.] Things are pretty hectic now.—I got your letter from Norfolk today and give you a good mark for withstanding the blandishments of the bell boy on all points. I hope they kept the telegram and letter that I sent you Saturday to Richmond[.] You probably did not get there until Sunday.—How can I lay your Daemon? When we are together again for a long while I can make you see. I am yours completely, body soul and mind.

I paid my rent on Friday up to July 1st[.] I do not think I can bear to keep the place next year, although it is a fine work room. I will try to work at home or at the playhouse, or God knows where. I must try to make time tomorrow to go about passports. I expect to spend a good part of my vacation working over your handwriting. Do you think I can teach you? We will have a half hour every morning, say from 8 to 8:30 or so, and you can get even with me from 8:30 to nine with poetry tests.—The weather has been unspeakably cold and rainy[,] very dismal. You would be miserable, and I do hope at least that you are having sunshine. I've been wearing a sweater to work in for two days. I hope things are better for you at home this time, and that you may keep a little more calm. And please please, not too much corn whiskey. You will find a flock of letters waiting for you at your sister's.[2] I hope she will not be alarmed. I hope you still love me, I love you— Aline

1. The letterhead for Mrs. Bernstein's home stationery. She had lived in this spacious brownstone with her husband and two children for several years.

2. Mabel Wheaton. In May, Wolfe had written to his sister asking if she could put him up if he returned home in June.

On 23 June, Wolfe sailed for Europe aboard the Berengaria. *Mrs. Bernstein had left shortly before, on business, and they were reunited in Paris. Once in Paris, he began working on his autobiographical outline for what was to become* Look Homeward, Angel. *For six weeks, he traveled with Mrs. Bernstein throughout France and England. While in England, Mrs. Bernstein worked on a production of* The Dybbuk *in Manchester. From here, they went to Ilkley for two weeks, where he continued to work on his outline. After a brief trip to Glasgow, Mrs. Bernstein sailed for New York on 19 August with Theresa Helburn, and Wolfe settled at Chelsea where he began working feverishly on his novel. He paused only for a ten-day vacation in Brussels in mid-September and his first trip to Germany in December before sailing home on 18 December.*

12. On Board S.S. "MAJESTIC"[1] / Sunday [22 August 1926]

My dear:

I hung around the radio office this morning, hoping to hear from you. Well, I did and naturally didn't much like what you had to say, it was meant to wound me and it did.—We did not leave Cherbourg until 9:30 Thursday night, and it has been very rough, so bad that until about two hours ago I could not start any work. I felt ill, and pretty low, and your radio gave the final touch. Terry[2] has been an angel to me. When I get downstairs to my room I go all to pieces, poor thing she has a rotten travelling companion, so far as company goes. I try to think of you at work, but I can only think of you in other ways. I see you again and again as the train pulled out of the station. I am one grand ache all over, because I cannot be near you, and because of how I know you are feeling. You love me and you miss me and you get these dreadful thoughts about me, and I cannot do anything being away.—I will go on with this tomorrow. The rolling of the boat has given me a bad headache.

Monday

This is the first really good day we have had, I got up early and tried to do some work, but no go. It will be a disappointment to Agnes[;][3] I am afraid I will fail her, unless I get an inspiration tomorrow, which I doubt. Can't bear to face her, after all my promises.

The day I left, you told me to remember only the things I loved you for. Please my darling do the same for me. For heaven's sake do not set your imagination against me. It is not fair. I am not there to stand for myself. Since I left you, there is actually not an hour of my waking time that you are not in my consciousness. I wish I had some sort of instrument like a ticker that could communicate with you. The ship is packed, and I am nearly crazy with nervousness. Thank heaven we only have two more days. Terry has stayed down in the room with me for some of our meals, when I couldn't bear to go into the dining room. She sends you her love, and wishes you were here. You can well believe that, if you could see the state I am in.—Some other time I will write you of all the celebrities on board.

If I get no ideas by tomorrow I will cable home to get another designer—Maybe I can never design any more and I will be a scrub lady. I'll come over and get a job in England and do out your room for you every day. Most of the time I can see you so clearly I can almost take hold of you.—Good night darling. God bless you[.] Aline

1. Mrs. Bernstein sailed on the S.S. *Majestic* on 19 August and arrived in New York on the 25th.

2. Theresa Helburn was one of the directors of The Theatre Guild and one of Mrs. Bernstein's dearest friends.

3. Agnes Morgan was on the Board of Directors of the Neighborhood Playhouse and a close friend of Mrs. Bernstein.

13. Chelsea / Sunday Morning, 1 A.M. August 22, 1926

My Dear:—

As I write this, I know you are somewhere out on the vast and moving waters, and since time goes faster than your ship, some two or three hours closer to morning than I am. It is a night here of stars and glorious moonlight. I have just returned from a walk along the Thames here at Chelsea—where Whistler loved to paint it. I saw the bridge all strung with lights, and knew it as his bridge. Where you are out there—already, I suppose, over the rim of the world, like a traveller who disappears over a hill, so that if I could see the necessary 1500 miles or so, you would be lost—I hope there is also moonlight, and stars, and that you have made continent use of them.

I found your cable at the American Express this morning; I went immediately to Marconi's in the Strand, and answered—the man assured me you would get it within two or three hours. After this, I returned to the Cavendish, packed my bags, lunched, and came here to Chelsea where I had engaged two rooms yesterday. I left Rosy Lewis[1] still aimlessly hurling invitations at me to come into the country with her.

I found nothing Thursday, but I came here yesterday morning, and spent five or six hours looking the place over. It is one of the most charming places in London: I found plenty of rooms, and two flats which could be let for as short a time as I wanted—one of three had a fine big long room, a bed room, bath, and a fair sized kitchen, beautifully stocked with china, for 2½ guineas a week. It was all furnished, but I would have to pay gas and electricity, and hire a woman for a couple of hours a day—9 d an hour—to do the place and cook breakfast.

My innate love of an establishment is so great that I may do it.

But I believe I am beautifully situated for the moment—I have two rooms (the whole first floor) of a house in Wellington Square. The place is very clean, and well furnished: I pay 45 shillings a week, which includes service. Breakfast is extra.

I have gone to the theatre every night since you left—After your train had gone, I went up and saw *Is Zat So?* I had seen it in New York, but I thought that Yankee talk again would do me good. To-night was the last night of *They Knew What They Wanted*; I went, realizing it was my last chance to see the prize winning, Be-Guilded Leviathan. Also, you told me it was exciting. I might have known you were lying[.]

I can't tell you very well how I feel—there is a sense of unreality about it yet, but I shall get on. For a night or two I have dreamed uneasily; I have only fear for a recurrence of that horrible past time when I was away, when my sleep was peopled with logical monsters; when I dreamed, and knew that I dreamed, with my mind rationally astride its own insanity. Then I dreamed most frequently of voyages; in a dark but visible universe, under a light that never fell on land or ocean, I crossed haunted and desolate seas, the solitary passenger of spectral ships; and there was always the far sound of horns blowing under water, and on the American shore, no matter how far, the plain but ghostly voices of the friends I had had, and the foes; rising forever, with its whole spectral and noiseless carnival of sound and movement, was New York, like a bodiless phantom, and my unknown home, which I had never had, but whose outlines were perfectly familiar to me; and thus I passed without lapse of time through all the horrible vitality of this strange world, all tumult but the ghost of sound, all forms and faces but the ghost of people, near enough to touch, but illimitably remote, until, returning in my agony from the place I had sought, voyaging again upon the haunted sea, under the unearthly light, I awoke with my hand upon my throat, to cry "I have voyaged enough. I will go no more[.]"

I am finishing this Sunday. Another fine day here—you are 300 miles further off. I walked again by the river this morning. The curve, the fine span of the bridges, the Bayswater Park, and the houses along Cheyne Row have brightened me up. The service here has been splendid—the father of the fat lady—a hearty old man[,] brought me tea: I was up before nine, and had breakfast on a snowy cloth in my room.

I shall not draw this out—believe me, I have not once been near getting drunk; I have had one whiskey—less to drink, in fact, than when we were together. Also I have had four letters. I heard from Carlton[2] and my mother the day after you left. His letter, of course, was cheerful—hers, more voices from the tomb—of the return home of my charming oldest brother—by name Frank—who has just been carted away to the hospital for treatment for whiskey and veronal.[3] There is, of course, the anguished cry over the hospital bill—money and misery are kneaded into their usual filthy cesspool.

In this fine sitting room of mine, I have shelves for books, already stocked with 75 or 100 volumes, a deep padded chair for reading, a large table for eating and writing, a cupboard for tea things: in my bedroom are more books and more cupboards. All I need now is someone to visit me.

I hope you are getting along with your designs for the play.[4] I know you will, for in spite of all you say, you have a place for everything. Write me as soon as you get this and let me know what news is to be known—

I cannot write very well or very sensibly at this time. So many things have gone, so many things must go that we think lasting—there are three thousand miles of sundering water, and all of the clamour and the lights—the local blaze of fame and tumult that seems so much over there. Against all this I shall make fainter and fainter music—and alone now, I am really sure that my charm is not so conspicuous that it may not be bettered—I know very well that better and more attractive persons are about; although I have sometimes felt that I have deserved a little more from your friends—from Miss Lewisohn on—than the kindly patronage with which their manner toward me was touched. Perhaps this is what you mean when you say no one but you will ever know how wonderful I am; or what Terry meant when she told you Day[5] "idolized me"—But perhaps he, and a few other people, have given me in the past a belief somewhat more objective—not flattered entirely by personal feeling.

Well, I must spin out my entrails again—this time, I hope, successfully—it is perhaps something of a beginning—or an ending—for me. My life grows sick and thwarted from lack of a hearing. But I shall not be too sick to heal myself.

Good bye, now. I'll write you again soon. You cried hard and frequently the last days—there is more wisdom in me than you think; I've been over the hedge once before: I know that a faithless world is not wholly bad. God bless you, my dear. Tom

Monday morning

I am posting this. I am not despondent. I feel like working. In two more days now you will be in New York. Good luck, my dear, for your designs. Remember me a little.

1. Rosy Lewis—youthful, exuberant, and charming—was proprietress of the Cavendish Hotel, where Wolfe was staying, and a fabulous cook. Her story is well known through its fictionalized treatment in the BBC television series, *The Duchess of Duke Street.*

2. Henry Fisk Carlton, one of the members of the 47 Workshop, taught English with Wolfe at N.Y.U. from 1925 to 1928.

3. A long-acting barbiturate, used primarily as a sedative.

4. *The Lion Tamer*, a satirical fable by Alfred Savoir, opened at the Neighborhood Playhouse on 8 October 1926. Mrs. Bernstein designed the sets and costumes. This play was one of the triumphs of the Playhouse.

5. Frederick Day was a friend from the 47 Workshop.

14. [London] Thursday / August 26 [1926]

My Dear:—

I am writing this at night, but I shall not post it until to-morrow, when I expect to have your answer to the cable I sent you this afternoon. I got your cable at two o'clock to-day when I went to the American Express; it has puzzled and distressed me beyond measure. Your message read; "Arrived pain worse leave" I could not construe the "leave"—I did not know whether *you* were leaving—or, what I thought likely—asking me to leave. But if you were asking me to come back now, why didn't you say "Come!" I hope I shall know more to-morrow.

If its absolutely essential that I should come back now, you may rest assured that I will come. Moreover, I can't work if I feel you are in any keen, overpowering distress of body or mind. I don't know what images you have been getting of my riotous life since you left—what drunken and lewd follies I have been engaged in[.] Well: here is the record—I have done a larger amount of reading and writing in the mornings; in the afternoon I have made enormous promenades, traversing vast sections in the East End, the Mile End Road, Whitechapel—yesterday I walked all the way to Hampstead Heath. I return home at seven or seven-thirty, bathe, and take a bus to Piccadilly and Soho—Then I dine. Later I walk several more miles in moonlight. Then I come home, write a little, and go to bed. The old man brings me tea at 8:15, and a paper; I am shaved, dressed, and seated at the table in my own living room by nine. I realize I am spoiling my story by this last touch but, so help me God, it's true!

Now, my dear, hark ye well to what I am going to say to you. I have tried with all my might to avoid thinking of being lonely. At the present time, the regularity with which my life is ticked off is an invaluable asset. Since you went, I have told myself that I will do the thing I came to do, and come home. I want to do it. The outline is finished. I believe, with my present energy, I can write it in two and a half months. I am willing, I feel like working hours a day. And I do feel most passionately that at this period of my life I should not utterly cast away this work of mine:—it sometimes seems to me that we have time after time dealt it cruel blows. I wonder why, when all else is present, we can not foster instead of harming it. There was something so preemptory in that message today. Even at a shilling a word I felt that you might be a little more explicit. For a moment I felt it was not quite playing the game—it seemed suddenly that my life had become something to be shunted about at the impulsion of desire—Listen, my dear, I am making no evasion now; believe me when I tell you that never had you had so fully what I have to give of loyalty and affection; only, a kind of steadfastness born of what I thought necessity, has grown up in me, which has made me ready to wait. It seems that you are not.

[August 27]

I am finishing this on Friday afternoon[.] I got your return cable today; after a bad night and day it relieved me considerably. I repeat, I am relieved. For I am one of those distorted natures who could not bear at all to know you were suffering constantly from belly-ache, or toothache, but who bear up instantly when they hear its only heartache[.] Heartache is that universal compassionate malady ladies have just at the moment of finding a solacement. Ahead, I suppose, the new Season in New York has set in. As I told you in the other letter, there's too much water between—my broadcasting set doesn't carry far enough; besides I was badly confused about my time—you are six hours earlier rather than six hours later. Now this, of course, absolutely destroys any hope I may have had of appearing suddenly, in the spirit, to give a warning or leave a curse—I should always have to continue to prepare for your mid-day adventures at six o'clock in the afternoon, and in order to meet your midnight ones, I should have to stay up all night. I suppose I may look forward with some fortitude to being gulled on that side of the Atlantic while I am asleep in my bed on this side, and to realize my translation only when I wake to find myself antlered like a mountain goat—You mustn't mind this—I am only having my little joke.

I didn't want your heart to ache, my dear—it is more to the point that it doesn't forget[.] Perhaps your feeling these last weeks has had too florid a tint—What Pater calls "recondite exuberance"—to last. I don't know. But I hold to it as the last and best thing I have to keep going on; the thing I care sufficiently about to believe in. I don't want to see the color of your blood. I want to see the color of your faith and endurance.

God bless you, my dear. I shall write very often—sometimes every day or so. Do thou likewise—For the present, goodbye[.] Tom.

P.S.—I am reading the *Carmina* of Catullus. Here's one (to Lesbia) you may be able to pick out[:]
. . . . nox est perpetua una dormienda, da mi basia mille, deinde centum, dein mille altera, dein secunda centum, deinde usque altera mille, deinde centum, dein—etc etc etc.[1]

1. A poet of the first century B.C. Wolfe's quotation is from the fifth stanza of *Carmina*. The entire stanza reads in translation:

My Lesbia, let us live and love
And not care tuppence for old men
Who sermonize and disapprove.
Suns when they sink can rise again,
But we, when our brief light has shone,
Must sleep the long night on and on.
Kiss me: a thousand kisses, then
A hundred more, and now a second
Thousand and hundred, and now still
Hundreds and thousands more, until
The Thousand thousands can't be reckoned
And we've lost track of the amount
And nobody can work us ill
With the evil eye by keeping count.

See *LHA*, p. 181, for Wolfe's reference to this quotation.

15. New York / Thursday / Sept 2, 1926
Dearest—

I cabled you today when I left the playhouse, and half an hour afterwards I was home and found your letter, paper that you actually had in your own dear hands. I have come upstairs to my bed right after supper so that I may be alone with you. I've had this terrible need all day to communicate with you, so that is why I sent the cable. There was no moon coming over on the ship, or if there was, I didn't see it. I am glad you are comfortably settled, it is such a relief to me that you are in a decent clean place, but your tale of the flat with the little kitchen just drives me wild. Today I had lunch at the fish place on 8th St. I had to do some shopping at Wanamakers. The waiters all greeted me and so did the proprietor. One of the waiters said it was very sad to see me alone, and asked if you had gone off and left me. It was dreadful, I might have known it, I was a fool to go there, and of course could not swallow a bite. I'll never go there again, unless you are with me. I wish you loved me. Tom dear whatever you suffered last year in that time before, I am going through the same thing now.[1] You have wanted to be loved. Now you are, more I am afraid than you ever wanted. Your letter says no word of ever wishing to see me again. You were being what you call objective. I know that even at your greatest feeling for me, part of your consciousness was looking into a future that did not contain me. I keep stating facts to myself over and over again, trying to bring my mind to some sort of order. But when did facts or common sense ever have the best of this sort of thing. You are a young man, I am a middle aged woman, but that gives me no ease or courage. You say I have a place for everything, but I have place for nothing now but you. I got my work through this week, bolstered up largely by Agnes. It is very poor and every one is disappointed. I had a rather bad time with Alice & Irene when I returned and have refused to do the next new production[.] They accused me most unjustly of pushing my own department last year, meaning of course in their round about way, my own work, and covering myself with undue glory. I was feeling down and out and sore at life in general, so I lay about me with a cudgel and we all went home with broken heads, more or less. Helen & Agnes[2] took my side vociferously. I haven't seen them since, just doing my work with Agnes and the technical staff. Winthrop Ames[3] sent for me yesterday, I have undertaken a small uninteresting job for him, in hopes of a better one later on. I only hope I can do it creditably. My poor head is absolutely congealed. I simply have to begin on it tomorrow, or else give it up. My other designing job is in abeyance (the dress designing one)[4] owing to a general strike of the tailors and women workers. It has been going on for 8 weeks and doesn't look like a settlement yet. But it can't last much longer, the men and their families are starving and all want to go back. They are really well paid and work under the best conditions, they get from $60 to $95 a week, easy hours and spotless work rooms. Every thing is being done but the magic thing that will settle it, whatever that may be,—I don't want to go back to them for a while, but I will tell you what. I want to come back to you if you will have me, or maybe you will come back to me. You see if I thought there was ever any chance of it, I could live along. I would come right over to you now, but there is no way I could possibly manage it, not till later in the year. Possibly you will get enough writing done, if you work very hard, so that you can come back.—I am glad you heard from Carlton and your mother. I guess it is better to hear from home than not, even if the news isn't so good. Don't pay any attention to their complaints, we will get the book written without them. I have such a longing to do all the physical things for you, your cooking and washing and cleaning (and petting)[.] I have no longer any strength nor pride, there is nothing I wouldn't do to be once more in the same place with you[.] Darling, do answer me this with your loving kindness, the way you have often come near to me after some stormy time. Or am I asking too much, more than you care to.—Chelsea is lovely, we should have lived there together. It is a magical neighborhood. I picked up an old copy of Vogue down at the theatre today, (1915). Strangely enough it had photographs of Whistler's house, inside and out. The one of his painting room was fine, two grand big windows from floor to ceiling, about 5 or 6 feet wide each.—I never said They Knew What They Wanted was exciting. I said the first act was interesting and rather exciting, but the rest was improbable and no good. Another time that you misquote me. But I love you anyway. I haven't been to the theatre since I came home, in fact I have only gone out once in the evening after dinner, with Edla to see a new film called Variety. Good in spots, very good in spots. I have been reading every night. I got an Everyman copy of Plato, and have been reading The Dialogues. Also a book of Chesterton I never saw before, another one about Father Brown, and some Walter Scott. I like the New York papers again, the news seems more intelligible to me than in the English ones, that is just one of those dumb things I can't explain but you will understand.—I wonder if you ever had your gray suit cleaned. Please do. Whatever you do, will you please send me a cable on your birthday. Maybe you will once in a while even when it isn't. A nice one. I don't know what I shall do on that day. How many years have passed since the last one.—Alice Baker[5] just phoned me that she is going to take our 8th St place to live in, and wants me to use it for work in the day time. I couldn't go into it again to save my life. I don't see how she can live there anyway, unless a lot is done to it. I have had the large purple chair brought to my room so that no one may sit in it. I shall try to work at home here, although the light is poor now, since the building has gone up behind us. The entire back part of the house is unpleasant now. The family wanted to move away, but I have prevailed upon them to stay another season.—Do you know your books never came from Boston. Of course I save all the stuff you left with me. I saw it all put away in the cellar before I sailed.—God bless you my dear. Keep yourself well. Write whenever you can, write how you feel even if it isn't what I long to hear. I want to know, I am bleeding frightfully where I have torn myself from you, it will never heal. Forgive me for being this way, but I am pretty well beaten. I thought I was the strongest woman in the world.

My love, Aline

I just read your letter again. There are no better nor more attractive persons about, no one who comes within miles of you.—I cannot account for the foolishness of my friends. That is the N.P.H. women.[6] I know that Terry understands something of your quality, and has the utmost faith in you as a writer. As for me, I will stake everything upon your merits. Besides the way I love you, I know the other thing will soon come to make you happy, the thing you have always coupled with wanting to be loved, to succeed with writing. This is morning now. I finished the other part of my letter last night. You said you would send me your outline when you have it done.[7] Will I ever kiss you good morning again? If you will—

1. During Wolfe's 1925 trip to Europe, he had fallen in love with a woman named Helen Harding, who did not return his affections. The experience is recounted fictionally in *OT&R*, pp. 680–794.

2. Helen Arthur and Agnes Morgan were business managers of the Neighborhood Playhouse.

3. A Broadway producer.

4. Mrs. Bernstein worked for Davidow's, a wholesale ladies' clothing manufacturer in New York.

5. A friend of Mrs. Bernstein's. She was the proprietor of an antique shop at 11 East 8th Street.

6. Neighborhood Playhouse.

7. The rough outline of *LHA*, now in the Houghton Library, Harvard University, in two large notebooks.

16. [New York] Sunday / September 5 [1926]

My dear—

This is the first day that I have really been able to do any work. Last night I spent up at Pleasantville with the Morgan-Arthur menage. I got up about 8:30 this morning, and redesigned all the costumes for Le Dompteur,[1] much to my relief. The first lot were awful. I worked steadily from 9:30 till 6, not even stopping for lunch. Lish made me some coffee about three and I had two cups. I had supper at my sister's little house, our car called for me and here I am at home, 10 P.M. My son Ted[2] came down with me, everyone else is still in the country, over Labor Day. I have an appointment with Mr. Ames and Winifred Lenihan[3] at 11 A.M. tomorrow. It has been pouring rain all day, such a pity for every one's last holiday. I am so relieved that I could work and so glad to be back alone in my own room tonight so that I may write to you. It is nice up at Pleasantville but my hostesses were so attentive, and I can't write unless I am alone. I had your two letters with me, and read them both over this morning before I got up. I hope there is another on its way. You say you do not want my heart to ache, you want it to be faithful[.] It is faithful, and it aches. At times I am completely overcome with the thought that you are gone from me forever. I want to cry out to you and how can I? Do you know, I had an intense feeling to call up your old telephone number Stu 4961 tonight. But I didn't do it. Tom dear do you think I am utterly mad? Here I am, every day charged to the utmost with love for you, I must write some of it. My fear is that some day one of these letters will come to you and you will not want it. I wonder if you are trying at all to release yourself. You used to tell me you would "pull out" some day. I go deadly cold at the thought—I am so afraid that you are going to be too lonely to stand it. If you are, for heaven's sake do not be too proud to come back. We can find some quiet place for you to work. But of course nothing would suit you so well as London, and possibly you do not miss me so much. I am going to ask you something, perhaps you will hate to answer. Do you think that you will ever want to be with me again? If I thought that you ever would wish to, I could have all the patience in the world. If not, I don't know. I suppose people have lived through these things before. When I say patience, I mean that I could wait quietly and try not to wail so loud and annoy you. My faithfulness to you will last forever, in body and mind.—My eyes hurt very much from drawing all day. I can write no more now. I'll finish tomorrow, it is nearly midnight. My old nurse, Margaret Stott, is staying at the house, and she is going to give me an alcohol rub. I am very nervous, figity, it will make me quiet[.]

Tuesday / September 7

My dear—

Yesterday I spent several hours over my Ames job, and about 5:30 went up to the country to call for my family. It was pouring rain, we stopped at White Plains for dinner, and on the way home were run into by a taxi. The car was pretty badly smashed, but no one hurt, I got a bad lump on the face, and Edla hurt her hand, but nothing serious. We are all right tonight, but I could not write when I got home, too much shaken. Today I shopped in the morning, and in the afternoon took Lenihan to order her costumes. It is a *very* poor play by Philip Barry,[4] enough stuff for one act, but strung along in a silly fashion. Mr. Ames thinks it will be a go, but I do not. I've never been so little interested in anything. It is now only 8:10 P.M., and I am already in my bed. I look forward all day long to the time when I need no longer talk to any one, and can come up here and close myself away. Your two letters are nearly worn out from constant reading. Several big ships came in today, and I hope that a letter from you is coming, I will know in the morning[.] I hope you are going to have the outline typed and send it to me. You and your book are always ahead of me, like a mirage. It is wonderful how clearly I see you. Every detail of your face, the way your hair goes on your forehead and behind your ears and the back of your neck. The way your eyebrows go together. Your nose, your two lips and your chin and your eyes that are always trying not to love me. Do you remember me? Do you see me ever? Tomorrow it will be three weeks since I left. In these three weeks, I feel as though I had passed an ordeal of fire, I feel burned absolutely clean.—

The great garment worker's strike is still unsettled. The streets down town are packed with haggard dirty men and women. They all want to get back to work but dare not. I am going to a mass meeting tomorrow night, at Cooper Union. I hope to find some settlement is made, both sides are down and out, and all over nothing. We have had two cool days but today it was roasting hot again. I just hate the weather. I shut my eyes and think of Ambleside, green and silver silk. I have had hardly anything to drink, it tastes so horrid after the good things we had in England, and I don't want to drink anyway.—I wish you would translate your latin quotations. I don't know anyone to ask what you have written. You forget that you are writing to a practically self made woman.—No Education. There are quantities of new books out, a life of Coleridge that looks very interesting from the review. Also a life of Donne (think I mentioned that before). I wish I had some technique for a literary life, my work is such a poor side of it. I am discouraged. I realize since I got home how little I know, and after all what an unnecessary part of the business I do. If only I had been an actress, but maybe if I had been any different I wouldn't have known you Tom—I will write a little to you each day or so. I wonder if you will like getting your letters as much as I do. Good night my dearest, God bless you, keep you well, believe how I love you. Aline

I have begun to pray at night again, never since I was 17 years old. I prayed in York Cathedral though.

1. *The Lion Tamer*.
2. Theodore Bernstein, Jr.
3. Actress, director, and playwright.
4. *White Wings*, a play in four acts, by Phillip Barry, opened at the Booth Theatre on 16 October 1926 and ran for twenty-seven performances.

17. Chelsea / Saturday / September 11, 1926
My Dear:—

I have waited to have more than two letters from you before I wrote, because your own second letter was such a little scrap, it seemed to me America and the Bright Lights had reclaimed you once more, and that I'd have to forget about it the best I could. I did write you a card from Brighton—I went there late Sunday night, and I came back Tuesday, but lost no time from work. I have been writing from four to six hours a day: and I have spent the rest of the time thinking about it—and about you. The regularity of my life has helped enormously. It has been quite warm—but I do from 2000–2500 words a day—almost a book [in] a month, you see, but mine will be much longer.

I have had a cold, but otherwise felt very well until to-day. Two days ago I got your cable asking if I am all right. I answered it, got the reply yesterday, calling for the Brussels address.

This morning I got up, and instead of writing, went to the American Express to arrange for Belgium—got some francs, my ticket, gave address, and so on.

I found your two letters. They put me into a terrific state of excitement; I read them twice there—your own distress and what you said about the foolishness of your friends for not believing in what I did, and I got quite sick from the pit of my stomach, so that I had to go out and vomit on the pavement around the corner in Cockspur street.

I do not know how you will feel by the time this letter arrives—I realize how like a fading coal most affections are—but I will not do anything farther that would add a single gray hair to your head, or cause you any more distress[.] This is a stupid, clumsy letter—I could have written a good one this morning, but my strength's gone out of me. Let me say this:—

With the vanity of young men I wanted to be a great man[,] a fine artist. This last year, particularly these past few weeks[,] it has changed. I'm not exactly done for, but for the first time I'm willing to eat humble pie. I know now that I can never be anything more than one of the millions of unknown obscure people who populate the globe—and somehow I don't care.

I get tremendously excited over my book—at times in an unnatural drunken ecstasy, it seems to me to be working into one of the most extraordinary things ever done; but then I realise that no one will care to publish it, few to read it.

Somehow I'm not unhappy. I am, on the contrary, deeply moved by the experience—I have gained so much wisdom this last year from you. I know that I shall never be a great figure now—but I [have] hopes of turning out a tolerably decent person, and I know that obscurity does not keep many people from having merry lives.

This book finishes it—it is a record of my secret life—somehow I want to get it done—it is a definitive act—and give it to you. I am rather sad at times when I think how many years of my life have been turned toward the will-o-the-wisp, how many of my friends have urged me on—but I know that many men have never *found* out in time; at twenty five it ought not to be hard to start over.

In spite of all the screaming jangle of nerves my life gets twisted in, I'm not a weakling or a coward. After my childish and silly nausea this morning I wandered around for an hour or two, and something of that Scotch granite, which has never let me break, came to my aid—I saw that it was mean and contemptible to go whining through life for something you can never attain. But one thing, my dear, you must *never, never,* do again, please God. Never tell me how much *you* believe[,] how *you* know—whether any one else does or not. You mean that well, but it is rather cruel. No, I know perfectly well now that my life, in terms of creation, has been an unlovely failure—I am simply one of those unfortunate people who develop keen judgement for everyone's work but their own; I have only the immense, the aching desire for creation—and no talent.

Don't think I'm whining. Will you do this for me?—see if there's any possibility of employment for me in New York—I don't know what; but say it's for a Young man who has read everything, can read with incredible speed, is fairly well travelled, can read French, and has classical background. God knows what you can do with this—I don't use a typewriter, but if you can find an opening whereby I might make some money—enough to pay my debt, with enough over to cover my improvident attempts at economy, I would work hard—do my best.

My dear, I can't have a great life, but I can have a good one. These last days I have thought of Socrates, and his insistence on "the good life." I am led to explain—one of the degradations I have submitted to is the explaining of thought, so that vulgar minds—people who go by formula—would not misunderstand me, and put me in the wrong hold—so that by "good life" I should explain that I do not mean going to church, I do not mean not taking a drink—and much other nonsense. But I am resolved to do nothing further to hurt or distress you—I realize now that my own life is not worth it. This has happened to me, too, you see—so I feel there may be some hope for me, after all.

I used to be greater than everyone and everything. Nothing could equal me, with much other fierce vainglory. That was because I was a child, angry and hurt at not being successful, cheered,—published abroad. Now that's gone. I know that you're a person of greater quality, of higher worth and calibre than I am—the knowledge has done me an infinite, a glorious good. And please, please, in God's name don't write me telling me I'm the Masked Marvel, the last and greatest wonder of the world. There's no wound to heal—only that deep and living wound that life makes in us all. I am not ashamed; don't think I will be afraid to tell my friends I have given up—and since there will be in me no evasion, since I will admit I had nothing to give, even the envious and bitter of tongue will have nothing to say.

Something gathers and chokes me in my throat as I think of that boy with his mad face[,] his ridiculous arms and legs, devouring life and books—borne up by all his drunken phantasies of love and glory —I wandered for hours in these comas, thinking of the great and lovely mistress, food, comfort, ten thousand books, a place of retreat from the world, of fame, of life with the great poets; sometimes in restaurants, I would burst out a loud laugh when I thought of something that had happened when I had rooms with Shakespeare—it was while he was writing Lear; or something Shaw had said to me one night in London, or most often, the pot belly, the innocent leer of Socrates. Having lived with the mightiest poets of all time—I have been honoured, great, successful among them—no one can ever take it from me; no one ever will.

I love you completely. I have never wavered in my feeling since you went. I have had to do with no one—once I took to lunch two women artists in Paris; one of them knew me in Paris. It was dull work. The mighty pageantry of London absorbs me when I go out.

I can't go on with this. My brain is entirely dead. I'll write you from Brussels. See if you can find the job; I'll come when you like.

Good-bye; God bless you[.] Tom

You are probably paying the penalty with the Lewisohns for knowing me. At any rate, even sophisticates can be guilty of sour grapes. You have never done a conspicuous design in your life. You are simply being asked to design less well. But now that I'm out of it, they may profess to see in your work a return to earlier virtues. For God's sake get from the woman my two plays,[1] and promise me, please, not to talk with her about them at all. You will be healed, Jew, by the time this gets to you.

I have never called you a bad word—you accused me of it in your first letter; nothing was ever designed to wound you. I said "I remember"—Well, Jew, I remember. Do you?

1. Alice Lewisohn still had in her possession both *Welcome to Our City* and *Mannerhouse.*

18. New York / Sept 15 1926

My dear—

I was much upset by a post card I found waiting at the playhouse for me today[.] Was it what you call one of your jokes? This is what it said—"My dear, by no means as genteel as this suggests etc—etc, I am by this time well (some word I can't make out) beautifully antlered with bulls feathers. But then I am not alone—Love, Tom."—Does this mean, "I am not alone," that you have already found some one else to your taste? I simply cannot believe it, I will not believe it,—I had another almost unbearable day, and sent off two cables to you. Why can't I stretch myself across the water? Then, when I found your card I just went to pieces. I might as well make up my mind to it, I suppose the thing will happen sooner or later. You will go from me to some one else. I have had no letter from you since the first two that came soon together. I want to know about you, how you feel and how the book. It must be fearfully lonely for you. Do you speak to anyone? Aren't you burdened and annoyed with these letters I write you? I am curious to know how you feel about them, but I can write no other way.—If I am to see you again in this life, I want you to know beforehand how things are.—You never would take in all this when I kept telling you this summer, by all this I mean the way I care for you. Apparently you think I can serve you best by being away. That may be so, but it is painful. I have moved myself up to the top of the house, to be more alone. It is nice. I wish you could hear the noises coming in from Riverside[,] freight trains shunting back and forth, the bell ringing, long thin whistles from the boat or engine. I don't know which, and every once in a while a terrible screech from a bad automobile brake. The same noises for years in the same proportion.—I really do not know where to send your letters. I will keep this one here several days and add to it. Now I am going to ask you something and for heaven's sake don't get mad. How is your money holding out. I will soon have a check from Mr. Ames and one from the playhouse, and I spend practically nothing. I have enough clothes, and I take my meals home, and [pay] no studio rent at all. You must promise me please not to ask for anything from home, please let me know just how you are fixed now, and just as soon as you need. I am so proud of you and so happy that my life has ever been a part of you. Good night darling, God bless you.

[September 17]

Dearest—

Yesterday afternoon late I got your cable from Brussels, you are still faithful, and still my dearest. Why did you write what you did about not being alone? Or did you mean something else that I do not understand.—This is the holiest day in the Jewish year, the Day of Atonement. We fast 24 hours, and I wish I were holy. It must be glorious to believe in God and through [sic] yourself on his breast. We fast 24 hours, not even a drink of water.—I go up to the Morgan-Arthur menage every Saturday evening, and stay over Sunday. It is nice and quiet, and the country smells so good. I am so good that I am growing little wings. I never even take a drink any more. I've only had something once, with Winnie Lenihan—Did I ever tell you how I planned Le Dompteur. I can't draw it very well this way, but water. — I go up to the Morgan Avenue menage every Saturday evening, and stay over Sunday. It is nice and quiet, and the Country smells so good. I am so good that I am growing little wings. I never even take a drink any more. I've only had something once, with Winnie Henihan — Did I ever tell you how I planned Le Dompteur? I can't draw it very well this way, but this is how it goes. The first act is outside the circus tent —

Tent

flats with circus posters painted on

Plan

Bar

The second act, I turn the entire works around and paint the room in Lord John's house on the inside of the circus tent, leaving the tent top to represent the ceiling, and the two doors in the flats at the sides. It is very simple, and not bad for the play, and

plan act II

Aline Bernstein to Thomas Wolfe, 17 September 1926 (By permission of the Houghton Library, Harvard University) this is how it goes.[1] The first act is outside the circus tent.—The second act, I turn the entire work around and paint the room in Lord John's house on the inside of the circus tent, leaving the tent top to represent the ceiling, and the two doors in the flat at the sides. It is very simple, and not bad for the play, and very very cheap to build and work. The little model I made turned out quite well, and I hope the scene will also—Dorothy is playing the lady, and she is as alluring as a dish of cold cream of wheat. I am dressing her in vile shades of pink. She came in to see me this evening for a little while, with John Mason Brown.[2] The very first thing they both asked for you. I was so glad to be able to even open my mouth about you. I am afraid I talked of you too much. They heard you had gone abroad forever. I hope not. They didn't stay long. They were on their way some where else. Dorothy is really a nice girl though—I had another call to go to Baker's to teach, maybe it's about what I'm fit for.—Very discouraged about my work. I can't do it any more and when you can do it, what then? To write is the only thing, or to act maybe, if it is lovely. But to write is the only thing. I wish I had the courage to start some thing else, I don't know what.—I think, to tell you the truth, that the very best I can do in life is to cook for a certain Tom Wolfe, to mend his clothes and make him generally comfortable. And to put on a gold dress in the evening and sparkle for him, so he will not think the romance of life is all gone. I feel the very center of romance now, a princess in a castle, in duress, and some day maybe a rescue and tight tight loving arms. I wish I would have a letter, I wonder if you have written and it has gone astray—I'm going to sleep now—I've been reading Amy Lowell's Keats all evening, I like it. Her writing is clear. I love you for all the time I will ever live— Aline

1. Mrs. Bernstein drew sketches of her set designs on this page of the letters.

2. One of Wolfe's friends from the 47 Workshop who later became a prominent theatrical critic.

19. [New York] Monday / September 20 [1926]

My dear—

I've been carrying a letter to you in my purse for several days, because I didn't know where to send it, I am relieved to know that you are going back to England, it seems as though you are nearer home than when you are on the continent. I have the other letter in an envelope so will pop it into the letter box tomorrow morning.—I had a nice quiet weekend in Pleasantville with all my Playhouse bosses. I cooked their dinner for them, and O it was so good. I took my grand mother's iron cook pot, and made chickens the like of which you never tasted. Helen christened them chicken a la Becky, and a very good name for them. I cook them for hours, very slowly, and lots of vegetables with them.—I went this evening to see "What Every Woman Knows." I went with Mr. Bernstein. It is the first time I have seen a play since I came back. Enjoyed it much more than I expected, Helen Hays is excellent. I keep plodding away at my work, it will get done somehow and then what shall I do? Something else will turn up though. Maybe Helen of Troy[.] I care for you more than ever, no not more than ever, but I feel it all the while. You cannot imagine how I want to talk to you. We lived a very intimate life, it was divine. I want to talk to you about everything. Darling, this letter will come to you about your birthday, maybe a little sooner. Do you remember what a warm day it was? And I looked swell in brown, and I waited for you on the library steps for 20 minutes, I can't believe it was only a year ago. You have come into that year and expanded it to four times its size. I am so lost without you, isn't it terrible to be a woman? We go to pieces under these things. I wish more than ever that I was a man. Just see how you can travel about, come and go at any time, go into a strange city and get the meat of it. Do you realize what it would be like if I went alone to Brussels and went to see the sights? If I go on this way I'll be advocating women's rights. There has been a fearful disaster in Florida. A hurricane destroyed millions of dollars worth of buildings. I wonder if you have read about it.—I am so anxious to get a letter from you. It is so strange that I have had none but those first two. Maybe you haven't written, but your postcard said you were writing. Maybe a letter has gone astray, that would be dreadful.—I write to you when I go to bed at night, it is the only time when I will not be interrupted, so I have to write in pencil, and sometimes I find it not too comfortable. —I am going to sleep now, good night Dearest, God bless you, how thankful I am that you were born.—1000 times, I love you[.] Aline

Tuesday 8:30 A.M.

This is good morning. I always end my letters good night. Possibly I will find a letter at the playhouse today. We have been having damp warm weather, but today is nice and clear.—Savoir arrived yesterday from France, and is expected down town at rehearsal today. Everyone is very nervous, but I am betting he will not show up. I am taking the liberty of speaking to some one about your play. I will get back the copy of both that your Miss Alice Lewisohn had. They must be at the playhouse.—I had a letter from Minna asking me to come to Northampton immediately after our opening. (Oct 7). I will go for a few days. They have a house way out in the hills. I think it will be nice. I could buy the most heavenly old place up there in the country for a song. If you were here to occupy it (with me?). I would find the money somehow. About 20 acres, so rich and green, and a lovely white farm house. Too lovely, I dare not dwell on the thought[.]

Aline

20. Brussels / Tuesday / September 21, 1926

My Dear:—

Just a short note from a wine shop—a longer one to-day or to-morrow. I cabled you yesterday that I should leave here Thursday and be in London the following Monday[.] I thought I should stop a day at Antwerp and Bruges. Then, I doubt if I shall leave England until I have finished the book.

I have written every day since you left with the exception of the Sunday I came over here. But I have done very little touring about[.] There are cars everywhere to Waterloo, the British Front, etc. but I have had no time for touring. It has been terrifically hot these last three days—today the sky is overcast: it seems to be over[.]

I am going ahead at a good rate, doing 1500 or 2000 words a day. I am afraid, however, that I can't get it written as quickly as I thought. I think of it all the time—when I'm not thinking of you. Your letters and cables have been the sustaining thing in my life here. You ask me if I can think of New York with you—I can not really think of New York without you.

But I reflect also that, in spite of the feeling which I know to be honest, which animates these letters, you left on schedule[d] time, after completing your summer's trip, and you never dignified my utter absorption by so much as a day or a ship later. And I know that you have carried the double-faced quality of the thing back with you —you bludgeoned me last summer by picturing yourself as being expelled everywhere,[1] but that was deliberate sob stuff. You always took care not to take risk[s].

It is no good protesting against my hard-hearted unbelief[.] I only face certain undeniable facts. My dear, you will have betrayed and cheated me time after time after time before ever I shall see New York again[.]

But I care for you more than I care for anyone. The town here is full of women—they have as much attraction for me as stuffed dolls. I have gone with none of them[.]

I am sorry you are doing the Barrie play. I knew the man slightly at Cambridge—he was always sufficiently cordial. But anything connected with the workshop gives me a pain now—I failed at it[.] Some of them thought I would come through, but I didn't. And I know you sneer at these people to me, but pander to them—as during the horrible meal with the man in Paris. Never speak to me in a letter again of a play—unless to tell me you did well with your work. You cannot have me back in New York now—it will be too late when I do come. Please betray me, won't you (in God's name!) with some one I don't know. I love you[.] Tom

1. In the summer of 1925, Mrs. Bernstein had traveled to Europe. Perhaps Wolfe is referring to some anti-Semitism that she had experienced.

21. [New York] Wednesday / September 22, 1926

My dear:

The park is filled with white clematis in full bloom, every thing is richly green from all the rain we have had. I came up from the theatre about 7 o'clock, it smelt so sweet[.] It was sad. I have never before seen so many rich beautiful colors. My eyes have been cleared of something, I see things like organ notes, and deep chords[.] The buildings are more beautiful, the new ones unbelievable in form and variety. But there is something ugly too. But I like it. I wish that you liked it. I believe you would if you didn't have the drudgery of teaching. You should have the top of one of the new recessed buildings to live in. Your head would nearly touch the sky, and you would have only a short trip to go to heaven. What I want to say is that there is tremendous physical beauty, so abundant, but a horrid spiritual poverty and no *form*, that pleased me so in England. Slipshod, and almost too much of everything.—I met Savoir today. He is very nice, he came over for the movies. He is a florid very Jewish looking Frenchman, about 45 I should judge, very jolly. He didn't like my designs, too simple, he likes the decor more decidedly modern in feeling. He leaves for California Saturday for about three months, so [he] will not see the show. I was a little disappointed that he didn't like the sets, of course they are not finished yet but he got a general idea. I've been discouraged about all my work any way. It's no good and no use, my one consolation is that you are doing something fine. I treasure you, and the thought of you at work. All your cables are so reassuring, working they say, and end up with dearest. I must say that I am disappointed to have had no letters, but maybe you couldn't write. Aren't you just sick of having me tell you how I love you? I want to write it all the time. It presses into me like a burn. Maybe this letter will be the birth day letter, I cannot calculate the mailing date. It was a Saturday last time, so will be Sunday this time. I will cable a day or so ahead, because of its being Sunday. I know it is Oct 3 even if the cable comes another day.—What do you think, I am going to the big fight in Philadelphia tomorrow[.][1] Some friends of ours couldn't go, so our family fell heir to 3 tickets (value something exorbitant)[.] I don't know who else will go. Do you know about the fight? I'll write you a graphic description when I get home.

I will not stay there overnight. I think probably Edla and Teddy will go. I am quite excited about going, mostly to see the crowd, although the crowds usually frighten me.—Will send this off in the morning. God bless you, my dearest.— Aline

My dear—

Just had your long letter. I will write a long answer to it tonight or tomorrow—It is terrible that I conveyed to you the meaning that people do not believe in you.—What I meant to say is this, that if they do not, it is because they are fools, meaning especially Miss Alice L. Terry thinks you are one of the greatest, also Helen and Agnes Morgan. Terry told me coming over on the boat that she thought you would find your place soon among the great ones.—I am afraid to write more now, for fear of doing it badly and getting you excited. I am off for the train to see the fight[.] My family are waiting.

God bless you[.] I love you.

1. The first Tunney-Dempsey fight.

22. Brussels / Wednesday / September 22, 1926

My Dear:—

I have not kept up with my correspondence since I came to Brussels. I have cabled you several times, however, and I shall do better after I return to England. I have been in this very gay city for ten days now, in over a week I have not spoken my own language, or talked with one of my own nation. My talk with nearly everyone has been impersonal—a month of buying and paying. It's not bad, save at night. I get rather lonely, then.

I have done a great deal of writing—my book is going to enormous length, and I can't get done as quickly as I thought. Today is the only day I haven't written—I am writing you this at dinner (8 o'clock) and shall try to get my day's work done tonight.

I took the day off and went to Waterloo in a bus—the first trip I've made. There were seven or eight of us only—two or three English, two or three French, and your old friend, James Joyce.[1] He was with a woman about forty (but not as young looking as you are, my dear) and a young man, and a girl. I noticed him after we had descended at Waterloo—I had seen his picture only a day or two ago in a French publisher's announcements: He was wearing a blind over one eye. He was very simply—even shabbily—dressed: we went into a little cafe where the bus stopped to look at the battle souvenirs and buy post cards; then we walked up what was once the Sunken Road to a huge circular building that had a panorama of the battle painted around the sides; then we ascended the several hundred steps up the great mound of earth which supports the lion and looks out over the field. The young man, who wore horn rim spectacles, and a light sporty looking overcoat, looked very much like an American college boy: he began to talk to me going up the steps—I asked him if he knew the man with the eye blind. He said he did, and that it was Joyce. I commented briefly that I had seen Joyce's picture and read his book; after this the young fellow joined me at every point. Walking back down the road to the café, I asked him if Joyce's eyesight was better—he said Joyce was working on a new book, but thought it impossible to say when it was finished. We went back to the café—they sat down at a table and had tea:—the young man seemed about to ask me to join them, and I took a seat quickly at another table, calling for two beers. They all spoke French to-gether—he told them all about it, and they peeked furtively at me from time to time—the great man himself taking an occasional crafty shot at me with his good eye. As they had tea, they all wrote post cards. As they got up to go into the bus, the young man bowed somewhat grandly to me—I don't blame him; I'd be pleased too. I judge the people are Joyce's family—he is a man in the middle forties—old enough to have a son and daughter like these. The woman had the appearance of a thousand middle class French women I've known—a vulgar rather loose mouth; not very intelligent looking. The young man spoke English well, but with a foreign accent. It was strange to see Joyce—one of the gods of the moment—speaking not one word of the language his fame is based on. The girl was rather pretty—I thought at first she was a little American flapper.

Joyce was very simple, very nice. He walked next to the old guide who showed us around, listening with apparent interest to his harangue delivered in broken English, and asking him questions. We came home to Brussels through a magnificent forest, miles in extent—Joyce sat with the driver on the front seat, asked a great many questions. I sat alone on the back seat—it was a huge coach; the woman sat in front of me, the girl in front of her, the young man to one side. Queer arrangement, eh?

Joyce got a bit stagey on the way home, draping his overcoat poetically around his shoulders. But I liked Joyce's looks—not extraordinary at first sight—but growing. His face was highly colored, slightly concave—his mouth thin, not delicate, but extraordinarily humorous. He has a large powerful straight nose—redder than his face, somewhat pitted with scars and boils.

When we got back to Brussels, and stopped in front of the bus office, the young man and two women made a little group, while

Joyce went inside. The young fellow was looking at me, and I was swimming in beer. I made a dive for the nearest place, which was under a monument: they are more respectable here than in Paris.

Anyway it was too good to spoil: the idea of Joyce and me being at Waterloo at the same time, and aboard a sight seeing bus, struck me as insanely funny. I sat on the back seat making idiot noises in my throat, and crooning all the way back through the forest.

I think really they might have been a little grand about it if they had known they were discovered. But they were just like common people out sight seeing.

I'm going on to Antwerp to-morrow, Bruges the day after, London Sunday or Monday. I wired the Am. Express to-day to hold my mail. I hope I find some from you when I get there. Your letters give me life and hope. My life is utterly austere, utterly remote. I have eaten well here—some of the restaurants are excellent. But I have [not] sat at table or anywhere else with anyone, save a little English merchant who came over on the boat with me: he was a funny little man, full of innocent viciousness, who conducted me, with many a sly wink, to a table at a most respectable dance hall: we drank orangeade, the little man looked at the girls, and winked at me, going off into fits of silent laughter.

You get nothing to drink in Brussels but beer and wine unless you buy *bottles* of the stronger stuff at stores. I drink beer mainly: there are places where you get iced sparkling champagne for twelve cents a goblet[.]

Last night about midnight—I had gone out from my room after working, for a walk—a woman stopped me, and began to wheedle me. She was a large strapping blond prostitute. I gave her money for a beer and sent her on. A few minutes later, I noticed a fearful commotion across the street. Prostitutes, with their eager delight in a brawl, came in magical hordes. My lady had cut a sizable hunk out of a gentleman's neck with a razor, and was fiercely mauling a small man all over the pavement. There were several minor brawls going on between the whores and their pimps. Finally, someone yelled "Police," and the army disappeared up four separate alleys. The police came up and arrested magnificently the man who had been cut.

You ask me if I can think of New York again *with* you. I tell you honestly I can not think of New York *without* you. And I say this knowing very well that you may have sunken your life elsewhere before I return, or that your "waiting" may ease itself in the passage only—someone I don't know, *please*! I love you, and honor you—you are better and finer than I am—but even the greater people, I know, have in them that grey lipped granite thing, which abides in me, and yet is not part of me, and which, weak as I am, in my moments of terror and desolation, arises and comes marching slowly forward in me.

I am going back to England to try to finish the book—it is a far vaster thing than I had thought, but it grows in clarity and structure every day. This letter is *stupid* All my energy, and most of my feeling for you, has gone into the book.

I may go to Oxford next month. Meanwhile I shall try to get back my old apartment in London. I have read of the terrible storm in Florida: it means that my people have lost money—which may help them—but I pray God it does not mean anyone I know has lost life[.]

The evidences of your affection are the most valuable things I own; thinking of them I forget that you were not a day or a steamer late; that the old concealment of everything remains, and that as I write this, entoured by gilded youth you live again, doing the settings for Barrie's play, dispraising them to me, but making the obeisances to fame you made to the man in Paris on that nauseous night—as I, an unpublished boy, sat choking my food down: and I know that listening to my dispraise in the mouths of your companions you have en-halved yourself by proclaiming belief in me (no—you haven't) but don't mind; it's over now[.] I know I shall never create anything worth while—the book's a great necessity but if you can get used to me after the Great Renunciation,[2] while I try to become an unassuming man, my heart, you'll find, is where it used to be.

Good-bye—God bless you, my dear[.] Tom

I'm tired after Joyce and Waterloo[.] Forgive a stupid letter. I just thought that I shall probably be 26 years old when you get this[.] At 23 hundreds of people thought I'd do nothing. Now, no one does—not even my self. I really don't care very much. Don't say "*I do*"—I'll have no more boasting.

1. Mrs. Bernstein had first met Joyce when the Neighborhood Playhouse produced his play *Exiles* in 1925. In August 1926, she had occasion to meet with him again, during which time Wolfe and Joyce shook hands and exchanged a few brief comments.

2. Wolfe later referred to his break with Mrs. Bernstein as "The Great Renunciation."

23. [New York] Thursday / September 23 [1926]

My dear:

I had given up hope of having any letter from you, when quite suddenly I got one this morning. It came up with my early coffee, and I was terribly excited over it. I seem to have done something dreadful to you, but let me go step by step and get it as straight as I can, in language as plain as I know. In your first letter to me, which was a beautiful letter, you trailed off into a sort of lament that in spite of the fact of my love and devotion to you, you had not had encouragement from my friends. My reply was only intended to make clear to you that I am not responsible for their foolishness, I could only be responsible for myself. I did not intend to convey to you that my friends (I really do not know just whom you include in that, probably Alice, Irene, Helen, Agnes, Terry etc.) had no faith in you. They have. Both Alice & Irene have spoken to me repeatedly of your writing. And I wrote you in a hurried paragraph today what Terry has told me. Also, I wish you to understand that my judgment of your writing is not tempered in the least by my love for you as a person. You should know me well enough by this time. It is the only unfeminine trait that I have, I am unbiased when it comes to matters of that sort. And I do not think you should think it cruel of me when I tell you that I believe you are a great creative person. If you do not value my judgment, you may leave it. But that is what I think, and, (here is a phrase I have picked up from you) I am not alone in that opinion. What is more, you are not finished with your work, you are just beginning. This is what I think is the most sensible plan. Why not finish the first writing of your book over there. There is nothing in the world I would love like seeing you right away, but I want you to finish, and I imagine you can work more steadily there. Then, I know you will need a great deal of revision, and if you want to be near me, and do not think it will interfere, come back then. At the rate you are going, you will probably make it by the New Year. I want very much to take a studio, but will not do so until you come home, then we will have a place where you can work as well. My work room at home is almost impossible, and I have moved my drawing materials down to the playhouse, and use the studio there. We have a new one now, on the top floor front, the floor where Lish and I had our little office[.] It is a room as large as the downstairs one, but ever so much pleasanter. Agnes Morgan has her desk there as well. If I have any idea when you are coming, I can get something I am sure and have it when you get back. I could always have our old place again, but do not think you like it. Maybe I can find another but it had its advantages.

You are not going to give up your writing *at all.* And listen to this Tom, between you and me there is no question of debt, *never*[.] We have elected to care for each other, and let there be no nonsense, and none of the over emphasis of what dollar does this and that. If that time comes when our position in that respect is any different, you know well that there would be no compunction or quibbling on my part.—My designing at Davidows has begun again, and in another week I will be fairly rolling in money. Also Mr. Gilbert Miller is seeing me tomorrow about doing a show for him. I hope it isn't right away, I can't do it till the Lion Tamer comes on. Then I really want to go on and do architectural drawing. I tried going to The School of Applied Design, but it didn't work out well, I had to stick to their hours—Carolyn Hancock[1] is back, and she says she will work with me if possible, she has quite a lot of jobs. I tried Columbia but needed a lot of mathematical training I never had, before they would let me in[.] I wonder if I wrote you last week that I had lunch with my friend who is scenario editor of First National.[2] She told me that there is always piece work to do, bringing in enough to live on, and for some one smart, endless possibilities. Of course it is no career for you, but might keep you going until you see your way clear. Of course no one who works for them has any thing like your capacity, and I think you could walk away with it, if you didn't hate it too much. I also know some one in Famous Players,[3] but not so influential. But your book is the chief thing and that must come first. This is the first day that I have seen any prospect of your coming home again, and I have been very much excited, almost as though I knew the date. Do not fear that I will ever be cured, or healed as you call it. Your fear should be rather the other way, that I will go through my years with my love for you. You will weary of it. I am sorry I cannot write better, you know your idea that we can say any thing is all wrong. I am afraid that I bungle and hash every thing before it gets down on paper, and then it isn't any good. Here is plain English though, I love you. I want your presence. I want to be next to you when you have rooms with Mr. Shakespere, and dinner with Mr. Shaw. I should like to be the great and lovely mistress of your dreams. I wish I had a quiet beautiful retreat and 10000 books. But I am only a Jew.—I must tell you what happened about the fight. We got as far as the Pennsylvania station, and I saw such a mighty crowd that my courage turned to water and I came home. I thought the station would be wrecked, and I had terrible visions of the flimsy new stadium being stampeded. I saw a long blue line, which turned out to be *solid policemen* driving in the crowd, so I just turned around. The cops put the finishing touch. You know crowds like that terrorize me. Teddy got a friend to use my ticket. I went over the way, and listened to the fight by radio. It was thrilling, the man who told it is a marvel. He never hesitated, what his eye saw his tongue immediately described, his speaking lasted only a few seconds after the bell sounded, it was so quick a record[.] I never thought I would enjoy a radio. It began to rain as soon as the big bout came on, and by the finish it was teeming and here I am in bed again. I will send you a copy of the morning paper, I know how you enjoy these tales. I wish you could have been here to listen to the wonderful tale. Apparently it was not an exciting fight, but it sounded alright to me, and Dempsey is no longer Champion.—You know, about the Lewisohns and their attitude towards me, I think they are perfectly sincere, in their own way. Helen seems to think that they were distressed in a measure at the amount of publicity I had last year, a sort of personal publicity that no one else seemed to get, and that I really did not deserve any more than any of the others. It is just in the nature of my job to be in the paper, not because of its relative importance. Any way, they are getting over it, and behaving somewhat like human beings. They had better. Did I write that I expect to go to Minna's[4] after the L. T.[5] opens, just for the week end.—I go to Pleasantville now every Saturday, and cook. I like it but O my God I wish I was cooking for you.

I am so frightened that you are misreading what letters I have written you. Or have I miswritten them?—I intended sending you a paper about the great Florida cyclone, but it was too dreadful. I hope your people did not lose much. Here is some news.—Patricia Calvert got married, I forget the name of the happy (?) man.—Edla told me, but it didn't stay in my mind. She can be a Scheherezade [and] soothe him with 1001 tales.—I hope I'll get a letter again soon, but not about your being ill or nauseated. God bless you darling, I am so happy at even an ever so faint prospect of your coming home. Aline

Isn't this a long letter—It took me nearly 2 hours to write.

1. Scenic designer, who in the 1920s and 1930s designed for such plays as *They Knew What They Wanted* (1924), *An American Tragedy* (1926), and *The Taming of the Shrew* (1935).

2. A Hollywood film company founded in 1917, which was very active in films featuring actors such as Chaplin and Pickford. It was taken over by Warner Brothers in 1929.

3. A production company founded by Adolph Zukor in New York in 1912. It was later absorbed by Paramount.

4. Minna Kirstein Curtiss was a close friend of Aline Bernstein's and the model for the character Lily Mandell in *Of Time and the River*. It was Minna Kirstein, before her marriage, who returned from Europe with Mrs. Bernstein when she met Wolfe aboard ship.

5. *The Lion Tamer*.

24. Hotel Bristol & Marine / Antwerp / Saturday / September 25, 1926

My Dear:—

I came here yesterday afternoon from Brussels; I am going to Bruges tomorrow, and from there to London. I got your letter yesterday in Brussels; I am happy to think there will be mail for me when I get back[.]

I have done very little writing the last two or three days; at this rate I won't be done for many months, but I have made good speed up to this, and finished last night the three Great red books I bought at Ilkley (one side of paper only, however). I am going on in a huge ledger I bought at Brussels.[1]

Antwerp is a very pretty old city—much less French, much more Flemish in its buildings than Brussels, and the people seem to speak Flemish—their native dialect—more extensively. I went through the cathedral this morning—it has a great soaring tower, and a magnificent entrance wrought with saints, sinners, heaven and hell: but very simple in decoration elsewhere. The interior is lined with Rubens masterpieces—this was his home town—including the famous descent from the cross. I went around with an old man who told me he was a Marine Artist before his eyes went bad: he was enthusiastic about Clipper ships.

My life has begun to acquire again the remote and lonely quality it had when I was wandering about before—I seem to be the phantom in a world of people; or the only person in a world of phantoms—it's all the same.

I think occasionally of my approaching birthday: I wish there was a lotus about, on which I could eat oblivion forgetting everything—Even that I ever wanted to be a man. But I can't—entirely.

Does it please you to be a romantic figure—to look mysterious grief? Think what a light you will throw with that when my successor comes. Or when he came.

I love you, my dear: your letters give me life. I can not yet swallow in my gorge the thought of night adventure. My life has withdrawn on a most high hill, within a wall. I no longer get depressed, as I did once, at being alone. I'm used to it now—there's a strange aerial coldness about it. Once, I loathed myself at heart, because I felt I was a spineless sensualist: I saw myself, a worn out whore master at 30, a battered rake at 40, with small red gummy eyes. But I believe now I may become some frosty hermit: with thirsty cheeks and eyes. I weave dreams no more about affairs with living flesh; but very often now I have thought of the antique figures—not coldly, but with passionate warmth—Not as symbols, but as great actualities. From my father, I came by Dutch blood, and the love of opulence has always been in me—the pictures of Hondecoeter,[2] tables groaning with fowl and fruit and fish; a butcher's shop hung with a dripping beef, the cows of Cuyp[3]—and, above all, the broad, deep bellied goddesses of Rubens, and all the others, their blond hair wound about their head, a pearl in the ear.[4]

I want eternal life, eternal renewal, eternal love—the vitality of these immortal figures: I see myself sunk, a valiant wisp, between the mighty legs of Demeter, the earth Goddess, being wasted and filled eternally. I want life to ebb and flow in me in a mighty rhythm of oblivion and ecstasy. Upon a field in Thrace Queen Helen lay, her amber belly spotted by the sun.[5]

I'll write you soon from London. There I shall go on with my work as quickly as I can. Good bye for the present. God bless you, my dear. Tom

1. These four ledgers are in the Harvard University Library.

2. Melchior Hondecoeter (1636–95) was a Dutch painter who specialized in highly colored paintings of still life and richly plumed birds.

3. Aelbert Cuyp (1620–91) was a Dutch painter who specialized in landscapes, animals and portraits. He is noted for his sun-bathed landscapes of Holland and the serenity of the animals he depicts.

4. Wolfe is probably referring to paintings he saw in the Musée Royal des Beaux-Arts d'Anvers.

5. In chapter 15, p. 161, of *LHA*, Wolfe used this poetic reference to Queen Helen. He changed it slightly to "Upon a field in Thrace Queen Helen lay, her lovely body dappled in the sun."

25. [New York] Monday [Late September 1926]

Dearest—

Saturday afternoon I went to Pleasantville and came home Sunday evening after supper. I have had a long arduous day with the scene painters, trying to get my stuff to look something the way I want it. I really have a naturally good disposition, and I am always having to tell people what is wrong with their work. I don't like it, and I wish I knew another trade. I have a bad cold, something I do not often have, I am longing for you and as I think of you my tears run down my face. I want you so much. I simply cannot believe that you will ever come home to me, and if you do, what then.—Last night when I came home I read the three letters I have had from you since I left. In the last one you say you will come when I say—I wrote you to stay until your book is finished. Don't you think that is the wisest thing to do? I have written to you often, I do hope that I have not upset you, that I did not say anything that is not clear. I only keep saying I love you.—I also lead the good life. I try to match myself to you. The time I have away from my work, I read poetry, or some fine book. I go every week end with Helen and Agnes, work all day, cook the meals, and take walks in the late evening with them. Last week we had a frightful hot spell, but today is like sapphires, cool. I grow so anxious to hear from you directly, I am going to cable tomorrow. Do you think it is foolish, cabling so much? I am trying to keep my self so well, I eat carefully, and sometimes I take very few meals of any sort. I have a great longing for milk. That is all I had today, not one single bite of anything else. I spoke to my friend Florence about a job for you. She can do nothing until you come yourself. Did I tell you about Gilbert Miller?[1] He wanted me to do a show at once, but I couldn't until the Lion Tamer comes off. He's promised me another later on. I don't know why my heart is so heavy. I seem to need something of your strong detachment. You see for some strange reason I cannot lose myself in my work any more.—Do you want to send any of the book on here to be typed? I thought you might send the outline but no doubt you need it to work from. I am crazy to see it. I try to imagine what it will be like. It will be a triple distillation of Tom. Do you look just the same? I wonder if you have had your hair cut. Will you do this, will you get yourself a nice warm winter overcoat. Have one made, a nice long brown one, and another suit, before you come back. How about a dark blue suit, double breasted? But you also look swell in brown.—I am lying still here in my bed. I am completely taken up with the thought of you. It reaches such an intensity sometimes that my body is nearly rent in two. Do you too want to be near me?

God bless you darling. Keep you well and faithful—Yours until I die[.] Aline

1. A prominent theatrical director and producer. He was noted for such productions as *The Captive* (1926), *The Patriot* (1928), *Candle Light* (1929), and *The Animal Kingdom* (1932). Between 1921 and 1965, he produced close to one hundred plays.

26. Antwerp / One A.M. Monday Morning / September 27 [1926]
My dear:—

I have just come back to my room in the hotel here with a skin full of champagne—it is the first time this has happened to me since I have been in Belgium[.] You cannot get at a cafe anything stronger than 10 percent. I was enclosed in a small luxuriously furnished wine shop, where champagne is sold on draught—there are many of them. I sat in a cushioned booth against the wall; all the women, even those with men, looked at me, and not with ridicule as they usually do. It was one of the evenings when I am God. I wrote frantically in a small note book I always carry with me now.[1] A woman came in and sat in a booth opposite to me. Presently she beckoned to me and asked me to come and sit with her. I went. She rustled her legs slowly and voluptuously crossing and recrossing them: she had on a short sleeveless dress which showed the hair under her arms. She offered to come here to the hotel with me[.] I paid for her drinks and sent her on[.] Now you can think of that, and gloat about it; if you have already delivered the knife thrust in the back, it should give you added pleasure. (Do not be afraid—Read on—)

If you went to the great prize fight I curse and loathe you forever. For years I have followed these things with gluttonous interest—at Boston I went often, going mad with rage and excitement, shouting

"Christ, Christ, Christ"—when a man was battered to the floor, and unconsciously attacking people around me, shaking and pulling them about.

The defeat and humiliation of that brute Dempsey I share in: the news of the defeat of a champion has always saddened me, and as of old, the exultant cries of the sport writers that "several thousand fashionably dressed women were present to see the new champion crowned, including the names of many prominent in the social register," fills me with choking fury—and "above the mighty roar of the fight crazed mob could be heard the shrill screams of women, urging the challenger to go on and make quick work of the reeling title holder"—this is enough to release my anger and bitterness in a flood of foul abuse and imprecation. Formerly, in Boston, on hearing this, I would walk about the streets, my face lurid with rage, muttering: "Oh yes, you sweet bitches. You dirty little whores sitting there with your pasty little pot bellied husbands who never struck a blow in their lives. Yes, I know you, by God, you gloat to see a young man beaten and battled insensible: you want to see the blood run down his face and among the hairs of his chest, his upper teeth stuck through his lips, his ear hanging by a flap, and his nose bone crushed to powder[.] I wish to God it had ended in such horror that your guts had frozen in terror, and that you would keep the picture of it in your mind as long as you live. I wish he had spitten his teeth out in bloody lumps, some of them flying out of the ring into your dress, I wish his broken jaw bone would have ground horribly before you in his blue face, that his eye had hung from its socket by a thread, that his cheek had been laid wide open, that he had vomited quarts of blood, and that he had collapsed totally insane, screaming in horror and agony at the top of his voice, drowning out your own screams of terror, and the frightened squeaking of the pasty faced little bastard who was with you, puking from sickness and fright. That'l teach you —By God!" (Do not be afraid—I write this late: I have decided to send it—You must get to know me)[.]

London / Saturday / October 2

My Dear:—

I am writing you this at five minutes before midnight. In another five minutes I will be 26 years old although, since I was born 4000 miles away, it is only six o'clock in North Carolina (and New York) as I write. Also, in England tonight the clock is turned back one hour at midnight. Finally, I have been told I was born between nine o'clock in the morning and mid day on Oct 3, 1900[.] That would give me until two or three o'clock here to-morrow afternoon.

I stayed in Antwerp until Tuesday, and went to Bruges for a day.

I came back to London late Wednesday night. I soaked myself in Antwerp in the great cruel vulgar Dutch and Flemish pictures that I love so well; there is also there a certain marvellous place—the great 16th century house of Nichlas Plantin, a Frenchman, who came to Anvers and erected one of the finest printeries the world has ever known[.] The place has been kept intact—the hundreds of books, the thousands of engravings, the old printing presses, the type—all is there stored in great musty wood panelled rooms[.] There are bibles printed in parallel columns of four languages, books of hours, classical authors, magnificent geographies, with their maps, the works, as all geography and the miracle of voyages ought to be, of inspired Superstition. Sunk in that place I seemed to sink too in the centuries, and to live again in the time when the making of a book, like its writing, was a holy labor.

I went to Bruges: it is an old place with lively, tortuous streets, canals, and vast aerial chimes in the great belfries. My room was small and cramped: I hated the lack of space—it was cold. I came back to London. I found here a cable from you and a letter; I got another yesterday, and two and a cable to-day. I held my cable until today for my birth day.

I am imprisoned in a remote world: everything about me passes like a parade of phantoms. People who serve me, and who have the most casual relations with me in shops are friendly and courteous, but I can not come out of it. I have had nothing to do with any one at any time. I am probably as safe from the millions of casual women who walk the streets of Europe as I am from Her Majesty, The Queen. I found out in Belgium that I could not go with them any more. I tell you I am literally and honestly alone 24 hours a day. I talk with plenty of people—on the bus, here at the house where the old man and the housewife gossip every morning with me, but no one knows the slightest thing about me, has the faintest hold upon me.

I've got to leave this place[.] The rooms were let while I was away to a woman who comes Monday; the people want me to take a room on the top floor and use their sitting room in the basement—but I am surrounded by other people up there. Here, I'm all alone. I'm going up to Oxford next week to find when the term begins, and if I can get rooms[.]

My dear, your letters are the only thing that hold me to the least reality in this world. I have determined to write more often—I don't know how well I shall succeed. You are the only person who seems to me to have flesh and blood substance:—I want you to understand that I am living in a kind of mighty dream, where I wander about extensively, examine everything, and find everything unreal[.] In this way my days pass, I enter and leave my room, write, fall heavily upon my bed for an hour, write again, go out on a bus, wander, rove, eat. Thus I think of you all the time, begin a letter, sleep, write, add to the letter, and finally, wondering in horror how it shall ever get to you, I remember suddenly that there are postage stamps, and strange things called ships, in which I don't believe[.]

I have read over the wild beginning of this letter from Antwerp in which I recorded my sorrow at Dempsey's defeat. My prophetic soul was right in telling me you would go, but I would not have hated you as I said, because you did.

I have recovered from the pain of the man's defeat:—the thing is a survival of Cambridge days, when I shared in every circumstance of a champion's humiliation. It was not he who was beaten, but myself: I saw myself beaten and battered to the earth time after time by a rival, in front of my mistress. I decided that I should get up at any cost—I would have to be killed first: I would get up blind and mutilated until he was filled with horror at the monster before him: if I could, I would crush his skull with anything I could get my hands on, smash his privates with a kick, gouge out his eyes with my thumb, or tear his ear off with my teeth. And in my hour of defeat, I drank down drop by drop the bitter draught, seeing myself mocked and ridiculed by everyone including the woman. I wondered if there really was a woman who loved a beaten man.

From this I passed almost immediately into a glorification of defeat. I felt immense pity for the winning pugilist, for his empty present brag, his stunted ignorance of the future, his faith in his entourage and his mistress[.] I came at such a time into complete absolution of the world, the web, all women. I drank the cup with a terrible thirst, for suddenly I saw clearly that everyone gets beaten; that against the tragic underweft of life one is always beaten, and that in the daily conduct of life the good man is beaten most of all. And thinking thus, I was drunken at once with a vast pity for all the world: I soared beyond all the small crucifixions of love, ambition, jealousy, fear, success—I understood very plainly that we are all damned together: we are forever proud and forever beaten; forever mighty, and forever cast down. And standing forever in a vast and unextinguishable dark, I saw Man, a tiny radiance, a glittering light, a preposterous flicker surround[ed] by the vast howling laughter of great unseen demons: and an exultant and animal cry burst in my throat because that light was so tiny, because it would not go out, and because it gained added significance in that enormous darkness. And I knew that Love could go; Hatred, Ambition, Pride—but this spirit of Valiance would remain—that we are forever beaten, but before we die we have the power to rise up and curse *Them*.

I have felt the agony of defeat more than most people: I suppose I am the sort the world likes to down, because they can see how it hurts. It has been hard for me ever to see myself playing second fiddle[.] But in my lucid moments, which are growing surprisingly numerous, I see now that I have always been beaten, that I have never won anything[.] Entirely without rancour or vanity, I believe, I have been beaten most often by smaller people. Everyone has gone ahead of me—for two or three years now I have accepted the empty specter of praise from a few friends who have adequately demonstrated that love is blind.

Do you know it has all become supportable. Don't think that I have lost spirit, or that I'm in a despairing mood. On the contrary. I have never felt greater strength. Thank God, I'm not a Christian, and I have no cheek-turning meekness in me. Something else has happened: I have seen a depth in me that shall never get to the end of, and a mystery that no one can touch. I'm not a man of genius, or an artist, or even a man of talent, but since that's out and freely confessed, what else have they to say about me? Having admitted this, let me also say that to call me a wonderful and extraordinary person is wild and hackneyed rubbish: I'm a miracle. And there's no one capable of getting within a mile of me.

Do you know, my dear, that in writing this book, the last thing I shall ever write, I feel for the first time as if I'm throwing my strength not at the empty air but at some object. I am deliberately writing the book for two or three people,—first and chiefest, for you. There is not the remote shadow of a chance that it will ever get published—if I cared to write salable stuff I would: I know most of the tricks, but something takes possession of me when I write, and I wear my entrails upon the page. I can't help it: I am writing, like any sensible person, for some audience—but unhappily my audience has never existed[.]

But, somehow, I am rather happy about the book. I am fashioning it somewhat as one of the men of Plantin's time might have fashioned his, or as Burton the Anatomy. I know that, at the most, it's one for two or three people. But it is evolving as a huge rich pageant, with a blending shift and interweave in the pattern. It ought to make good reading for those two or three.

—This is Sunday, Oct 3. I have just finished lunch here in my room—it is about 2:30. Tomorrow I have to look for new quarters, or find out about Oxford. I don't want to go about much for six weeks or more now. By that time I hope to have the two longest and hardest books written. There are four in all with an introduction.

I love you, my dear: I value your letters above everything. People write me a great deal more frequently now, but I hardly ever write anyone. You must not listen to inquiries about me from people unless you are sure they are genuinely my friends, and not hostile toward my life. No one has at any time been told that I was never returning: Brown and Miss Sands were pumping you in order that they might feed the Workshop circle, that group of meet-togethers and art for arters, who are not intentionally, but unconsciously, vicious—since their lives have been based on art without having in them any basis for understanding or creating it. The Yankee curse. At any rate I'm beyond that[.]

If my book breaks down, and I can't finish it I don't know what I'll do. I shan't stay in England, and I don't think I'll come home. Find out more definitely from your lady friend what "piece work" is, and how much it pays. Let me know about it.

I have about $600 left. I'm not in need of anything. I notice the note of awe and reverence in your letter about the visit of Savoir, the fluster of the company, and your own natural disappointment because he didn't like your designs. Forget about it—posterity will not care about it. Your designs will be better than those of any Frenchman, and better than most Frenchmen's plays[.]

Monday / October 4

I'll send this to you presently when I go to the Express. I'm just finished packing[.] I've got to leave these rooms this morning[.] I may go to Oxford this afternoon to find out about things there, or I may find rooms in London for 10 days more. I celebrated my birthday by working all day long. Last night I went to the Spanish restaurant off Regent street and had my party. I ordered a bottle of sherry with my food and filled a second glass opposite me. The waiter asked me if I was expecting someone. I said: "Yes—a ghost." He was so frightened he didn't come near me the rest of the time.

And you are a ghost, my dear, that will walk down the passages of my heart as long as I live. That pattern we wove together is fixed, absolute, like infinite time: that pattern you weave now has no reality for me. Goodbye for the present; God bless you forever. I never say a cruel thing to you in a letter—remember that. Badly and clumsily, because so much of me is going into the book, I unspin part of myself to you. Tom

I got a cable from you this morning, saying that you were spending my birthday in solitude. With my beautiful trusting nature, I picture your sniggering up your sleeve as you write it, reading it to the vast laughter of your companions. But still deeper than that, I love you anyway, and I don't expect you to spend your time in solitude. No more do you. If I had friends here I should probably see them. This letter is like a symphony which begins with bestial snarling notes, and ends in mighty soaring triumph. I want you to know something of what I feel—even the terrible things[.] Do you want to change that in me?

1. Wolfe had begun carrying a small pocket notebook with him so that he could immediately record observations or material for his book.

27. [New York] Saturday / Oct 2 [1926]
My dear—

I got your letter from Brussels in this morning's mail, so I did not send off the scrap I wrote last night—I am here at the playhouse, and have closed my self off in the new studio. The rest of the building is in a hubbub of work but here it is quiet—You cannot go on this way considering that after your book is finished you will write no more. You will[,] you will, if it takes every ounce of my life to get you to. I am beside myself at my helplessness to reach you now. Did you say that the book grows so much longer, which means you will stay away indefinitely. You seem to be possessed by the idea that my friends dispraise you. It isn't true at all[;] it just isn't true. I am helpless writing a letter, I seem to put down half of what I want to. How can I put down the ache that tears me in two, a groaning pain from my throat down? I felt from this letter of yours that you are putting me away from you as a reality, and I cannot face it. Is it true that you prefer me this way—across the ocean, to write you letters and not hamper you in any way? I am heart sick. As to my coming home when I did, what else could I do? You know well that I was unable to stay longer, and I have begun to think that in your deeper feeling, you wanted to be alone to work. I think that is perfectly understandable[.] Have you forgotten how often you told me that the creative person had to be alone? I think you used to tell me that when I annoyed you. Dearest, I want just to try to get at some sort of understanding with you. I go on in a blind way hoping that some time we may be together again. And now when I write this, I feel what right have I to impose anything of myself upon you. I have no right. I think I am very weary of life. I am about finished as a designer, I have no ideas whatsoever. You must never write me again that I am a better person than you are. You know it isn't so, and you do not believe it. Let us think that we are on a level, but who is to judge. I am going to Northampton to Minna's after the show opens to try to get hold of myself. Do I frighten you with all of this love? I wish I had some brains—I was just called to the telephone, it was Terry. She sends you her love. She wanted me to come to see her tonight but I have to stay here for rehearsal. Is it true that we were at Ambleside?

Could it have been so heavenly as I remember? Your encounter with Joyce is interesting. Why on earth didn't you speak to him? Do you think the young man was his son? I never heard of his having a son.—

I wish I knew some way of taking every thing of any value that I have in my soul or mind or being, what ever you choose to call it, some way that I could distil it and send it to you in a little bottle. You could take a drop now and then, if it were any good, and then what a beautiful use I would be. Would you like it?

Some day you are going to have all that you are longing for in your writing. I mean you will have the recognition that you crave. You wanted to be loved, God knows you are, but I have the conviction that you are not wholly pleased with it. You had dreams of some one so different. It is only because I am not young, I think, otherwise you would be happy. Will you try my dear to write me an answer to this letter? If you feel that you do not want to commit yourself in any way, just say so. You want just to go along. All right, if so, maybe I can find some magician to make the elixir of Aline to send you in a flask.—It will be your birthday tomorrow, what shall I do? It is a hundred years since the last one. Alice begs me to come and see her at 8th Street, but I just cannot do it. I went to the house one day but was physically unable to go up the stairs. It was about two days ago, the day I sent a cable. How can you keep on writing that I am what you call won over by anything else than you. I'm quivering with fatigue and worry tonight. I never used to be tired like this last year, did I? Some of those nights toward the end of the Dybbuk maybe. I shan't let myself get this way again[.] This year, it has been steady grinding work since the day I left you. If you only knew how clearly I see you standing on the station, you were white, and so lovely to me. I never saw you so pale as that. It was a frightful wrench, O but Tom dear you will be back again with me.—God bless you, I love you forever. Aline

I have slept with this under my pillow all night. It is warm with my sleep this morning.

28. [New York] Tuesday / Oct. 3 [1926]

My dear—

I had intended not to write to you tonight, but I am so filled with you that I cannot refrain. I wanted not to write because I go on in the same way each time, I fill page after page with laments. I started to read but it was no use so I put down my book and here I am. I have been in bed since 9:30 and tried reading for half an hour[.] I went last night to the opening of the Theatre Guild show, Juarez and Maximillian. It is a mighty dull play in the acting, but I imagine [it] would read pretty well. I bought a copy in the lobby, and left it on my seat before I came home. Simonson's[1] scenery is very handsome, but they tell me it cost thousands to build and is almost impossible to handle. It was a regular Guild first night, all the Jews in the world. You would have made a lovely pogrom, you could have cut all their throats and seen the dollars trickle out[.] I sent you a cable before I left for Northampton. You didn't answer it. That is the first time you haven't answered, I am hurt about it. Then I thought maybe you have started to come home. I wonder if some day the telephone will ever ring and you will be [on] the other end. It would not just ring, it would peal out wild chimes.—But I would rather know when you are coming. I must meet you at the boat and think [a] long time about it. In one letter you say you will come back when I say so. Is that what you mean? Are you waiting for me to say so or are you waiting for just yourself to decide—I spend hours and hours up here in my room thinking of you and writing to you. It is like a cell. You were never in this room. I have to go through one of the maid's rooms to reach it, I don't care much for that.—I wonder what you did on your birthday. If I do not hear from you tomorrow I will cable again. I think that the arrangement of everything in life is strange and ridiculous. I can see no way out of the labyrinth. I seem to be going back into my childhood confusion when I could find no reason for anything[.] I am winning myself back to a sort of virginity. Can't there be a second virginity as well as second childhood.—I have been able to go back day by day along our summer the way you like to unwind your life. I think I can see even more what I was aware of at the time. But there are spots illuminated by flashes of inner lightning, one night that I lay beside you at York, I looked at you in your sleep and I will never forget the premonition of anguish that kept me even from putting out my hand to touch you. The time we first went to your pub at Ambleside your face glorified with friendliness for all the men, the day we came down to London from Glasgow, the time we came home after our ride with Terry & Phil[2] in the lakes. Do you remember that time, you were sad, we went to your room and I bathed your eyes, and the first night we were at Chartres we walked along at one side of the Cathedral and you loved me a great deal then. You even said you would come back to be near me, do you remember that? And one of those last days in London. —I've gone off into one of my bad times, I'll stop until tomorrow—God bless you darling—Good night—. Dearest, it is morning now. I dreamt about you last night. I had to go see the doctor about earrings (funny?) I was buying, somewhere on 10th Street. You were waiting for me on 14th St., I tried to hurry and my feet clung to the ground, I could scarcely move a step, finally called to people passing to pull me along, a man asked me to take a cinder out of his eye, I just laughed at him, finally I saw you towering up in a crowd. You were dressed in khaki. I woke up just now with both my hands in yours.—We are taking out the Clay Cart[3] production, I have to make over a great deal of the stuff, it is nice to be at it again. I wish you were back in time to see it. We open Nov. 7th and run alternately with The Lion Tamer[.] It is awfully good entertainment. Since I go to bed so early I wake up earlier than ever. I love you so much, the beautiful early morning comes in the window and tries to help me. I wish I knew just how you are feeling, if you have gone back to your nervousness when I first knew you. You were so much better with me. Why did you ever let me go—It is not possible that you miss me so much as I do you—Forgive me for loving you this way. If you can think of any thing but your book, try to think of coming to write plays again. Here comes my coffee—God bless you dear. Aline

1. Lee Simonson, scenic designer for the Theatre Guild and a member of the Guild's Board of Directors.

2. Theresa Helburn and Philip Moeller. Mrs. Bernstein writes of this incident in her book, *The Journey Down*, chapter 2.

3. *The Little Clay Cart.* A Hindu drama, translated from the original Sanscrit by Arthur William Ryder, was revived at the Neighborhood Playhouse on 8 November 1926. The show ran for thirty-nine performances. Mrs. Bernstein won many critical accolades for her work on this play.

29. [New York] Wednesday/Oct 6 [1926]

Dearest—

I have not written any for four days, not since Saturday[.] I wanted to wait until I could write you more cheerfully, but I cannot, I cannot write more cheerful things.—Your birthday came and went. I thought of you, literally every minute of the day. I staid all alone, did not go to Pleasantville at all, and had the house quite to myself all day. I took a walk in the morning for 2 hours, came home and had lunch, and spent most of the afternoon at the museum, with the Egyptian things. I had supper home, and went to the playhouse for rehearsal in the evening. I come home immediately after rehearsal at night, do not even stop to have any food with my associates. I go right to bed and read. I am growing stout from such a regular life.—I come home as often as I can for dinner and drive down immediately after. Tomorrow night we open with The Lion Tamer. It plays more interestingly than it reads, but I think our company is unequal to playing it. Dorothy gives a remarkably good performance as Arabella but that is all it is. Not a bit of excitement and sicklied o're with the pale cast of Cambridge. Thank God this is the last dress rehearsal tonight, I don't want to sit through it again and watch how like a wig Dorothy's wig looks, and how remote the possibility is that

Carroll[1] is a charmer. Yes, Tom, he plays the Vicompte, the man who should have done it. Harold Minger[2] went away to California. The sets and clothes are about 65% my standard, although M. Savoir liked them enough last night to write me a message. I just found your letter and card from Antwerp, when I came home. But I have heard from you since, by cable from London. You made a silly remark about your successor. Do you not realize that with me you will have no successor? Hasn't it penetrated yet to your consciousness that my entire self is dedicated to you? I am really sick with love for you, I don't know what to do. Each letter you write, you seem to say that the book will take longer and longer to finish. I am almost hopeless that you will ever want to come back to me again[.] You write that you love me, so I must believe you. But my heart misgives me. I feel tonight as though I could tear myself to pieces, anything for some sort of release. I wish for the Lotus blossom. The thing that constantly torments me is that how on earth we can have any life together, with all these years between. If it were not for that, I know you would not allow us to be separated even now. My hard work is over now, what shall I do? I meant not to write this way again, but here I am at it. You see it is the way I feel all the time. My one hope is that your roving spirit may bring you home again some time. I love you with the last drop of my life— Aline

Thursday A.M.—Dear, will write you more tomorrow after the opening. I have to be off down town—Love Love[.]

1. Albert Carroll was one of the ten permanent actors of the Neighborhood Playhouse Company. In the annual productions of the *Grand Street Follies*, he was very successful as a female impersonator. Wolfe disliked him intensely because of his foppishness.
2. An actor with the Neighborhood Playhouse.

30. Massachusetts / Chapelbrook [Saturday, 9 October 1926]
My dear—

I am enclosing a few notices of the play that came out yesterday morning. It had a very fine reception the first night, much better than the acting deserved[.] But the play itself I think is a very good evening's entertainment. People seemed to like my work, at least they told me so, but I should say it was far from being a triumph. The second act, which I had painted on the inside of the first turned out quite well, it is funny and not too ugly. I was frightfully nervous, but you should have seen Savoir, he was nearly as nervous as you would have been. He didn't come down until it was half over, and then paced back and forth in the lobby until Alice Lewisohn hauled him in for part of the last act. I hope he was satisfied with the notices, he goes to California immediately. I packed my bag early yesterday morning and came up here to visit Minna. The place itself is lovely, I am in a little guest house all alone, and it is now about 6:30 A.M. I went to bed at nine last night, I was so tired and slept through until 6. This little house is freezing cold, I just got up and made a fire and crawled back to bed again. As soon as I can get some coffee I am going out for a long walk. It seems as though I haven't breathed since I left England.—Today is the apex of the time of gaudy color on the trees. I have never seen anything like it, so gold and so scarlet, dripping. The sky is gray and all the colors are beautiful with it. But what are they to me without you.—I wish you could see this room, it used to be a blacksmith shop. It is made of great honey colored pine beams and there is a bed 7 feet long, built along side of a window looking out on a garden and hills beyond.—I went off then, to dress and breakfast. We took a long motor ride yesterday through [. . . .]

31. [New York] Sunday, 11:30 P.M. / October 10 [1926]
My dear—

I intended taking the midnight train home tonight, but decided it was too uncomfortable so I took one at 5:30 and got in to N.Y. shortly after ten. I just couldn't bear the thought of a sleeper. I had only two days in the country, but they were beautiful, cold and sparkley, and I had two nights of rest. I had done practically no sleeping the past week. You know how it is with me before an opening. I just called up the theatre. Helen Arthur tells me the show is selling wonderfully, they had 50 standing tonight (where they stood I don't know) and are selling out all next week. I hardly think it will keep up, though. Dorothy has made a hit, and she is so happy, we all are, she is really an awfully nice person. I didn't write you did I, that Maurice Wertheim,[1] at our opening, told me he had such fun the day we had lunch at The Old Cock Tavern. He was tremendously interested in you and wanted me to make an engagement with you for dinner. The same quartette, but I told him you are not here, and promised to let him know the minute you come back. Also, about your plays and Alice Lewisohn. I sent her a note asking for them. She read them, and asked if she might keep them a little longer to read again as she was much interested[.] I said she could have them a little while. I wish you were here to talk to [her] about [it] yourself. You know I am always afraid to say anything to you about your writing. I never seem to be right in your opinion, but listen to this, please try and make your book not too long for publication. Write as long as you please at first, then bring it home here and let us see people about it, and then maybe work it to a publishable length. Is that a bad thing to say? I am in such fear that you will not understand what I write, or rather that I do not write clearly, or that maybe you will not like what I say. Also I wish you could finish and get to writing plays again. You must. It is the one thing that will satisfy you and be right for you. And I know you will get on with them eventually.—I wish I could work with you. But I am no good at it. I read "Welcome to Our City"[;] I took it away with me. (You let me have a copy). It is wonderful writing. I want to talk to you about it, not to you but with you, and I can't do it on paper here. I seem to take for granted you are coming back. Will you? It is the greatest gift in the world, writing. I'd give my ears to be able to. All I can do is to love very much a writer—There is a charming place for sale near Minna, on a hill over looking a peaceful valley—40 acres, a nice little house, noble trees, such a place to work. But not in the mid winter. This morning it was like fairy land, the trees a glory and the ground a glory with purple asters and red and gold leaves. I brought home some leaves and pinned them to a sheet of paper. Maybe I will send it to you.—I feel a little better for my visit but the ache for you has not abated an inch. It goes on and on. I am in a hopeless morass. My heart stops every time the telephone rings, I think maybe it is you, come back on one of your wild impulses. But of course it isn't you. —It is always for Katy[2] or the playhouse, or Mr. Ames' secretary.— Good night dearest, all that is good in the world for you[.] Aline

1. An alumnus of the 47 Workshop, member of the Theatre Guild Board of Directors, and New York investment banker.

2. Mrs. Bernstein's maid.

32. [New York, October 1926]

My dear:

I am in such a frightful state of mind that I hesitate to write you. I got your long letter this morning, from Belgium and then England. You tell me quite plainly that I am a ghost to you, and that you are not coming back to America. I have been trying to conceive [of] the possibility of life without you any more, and I cannot. I take it from your letter that you have no desire and no thought of any union with me again. I have read your letter three times and that is what I make of it. I have walked all the way from home to the Playhouse, I stopped in the park to read again, and fairly shrieked with laughter when you wrote you love me. I will hold out the best I can until your book is finished, and then make my exit from life as quietly as possible. I will write again, I am half dead, My dearest love[.] Aline

33. London / October 14, 1926
My Dear:—

I had two letters from you to-day—one was a one page note. I got a cable from you the other day.

I moved to Bloomsbury from Chelsea 10 days ago: I am living at 57 Gower Street; I have a huge room; much furniture; red curtains on my bed; plaster statues under glass, engravings of the Crimean War—but there's room to move. I have worked well.

I will tell you how I feel. I live in my pyjamas until about one o'clock, when I go to the Express[.] I write in the mornings—I am heavy after lunch and beer; I wander about the book shops in the Charing Cross Road until 4 or 5. I go home, have tea[,] from six to eight or nine I work. Then I eat and drink. After this I work from 11 or 12 until 1.

Your letters describe your desire for me, and then you add, as if you wanted me to deny it "but perhaps you are better there[.]" I am sunken; I am about incapable of action; I am the super-Hamlet pinned beneath the weight of his own spinning; I live under the sea, I think of you continually, I do not know how I shall emerge[.] I intended to go to Oxford last week; I think I shall go at the end of this one.

I have had a great deal of whiskey today—the first time in a long time. Your letter excited me; last night in a pub two crooks from Soho tried to work me, not daring to become positively abusive, but skirting it. One, a little man, pretended to be drunk; he introduced himself to me surlily, then boasted that he could read character, that he was a phrenologist. His game, the woman publican told me, was to arouse curiosity by hinting at some extraordinary characteristics, and lead you where he would—to some Soho joint he touted for. He kept making hints and promises until I told him that any prophesy he made, he had better make for himself, and about himself: that I would stand for no insolence. He became very ingratiating then and said he saw in me the face of one who would never break his word: [Instead?] he and the huge brute with him tried to induce me to go to a place they knew and get a drink; it was after closing time. I brooded over it today, and began to drink early: I have been into the pub three times looking for them, and if they ever approach me again I'll have it out with them[.] As a result tonight, hot with whiskey, I waited for them, and they didn't come: I took it out on three men who were leaving the place, running violently into the last one at the door, and seizing another by the arm and chasing him to a fruit stand where I bought him a pear—ridiculous childish conduct which fills me with shame and self-loathing. Your letters are almost wholly beautiful and tender, spoiled by what I imagine to be occasional sniggering jeers: "As I write this the tears are trickling down my cheeks"; "I hate the stage—what else can I do:"; "my designs are rotten—I wish I could write. It's the only thing"; "I console myself by thinking of the fine thing you are doing," "I am in bed by ten o'clock almost every night, reading poetry or some *fine books*"—I tell you, Jew, that "fine book" got me. It was the touch too much of laughter and contempt. I got your cable this morning—you said you were hopeless and tired. My dear Jew, my life is yours. I am held from submission because I believe sometimes that during the ten days between the writing and delivering of this, trickery has crept in. But I believe in you at bottom. I am terribly depressed to-day. The rainy weather has set in; a leaden drizzle falls constantly—London reels with mist and fog[.]

Since you left I have written over 60000 words of a book that may be almost 200000[.] I cabled you a long message this morning in which I said I would come back without complaint whenever you want me. I think now I shall go to Oxford to-morrow, if possible stay a month, and do all I can. Then I should like to go to Germany for a few days. I don't know—all I do know is that I want to get on with the book. Your letters about New York have depressed me—I found that even the easy promises of work in the movies went the way of most easy promises—faded. When I call you for information. When I finish the book I want to earn my living in some way[.]

The thing we have got to find, I suppose, is whether we can be together and work, too. I am so low today I hardly know where to turn. Your letters are the only things I have left—I have lopped off everything; and your letters have almost taken the heart out of me[.] I do not mind being in anyone's employ as long as I can render faithful service; I can hold my head up as long as I write honestly and hard for four or five hours a day[.]

Saturday / October 16

I am finishing this at 11:30 tonight. I am going to Oxford to-morrow afternoon to stay, I hope, a month. I have raised Hell in this house here to-day: I found the two little maids, who had been popping alternately into my room every 15 minutes since I have been here, huddled silently outside my door yesterday morning. I laid them out and sent them about their business. I demanded my bill and they gave me one for a full week—the week's not up till Monday; the old girl who bears the name of Brundle said I had promised to give her a couple day's notice—which I don't remember[.] I denounced her for not putting clean linen on my bed, which I made the maid confess was done once a week[.] I spoke passionately of honor and justice, remarked that I was a stranger in a strange land, but that I would defend the right to the last, and then told them grandly I was done—that they need fear no more unpleasantness, but that I spoke for principle and not for bed linen[.]

I got a letter and a cable from you this morning. You tell me in the cable to stay until the book's finished. The book won't be finished for several months: but I'll push it through as best I can[.]

You spoke grandly of having stayed alone my birthday. My dear Jew, I stay alone from waking to sleeping to waking every damned day[,] though of the other days when you jig about wantonly with your retinue[,] you say nothing. I care not. Shake your grey locks and your shimmy. I do not expect you to be alone[.]

You say I do not really believe I am a better person than you[.] "Let us say we are equal[,]" you say smugly. But you know very well that you look noble, plead my cause with trusting loyalty, and so on, when your friends tell you how unworthy I am. But, curse you all, I shall enjoy my humility. "You say you love me, so I must believe you"—you remark pathetically. Why, God's wounds, His liver and His guts, I have torn my accursed heart away from its moorings, I have ladled it up to you with smoking blood; I have unspun my entrails, counted my slow pulses, distilled my brain for you[.] And so you are "sick with love of me[.]" Is this, Jew, not merely a way of saying you want to keep me on *tap*? You have given up nothing; you have had me in secret; I gave you the ticking minutes of my life and all of it has never weighed as much as a pair of ruffled drawers, a wig, a flowered waistcoat for your man Carroll; a room and dresses for a play.

Sunday Morning

I am going to Oxford this afternoon. The sun has come out: I want to do nothing tawdry, nothing mean, nothing common.

Oxford / Wednesday / October 20

My dear:

I came up to Oxford Sunday afternoon; I have stayed ever since —on this High Street at the Mitre Tavern, a famous old and chilly place[.] The term has just commenced; all up and down the High Street and in and out of the colleges swarm apple cheeked boys. I feel very old—I can never be a part of this again. I went out looking for rooms. Those I found were far out, miserable, cold, dispirited—there's very little coal. Yesterday I found this place—it's called Hilltop Farm; it's 20 minutes walk from the center of Oxford but like the country, up a noble avenue of trees, flanked by green playing fields. The house is a fine residence; I have a sitting room and bedroom—both magnificent places—I get breakfast and dinner at night as well for 3:10 a week[.]

Thursday Morning

I am settled here now in my sitting room, with a cheerful fire in my grate[.] The weather here has been raw & cold, several heavy frosts. Last night there was a blazing moon, but today rain is falling, there's a mist low over everything. I am going into town presently to the Post Office to see if I have any mail from you. Did you get a cable from me saying that my address until further notice was Poste Restante, Oxford. I got one from you, telling me to finish the book before I came back. I'm afraid my dear, it will be several months before the book is finished[.] I want to stay here a month, and work like Hell. By that time I hope to have on paper roughly three parts of it—There are four parts—but one is an introduction that will be comparatively short. I have almost finished the third part; I am well on with the first. I am fairly sure I have done more work since you left than most of the Oxford boys will get done during the entire year[.]

I met more people at the Mitre than I have since you left—but no women. The boys are rigidly guarded, have to be in at night; the place is controlled by the university proctors. A young Englishman who was in the service during the war, and ever since until a few months back, is coming out here today[.] He got a room here—I think he's a good sort, and perhaps he'll be company for me. I met some undergraduates and several Americans. One of them is a young New York Jew; he is my age but he tells me he's one of the Assistant District Attorneys. He was reverential in his attitude toward the English gentry; he had the secret desire of all Jews to be gentlemen; and he had letters of introduction to one of the Dons and some of the students. He concealed his name from me, but before he left he sent it up by the little hotel boy—there was a *Berg* to it. But he was kind and decent; he wanted to take me around to the places he had discovered. I went with him. He's probably sharp as a gimlet, and will make a huge success in law[.]

Oxford, of course, is a beautiful place, but England is a sad, cold, desperate country. After I leave here I may go back for a period to the hated and hating French: I should like some of their food and wine and tinsel. I suppose my reverence for holy ground has waned as I grow older and wickeder: I had half hoped to see the streets of Oxford peopled with the flaming faces of future Shelleys and Coleridges, but they look very much like the people at Harvard and Yale, only younger, fresher, and more innocent. They all wear a sort of uniform—light baggy flannel trousers of grey, a dark coat, a striped shirt and collar. I fear that their ideas upon examination would also wear a uniform of baggy grey flannels. For this is what it all seems to mean. They are up here twenty four weeks a year for three years —about 18 months. In the morning, if energetic, they go to a lecture, in the afternoon they play games and have tea, and from tea time to seven o'clock, they read[.] The night is given to eating in hall together, chatting, and paying visits. All of this is supposed to weave a mysterious charm about them, to impart delicately modern wisdom, to put a chrism on them. I have watched some of the American students here—they submit reverently to all the constraint of the life, hush their voices, and try to be as unlike themselves as possible[.] No one seems to have thought yet of the possibility of becoming a civilized person at home, yet we have, it seems to me, the materials from which civilization ought to be made—abundance, plumbing, warmth, light, comfort—the nasty little people sneer at these, but fine people, like fine horses, need them—even plumbing[.] Also, when any of our people have ideas, it seems to me they are likely to be quicker, truer, and less worn[.] I have been away four months, I wonder how much longer I shall stay[.] Have you been able, in the midst of your woes, to perform the single little errand I asked of you —namely to get from Miss Lewisohn without talk my plays? Have you been able to realize that I get sick every time I think of them in conjunction with the rather interesting reptilian face, and that I no longer want them to pollute the air near this very extraordinary, sensitive, although somewhat inarticulate-because-what-she-has-to-say-is-so-unusual person? You have not, but please, *please* do. Do you remember the time you thought I was away and lied to me about your doings, the night before? You said you had worked late at the Playhouse. I lied back at you, and said I had called there and was told you had been gone for hours? Do you remember how you wept then, and said you had been at Irene's, where, I believe, you sat in a corner and talked to her grandmother while everyone else played checkers, dominoes, and hide-and-go-seek? At half past one milk toast and cheese sandwiches were served and the happy group disbanded. Furthermore, you had *just* come in after I called. I thought of it all the other day, but without rancour. Shall I be laughed at because I cleansed my heart at 25 and took monastic orders for a notorious wanton? (I said 'shall'—I don't believe you are). I do not know. And it does not matter as it once did. I am a better person than I was: men have given their greatest faith to a myth. I am not ashamed to affirm my love for you, and my belief in you. No one can triumph over me.

*I have been in to town and found two letters from you—one from your friend's house in Mass, the other from New York, containing notices of the play, which I shall read later. I am glad it went well, and that they praised your work. I knew *your* part of it would be good at any rate. I am glad to see you are back on your feet again. It gives me an added incentive to get on with my work. You are right: I ought to stay until my book is finished, and I shall, if it takes eight months longer. I note that you had *written* Alice Lewisohn to get my play, and that she has asked to "keep" it a few days longer. Now you know perfectly well the woman has never read it, and she has no intentions concerning it, has never had, and further that I did not write hinting that you should ease negotiations along, but *solely* and *simply*, *solely* and *simply*, *solely* and *simply* to get it back[.] Since your own timorous conduct reveals to me only to [sic] plainly that disloyal and half hearted disparagement of your attempts, I am taking matters in my own hand and writing her. I shall ask Carlton, who has been small in professing, but who will be somewhat more adequate in accomplishment, I believe, than the Loud Speakers. You must know that the failure of my plays, even to get a reading, has sickened me of ever trying another; Good God, can you not have kindness and decency enough to refrain from writing me about them again, with slobbering generalities about "going on," "eventually," "wonderful writing." Must I be depressed and nauseated helplessly when I'm trying to forget them in something else? As to my book, you say vaguely that we will "take it around[.]" Yes, as we took the plays around. I have admitted that they were failures, that I was a failure as a writer; and I have told you that I'm willing to face it. The play you mentioned I wrote four years ago. I've done nothing since—no one ever saw anything in the other[.] Goddam it to Hell, be quiet about it. If I've recognized my failure I owe the recognition to your help—it's a good thing for me: surely you must recognize that the sooner I'm out of it the better. If this happens again I'm off to Paris.

Monday / October 25

My Dear:

I will not scratch a word out of my abominable ravings. They are part of the evil texture of my soul, and you shall know me for the half-monster I am. I love you truly, my dear Jew—below the dark wilderness is my heart: you are run into it like a thorn[.] I thought the other day of a meal we had at Scott's in Piccadilly: it was a day or two before you went home—I made you cry, you couldn't stop, we had to leave. Your nose grew red and big: I thought of it often. I see you as clearly there as anywhere: I told you my Furies would come back to torment me[.] Perhaps the God will do for me what he did for Orestes—turn the avenging spirits into good demons—but only after a period of purification. And I think I am going through that now: Your instinct was right when it bade me stay in England. God knows, their vice is a sordid and gloomy business, and their nice women have long teeth, or false teeth, red leathery cheeks. My powers of resistance are never tried: I wonder how they engender fire for begetting children. The adventuring of the students looks doleful enough: —a sneaking arrangement with a grinning threadbare girl, with cold chapped hands. They have a magnificent sense of ritual these people —gowns to class, dinner at college, hours and traditional rules, but no comfort. We have comfort and no ritual. Thus they have a ritual of roast beef and Brussels sprouts, but both the beef and sprouts are tasteless. The food at this place is splendid: I have dinner in my sitting room every night. I am buying more books—here are some of them: little books of poetry of Thomas Campion, Marvell, Sassoon, Blunden, Davies, Gilbert Murray; and little Greek and Latin texts—the *Alcestis*, the *Lives*, by Cornelius Nepos, Ovid, and little books on Greek and Latin antiquity[.][1] I spend a couple of hours after lunch in book shops. I am writing steadily but I can do only about 1500 words a day. If I stay here a month I shall have over 100,000—more than the average novel—; but the end is not in sight.

I got your cable today asking if I am happy here, and [saying] that you are faithful[.] You seem to throw this at me nobly, as if you preserve yourself against desperate enticement and above my desert. Do you not think that if I can maintain steadfastness in this deep grey solitude, you, attended by warmth, comfort, the excitement of your work, and your friends, can return as much? Or do you doubt me when I tell a plain straight story. That depends, I know, upon the present texture of your heart: you will affirm or deny *me* there only after you have affirmed or betrayed yourself. I am invincible in defeat, supreme in my victory over all lost faith: you have given me that, it cannot be taken from me. O great lost demon of my youth, wild boy that beat across mysterious seas, strange seeker of enchanted coasts, I haunt around the grey walls of my house to find you. Where is the apple tree, the singing and the gold? Where are the moonbright feet of the running girls—the Arcadian Meadows—the goat hooves and the glimmering thicket faces? I will sing of him and celebrate my sorrow; I will invoke him, over all loud laughter, for he was godlike, deathless faith, unending beauty hung like lanterns in his eyes, and he is gone.

All men must lose a god to gain a castle[.]

Good-bye, Jew. I remember with dull horror that it has been three weeks since I wrote you. Do you take this as an indication of my growing laxity? Oh but I speak to you presently and immanently as I write; the sea is too wide, too deep, too dark for me ever to reach you with my words. And I think as I go to bed here in ominous midnight that darkness drops, the revelry begins, the flashing lights blaze on the sky, and women, fatal, false, silken, soft breasted cushion-bellied women awake to lust. Meanwhile my dear Jew the rind of this spinning orange wheels on through desolate eternity: I am whirled daywards burnt to a flame with my passion, hurling my prayers back that might reach out to God if he were there and had remembered us —to absolute and timeless God who never can be five hours off—at what? At slender, groping truth housed desperately behind the hungry flesh of forty; faith competitive against the blowing horns of jazz, the three lines in the inky morning press, the thousand needle titillations of your world. Why I would go to China and ther'd be a day between our thought, but what's a day? And where dies faith? Where does the heart go rotten? Why, when a woman lifts her skirt, behind the door; with sow grunts and belly burlesque. By God, I say that this is good, for poetry must *live*, the good man speak, high passionate thought survive, through the enormous subtle masking of a clown. Christ and Galahad will not do for this: I summon mighty Socrates—pot bellied Silenus-like Socrates, the prince of [shores?] the god of man.

Tuesday

So help me God, I'll send this to you now—today. It is four minutes to one o'clock by my mantel clock—I am going into town for mail and food, and a book or two. I have written since ten o'clock. You are probably not out of bed yet—it is eight o'clock. Perhaps you are getting out, bathing, and have bound your hair up in the little girl's knot behind. What shall I do? I can't finish before I finish—that is to say, I am working inexorably, but I can push or sketch it. I love you, my dear. I think you know that. Go your way: act according to your God and your heart. You are better and greater than I am—I will never forget you or despise you. God bless you. Write me when you get this— Tom

1:15

I'm going now. I've put the pages together and read them. Parts are terrible, but you shall know me. And people go by the final word[.] Here it is: *I love you.*

I have had a letter from you, and a short note in which you acknowledge the receipt of my long letter. You make a terrible threat and say that you "shrieked with laughter" when I said I loved you. In the name of God, be honest. You have never done me any fairness in my letters, ignoring their import in order to make your point. What in Christ's name do you want? Do you think I am staying here from desire? If you want me back, and believe I can work there speak up like a decent honest woman[.] I am not trying to bludgeon you—my life's lost—I don't know where to turn—you taunt me vaguely by saying I "must" write more plays[.] Do you want to drive me mad? I will die without your love, but, God damn it, can't you see I will die if I have nothing else! Don't you see I must hold my head up? You think you will play up to my idiot impracticality? But you're a woman of the world—for God's sake talk decent fact. *What can I do*? Why do you not only distort but lie in every letter about what I've said. I never said I would never [evade trust.] You have invented it deliberately. For God's sake imitate my honesty instead of my luxury—Speak up and be worthy of this thing like a decent honest woman. Do you want me back[?] Some of my heart's in this letter. I wonder now how much of *yours* has been in yours. I love you. "Shriek" over that.

1. Thomas Campion (1567–1620) specialized in song lyrics in both English and Latin; Andrew Marvell (1621–78) was a poet and satirist; Siegfried Sassoon (1886–1967) is most famous for the ironic treatment of war in his poetry; John Davies (1569–1626), Elizabethan poet, is best known for his "gulling" sonnets and his intellectual versifying in *Nosce Teipsum* and *Orchestra*; Gilbert Murray (1866–1957) wrote many of the translations of Greek drama which Wolfe so greatly admired; *The Alcestis* is by Euripides; Cornelius Nepos, Roman historian, wrote in the first century B.C.; Ovid, Latin poet, first century A.D., is best known for *Metamorphoses*.

34. [New York] Thursday / October 21 [1926]
My Dear,

I am so happy that you are in Oxford. I think of you there, in that beautiful place, I wonder if you have a pleasant room and good food. Are the days cold now? Do the trees turn such wonderful colors as they do here? This autumn has been a triumph and now things have reached the bronze age. New York is packed jambed pushing with people, and all the streets are torn up to make new subways, and there is no place for people to walk or ride. It seems terrible for you to have to come back to it, but it is grand also. I wish you wanted to write about New York. It seems to me that it is being entirely rebuilt, very little left of what was here ten years ago. It is too much for me since I came home, I can't stand the objective life in such quantity. My one thought all day is toward getting up alone into my room, and not having to do anything or make any arrangements. I remember your saying to me in London one day, with a scathing tone, that I liked getting things done. Well unfortunately that is 75% of my work. The designing is a small proportion, and I am sick of it. I got back into the necessity the moment I landed, and it requires the utmost effort to keep it up. I want to lead the thoughtful life for a time, wasn't it grand when we were together at Ambleside. All day long there are countless things that remind me of you with stabbing reality. I pass the old hotel Albert often going down to the Playhouse.

Places have the most poignant association for me. I can't believe that you will not materialize, when I want you so much. I want you here, and I want you to finish the book and write plays again. You must never again say you will write no more. It is the most heaven sent gift, I envy you so, and I am going to bend all of my strength and all of my love for you to make you do it. And I am going to try to give up what I am doing and try some other thing, what good is a scene designer? Helen Arthur has been very ill since Sunday. Tonight we took her to a hospital for observation. It is very strange, she has been asleep since Sunday night and we cannot rouse her. She wakes up occasionally for food and then goes to sleep. No doctor seems to be able to find out what it is, she has none of the symptoms of sleeping sickness, we are all so worried, it is such a strange thing. She has no pain, only says that her head and arms don't belong together. Lish and Agnes and I have taken turns looking after her. Isn't it strange? Tom, dear, I love you and I am living to see you again. Do I frighten you when I write of my feelings?

God bless you my dear. Aline

This is good morning now. We are having beautiful days. You know how fine October is here. It is cold and clear and sometimes a little thin sheet of warm haze comes over every thing. I walk a great deal.—There is terrific excitement over Queen Marie being here.[1] You should see the papers. She is a lively dressy sporty Queen and very handsome, according to her pictures, I have not seen her though. Dearest love.

1. Queen Marie of Rumania, consort of King Ferdinand, arrived in New York aboard the S.S. *Leviathan* on 19 October 1926. She was very popular in this country because of her pro-American position during World War I.

In an undated letter written during this period, Mrs. Bernstein spoke of the desire to put some of her physical self into her letter to Wolfe: "I have thought of pricking my finger and staining [the letter] *with a drop of blood, or pinning a piece of my hair to it." In late September 1930, she was to send him a letter dramatically imprinted with a drop of her own blood.*

35. [Oxford] Thursday / October 28, 1926

My Dear:—

Unfortunately, I'm going to write you a nice letter, which will explain its brevity. I'm writing you this in my sitting room at ten o'clock in the morning after breakfast. I got your letter yesterday in which you speak of your relief over my cablegrams. I am relieved to get the letter.

I have been thinking of getting home in time for Christmas or New Year's. The book stands thus: I work five or six hours every day on it now—I see my way through the first three books as straight as a string. I brood constantly over the fourth and last—the book lifts into a soaring fantasy of a Voyage, and I want to put my utmost, my most passionate in it. The prefatory action to these four books I can write down in ten days.

I am confident now I can get the central body on paper by Christmas—that is, the first three books. But I am also confident I can *not* get the last book in by that time. But if then three books are done, I know that the *whole* will get done wherever I am. Listen, my dear: last night I worked till past midnight, a late hour for me now, and did over 2000 words. The book is swarming with life, peopled by communities, and governed by a developing and inexorable unity.

I think I shall stay here until late in November: it is a fine house, out in the country, a quarter mile off the road that goes from Oxford to the village of Cowley. "There was a roaring in the wind"[1] last night. After dinner at night I walk down the Stygian Avenue of trees to the Cowley road, get a drink and cigarettes at the pub, and come back and work. I have been in to the town at night only once since I came here—that was with the Englishman who followed me out here when I praised the place, and who sometimes comes in to eat with me. He entertains me with stories of his efforts at seduction: last night he took a little girl, freshman in one of the colleges here, to a room in a pub, got her drunk, seduced her, and brought her back to her college at eleven—three hours after she is supposed to be in. This means they must appear before the authorities—she before her principal, he before the proctors[.] Nothing will happen to him, except perhaps a fine of a pound, but she may be expelled. There is something very nasty about the English when they do these things—do you remember the very elegant plays about the beautiful and lost Jessica or Iris or Godiva sweeps in and someone says to someone quietly that he has known her at—Monaco, and someone else in the pause says "Oh *that*!" and you feel that quite enough has been said. Well, I saw the upper classes on debauch at Brussels, a red-faced oldish man with a preposterously accented voice with the Colonel's wife, or some such person, with longish white flaccid arms, streaked with blue, and a sloppily elegant evening dress. He told her dirty jokes, evading and hinting at the final point; after a moment she laughed and said "Jolly good, that!" God what a business!

I think they love to think of themselves as they are shown in these plays—Elegant, witty[,] seducing in a high hat; *it is* not pleasant to think of bad teeth, and large feet and hands[.] And these future elegants who attend this most ancient university get their clumsy practice on green dirty little girls.

Monday / November 1 [1926]

My Dear:—

I have been in Oxford two weeks yesterday, and at this house for 12 days, where I have got a great mass of work done[.] My life is running with horrible precision—I have lunch here now; go into town for my mail at two o'clock, haunt book sellers, and come out again at four thirty. Then I go out no more save for a walk after supper, and a visit to the pub. I go to bed at midnight or 12:30.

I shall stay here two or three weeks longer. The first book will be finished in a day or two—the Third book, which is twice as long as any of the others will be finished in a week[.] The second book I shall try to get on paper this month.

I got your letter to-day. Please give my dear love to Terry. She is the real right stuff, your true friend:—how has so much gentleness and wisdom lasted out over all the cutthroat venom of the theatre?

I am beginning to have the decent heart of a child. I have been a bawdy and unlicensed fellow, but I believe I have always been a man of honor. Now this régime, not only of my body but of my spirit, has lifted me up to some strong rock. I am like a man who might say at 20 that God had a long grey beard, and who is laughed at by the kind of person who thinks Jurgen[2] a great book; he thinks God has a long grey beard, too weary, too indifferent to [sic] remote from their opinion to care to explain or equivocate, and the same people are silent, because their little tagged minds find what puzzles them, and they see a sign upon him. And thus I will not explain even to you what I mean by a man of honour.

Monday / November 8

Here I am, my dear, two weeks behind again in my letters, but I have meanwhile sent you several cables—one to-day saying that I shall certainly be back in January. I shall not give myself more than two months more. My dear, I want some place to work, and some place to live when I go back. None of your Greenwich Villagey places if you please, not even the old Albert, convenient as it was, I think of some big room at the top of a shabby old building such as the one on Eighth street; but I want to live there too, and I like to be warm during the winter, and have a place to wash my dirty hide once in a while. Do you think such a place exists? New York is a place of trade, of money making—it excites me, but I feel the money lust going on around me and I am depressed if I am not joined with it. It is something that was riven into my soul as a child when I was taught that no work was work unless it gained *money*. Good or bad, the book, I think, will save me from that depression, for a great deal of work has gone and will go into it. And as long as I keep it before me always and work my five or six hours a day on it, I shall feel that I am honestly employed. I have less than $300 left—I am having a suit made which, with trousers, will cost me ten guineas. I do not think that I shall get away from Oxford with $200[.] I want to go for a few days into Devon and Cornwall, then to Paris for two or three days, then to Strasbourg, then to a few of the nearer towns in Germany, and then home.

I have done an immense quantity of work here—Do you know I have been at night into Oxford only once since I came to this place three weeks ago? I shall stay here two weeks longer and try to get as much of the Second Book on paper as I can[.] The first is done, the third almost done. I shall finish the last one in New York. I have written 100000 words, or almost that, since you left—it is an unusual quantity of writing, and however bad it may be, I have said a great number of things I have always wanted to say. It is going to be for you, I think, if for no one else, an exciting book: I have somehow recovered innocency—I have written it almost with a child's heart: the thing has come from me with a child's wonder, and my pages are engraved not only with what is simple and plain but with monstrous evil, as if the devil were speaking with a child's tongue. The great fish, those sealed with evil, horribly incandescent[,] hoary with elvish light, have swum upwards.

I have been very tired of writing the last two days: it has rained interminably—the appalling English weather, dewy, foggy, physically depressing has set in. I shall be glad to get out of England: there is something here that renews and fills the spirit—there is something here too that is ugly, base, degraded. I want to look on gaiety once more: I want gay food, gay fires, gay lights. And I, who am at heart the most conventional person that ever lived, know that I can never be a Tory—whatever comes to supplant it, I want to see this ugly ancient palsied thing that lies and cants wiped out—its got to go. Not only the old toothless thing that sits upon the land and uses all the words as liberty, patriotism, God and king, and so on, but the same thing in all criticism of letters and the arts[.] The newspapers have lied so systematically for months about the coal strike that my sympathy has gone over to the miners and their mad fanatical, but valiant leader, Cook, who is cartooned with a swine's or an idiot's or an animal's face, in league with "Russia" and "Bolshevism"—insensate hysterical words which they brandish like death's head at the frightened people. I have never before realized how evil and rotten a thing desperate and panicky wealth tied up to government can look—these poor men, the miners, who have fought like animals to save the poor standard of their living are attacked as traitors, Bolsheviks or fools for listening to Cook. And there is a kind of horrible satisfaction about that they are to be forced to surrender, which means of course that the lords and masters have done for themselves: these men will turn on them like wolves some day, and goodbye Torys. "Then," say the Torys, "goodbye everything—freedom, life civilization," but I think not. Other people will begin to use these words for their own things. In the same way, they hate their best writers—Wells they are covering with vituperation for his new book—*The World of William Clissold.*[3] I went through the last volume in a bookshop today. It is certainly not a novel—which will be all the American critics will be able to say about it, until someone else sets a new fashion in Wells' criticism: but it is one of the most interesting books I've seen in some time, sparkling and bristling with facts, ideas, schemes for setting the world right and so on. I picked up a volume which your kinsman Gilbert Frankau[4] has written about America[.] It is called *My Unsentimental Journey*: it is written with the submerged jealousy of a small cheap man: it has in it something of the terrible and degrading bitterness and jealousy towards us which is gnawing the liver of England today, and doing a far more irreparable damage to her spirit than to her wealth, position. He is heavily sarcastic toward any manifestation of "socialism" which he weaves in vaguely with what he calls the "highbrow," seas on to Russia, and includes in it everyone who does not read the Daily Mail.[5] He whoops it up so loudly that he ought surely to be knighted before long. He makes one or two jokes about the Jews, also. You ought to excommunicate him from the synagogue.

Some of the young men in the university have had me to teas and breakfast, and in their rooms several times. My criticism of their college life is not that it is idle, but that it is dull. What Wells says about the place in his book is remarkably true—it is a magnificent architectural monument of the Middle Ages—it is stuck in a river basin which steams with mist and drizzle, and is undoubtedly sodden to the mind if long endured. It is the crowned throne of Toryism. It affixes a label, it establishes a manner of baggy trousers, casual lack of enthusiasm, and preposterous accentuation—what is called the Oxford manner, by which, you are told, you may recognize an Oxford man the world over; but by the same token can you recognize a London cockney, an East Side Jew, a Middle Western farmer. Unfortunately, it seems to have little to do with the heart and the head. I am fed up with universities everywhere[.] I am fed up with people who write like clever boys. Give, oh give me Joyce, but don't make me swallow the Sitwells.[6] The Sitwells, by the way, are the university contributions to literary "radicalism," the kind of thing that will go on writing heavy satire against Victoria when George VIII is dead and buried[.] Let the dead bury the dead. The London papers are bitter against American plays at present not because they are bad plays, as most of them are, but because they are American[.] I am sorry for these people: they are in a desperate fix, and they are behaving badly. I have a deep interior affection for them which I think I shall never lose.

I am very sorry to hear of Miss Arthur's sickness, but glad to see from your latest letters that she is better. I can well understand the anxiety you must have felt, and the gap her absence must cause in the business of the theatre. I note, too, that you have a new commission from the Guild, and that you have taken it because you did not know what else to do in your present frame of mind. That is not true: you take it because it is the most important thing in the world for you—my presence or absence has very little to do with it. I am glad you have found the work.

I am sorry to hear of the failure of *Juarez and Maximilian*. It serves them right, you say, for being so pretentious. I am glad to find you are a person who does not like pretentious things. I have known many of them—they use the word "pretentious" frequently to down any effort they do not like, and to show what simple earnest fellows they are. I agree with you—I like unpretentious things myself—like Homer's *Iliad*, *King Lear*, *Paradise Lost*, Joyce's *Ulysses*, *Jean Cristophe*, *Peer Gynt*, and so on.

So much for our two good friends who rule the roost: Professor Cant and Doctor Twaddle.

This is a dull letter—I have worked hard here and begin to feel it. Also the drear November. My daemon is waiting to speak: and he will speak some time soon so that I may know the truth about your vows. And if you lie, why not good ones? Why insult me with the clumsy ones? Why do you say in one letter you have been to see Terry night after night, and in your latest, only once? I do not exact prison for you—I never have.

It's a strange thing how all the sensitive plants, the fine flowers of aestheticism, I have known, have looked at my great body, and my devouring appetite, and accordingly, with the usual perception of sensitive plants, attempted to use a whitewash brush upon my soul.

O Jew, I have lain such a long lifetime under sea. When shall the dead awaken? And I am old and sodden—I have lived three times as hard as any one else: therefore, I am nearly eighty now[.]

I'll write or cable you when I leave here giving you an address for my mail. Your letters make a big stak [sic] now—they bolster up my heart. When I come back you must make me some rich coffee—that will serve acceptably to intoxicate me. I will not take you by surprise:

I shall give you time to put your house in order, to take the veil, and to smooth out your eyes like a nun.

I am a dull fellow: I'm going out into the yard and let the rain fall on me a while. Good bye, my dear. I love you. Tom

I picked up one of your first letters just now, noting with interest how much fatter and longer it is than your last—But two months dead.[7]

1. "There was a roaring in the wind all night." Wordsworth, "Resolution and Independence," I, 1. 1.

2. A novel by James Branch Cabell which was widely read in the 1920s.

3. H. G. Wells was a lifetime favorite of Wolfe's.

4. Prolific English novelist and short-story writer. Although Aline Bernstein's maiden name was Frankau, Gilbert Frankau was not a relative.

5. A London newspaper, located on Tudor Street.

6. Though many considered Edith, Osbert, and Sacheverell Sitwell to be famous for their unconventional views, Wolfe obviously considered them traditional and dull.

7. Shakespeare, *Hamlet*, I, ii, 1. 137.

36. [New York] Sunday / November 3, 1926

Dearest Tom—

It is Sunday night about 12:30[.] I have been down at the playhouse all day[,] rehearsal this afternoon, and made drawings for The Guild show all evening. I went into a Western Union office this morning to cable you, but I walked out again. I cable you too often, you'll get tired of it and then what. It is a great temptation to send such an immediate message to you, and it is so grand to get a reply. Letters grow cold I am sure, on the way over—It was Agnes Morgan's birthday yesterday, and the company and staff had a party for her last night. It was a mild party, suitable to the occasion. The only people outside the immediate playhouse family were Mr. & Mrs. Ernest Boyd,[1] and a young lady whose name I did not catch.

I questioned Mr. Boyd very closely about possible work for a brainy young friend who is now at Oxford. He seemed to think that movies were the only solution. He apparently makes his living doing translations, and says it is a poor living. Writing short stories is the thing that makes money, he says. A good one will bring $500 or over. I am simply passing on information to you. I want you to meet him as soon as you come back, he knows all the works of that world. These last few days it has seemed impossible that you would come back. The thought of seeing you is like this, sometimes when you take a walk at night, you fix your eyes upon a star and as you walk the star seems to go farther away. Have you ever done that? Have I fixed my eyes upon a star? I have to shake myself out of my despondency.—I have a friend here, an English actress named Gertrude

Kingston. She is sailing on Saturday, and I am giving her a small package for you, to leave at the American Express Co. Will you call for it. It will be nothing much, just nice to have some one take it over. Miss Kingston is a lovely woman. Well on in years now. She used to be a very successful actress, but I fear now is having a difficult time. She is most distinguished.—I haven't had a letter from you for a long while, but no doubt you write every thing in the book.—Here I went to sleep, and it is now Tuesday night, or Wednesday morning 2 A.M. Just got in from The Clay Cart dress rehearsal, and I'm dead.—There are about 15 new people in the cast, and you should have seen what a sight they looked, they had their beards on upside down, their coats hooked up the back instead of front, O just dreadful, Lish and I got hysterics on the top floor. My eyes hurt so from looking intently, and setting lights, I will not write very much. I hope I will get a letter soon, it means so much to me. If there is none tomorrow I'm going to cable you. The only time that you are not in my mind is when I have to do a very concentrated piece of work. The moment that is over, I am walking with you, talking, and living over other times. I often say your name aloud, and I find myself actually stretching out my arms to you. I am very tired tonight, my working hours lasted from 9:30 A.M. until 1:00 A.M., pretty long day, and these last few days I have had a cloud of depression all about me.—If I can get away Saturday, I may go to Westport with Lillian, possibly the country will cheer me up. But there is only one thing will cheer me, that is you.—God bless you Tom dear, I kiss you good night. I am crying the way I used to when you said awful things to me. I love you, true to you forever[.] Aline

In the Dybbuk there is a character called the wailing woman—that's me—sounds like it—

1. Ernest Boyd was an Irish literary critic, best known for *Studies From Ten Literatures* (New York, 1925). His wife, Madeleine, was to become Wolfe's agent for the sale of *Look Homeward, Angel.*

37. [New York] Thursday / Nov 4 [1926]
Dearest Tom—

I do not quite understand the cable I had from you today—It said among other things Continent December—does this mean that you are faithful, and returning in December, or does it mean you are going to the European Continent for December. This sort of communication is so difficult. I sent off a letter to you this morning. God knows what you will make of it, I tried my best in simple language to ask you to come back. Of course the pity of it is that you do not care enough to come back. I went out at once and answered your cable, thinking it meant you were coming home, and then found after reading it again that I may have been mistaken, but you said before that you wanted a month in Oxford and two weeks in Germany. I lived in happiness for about half an hour. I think you need to be near me again. Your letter is wild and nervous, I want to be with you and make you happy. Surely you must know by now how great my love for you is, how deep and strong is my affection. You have written some bitter things to me in this last letter, and if I didn't know so well the working of your mind, I should be angry.—What you do when you get a pencil in your hand is to write, and these weird and terrible things come tumbling from your mind. And here I am, hyper sensitive to every word you send me. I hold so many conversations with you during the day.—You said in your letter that I have never given up any thing for you, what is that, you know I saw nothing of my friends last year. What exactly you mean I do not know. There is nothing in the world I would not give up to be with you. Do you think that I care for anything here? I'm not even interested in my work any more, that is what fed me these last few years. For the first time in my life, work is not a delight to me. It is drudgery and I can scarcely get through with it.

The Clay Cart opened again tonight, I think it went pretty well. I've had a ghastly headache all day long, I wanted to stay in bed but had to get up to work on the Guild show, and I had to go down tonight. We all went to Irene's for the usual frigid supper. Your transcription of my description is nearly correct. They are frightful parties, you said I lied to you once about working at the playhouse late, I did not lie to you[.] You love to belittle me, you know very well I am truthful, honest, loving with you. How can you waste me the way you do, why are you not here with me, I love you, you love me, and you let the ocean stay between us.—

I am sick, miserable and do not know where to turn. I used to wake up so happy in the morning, now I wake with a dull thumping pain all over me. All because you are away. Isn't it shameful of me to write you this. If you don't come back soon I do not know what I shall do—Love you forever[.] Aline

You must think I am crazy to have cabled beautiful December—I thought you were coming home then,—good morning darling—I kiss you—

My dear—

Just got your letter, it is really a package, how did you find an envelope like that? I am not well today, I have a frightful headache and decided to stay in bed until noon, something I rarely do. I can't imagine what it can be[;] it is really a pain in my head, different from a headache.—It may be my eyes, we have had three late dress rehearsals of Clay Cart, and I look so closely at every thing, and trying lights etc.—

Now listen carefully Tom to what I say—I have read your wild letter twice, it has taken a full hour because your handwriting is so illegible, but I think I know what you have written. You say I should write like a decent honest woman.—I have—You cabled me you would come back in six weeks, and now you say 8 months. I want you to come back. Spend your month in Oxford and your visit to Germany, and if you love me, for God's sake come back. You can finish your book here, why must you write only on the European Continent? I will take the old 8th St. place and make it nice for you to work in, it is large and quiet, and you might not mind if I work also, off at one end. If you do not like that, I can go on working at the Playhouse. I hope I am saying all this clearly—I love you, and I am miserable without you. If you feel that you cannot come back to me, I want you to tell me so at once. I am ashamed to have to ask you this. You have told me how you always wanted to be loved, now you are. Why must you stay away?—Everything I write you of my life is true. I also live a monastic life.—You write of me as though I live in a constant glitter of sight and sound. You know how quiet the playhouse is. And now since Helen is ill there is a gloom over every thing.—I got your play from Alice Lewisohn about two or three weeks ago.—I did not know she had two. I will ask her tonight for the other. I have it here at home in my desk.—Here is something else in words of one syllable[.]—If you come back (soon, please) you must not look for work until your book is finished.—I have saved all I earned this year, but a few hundred dollars that I use for daily expenses, and I will probably have other work. I'm always afraid that you will get angry when I mention finances.—You can live wherever suits you best, and have a quiet place to write, and let me see you when you will. I wish that I could be perfect for you, all I can be is the way I am, and as true as the sun. I hate to write, I want to talk to you. Please dear come back. It certainly will not be too bad for you here. I love you more than any one else ever could. Aline

38. [New York] Monday / Nov 8th [1926]
My Dear—

Your letters and cables have grown to such bulk that I have had to put them away in a box. I carried them in my hand bag, until it broke apart. So now I have them in a nice wooden box on my table.—Terry has been frightfully ill. She has pneumonia, and two nights ago her life was in great danger, but fortunately she seems to have come through the worst. Last week she was laid up with a cold, and I stopped in to see her a few times, on the way up town, and suddenly on Friday she became very bad. It seems as though I write letters as tragic as your own family. She still is running a high temperature, but the doctors seem to think she has passed the worst. I have just come from her house, her husband is nearly crazy. They are very very fond of each other, and I thought he would go out of his mind these last two days. He is just about the way you would be under the circumstances. Helen Arthur is a little better, I went to see her last Saturday. She is still in a sleeping state, but more wakeful, stays awake about three or four hours out of 24.—I am hard at work getting the Howard play through, there is little or no chance for any interesting designing, I don't know what they have me on it for, couldn't design a good one any more any how. But the Clay Cart is beautiful, I am so sorry you will not come back in time to see it. I am sending you a cutting from the evening Sun, I know you hate me to send you these things, but this one may please you. It makes me so sad because I can never do anything else again so good.—Yesterday was Sunday, and I did no work, stayed in bed until lunch time, reading some stories and the papers, went to a concert in the afternoon with Lillian and her husband, and then went down to the playhouse for the show. Now that Helen is away, I take charge of the house twice a week, some one always has to be there. I heard a beautiful concert[,] all Bach, it was grand and I sat holding your hand the whole time. Saturday night I had gone to bed, when Lish called me up about your cable arriving. So I got up and took a taxi down and got it. I had asked you to answer me at the playhouse because I was there all the time working. That was the 6th of November and now I will count the days within two months. Of course I am frightened about your going to the continent. I know how you drift, and I fear so that you may be caught up in the life there. At first you told me a certain time and now you tell me another. I shall have to be as patient as I can, how can I beg you again to come back? Might as well ask the West wind to turn and blow into my face. I dread having the New Year come and go without you. But what can I do? I wanted to write you the loveliest thing in the world tonight, the only thing I know is I love you, and I have said it so many times. But maybe it will be nicer for you this time, maybe you will be in such a mood that it will go deeper into you. I have turned and turned within myself today, trying to find a word that would mean the innermost crimson drop of blood in my heart.

I shall not write any more to you about your work. Either I do not make myself clear, or if I do, what I say is wrong and sets you into a fury. For God's sake don't you know that all I say and all I think is for your self, it is always the best I know.—My life is yours to do whatever you like—I am lonely and miserable without you. Dearest will you ever be here to comfort me and love me again.—Your letters torture me at times, and you are not with me to finally ease the pain, as you have done when you made me cry. God bless you, Keep well, be faithful and come home to me— Aline

I hope you will get yourself some more clothes in England. Please don't neglect it. You know how much better they are there, and a good warm coat. My friend Gertrude Kingston went off without the package for you, she left it behind in the automobile. It was a brown muffler. I'll keep it for you. Won't you please attend to the clothes. I will cable over some money.—The only thing that has made me smile for days is your description of yourself in your pajamas all day.—Do you ever have them laundered now that I am not there, and how are the blue striped ones holding out. And your socks!!!!!!! I love you; my heart is bleeding for you[.]

39. [Oxford] Tuesday / Nov 9 [1926]
My Dear—

I went off to the Post Office to day leaving this letter behind me. I shall certainly get it off tomorrow. I had a fitting of my new suit—it is a mixed blue stuff, with a faint stripe—very pretty. I lost my little fat notebook which I carry everywhere with me—went to the office of the bus company.—They sent me to the Police station.—Found the sargeant reading in it with a bewildered face.—He treated me with all the courtesy one extends to the insane[.] But, thank God, I have it back, with such damning items as "in my Jewess-haunted blood; green lily depths; gaseous ripstink; revolt of the tailors; a shrivelled pelt; the little golden apples of delight; bronchial horse-cough; King Poseidon; Frankau's a Fool; The Hills Beyond Pentland; The Novelist with a pipe and a boy or a rabbit called Artaxerxes, Foch, Genevieve; Dark Helen; moonwards the camels seek Bithynia; Grey Rebecca."[1]

I have thought of us today—how you are a Jew, and like success, and how success and I are strangers, and how short my respite is, and how near the time of the final rooting up of all my desire. I am quitting finally, cutting myself away with a sword: I will not linger on the fringes, becoming grey, picking the sparrow crumbs of hope. But I would finish this first.

I got a kind letter from Day asking me how my three verities were—the world, the flesh, and the devil. Poor good grey man; I have lost him too, and he will never suspect I am the greatest ascetic he has ever known. Do you know the Boston sign: It is this—I thought of it the other day: a man is of the spirit when he does not bleed. Blood, you see, is worldly—that's how they know.

It is almost ninety days and ninety nights since you left. I think how many times grey light has come across the viscous and interminable seas at dawn; the lonely death of all these waters; the strange cold fish that prowl below our ken; and the disjointed wakenings of two earths five hours apart. And I saw time astride a horse, a grinning death that lashed on the pounding hooves; but it was the ghastly world behind that shifted past—they race a treadmill race. Is it not strange how this small earth is built in pieces, but all eternity is one?

There is a land where this strange life shall find a home[.] I am going into Germany because there—I will tell you—below old dreaming towers a river runs; upon the rocks Loreli comb their hair; the winds about the castle crags at night are full of demon voices; and the gabled houses of the toyland towns are full of rich and gluttonous warmth.

I am quite sure that where God looks all the seas and lands are in their order: how should He care for more, or know the seas that storm, the cities overthrown, the heroes dead and the old wars that wage in this small prison house of life? Your hair is grey, Penelope, but ageless beauty rests upon you, and I know young suitors wait within the hall. Do you unweave the loom at nights? Troy is burned to ashes in my heart, Achilles dead, Dark Helen quenched within my blood. But wine-dark still the seas.

Wednesday Morning

My Dear:—

It is a grey fierce morning: the wind is howling against the trees. I have been standing at my window watching the dead leaves which fill the air in flocks, and the trees growing visibly bare before my eyes, and the blown rain which spits against my window. I have in my heart the wild exalting the wind and the rain always bring, and a nameless terror. I am going to tell you how I have felt since you left. When I was ten years old, I read myself blind and dizzy in all romantic legendry:—the Iliad and the Odyssey at the same time as the Algers, the Hentys, the Optics, and hundreds of the popular English and American writers of the time—Louis Tracy, Chambers, Philips, Davis, Locke, Farnol, Churchill, McCutcheon, Major, Hope—scores of others.[2] Sometimes I was the valiant young minister of the fashionable church, arrayed in warfare against my wealthy congregation in my fight against slum conditions, and aided by the millionaire's daughter, othertimes I was the bronzed captain of the Yale crew, fullback of the team, the wonder of the world, adventurously adrift across Europe, Asia, South America—the vanquisher of Dago armies, the leaper over garden walls, the climber of moonlit balconies. I was always 25 and she 22 or so. And the trees were always green.

But I was born, my dear, with an autumnal heart. With me since I was twenty ripeness has been almost all. I began then by endowing my princess of 22 with the golden wealth of 35. But for two years now I have been unable to think of the running maenads without boredom. I think only of Helen and Demeter moving their rich bodies in the ripening fields. Or of Peer Gynt's wife, Cid,[3] in the grey English autumn, I think of my childhood autumns at home—the pain, the desire that was so much deeper, so much more nameless than Spring, the sharp knife—the maples burning red, the smell of ripening persimmons, the tired rich smell of the earth. Once, when I was reading Homer—I was 16—I asked the Greek professor if Helen was not very old when Troy was taken: it had worried me so much that I had figured it out, and knew she must be more than 50. And that old man, who had lived so long among this ageless and unwasting beauty, flayed me with his bitter tongue. I am no longer that bronzed young giant who was empeccably handsome, and always victorious. Too much water and blood has gone under the bridge since I was 10. The young man bores me, as does his doll faced queen. And like God, I see myself always beaten, forever lost, forever hunted, forever driven by the furies. I am beginning to get a jowl, a bit of a paunch—I swing heavily along now with a man's stride—the racing thin boy who leaped into the air is gone; but through all this gathering flesh, this growing heaviness[,] I exalt to see the faun's face shining yet—the ancient eternal morning madness that grows wilder, younger as my body ages. I sat with the young men in a college room the other day:—all of the young men talked to me like clever boys, I talked plainly, simply, and I realized suddenly that three years ago I should have wanted to talk like a clever boy, and write like one. But they all turned their chairs toward me, and I would say something about the weather, and they would talk like clever boys about the weather, and I would speak of poetry, and they talked like clever boys about that. They performed for me eagerly, and suddenly I knew that I no longer cared to shine in that way—I seemed somehow to be sitting on a good-humored but unpatronizing rock, laughing deeply, caring for nought but to have the clever boys amuse me, enjoying myself. And I think most often of your hair flawed with grey, but not in the way you think. It seems to me that this great pageant of my life, beginning in cheap legendry, in which all was victory, faultless perfection, has led my dark soul across perilous seas, scarring me here, taking a tooth or an ear, putting its splendid blemish on until now I come to my autumn home, the streaked hairs, the rich widehipped body, the brief repose which lasts forever for it is founded on sorrow and the skirts of winter—beyond youth, beyond life, beyond death. You live timelessly like Helen, like deep-breasted Demeter, like Holvig.[4] My head is no good this morning[.] if it were I could put all this into a few words, but perhaps I have made you understand a little of what I feel. I feel that I have pierced in to the deep rich heart of romance: with you in New York I never felt embarrassment in being seen—you, poor woman, did—I was not 25, you 40; I was in the young man's age, for me you were timeless—the home, the harvest of all desire: when we were together I was in a world-forsaking, world-oblivious spirit.

As I live here, going daily through the punctual pattern of my life, I seem to myself a richer, a braver adventurer than I ever dreamed of being in my childhood. The world's parade, the phantom show of faces pass me by: I live courteously and conventionally, having that in me which may not be revealed nor understood in their stale legendry: at the time of life's heat my rich fidelity to you, my grey haired widehipped timeless mother.

I do not think I shall return to England before I sail. I shall cable you an address—probably the American Express in Paris, and I shall cable you from various points beyond[.] Perhaps I may get home by Jan 1. If I do, can we be together New Year's?

Goodbye, my dear. Forgive this wandering nightmare. Do you think I'll ever sight land? Or do you believe there is a land? I would write you good letters, but it goes into the other thing. God bless you. Tom

—The ships came home; he was old—do you remember?—Troy a grey ember in his heart, the lotus isle a memory—but he was the only one who could draw the story honestly—you have asked me what I expected you to do, as if remedies could be stated in paragraphs. And you have told me how you spent all of your time with me and saw none of your friends. But it might be better for our lives if we had less time but a great deal more brave and honorable resolution. Whatever door you and I may enter, let us write up upon it before we close it: "Unashamed[.]" Except your love, I ask you no more than that[.] But be advised that I will take nothing less, as you shall find.

1. See *Notebooks*, 1:72–75.

2. Horatio Alger, George Alfred Henty, and William Taylor Adams (Oliver Optic), authors of juvenile books for boys; Louis Tracy, twentieth-century writer of historical fiction; Robert William Chambers, modern American novelist and short-story writer; David Graham Phillips, American novelist, journalist, and reformer; Richard Harding Davis (1864–1916), popular American journalist and short-story writer of the period; William Locke, British playwright and novelist of romantic tales; John Jeffry Farnol, British adventure novelist; Winston Churchill (1871–1947), American novelist, playwright, and short-story writer; George Barr McCutcheon, American writer of roman-

tic fiction; Charles Major, American historical fiction writer, best known for *When Knighthood Was in Flower*; Anthony Hope (Sir Anthony Hope Hawkins, 1863–1933), British novelist, most famous for *The Prisoner of Zenda.*

3. It is questionable to whom Wolfe was alluding, as Peer Gynt never married.

4. Wolfe is referring to Solveig, Peer Gynt's ideal love.

40. [Oxford] Saturday / November 13 [1926]

Dear:—

I have gone dead and flat. During the last two months and a half I have written 100,000 words. This is a terrific amount of writing. My mind has gone to pieces these last three days. It is scattered and cannot follow either reading or writing. It will all come back in a week or so, I am sure. I am going to leave here at the end of next week and go to the continent. I cabled you to-day that I would get home if possible by the end of December. I will do all the writing I can between now and then, but the book has not been finished. Dear, you must see that I have a place to work when I get back:—don't blame me for not finishing—I have worked awfully well. Have no regrets. Don't you know, dearest, that my book can't be done in three months[.] I love you, my greyhaired Jew, and I am coming back to you. . . .[1]

Tonight I am sick. I went down the road to the pub at eleven this morning; I fell in with a poacher, a sailor, and a huntsman, amusing people. I went on a frightful beer drunk, and when the pub closed at 2:30 I tried to ride the sailor's bycycle[.] I had never ridden one before: I have bruised and skinned my hands and face in the wet street, and I have torn my trousers. But I finally rode the bycycle. A crowd gathered and laughed at me but finally applauded me. I cannot walk upon my left leg tonight[.] The knee joint is strained, but it will be all right. I had a young undergraduate out for dinner; he wants to go to America. I am fat and old, Jew—you want the young ones, don't you? Why, when you answer me, do you not answer me? Your letter was a heavy accusation that I did not care for you because I was not in New York with you—the sick wisdom, I dare say, of your fine friends.

Sunday [14 November]

My Dear—

Today I have limped around on my stick[.] I am in high favor at the pub, but I have paid for it with my bruised bones. Tuesday I get my suit—it's very pretty, I believe—Tuesday night I am having two young men out here for dinner—I want to leave Oxford later in the week. From then on until I come home most of our communication, I suppose, must be by cable. You will not tell me, after I get home, will you, that I have had my chance and that I should have finished my book before I came back? That would be a bestial and unfair thing. Somehow or other, you must see that I finish it there. I have failed at the other thing, I shall never attempt another play, this is the end, perhaps. Your letters the last month have simply raised hell with me. I sleep of nights in a land of nightmares. I want with all my heart and soul to see you again, but since I am here, and you there, will you not attempt to arrange some method of life and work for us? Don't you think it's only fair? Or, is having me back again, owning me, all that matters?

I have been in Oxford four weeks today; here four weeks Wednesday. The first book is finished the third almost finished. I must do what I can on the second before I come back.

Your letters are incomparably superior to mine, but I believe they are less honest. I find when I write you the greatest difficulty in coming to an end—and usually somewhere I spin a part of my entrails into it. Your letters have a beginning, a middle, and an ending—they do not sprawl—they work up swiftly to a note of passion, and decline accurately to one of hope or despair[.] And all of this seems to me extraordinary: you have always, since I have known you, belonged to that large number of simple but sincere souls who boast that they are inarticulate, unable to put what they mean in words (because, they suggest, it is too fine)[.] And yet while I grope darkly about in these letters, you obtain a sense of form, proportion, perfection of your woe into two and a half pages and all according to the most approved laws of dramatic and fictional technique. Isn't it queer?

The day I arrive I want you to make me some rich coffee, and, if possible, cook me a meal. Perhaps in December you will find some place that is suitable for work, where a stove may be rigged up. I should like some succulent Jew's food with melted butter, spices, and fragrant sauces. You will probably be in the middle of a show—which you will regret, of course, but which you must do, and I will feed as usual upon the crumbs of weary time that fall from the groaning board of art. The trees are stripped bare now—all this within the last week. For the first time in my life I have stood and watched it happen[.] All through the night the huge winds howl about the house, clashing the boughs. And something creaks and whines forever in the wind. It rains all day, at night the sky is blown almost clear, the stars look through, and the bright moon drives along through ragged clouds. Last night lovely. I live a great deal in old legends. The other night I wrote something for you which I am sending to you. It is called "Super Flumen Babylonis," which means "by the Waters of Babylon."[2] The name is not mine; it is the title of a poem of Swinburne's which I read long ago, but I believe it comes originally from the Latin Bible. What I have written is not a poem—you know I believe poetry lives silently in the hearts of poets who are too loyal to speak at a time when only the small cad, who has never written poetry, is called one. America is full of them. I wrote the thing because it is about you and me—my head and my heart and my bones are sick and weary—I must leave here—but it may have some meaning for you, only remember, I do not call it poetry. I have enough religion for that. It is for you.

God bless you, my dear,
Tom

I'll cable my address when I leave here[.]

It's a little after ten o'clock. Again—this strange wonder—a grey wind blowing day, and a moonlit, cloud-driven night—I have just come back from a walk down to the pub for cigarettes. The puddled rutty road under the great glowing trees gleamed in the cloudy moonlight—oh, the wonder, the wonder of it—this fiend-haunted road:—

Like one that on a lonesome road
Doth walk in fear and dread,
And having once turned round, walks on,
And turns no more his head,
Because he knows a frightful fiend
Doth close behind him tread.[3]

It is that same road—the heart, the core, the spirit of dark romanticism[.]

When first the snow comes you must cable. I desire the blown windy moonlight, the driving sleeting snow, and windy bells across the sleeting snow. I want a house in the remote North, and a howling wind, and the windy bells; there Jew, I will lie of nights with you in the warm dark[.]

You fool, do you ever pay any attention to what I say, when I wreak myself out for you, however clumsily, or have you grown into one vast writhing belly, one crying wail, saying something of my "wild nervous letter," but understanding or caring nothing?

Monday [15 November]

I got two letters from you today—I'm carrying both[,] dear—I'm leaving here at end of week and going to continent. I'll sail for New York in time to get back by New Year's if possible—I love you, my dear—What you think is a star is a wandering flame in hell[.]

Tuesday Morning [16 November]

It occurs to me to say this:—I get letters from time to time from other people—once in six weeks or so from my family; but I could rot and be buried before most of them would ever think of asking about me. I can not deceive myself therefore that there is any one besides yourself in the whole world who has any genuine affection for me. Nor do I any longer care very much. I have turned these past two years more and more to a vision of the Happy Isles—to a belief in life that is forever beautiful, but more and more, no matter where I am, does the world around me cease to draw my interest: I have a kind of terror in going now to some renowned place for the first time, because of the terrific attack of boredom that lays me low for a day or two. And of All God's Children, as you can perhaps testify, I am the least blasé. I simply want to get back to the Toy Room and play. That is why I still believe in New lands. They will be better than the old. This is the last letter I shall write you from here. I'll cable you when I leave, giving you an address. Good bye, my dear—it won't be long now. I get weary thinking of the sea, trains, ship, travel. I wonder how I'll ever get there, but I will. Tom

Tuesday Afternoon / 5:30

Dearest:

I've just returned from the town with my new suit of clothes. I had your letter telling me of Terry's serious illness. I am deeply shocked. It is so short a time—save for us—since you went back. Ever since Ben died, and I looked for the last time in his aqueous grey death-haunted eyes, I have hated and feared that accursed disease worse than leprosy. And when I hear that someone has torn his life away from strangulation a great cry of joy and triumph bursts from my throat—I feel as if Alcestis[4] has been wrested back from Death. You said she was through the worst—I hope to God the absence of cables from you does not portend evilly. You have not answered my last one. Nothing must happen to you. I have groped and blundered so with what was precious in my life, I have intended so much, and done so badly, that the perilous hand of chance upon my own misjudgment would be devastating. I am but an inch away from madness—I do not hover on the brink, but some dark blow would hurl me in.

I am preparing with heavy foggy steaming November dulness to entertain two young university men here tonight: in a day or two I am off on that last orbit that will swing me home to you. As my heart and my head revives again in higher more passionate air, I will write you such a message as you deserve[.] You call me the west wind. And which way does the west wind blow? The most marvellous thing about these weeks in Oxford is the amount of work I have done, and the stodgy routine of my life[.] In a month here I have been into town just twice. I am beerfat and heavy—the wild thing is drugged, the cry does not break from my throat now. But it will again.

Some of your letters have come with enormous speed[.] The one today was dated Nov 9—today's the 16th[.] Don't send the muffler —keep it for me, dearest. I paid for my suit getting 5% discount—10 pounds instead of ten guineas—I have now just $80 in checks left, and a pound or two in money. I do not think I shall buy an overcoat —I'm making the one I have do. But I'm going to get two or three of these new shirts and another hat.

After I finish the book, I'll try the stories. I think I may do that[.] For the first time in my life I will be writing without equivocation exactly as a great many people would have me write.

There are some thrilling things in the book, but these last days my writing, like myself, has been tired. God bless and keep you, dearest. My name, I suppose, is a jest and jeer and anathema in the mouths of the righteous, but I am not losing hair about it[.]

[Tuesday night] 10:30

The young men have come and gone[.] One of them talked Catholicism violently to me and condemned the general American lack of "a soul"—Have you got one, Jew? We must see to it. It is something, apparently, that all the nations of Europe are bursting with. I feel so old. The boy wanted to argue fiercely; I was temperate, benevolent, and sad. I confessed to a religious faith in my countrymen. I did the most amazing job of flag-waving, but with such balance that they both went away almost unashamed that they were American.

[Wednesday Morning, 7 November] 12:20

My Dear Jew:—

I'm getting too popular. These people are taking too much interest in me. Several men in the house—ex Colonels and officers who are jazz crazy and sing American songs all night long have had me in their rooms playing their songs to me and performing slight-of-hand tricks. It's almost 7:30 in New York—the hour of—what, Jew?

I am glad to read of your success in The Clay Cart[.] The man seems to think it was your best work. It was done before you met me; may it not be that my best work, poor as it is, was done before I met you? And shall we not take what's left without regret? But it seemed to me that his scant reference to *The Dybbuk* was typical of the people—do they not always take the present thing—either for great praise or blame; and is not the piece they called "epic" a year ago, "interesting" or "amusing" now? I do not know. I have not seen *The Clay Cart*; my greatest interest, my dear, is in *The Dybbuk* because I knew you then[.] But I do not envy you your little triumphs.

All the praise we hanker for is small and pitiful enough. I have just thought that one difference between us is that I should like to be written about in print, but that after it was done, I should be weary and bored with it, and the great shame I have in me would keep me from speaking of it. You live very intensely in your world: I should think you send me these things with a little girl's delight. I have so much horror of the theatre—I am beginning to hate to talk of it[.] I picked up a book by Gordon Craig[5] the other day—he's the highest prophet they have, and the book had all the aestheticism of the undergraduate. Talk to me of your friends, but do not talk to me any more of plays and the theatre[.] You said once that you could talk of nothing else—it was your life. Yet I think you can. You have another life—with me, you say. Let's live in that.

Wednesday [17 November]

I have been thinking this morning what strange things words are —how I sit over my table writing them to you across three or four thousand miles of water; how we send replies, messages to each other; and how each of us may fall into a *manner* when we write—a manner of passionate declarations, a framework on the surface of the great well of our hearts, which repeats itself, while all the strange fish, the myriad communication in the pool below, is left unseen.

I want you to burn these letters. I will be home soon[.] I do not want what I have written to be kept—I do no[t] like the box.[6] These things have a way horribly of being found. Good-bye dearest. It is not long now.

Had your cable—you said you're happy. Friday Torquay—Leaving tomorrow—London Wednesday—Paris Saturday—I'll cable—

Tom

1. A portion of this letter has been omitted at the family's request.

2. Although this poem is no longer extant, some of the stanzas he was working on can be found in his notebook. See *Notebooks*, 1:78–79.

3. Coleridge, *The Ancient Mariner*, pt. VI, ll. 446–51.

4. The heroine of a play of the same name, by Euripides.

5. British scenic designer, actor, director. Also a prolific writer of theatrical books.

6. Mrs. Bernstein had written earlier that she kept his letters in a locked box by her bed.

41. [New York] Friday / November 19 [1926]

Dearest Tom—

I haven't had a letter from you for so long, but then I do not expect any, any more, except every great while. I am living by the last cable I had. I wonder if you will still be in Oxford when this gets there. Sometimes when I don't hear from you in so long, I think maybe you are on the way home.—I spent the evening at the regular monthly meeting of my union.[1] It is the first one I have been to since my full membership, and I liked it, never felt so important, just as though I was managing the nation. Carolyn Hancock[2] and I were the only females present and I was never before the object of so much politeness. Carolyn and I sat together, and we were offered cigarettes and life savers and chewing gum at intervals of 15 seconds. —I've had three wearing days, but finally we are all set on the new show. I can't do lights until Sunday, as there is another play still going at the Golden Theatre where we open. I am so tired I ache all over. Thank goodness for a little rest. The Theatre Guild board are very trying, I disagree with them so much, and yet I hate to have friction during rehearsals. It takes a lot of patience to keep quiet and still have things somewhat the way I like them. You know how unimportant I think my end of the work is, unless it is done with economy in all directions. My head has passed the thinking stage, and I'd like to bury it in the sands for a few days, or unscrew it and drop it down a nice cool mossy well. I may go out of town with Terry for a few days, when she is able, maybe next week, over Thanksgiving. I have worried about you so much of late, I want to see you so much, I can't believe the time will come when you will be here. I am in this constant sort of agony, you love me and you mean to come home, but there is always a fear that something may take you away. I want to put all the rest of my life into one small complete space of time with you. I want to talk to you for hours at a time, and I want to sit still in the same room with you where you write.—I finally met Miss Rebecca West. She is very attractive, brilliant, but rather hard. Somewhat the style of Minna Kirstein but I did not care for her so much, and rather uppish. Maybe I have written you this before. I do not remember when I wrote last.—My dear daughter Edla is going to Europe with my sister, they sail Dec. 27 for about 6 weeks. They just decided about it this week. Edla is awfully excited, she hasn't been over since she was a baby. She is being presented the trip for a birthday present by the family.—

I imagine that after I've rested a couple of weeks, I'll be weeping for another job. Maybe there will be no more.

1. Aline Bernstein was the first female member of United Scenic Artists.
2. Costume and scenic designer, wife of Lee Simonson.

42. [New York, Monday] Nov. 22 [1926]
Dearest Tom:

I had your lovely long letter from Oxford today. It came with my coffee this morning. It is such a nice letter, almost the nicest one you ever wrote me, with many things in it. Also got your cable yesterday,

(Sunday)[.] I had planned to telegraph you some money today to Oxford, but I have sent it to Amexco London instead. Hope you find it alright and enjoy it. I am so glad you ordered yourself some clothes. Will you need more to come home with? I will have more in a couple of weeks, from the Guild. Our play should have opened tonight, but has been postponed until Wednesday, owing to Claire Eames[1] having the grip. (My sentence construction grows more faulty all the time.) It is the most uninteresting piece of work I have ever done, it could as well have been ordered from a builder. But I have learned a few things any way. It is such a small show but there are more things in it than any thing I ever tackled except the miracle about 1000000 props and 5000000 pieces of furniture, I ran myself thin for two weeks getting them. Isn't there a piece of poetry about calling for madder music and redder wine? That's the way it was, more props more furniture every damn rehearsal. I have to do a light rehearsal this afternoon, then finis! I wanted to go away with Terry this week, but they are taking out The Dybbuk again this week, and there is a great deal of overhauling to do. I am very very tired, but feel so much better since I expect you back. I'll tell you what I have done, I telephoned to the landlords that I would take the 8th St. place on from Dec. 15. I thought you would prefer to live in a hotel. You see I have to have a place to work in myself, also. It is very inconvenient for me to go way down to the Playhouse. I will rest for a day, tomorrow, I want to stay home in the house all day if possible [and] lie on the sofa and read. Then I will go about and see what I can find in the way of a nice room and bath. I wish there was a bath there, I could have a fire place fixed, and corner off a little place for myself to work. But possibly you would not find it convenient to have me about if you live there. (That is, to work)[.] I will see what I can find. We can always take the other place, and make it nice.

It must be very dreary and cold in England. I was sickened by the tale of the young man who made the girl drunk and seduced her. It keeps knocking at my head all the time. Hope the girl has strength enough to hold up.—I wonder what will happen to her. Isn't it wicked to make her go?—The only reason I hope you do not surprise me is that I want to meet you at the steamer. My daughter sails Dec 27, I hope she will have a lovely time.—Tom dear I wonder if you are not keeping too beautiful an image of me. Your letter was filled with it, Can't you remember exactly how I look? Just now I look tired, I have lost about 8 pounds, but really look about the same. I have come out of my terrible state of gloom since I knew that you are coming home. If your demon comes upon you, just choke him off. How can you doubt me, what way can I show you more how dearly I love you, it seems that every thing I do or say about it is not enough. My letters are only variations on that theme, not even variations, I even fear I will weary you with it. I have given myself to you in my own mind—I wish I could transport myself on a magic carpet, to you in Paris. I should love to go to Germany with you. I will have to dream it, and be patient to wait for your own self. I have seen very little of Germany, and that under unhappy conditions. I think you will enjoy it. Wasn't that week we had in Paris at first a strange time? You frightened me. Will you ever care so much for me again do you think? The days in Chartres were heaven. Now it seems to me that it will be heaven to look at you again. Have you really a fat belly? I am losing mine but will probably gain it again when I take some meals with you. I will have to practice my coffee making, I will love to see you drink it down and say "Pretty good, my girl." You know you used to say that.

It would be lovely if you could be here Jan. 1st[.] I will spend it with you. I will most likely have to stay at home to see the New Year in with what is left home of the family, they would be frightfully hurt if I didn't, but I could be with you the rest of the time, and if we had the facilities I would cook you a New Year dinner. Do you ever hear any thing from home?—I am sure you can write here, and I will promise not to intrude upon your time. I will be quiet and good about it and see to it that you are not distracted. It will take me weeks to read what you have written, it took me an hour and a half to make out your letter this morning.

I'm going on down for my light rehearsal now, and will mail this. I have a cold, and feel what we call all overish. I'll be busy about three hours and then come home and probably go to bed. I often get this way at the end of a job.

It is very difficult to get any good stuff to drink, you will miss it when you come home. Any decent whiskey, when you can get it, costs $15 a bottle, or more. Take care of yourself dear, my whole self is in your keeping.

Dearest love[,] Aline

1. Principal actress in *Ned McCobb's Daughter*.

43. [New York] Wednesday / Nov. 24th [1926]

My dearest Tom—

I am so glad you got the money cable all right—is it enough to see you through, or do you need more for your passage. Please let me know at once if you will want more. I have a big check ($750) coming in Monday for my Guild Show. I wish you would get a warm overcoat, the one you got here in the Spring is not heavy enough. I'm so happy about your coming home that I walk on air. Tomorrow is

Thanksgiving day—I went down to the Washington market and bought a 23 lb. Turkey today. And tomorrow I will give thanks that you are coming home. I wonder if you know how much you find fault with me in your letters. I don't care, you've always found fault with me, but you tell me also such wonderful things, I am a thorn in your heart, but a blossom too?—On Monday afternoon I will go downtown and look for a room[.] If I am uncertain, I will wait until you come. You can stay at a hotel for two or three days. If I find something awfully good, I will take it[.] The trouble is, most nice places have to be taken on lease and are unfurnished. But I may be able to get enough furniture together. I will tell you just how I am fixed, so far as work is concerned. Some people called The Playshop, have asked me to do setting [sic] for a lugubrious Irish play.—I refused, and this morning they telephoned me again, so I went to see them. They offered me $750 for the job. I am taking tomorrow to consider it, but want very much to give it up, only for the money. I am so tired I can scarcely walk. You know our Guild show was postponed until Monday next, that means more rehearsals for me, and we are getting out Dybbuk again. I was also offered an extremely interesting piece of work, to design some private offices for a big advertising firm, but that will be a little later—about February. If I take the damn Irish show, it means heavy work the end of December when you are due, and Edla sails. So I think I will chuck it. I hate it anyway, it is a beast of a play to design. And I want some time to read and think. I wish you were here to talk to about it. Don't you want to talk to me? Can you believe that not too far off we will see each other, touch each other, breathe the same air. I will be reading your book, we will go away for a few days, as soon as you like. Or you can settle right to work again[.] Whatever it is, I am your devoted love, my whole being is in your keeping.

I have a bad cold, it was in my chest, but now is in the head, and my nose is red and ugly like the day I wept so hard at Scotts'. Our summer was wet down with tears from time to time. But wasn't it lovely. Whatever time God gives us together again will be lovely too. Your long bearded God that you speak of so often. He is the same as mine—I have read William Clossold and like it enormously. When Mr. Wells digresses so much he is best. It is so wise and so meaty.

You must have missed a lot of my letters sent to Oxford, if you left a forwarding address you will get them. You know, sometimes they catch a slow boat. I hope you will cable often where you are. I would give anything in the world to be with you now in Paris and then Germany.—I am going to find out what would be a likely boat for you to come back on. A fast one I hope. Will you let me know when you make up your mind? Terry went to Atlantic City today, and if I do not do the Irish play I will go down next week for a few days, Monday most likely. I'll cable to you to Paris Monday in any case[.] Tom darling, You must know by now how I have cared for you, how way above all others I hold you. Beyond the love I have for you, I care for you, respect, admire, and prize you more than any man that I have known[.] When you come back, let us have comfort and joy in each other. No doubt there are plenty of other females who would love you, but will you not take for yourself and treasure, the whole sum of my affection. Good night dear. I will add to this letter tomorrow.

Thanksgiving Day

I took a lot of aspirin last night, and slept through until about 9:30. My head is buzzing and singing and nose redder than ever. I am going to stay in bed until dinner, and I look forward to resting my bones. I wanted to take a rest last Tuesday, but my Aunt arrived from Cincinnati and I had to go to meet her. This is the most beautiful day, I have just looked out of the window, clear and cold, and from some unknown reason our pesky old furnace has taken a new lease on life, and my room is warm as toast (American toast)[.] I put some ointment on my nose, I have on an old wadded red silk wrapper and a cold compress on my neck. What price Helen of Troy! But I look alright anyhow. I'm getting a new brown dress for when you come home, and I've had my sealskin coat fixed over, it isn't finished yet but will look like new. My face looks about the same as ever but not quite so stout, and when my nose recovers, it will look nice. I hope you will like it.—I'm going to make a speech next Tuesday, for some girls' clubs. I hate to do it, but I am taking Helen Arthur's place, who is a shark at speaking, you know I will have to talk to them about costuming, and they will not know what I am talking about. I think we will still be doing The Clay Cart when you return. I've done so much grumbling about my work this year, and I want you to see what I think is really good designing. I have really lost interest in it, in spite of what you say, that I do it because I like it. I have always loved it until this year, and possibly I will enjoy it again. Just now I can only occupy my mind with your home coming. I wonder if you will find a piece of Turkey somewhere to eat today for patriotic reasons[.] Wish I could give you a slice of the noble bird I bought yesterday, it is proportioned like an eagle. The cook says she will never be able to make enough stuffing for it.—Dearest love to you, I will send letters along to the American Express, Paris until further notice[.] No doubt you will arrange to get them. God bless you— Aline

44. [New York] Wed. Dec 1 [1926]
My Dearest Tom:—

I write this on the chance that you will get it, but I don't know, with you skipping all over Europe. I wrote you, I think that I was laid up Thanksgiving day with a cold. I stayed in bed until the Saturday afternoon following. That is why I did not answer your London cable immediately. I went yesterday looking for a place for you to live, and for me to work. I went to a thousand places, and you never saw such dreary holes in your life. I simply cannot let you go into one of these furnished rooms. I finally found a place on 8th St. two doors from our old one, No. 9. It is a fine building, and the place consists of two rooms, a bathroom, (fine one)[,] and a little place like a kitchenette. The rooms are not awfully large, and are on the top floor, but the whole layout is so nice and convenient. Of course I do not know whether you want me to be with you at all to do any of my work. I think you could stand it if you have two rooms. I haven't taken it yet, but it is by far the nicest place, and you can have your friends there and be very comfortable. There is plenty of hot water all the time. I gave up the idea of the old place, when you said you wanted to live there, where you work. I will have to find some furniture, I have some chairs at home, and will find you a nice bed to sleep on. How I wish you were within consulting distance. You might not like it, and then what shall I do. But I assure you it is the best place I have seen.—I was excited over your last letter. Do you know it was a wonderful letter, a love letter. You probably have been writing too much, and I am glad you are stopping for a while, you are bound to go stale in time without a rest. Of course I would not chide you because the book isn't finished, and I will make it my business to see that you finish it here: I will never willingly intrude upon your working time. The new quarters will cost $85 a month, about what your hotel and my studio came to. Not nearly so large, but very convenient. There is a much larger room in the back, but only one. I think I will take it on a chance that it will suit you. Rooms are so much smaller here than in England. There is a funny little place where I can cook, and hot water for dishes. I am looking every day for the piece of writing you said you are sending me.—I wouldn't destroy your letters for anything. I have them in a wooden box locked, beside my bed. I don't think anyone would open it, I carry the key in my purse, and your two pictures and do you remember one day I cut a piece of your hair. I have that in a little gold locket. I wonder how you will love me when you come home.

My Guild play opened Monday night, nothing exciting.—I think it will run, most people will find it entertaining[.] I grew so tired of it before it opened that I didn't even go the opening performance. I know you will find it hard to believe that I would miss a first night of my own, but it's the truth.—Jacque Copeau[1] is here, and I met him Sunday afternoon at a tea party given by Boleslawskey.[2] Copeau was interesting and seemed a powerful sort of person. Of course I did not speak much with him, there were loads of people there. Among others was Prof. G. P. Baker.[3] He came and spoke to me, and for fully ten minutes I thought he was an old actor I know named Francis Wilson. I started talking about a play he was in called Erminie, and The Rivals, G. P. must have thought I was a lunatic, I only found out when some one else came up and spoke to him, so I just vanished. Dorothy wanted me to invite Carlton to see The Clay Cart, but I haven't had time nor inclination. I'll wait now until you come back. —I went to a party given by the Ernest Boyds, the first evening party I have been to. It was very pleasant, very literary, and elegant. Ernest has a new brown dinner suit, and that was the occasion of the party. The guests were like a book list in a periodical. The only one I knew at all was Tom Beer,[4] who just returned from California. He comes down to New York once during the winter, and that was the once. There was another one I knew, too, Mr. Liveright.[5] I should like very much to have been able to hear what every one said to each other, but I couldn't. I fancied they were brilliant and entertaining, but may be not.—I made an hour's speech yesterday, and the first ten minutes I nearly passed away with stage fright. I caught sight of a friend of mine in the audience, and I fastened my eyes on her and it went much better. I'll tell you something else, I have refused to do a play, because I didn't like it and I'm weary to death. I want to rest up before you get back. I've grown a lot thinner, but look well, it is becoming to me. I'm crazy to see you. It seems as though I never would stop talking to you. I can't imagine that I have found so much fault with you as you say I have, in your letter. I love you so, I probably made a lot of moaning that you aren't here with me.—I'll get the new place in order soon, there is a nice workable open fire there too.—I'm writing at the playhouse, we had a staff meeting this morning and a Dybbuk rehearsal this afternoon. I have to go downstairs. God bless you dear, keep yourself well, and come home to me safe and sound.

Love[,] Aline

I'm in an agony of longing for you. To think of soon sitting in the same place with you: I hope you buy an overcoat. I read in the paper today that they predict a very cold winter. Will you need funds to get home? I got my Guild check this morning—

1. Playwright, director, and actor.
2. Richard Boleslavsky, director, choreographer, and costume designer.

3. George Pierce Baker was Wolfe's Harvard professor. Wolfe's desire to enter into Baker's 47 Workshop, a seminar that specialized in the techniques of playwriting, was the major reason he went to Harvard.

4. The biographer of Stephen Crane and brother of Mrs. Bernstein's friend, Alice Beer.

5. Horace Liveright, producer and book publisher. Wolfe first submitted *LHA* to Mr. Liveright, who rejected it. He later satirized him as Mr. Rawng of the firm Rawng and Wright.

In her 4 December letter, Mrs. Bernstein wrote that she had been unable to rent the apartment to which she had referred in her previous letter.

45. Stuttgart / Friday Night [10 December 1926]
My Dear:

I went to Strasbourg Monday, and came here yesterday. Before I left Paris Monday morning I found a cable from you which I answered. I got another one at Strasbourg, and I cabled you from Stuttgart today asking you to answer me at the American Express Co., München, although I am not sure whether there is an office there. If there is not I will send you another address as soon as I get there[.] I am going tomorrow. I have been in such a typhoon of excitement at getting into Germany that it made me a bit sick yesterday[.] I got up to the German frontiers at Strasbourg, stayed there two or three days, losing myself in that grotesque gabled city: I ate goose liver pie and drank beer and wandered everywhere. But I did not know where I was going in Germany; I was doubtful where I was geographically, I bought at last a map of South Germany, and decided to stop off at this place, and then go on to Munich. I have not time to travel wildly about—I shall stay at Munich until I return to Paris. I got up yesterday morning, packed with a stamp and a curse, got some marks at a bank, and left Strausberg at 10:40[.] Fifteen minutes later I was crossing the Rhine into Germany. I went nearly crazy with excitement and exultancy, rushing from one side of the compartment to the other to look down at the river, and crying out "I have fooled you, you swine!" because I get these obsessions that I am being hunted, thwarted, checked[.] I had to change at the little border town of Kehl where my baggage was examined, and at Appenweier and at Carlsruhe[.] At first the Rhine country was vast perfectly flat steaming with mist in the illimitable distance[.] After Carlsruhe all through the afternoon we climbed up slowly through a steep valley: the little hills rushed down to the train, the little villages—the gabled toyland of which I have always dreamed—fell crazily away from the train and up the other slope[.] I got here at dark[.] It is a place of 400000 people built in a valley and completely girdled with close fitting hills[.] At night it is bright with light—the hills about are studded in the concept (the essential, indestructable and eternal *idea*) of wheelbarrows from which it and all the wheelbarrows that ever were or ever will be must come. Well, this new building of theirs, is, architecture by concept[.] Do you see?

From the station place the main street—Kaiserstrasse—goes up straight as a string, full of cold hard light in the evening, electric signs, but on the streets that go off I came into toyland again this morning—the Market Place, the Rathaus, and gabled bright painted elfin houses[.]

The book shops are full of editions of English and Americans—Galsworthy and Shaw, Wilde, Chesterton, Cooper, Mark Twain[.] I saw their theatre program tonight— they are doing *Frau Warren's Gewerbe*[1] von Bernhard Shaw, and one of the comic journals has a front page cartoon of Shaw in a bathing suit.

I have lost myself in the place today; I bought a dictionary this morning—I get along uncannily. I began to speak German as soon as I went over the Rhine yesterday—I am alone in the kind of adventure that excites me, discovering, voyaging, renewing myself, soaking in it. When I was 13 I read some little stories in German under a teacher who knew less than I did—my remarks are confined mainly to "Give me this," "Where is that?" and so on, but they understand me, answer in German, and by some queer intuition I understand them. I am not good at speaking a language, but I have a strange power of instinctive assimilation and understanding[.] This winter when I return I shall learn to read the language as well as I read French, which is about as well as English[.] I shall buy some of the books those chiefly by Mann, and Wassermann, a new play by Hauptmann, Kayser and their other people.[2] I think I shall like their ugly powerful language, for they build in it as a child builds with blocks, and as their towns are Toy towns. Their windows are full of jolly Christmas signs and Santa Clauses and piled sleighs. Apparently you can invent what words you need—a building firm putting up a building opposite the station has a sign out with a marvellous word it has created to explain its activities—something like Bahnhofsplatzbauarbeitengesellsehaftverein or to that effect "the rail station construction company union[.]" I carry my book in your green case —the twelve great ledgers fill it up—I have done nothing to it since I left Oxford and felt like doing nothing[.] Don't worry—when I get to it again it will be to finish it. Already I have written beyond the length of most novels—I think part of it will interest you very much —The last part which I shall do at home is most important of all[.] I am loaded to the lips—I want to get behind four walls again and write it out of me: do you know, I am at home only when I am homeless? And I have always been homeless save with you. I am tongueless, friendless, houseless here—I do not mind it. In England the *size* of things finally began to worry me—there was no place to get to, and I have constantly been worried by the fear that there was no abundance left—that everyone was measured out eleven ounces of chump chop, three boiled potatoes, and forty one marrowfat peas[.] I think again of the vast uninhabitation of America and the wind moaning pines[.] Do you know that I will always be a wandering ghost who will always be as American as Kansas? The psychologist once asked me the old question: When the forest tree falls and there's nothing to *hear*, is there *sound*? I think I will take over your own form of boasting—and that of the Simple souls. I'm not very bright in the Bean—I see this very well, now that I'm too old to be a clever boy—but I've got something. And that something is a simple incomparable sense of everything in the world. I have wondered lately in what deep sea Icarus fell, where now his hair floats above his drowned face, and where Poseidon is buried, and I think then of the great sky-towers that float on the American shore so far from where drowned Icarus is[.] I wonder most of all because he never saw them coming along through Germany[.] Yesterday I met the hills, the woods, the crazy villages for the first time—they *sounded* in me, I gave them life that had never existed before.

Munich / Sunday Night
[13 December 1926]

I came here yesterday afternoon from Stuttgart. If I do not get this letter off to you at once, I may deliver it to you in person. I shall stay here until Wednesday or Thursday and return to Paris stopping off, perhaps, for the night, in Switzerland[.] I want to get back to Paris Saturday in time to get a steamship ticket. I believe the *Majestic* sails on Dec 22nd—I shall get passage on her. This will bring me to New York before New Year's.

I like München; I like what I have seen of Germany—the people, I believe are simple, more honest, and a great deal more friendly than the French. And I do not think their kindness and honesty is the result of a malevolent conspiracy to dominate the world through trickery—We live, apparently, in a world in which it is necessary to drain all one's strength in fighting through a wilderness of absurdity in order to arrive at a very simple and obvious fact. Last night I went to the Hofbrau Haus and drank a great mug full of the best beer I have ever tasted. In this vast smoking room there were seated around tables 1200 or 1500 people of the lower middle classes[.] The place was a mighty dynamo of sound[.] The floors and tables were wet with beer slop; the waitresses were peasant women with smooth hard kindly old faces—the beer slopped from the foaming mugs as they [whisked] through this maelstrom—A choir of drunken voices sang beyond the doors—Women and men—ugly and hearty swung toward each other in a thousand natural powerful mug-lifted postures, as they do in Teniers.[3] The place was one enormous sea-slop of beer, power, Teutonic masculine energy and vitality. It was like watching some tremendous yeast unfolding from its own bowels—it was the core, heart, entrails of their strength—the thing unfolding and unpremeditated that cannot be stopped or stoppered[.]

Tuesday Night [December 15]

I went to one of the municipal theatres tonight—I saw a play of Hauptmann's[4]—a very dull comedy, but well acted, with that kind of naturalism which our people thought was the tip-top pinnacle of everything with the Russians[.] As I looked at these people tonight, doing so well the thing they have done so well so many hundred times before, as I looked at the old scoundrel-peasant coughing over a strong liquor as he had coughed for years, talking so peasantly with a mouth full of bread and meat—doing it all as the great Stanislavsky had *trained* him for years to cough—it occurred to me that all this was a very pitiable business for people to write books about—and that an aesthetic did not result from twenty year's practice in belching. You are all a poor sad lot of little scoundrels and fools—tell your people to show their wares after a week's practice but not after *ten* years—then again there may be poetry—certainly there will be life.

I cabled you from Stuttgart to send a cable to Amexco-Munich. They have no agency here. I didn't know this—but I found two cables from you this morning inquiring into the state of my health. "Worried about you[.]" Do you know that one hides less easily before a few words than behind many—just as I see the world's Great Harlot like a Dürer legend always barred behind a skeleton. Did you read France's[5] story of the saint who sent his maid to the tavern for wine and drove her out when she came back 20 min. later without raising his head? She thought he was God-or-Fiend informed, but he only heard her voice.

This place is speckled with large solid-looking museums—I went to the Slyptothek[6] today to see their sculptures—they have a half-dozen great things in the Egyptian and Greek sections—two Apollos that are the best I have ever seen[.] I have begun to draw them—I drew those in the Louvre last week and here is the devastating bullock leg of one here—better work then you'll find outside Picasso: This is the leg from the side—the way the lines go[.]

Have the Guild done a Werfel play called *Paulus Unter Die Jeden*?[7] It is advertised here at the Theatre for Sunday next[.] I won't be

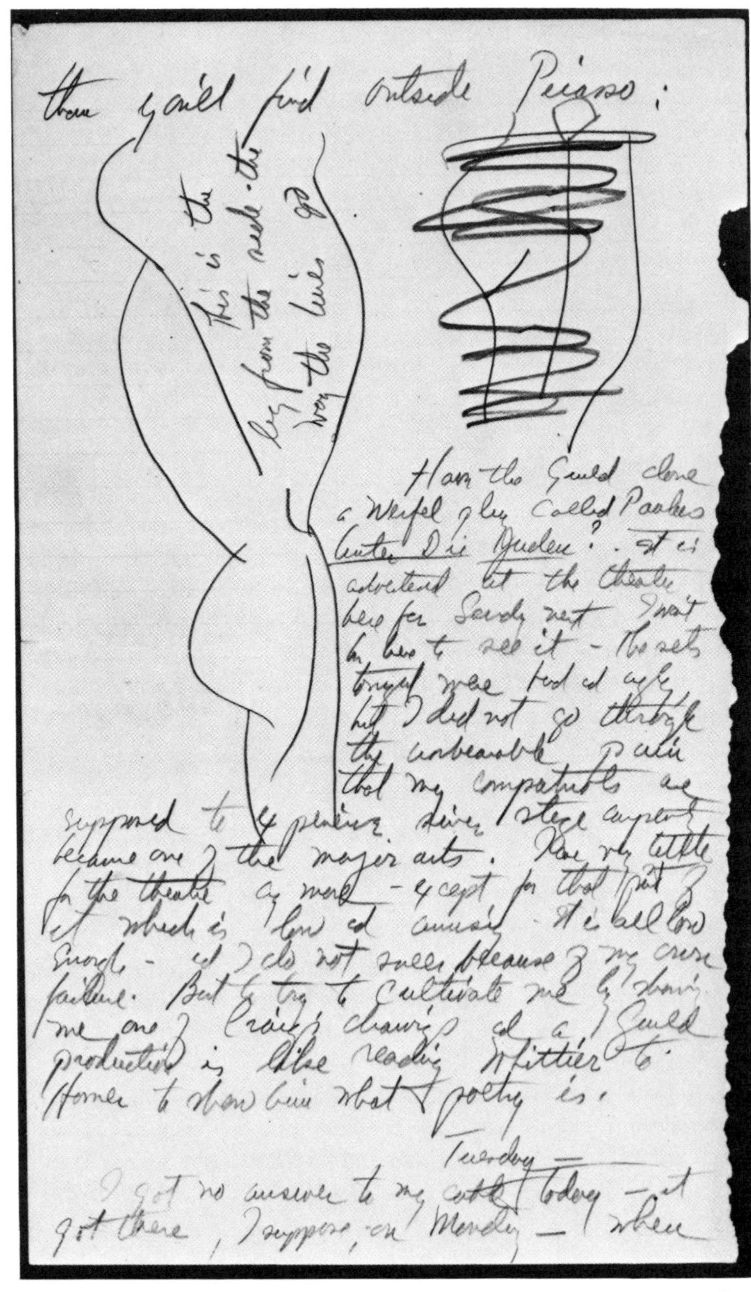

there you'll find outside Picasso:

This is the leg from the neck—the way the lines go

Have the Guild done a Werfel play called Paulus unter die Juden? It is advertised at the theatre here for Sunday next. I won't be here to see it—the sets tonight were tired and ugly, but I did not go through the unbearable pain that my compatriots are supposed to experience since stage carpentry became one of the major arts. I have very little for the theatre any more—except for that part of it which is low and amusing. It is all low enough—and I do not sneer because of my own failure. But to try to cultivate me by showing me one of Craig's drawings and a Guild production is like reading Whittier to Homer to show him what poetry is.

Tuesday—

I got no answer to my cable today—it got there, I suppose, on Monday—when

Thomas Wolfe to Aline Bernstein, 15 December 1926 (By permission of the Houghton Library, Harvard University)

here to see it—The sets tonight were bad and ugly, but I did not go through the unbearable pain that my compatriots are supposed to experience since stage carpentry became one of the major arts. I care very little for the theatre any more—except for that part of it which is low and amusing. It is all low enough—and I do not sneer because of my own failure. But to try to cultivate me by showing me one of Craig's[8] drawings and a Guild production is like reading Whittier to Homer to show him what poetry is.

I got no answer to my cable today—it got there, I suppose, on Monday—when there was no play at the theatre and one can commit adultery carefully in the country[.]

I am going to leave here Thursday or Friday, and go back to Paris. I shall get passage if I can, on the *Majestic*[.]

I went to a great church today—the great Frauen-Kirche which has two terrific towers like this. And I went to a great vault called the Maximilianeum:[9] it was closed, I went in, and fell down a flight of stairs, spraining my foot. It was very dark and cold. Tonight I went to the Shauspielhaus and saw Shaw's *Mensch und Uebermensch*,[10] done with German thoroughness, including the Hell-Interlude[.] The sets this time were painful, the men unpleasant, but the women attractive. And the Germans laughed and laughed.

I should like to see people I have known again; breathe the air of my own soil; return, return. I have had all I want for this time[.] I am head-and-heart tired[.] Germany has been kind and passionately interesting. I am loaded and I am weary[.] I have almost lost wonder except in my own heart—there is little in books and pictures, or even, God forgive me, in new lands, that excites me any more. I remember when I see or read that I have known and put away what they say. This sounds like the saturation point, doesn't it? But I know the other thing will return again. Always the death, always the life again[.]

I have done no writing in weeks—that is the life that must be born again in me.

The necks of the German men do this. I wish they wouldn't—it's so easy for the cartoonist. And so very many of them look like this —sword cut from sword days.

This will arrive with me or just before me. It is a wretched stupid letter. Something in me needs to kindle and burn again[.] I think that on the sea my heart will lighten[.] I think that I shall seize you when we meet and eat some of your delicate fingers[.] I need women again—I am dull, dead lifeless[.] I need you. I kept the faith, Jew—whatever dies, faith will live in me ever after—what a hell, poor woman, you have to go to.

own heart — there is little in books and pictures, or even, God forgive me, in new lands that excites me any more. I remember when I see or read, that I have known and put away what they say. This sounds like the saturation point, doesn't it? But I know the other thing will return again, always the death, always the life again.

I have done no writing in weeks — that is the life that must be born again in me.

The ladies of the German men do this & I wish they wouldn't — its so easy for the cartoonist, and so many of them look like this —

round cut from the dough

This will arrive with me or just before me. It is a wretched stupid letter. Something in me needs to kindle and burn again. I think that on the sea my heart will lighten. I think that I shall seize you when we meet and eat some of your delicate fingers. I need women again — I am dull, dead, lifeless. I need you. I kept the faith, Jew — whatever else, faith will live in me ever after. — What a hell, poor woman, you have to go to.

Thomas Wolfe to Aline Bernstein, 15 December 1926 (By permission of the Houghton Library, Harvard University)

1. *Mrs. Warren's Profession.*

2. Thomas Mann, Jakob Wassermann, Gerhart Hauptmann, Georg Kaiser. Hauptmann was the most frequently performed dramatist in Germany in the 1920s.

3. Teniers, David the Younger (1610–90), was one of the foremost masters of genre painting in seventeenth-century Flanders and portrayed a wide variety of ordinary people in everyday scenes and occupations. Wolfe is probably referring to *Drinkers*, located in the Antwerp Museum.

4. Probably Hauptmann's *The Beaver Coat*, a folk comedy.

5. Anatole France (Jacques Anatole Thibault).

6. The great sculpture gallery in Munich.

7. Franz Werfel. *St. Paul Among the Jews*. The Guild did not produce this particular play, but had produced the English translation of his popular play *Juarez and Maximilian*.

8. Gordon Craig.

9. A nineteenth-century school for royal pages which houses an extensive collection of historical paintings.

10. *Man and Superman*.

1927–1928: The Grand Renunciation

Although the relationship seemingly continued as before, Thomas Wolfe's doubts about his life with Mrs. Bernstein began to plague him. He had written in his notebook aboard the Majestic *in December, "What rut of life with the Jew now?" For the most part, however, 1927 was a year of work and steadiness, punctuated by increasing arguments. By the winter of 1928, Wolfe was working himself into exhaustion, teaching, writing, and dictating his finished manuscript. The arguments and recriminations became unbearable, until finally Wolfe refused to see Mrs. Bernstein at all. Each went to Europe alone. Wolfe later referred to his European trip as "The Grand Tour of Renunciation." Mrs. Bernstein yearned to meet with him in Europe, but he consistently avoided her, although he maintained a steady stream of letters. After his injury during an Oktoberfest brawl, his letters began to show a spark of that earlier devotion. In the meantime, Maxwell Perkins, from Scribner's Publishing Company, had expressed interest in his manuscript.*

Wolfe once more settled into his old Eighth Street studio. Although N.Y.U. had offered him a teaching job, he turned it down, for Mrs. Bernstein had agreed to support him while he continued his writing. During the next several months, he worked feverishly, and when the heat overcame him in June, he spent three weeks writing at the Rhinebeck estate of his friend Olin Dows. In the meantime, The Neighborhood Playhouse, which had provided Mrs. Bernstein with her primary source of work, closed its doors in May 1927. She continued to work steadily on Broadway, however, often for producers Gilbert Miller and Eva Le Gallienne.

46. [New York] 333 West Seventy Seventh Street [June 1927]
Dearest Tom:

I am so disappointed not to hear from you, hope you are not sick. I came down early from Greenwich yesterday thinking there might be a telegram or some message. Aren't you coming in this week? Or is the work going too well. I know you called me up at Westport and at home but you were easily discouraged. I am designing costumes for Lynne Fontane for *The Doctor's Dilemma.*[1] She is coming up this afternoon to work on them with me. Also I have to design two more pieces of furniture for the J. Walter Thompson Co. before I go away. I am caught in a steel net and feel as though I should never get free of work. But I have only myself to blame.

Tom dear I am so sad to be away from you. I know you had to go. I know you wanted to be by yourself. I guess it is best for you but it is terribly hard, for me. You see I cannot free myself of the thought that you are really separating yourself from me. God bless you, I love you forever[.] Aline

1. *The Doctor's Dilemma*, by Bernard Shaw, was produced by the Theatre Guild at the Guild Theatre on 21 November 1927 and ran for 115 performances.

47. [New York] 333 West Seventy Seventh Street [29 June 1927]
Dearest Tom:

I've been having a bad week since you left; and it seems to me that I do nothing but complain that I do not hear from you.—In the first place, Terry's father is quite ill and she cannot possibly get away, so we have given up our passage. I am working harder than ever, all the Swedish stuff[1] is arriving this week, and I am getting Miss Fontanne's[2] costumes made. I am actually so tired that I cannot think. Will you come down to see me? If I don't stop work soon I'll break in half. I stayed down at 8 St. a whole afternoon cleaning with Joe. It was a terrible mess, and flies by the 1000, because of the food that was there. We cleaned it all up though, and threw all the food stuff away, and now the flies have disappeared. I found upon the floor under rubbish two ardent letters of mine, to you. I tore them to pieces, it made me feel so sad, to think you could throw my loving letters to you around. I also found a check from your uncle, which I am enclosing.—Please come down, I want so terribly to talk to you.—

Dearest love[,] Aline

Would you like to go to Europe with me?
Vienna, Prague, Budapest?

1. *An Enemy of the People*, by Henrik Ibsen, opened at Hampden's Theatre on 3 October 1927. Although she was not the principal scenic designer, Mrs. Bernstein did work for this play.

2. Lynne Fontanne, renowned stage and screen actress, was the star of this play.

On 12 July, Wolfe sailed aboard the George Washington *for Europe, meeting Mrs. Bernstein, who had sailed aboard the S.S.* France, *in Paris. Together they toured in Paris, Strasbourg, Munich, Vienna, Prague, and Nuremberg. Wolfe remained in Paris for a brief stay after Mrs. Bernstein returned home.*

In September, upon his return from Europe, the two rented the second floor of an old house at 263 W. Eleventh Street. Mrs. Bernstein used the front room as her studio. Wolfe resumed his teaching and continued working on the last section of the manuscript, dictating finished sections to Abe Smith, a young student from N.Y.U. who was typing for him.

By late March, the book was completed. Meanwhile, the arguments between the two had grown increasingly frequent. Beset by irrational fits of jealousy concerning Mrs. Bernstein's fidelity which plagued him throughout the relationship, Wolfe began to call the Bernstein home at all hours of the night to determine her whereabouts. Mrs. Bernstein submitted his huge manuscript to several publishers, but no one expressed any serious interest. Wolfe, in a state of frustration and weariness, told her that he could no longer live with her and that he wanted his freedom.

48. [New York, May 1928]
My dearest Tom:

Things have come to a dreadful state between us, and I know that it is impossible for us to talk. There are things I must say, and this is the best way to do it. You are in terrible shape I know, you are tired out and badly hurt by what has happened thus far to your book.[1] You are hurt not only for yourself but you feel it for the people to whom you hoped to say good news. I do know how you are suffering. I know because I love you so dearly, and now I am only trying to lay my heart open to you. I wish that there could be some way you could be spared the other pain caused by the dreadful black clouds of fantasy that have embittered you towards me. With all of your imagination, you do not seem to know how it is to be constantly vilified and beaten by a loved being. You talk to me as though I were the lowest of the low, and I cannot stand it any longer. By all that is sacred to me, I vow that I have been a loving and faithful woman, and I have been a true and good person to you in every respect. I have done all that I knew how to help you, I have given your book to the three people that I considered best.

My presence seems to be so painful to you, that I will make no attempt to see you or speak to you again. If you care to see me before I leave, will you let me know? It is so sad, but my dear I cannot go on this way. Remember I love you beyond any thing you dream of, and I do hope that you will want to part from me in love and tenderness. I will never be anything but your true and good friend so long as my life lasts, and I will have no lover in this world but you.—

I have to finish my work, but will try do that at home. If you will let me know when you will be away I'll come down and get my materials or send Miss Stott[2] after them. In case you do not wish to speak to me, will you let me know how I can communicate with you later in the summer?—

Things are bound to come right for you for you have a great mind. Later I want to tell you what I think you need for yourself. Tom dearest, God bless you, this is too terrible. Aline

1. Wolfe, with Mrs. Bernstein's help, had submitted his manuscript to T. R. Smith, an editor at Boni and Liveright; Ernest Boyd, literary agent for Little, Brown and Company; and Cleveland Chase, of Longmans, Green and Company. All had rejected the manuscript of *LHA*.

2. Margaret Stott, Mrs. Bernstein's former nurse, was to sublet the apartment in their absence.

49. [New York] Harvard Club / Thursday / June 7, 1928
Dear Aline:

I suppose you are very near the coast of France as I write you this, and I hope your six days on the water have rested you, and got you ready for the good time I hope you are going to have when you arrive.

I feel much better since school closed—I am quieter, less nervous, but already a little impatient to get to work again—this time, I hope, with better success. I went to see Koller, the eye doctor—he found nothing wrong, and said I had very good eyesight. But he gave me some drops to put in the eye—I believe it is silver nitrate, which is what they put in the eyes of new-born babes as a protection against venereal diseases. So you can draw your own conclusions.

Stott has been in twice and is coming back again today. We have cleaned up the books, thrown away all the trash, and packed the papers away. I have also seen Mr. Greenleaf.[1] I have had a letter from home: I have decided to go down for three or four days, but they must bear part of the expense of the trip.

The people I met in the speakeasy called me up Sunday and insisted that I come over to their apartment. I went over. There were two women and three men—all about forty or over. One of the women was jealous of one of the men: she was using me to arouse his jealousy—she called me up and asked me to meet her—and he invited me over for the purpose of making me very drunk so I couldn't meet her. This sounds incredible, but it is literally true. Well, I did go over, I did become very drunk, but I did meet her. I cried out in my throat and cursed them all—as they deserved to be. But I went on and met the woman, bought her a meal, and told her what she was. In my suspicion I accused them of being criminals and blackmailers —I think this worried them, for they insisted they had big jobs with a big construction company. The woman was enraged at the man because he had told me she was a grandmother—which is true. The next day she was at the phone again, insisting that I come over and meet her son-in-law and her daughter, and eat with them, to see how nice they were. I did not go, but I went by and spoke to her, and I told her good-bye, because I was very sorry of the way I had spoken. But I have rarely seen people caught in such a loathsome web as were these middle aged men and women. This is the greatest excitement I have had, but this is the truth of it, and I shall have no more to do with them.

The pyjamas were lost; I made Stern give me new ones—I went up and picked them out. I have looked at the magazines for write ups of the Follies—there is nothing yet in the *Nation*, but I read a big piece by Stark Young in the latest *New Republic*. His comment is ecstatic —he begins with a few minor reservations—political skits didn't wholly come off. *Strange Interlude* one good in intention, Spanish Dances not so good, etc—then he bursts into lyrical song. Of course, I think he spoils things by his big talk—he talks of all his sardines as if they were whales, but there's no doubt how he felt: he said D. Sands "carried burlesque to a kind of tragic farce, and wit to inspiration" and said Mary Nash[2] ought to study Carrol's imitation "for better movement and more design." He did not like Dorothy's "rhythm" here and there in the May West thing: perhaps you can design a rubber butt for her when you come back. He has a good bit of praise for the *settings*, although he foolishly omits mention of their designer. He says that the new Follies reflects the times, because three or four years ago, when everyone was agog about settings, the Follies parodied them: "there was Mr. Robert Edmond Jones' brilliant "Macbeth" for one instance, or his "Hamlet," to be parodied, and who will forget that ladder mounting into space, those mounds, those planes of madness to be seen in Grand Street then?" This year, according to the trend "the settings strive mostly to be diverting and expert for their own sakes." I am quoting all this from the Harvard Club copy: I'll buy one of my own and send you the clipping.

But I suppose your show is a hit—after reading all the big words in the article I feel like the fellow in Molière's play who discovers he has been speaking *prose* all his life, and didn't know it.

Since you have gone, I have thought more clearly about you. I think of you with pain and with love, and I think I always shall. And it is very bitter for me to know that I have acted meanly and badly to you. But the snake headed furies that drive us on to despair and madness are inside of us: how to unroot them from the structure of our soul is a problem that gets me sick with horror. What I mean to say more plainly is that, no matter what you did or are about to do, I acted badly. That is as far as I can truthfully go now. I wish that I had had strength to be finer, but I felt like an animal, who had to endure mockery and torture until it got out of its cage, and it made me crazy.

Now, I think of our four thousand hours of love and goodness. I know that I loved you and still do, and I believe that you loved me, and preferred me above all others for a long time. And I love you for that, and for your good and beautiful spirit[.]

You used to tell me that "I talked like a book," and you were right. But it seems to me that I have only put down plainly some of what I feel. It is not very smart or very deep, but I think it is true. I think it is true that books and poetry have influenced my life. Love to me is still the fantastic and absolute thing that it is in the books, and never is in life. And the way I should like to be, the way I should like to act is not meanly or badly as I often do, but in the grand and heroic manner of people in books. When Stott and I were cleaning up my papers, I kept stopping to read letters I had written several years ago—to my family or to the girl in France. And I almost choked with shame when I came to the fine and flowery phrases, when I struck up a high and mighty attitude, and ranted about either to impress myself or others. And I wonder now if we never come to anything real—if we never put what we feel and think down so simply that we can come to it years later without regret. I think it may be partly an over-sensitiveness to what you have yourself felt. I have learned some humility, but I do not yet think I am the only jackass that ever lived, and I believe if I wrote in the fancy and affected way of dramatic critics, or most writers of novels and plays, I should not have to wait years to choke over it. At any rate, in those old letters I was always passionate about something I thought at the time mattered—love, anger, honor, and so on, and I tried to express it in fine phrases.

What good or evil we have done to each other I do not know now—but I think you have given me a great desire to be as clear and as plain as possible—to be myself and not a lot of other people.

I believe you had an honest person to work with, and I believe I still am. In those old letters I saw an honest and excited child, full of books and poetry, who wanted beauty and heroism and glory from life. I still want them. The fancy phrases were bad, but the thing that caused them was good. And as for believing more in the way people act in books than in the way they act in life—why is that so wrong?

Now that you have gone away I see you as if you were in a book—if you have any blemishes I don't remember them, if you wore a different suit every day, I don't remember them all—I remember green and grey, and the white blouse[.] The thing that lasts is the thing that you really are—I am still a great deal better than this bad tooth the dentist worked on this morning: that tooth is part of me, but I do not think it is the thing people will remember about me.

The thing I remember about you, Aline, is that you are a good and beautiful woman. If a person is *good* and *fine*, according to our understanding of those words, for forty hours, and not *good* and *fine* for forty minutes, then I think we must say the person is really good and fine. I hope I may be shown even more charity, for my own average is hours short of this.

I believe I have seen this much of life clearly. It's like one of those statues of Rodin in which something beautiful and strong is emerging from a mass of granite—but still blurred and undefined. That's the way things are, but meanwhile I shall stick to the books where things have emerged whole and clear and beautiful.

I hope I am not trying to be a philosopher. I don't want to talk wise, or to try to appear detached. I am still stupid and numb over what has happened to me. But I have lost my ugliness and bitterness, and I can not deny, Aline, that I love you more than anyone in the world. This is as honest a record as I can make at the present time.

Tom

1. The landlord at 8th Street.
2. Actress in such 1920s productions as *A Lady's Virtue* (1925), *The Two Orphans* (1926), and *A Strong Man's House* (1929).

50. Paris / Hotel Westminster [14 June 1928]
My dear:

This is not a tear, only a damn French pen.—We have had the best luck with weather, our crossing was very smooth but not sunny. Both Terry and I were worn out, and we did little but sleep all the way over, and eat. The food was too good to be true, and as the ship was not over crowded, we had the best of attention. I had a number of acquaintances on board but we spoke with very few people except Bob Chandler, and a lady who had an introduction to me, and her name is no less than Mrs. Vanderbilt (Mrs. Wm H. I believe). She is beautiful and very clever, and made a delightful companion. Terry is still terribly tired, and the first two nights we were here she could not even go out to dinner, so we dined in our room. I was terribly worried for fear she was going to be ill, but she seems better now, but has decided to go to Carlsbad for a cure, so there I will be for three weeks, in July, and a very dull place it is. But I will do some drawing and try to get rid of my adipose deposit. I believe there are waters to drink and baths to take there. It gives me a pang to be in Paris without you. I keep looking for you and would not be at all surprised to see your dear face some day. The strain those last two weeks in New York was terrible and I could not have stood much more. What with the show,[1] and home, and you or us, I should say—I could not help but feel that I might not see you for so long, for a year or more, and you did not seem to care about that. I love you, and long to see you and will be true to you as long as I live. I really think that it is necessary for us to be away from each other now, the wisest thing we can do. I am sure it must be a great relief to you.—I went with Mrs. V. this afternoon to look at pictures, nothing very interesting except one superb portrait by Picasso. I bought a photograph of it to show you. Lish is here and spends all her time with us. She is a darling. Her family do not come till the end of this week. Her brother took sick in London and has had a hell of a time.—We leave for Rapallo Friday (this week.) The only nice thing here is the Russian Ballet, it is lovely, quite different from what it used to be 10 years ago. Much more simple, with decors by Picasso and some of the new artists. But O my God this city is magnificent and O my Tom, the food! It is just a[s] well we are leaving. I'll look like a barrel. You will be glad to know that I haven't cried but once since we left. That was the day we came into Plymouth, it was so beautiful and made me think of you and long to have you with me. We were so happy in England. You are so deep in my heart.—I do hope for some news of you soon, and I must say I was a little disappointed not to have a cable from you here.—

I bought delicious paints brushes and paper today. Lish and Terry both speak French, which is a help to me.—

My dearest love to you, I will write as soon as I reach Rapallo.

Aline

1. *The Grand Street Follies* of 1928 opened at the Booth Theatre on 28 May 1928. The Neighborhood Playhouse had been forced to close on 31 May 1927 because of financial pressures.

51. Rapallo/Grand Hotel Excelsior & New Casino [22 June 1928]

My Dear—

Your letter came and gave me great comfort. I had been looking every day for some word from you, and I wonder if you have left America. But you said you would cable me when you did. Our life here is so quiet, the air so soft and humid. It is not the season, and I believe that there are not more than 20 visitors here, none under the age of 90. I am sending you a couple of post cards of Rappallo, but nothing can give you an idea of the sort of perfection in every thing. It is more rugged than the French Riviera, no beaches, but sheer rock up from the sea. (One or two, very small beaches along the coast.) We go swimming right off the rocks. This is our last day.—We have tea in our room about 8:30, read until 11, then swim until lunch time. After lunch, we read again, or, one day we took a small motor boat, and went along the coast, putting in at little ports just like opera bouffes. Then, Terry starts out to climb a mountain and we do that until dinner time. We dine later about 8:30. Mrs. Vanderbilt has come down to join us, so we are a trio. Yesterday was cloudy, so we went to Genoa for the day. It was very interesting to walk in the old city, but otherwise rather disappointing. But I am having the rest I so badly needed. Today I began to do some work, and made some costume drawings for the Bourgeois Gentelhomme.[1] (The man who found he had been talking prose all his life.) The climate here, while not too warm, is terribly relaxing, and I find I can sleep about 10 or 11 hrs.

Terry and I have a great big room, overlooking the sea, with a huge terrace outside, for about 1/3 the rate during the season, and very good meals, too.—My heart and mind are full of you, all the time when I swim out from shore, I wish that I could swim into a place that would hold us both. Maybe that now I am away from you, you will feel more or understand more, what I am for you, but I doubt if you will ever know what you are for me. I adore you and will always be thankful for the time we have had together, and if we can meet again, I will be anything you want, your lover or your friend.—I wish I could tell you in fine words, the beautiful pain I feel about you all the time. All of this even remembering the bad times, the heartaches and misunderstandings.—I am glad that you felt like writing again.—I hope to God you will and that you do not get mixed up with people you pick up here and there. I groan and worry over what might happen to you.—Tom—so long as I live, I am faithful to you in body and soul. Nothing could ever touch me again, no man will ever come near to me. I am afraid that you never fully realize this, you never have all the time we were together. Now you are beside me every minute. Please don't worry that Dr. Koller gave you nitrate of silver for your eyes.—I have had it often, it just relieves inflammation of the eyelids, sort of cauterizes them. I hope your bad tooth is better by now, along with your other ills. I must have been a sore trial to you, crying so much this past few months. But I have been your love, too.—I expect to stay here for some time, until we go to Carlsbad for a cure about July 5th. We might motor up from here if we can get a car not too expensive. The concierge has a cousin or brother in law or something, who has a car or something, and we may have it. It will take us through the Dolomites, Terry says they are grand. We will be in Carlsbad 3 weeks, and Terry's husband joins us there. Also Phil[2] at the end of the time, maybe the Wertheims, and they want to go to München and Vienna. So I will see all my beloved places again.—We sail back Aug. 14 on a small German boat, the Reliance, an 8 day boat. I will probably get my work finished while in Carlsbad. Maybe I will take a little cure and come out thin, who knows, then I will not have to be your aunt. I have grown thinner here, swimming I guess. But also, I have had a bad case of hives again, the way I had in Vienna, do you remember? I am afraid I will have to give up the nice Chianti, also the good spaghetti.—Max

Beerbohm[3] lives here, also Gerhard Hauptman,[4] and the Infanta of Spain.[5] I've saw [sic] the Infanta taking tea at a cafe this afternoon, not so very noble looking, very simple, no uniforms or anything in attendance just plain tennis clothes, not even a neck tie. I should love to call on Beerbohm, but it would be a nerve, I guess and what would he want to see us for?—If the weather is alright tomorrow we are going down the coast to Pisa. I read in Baedecker[6] there are some Cimabue's[7] there, in fact he decorated the whole cathedral.—Terry wants to put a p.s.—

Dearest love,
Aline

She's not getting as thin and sveldt [sic][8] as she pretends Tom—I'm having a hard time substituting for her last summer's pal—But at least I make her go to bed early—How & where are you? Best—

1. *The Would-Be Gentleman*, by Moliere, opened at the Civic Repertory Theatre on 1 October 1928, and ran for thirty-four performances.

2. Phillip Moeller.

3. Noted British cartoonist, humorist, and literary critic.

4. Gerhart Hauptmann, German dramatist, was a winner of the Nobel Prize.

5. Son of King Alfonso of Spain.

6. Baedecker's *Handbook for Travellers*.

7. Giovanni Cimabue (Canni di Pepo), forerunner of the Florentine school, regenerated Florentine art by breaking with the Byzantine tradition.

8. Theresa Helburn added this postscript. The "sic" is included in her message to Wolfe.

52. Rapallo / Grand Hotel Excelsior & New Casino [26 June 1928]
My dear:

My impulse always is to write and tell you that I love you. For I do, every hour and every minute. It is strange not to be part of your life. I want to know what happens to you and what you do. And whether you are more contented [now] that we are away from each other. Tom, I go through thoughts, and times of the most awful pain, thinking that you have gone from me. I love you, and wish to be of you and with you more than ever before.—We are leaving here early tomorrow morning, I have just telegraphed the bank to forward my mail to Carlsbad. We are going to stay two days in the Dolomites. Terry sends her love to you, I think she is weary of my repining. To-day I read most of your favorites in the big poetry book. I hope I will have my mail E.R. En route, Dearest love, I love you forever[.]

Aline

I saw this embroidered on a priests robe in a church near Balzano. It is an inadequate picture of my feeling.—One more sword and I'll bleed to death[.]

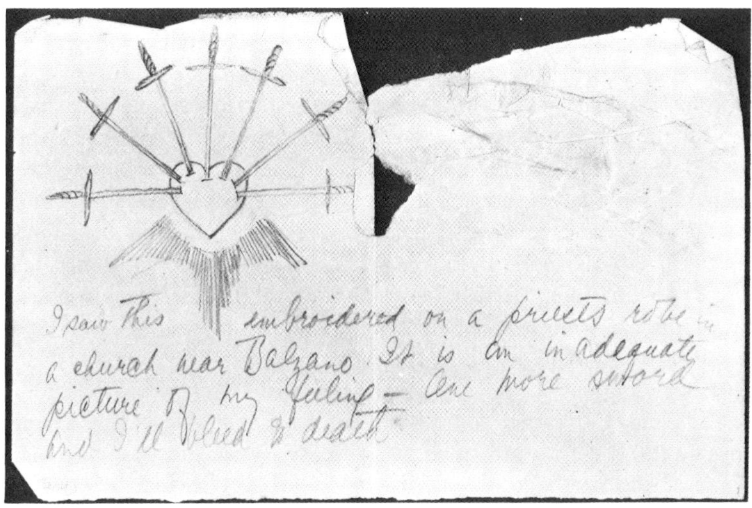

I saw this embroidered on a priests robe in a church near Balzano It is an inadequate picture of my feeling— One more sword and I'll bleed to death

Aline Bernstein to Thomas Wolfe, 26 June 1928 (By permission of the Houghton Library, Harvard University)

53. [New York, Thursday, 28 June 1928]
Dear Aline:

I have just returned from a midnight performance of *Diamond Lil*, which was the main reason I went. I wanted to see what the theater is like at two in the morning. I enjoyed the show a great deal: everything is so bad that it is very good. When I came out in the street I read the news that Al Smith had been nominated for the presidency. That will be a good show to watch too. I understand the Democrats have a plank in their platform that seems dry to the drys and wet to the wets. I wish we could get beer like that.

For the last two or three days we have had New York heat. Today the walls, the pavements, and the people all sweated. But before it has been almost uniformily cold and raining. I went home for a week —got back ten days ago. Found family well, but everyone very poor, and the town flat on its back after the boom. Everyone has lots of land but no money. My mother well, but it seems to me she has grown much older. Her mind is still quick and active. She has much good property, which will be all right, they say, and a good deal of bad property which she bought during the general lunacy. I had only one or two blow-ups and I am glad that I saw them. Mabel has improved amazingly, put on twenty pounds, and looks a different person. Fred came in from the South two hours before I left.

I have had a long siege with the dentist, but he is about through now. He drilled through my bad tooth, punched a hole in the gum, and scraped the bone with a knife. It hurt like hell. But it was a good job, and I think it will be all right now. I have seen Miss Stott several times. She was up again today. She gets on my nerves terribly at times with her incessant Board of Health mania, but she is a good soul, I believe and she loves you very much. I am giving her the place as you asked, and I introduced her to old man Greenleaf today. I have cleaned up my books and papers as much as I could, but I'm afraid it's up to you and her to dispose of the rest as you see fit when you return. If you are back before September I hope you will do all the work you can here, because I should like to think someone was getting some use from it. I have written a number of people letters and asked them to write me when I am away, because I know one of the ugliest feelings in the world is to come away from a foreign mail-window empty-handed. Since I want to be alone, I should be strong enough to do without this contact with the world. But I am not.

I have told Stott to make full use of everything she finds, but not to pry in to my letters and mss. She has promised that she won't. She was very funny with old Greenleaf. She had a long letter from her sister saying her brother-in-law might come to New York. She read it to the old man to prove that any man she might have around the place would be proper kin, but I think her manner conveyed the impression that she was going to keep her beau up here. I told her this later and she seemed very much worried. I got her a bottle of Harvard Club gin because she said it was good for the nerve in her back, and another for her fellow who is, she says, your second cousin, and is hot after her. She insisted on paying for both.

I am glad to know that you had such a pleasant crossing, and have had such good weather, and met such elegant companions as Mrs. Vanderbilt. But I am sorry to hear of Terry's illness, and that you have been confined so much to her sick room. I am sure she could excuse you for a half hour now and then, when you could walk in the gardens, or perhaps both of you might go occasionally to a performance of the Comedie Francaise by way of diversion. And at Carlsbad you could drink the waters and get a great deal of embroidery done.

—This is the next day, Friday morning. Raining buckets again. I've been to Macy's and bought some shirts and a pair of suspenders. I'm about ready to go away. The only thing I hate leaving in New York is this fine big place. Please try to do some work here when you get back.

I feel immensely better than I did a month ago, and anxious to get to work again. I stopped off in Wash. to see Olin Dows, but missed him. But I met him a few days later at the Harvard Club and had a long talk with him. He is a fine person, and I am glad to know him. He will help me at any time—I asked him if $500 seemed a lot and he said he spent more than that on a picture. But I said *later*. Told him I was going to write a book about him as he ought to be—always grand, noble, and romantic. Seemed interested and amused. He went to Grand Street Follies with a girl [the] day I saw him. I told him to call up your daughter for tickets, but he already had them.

Thursday / July 5

Dear Aline:

I have been wallowing comfortably across the ocean for the last five days in an old Dutch tub called the Rotterdam. I intended to send this letter to you before I sailed, but I came so suddenly that I decided to mail it when I landed in Europe. I got my ticket the day before and got on the boat five minutes before she sailed. Saturday morning Stott came around to Eleventh street and I turned everything over to her. I had previously seen Greenleaf and paid him and told him she would come in. She found me asleep and unpacked at nine o'clock—my boat sailed at eleven—we worked hard, and I finally got away, after she had driven me crazy by packing, unpacking, and wrapping everything in newspapers. This old boat is crowded to capacity, but I have been comfortable enough. Got badly sunburned on top deck, and my face is peeling. Have let myself go and talked to everyone. Found out a great deal about the Dutch—a great many of them going home for a visit. A very interesting and honest people. Many of them are florists—they load me down with beer and cigars and invitations to stay with them in Holland; I think I should get off at Boulogne but I may go on to Rotterdam. I think I shall stay at Boulogne or Amiens a few days. I wanted to go to Rouen and up the Seine to Paris by river boat, and may do it yet.

I wrote you a great long letter shortly after you went away—

Boulogne / July 9, 1928

Dear Aline:

I landed at Boulogne this morning after a comfortable trip over: I could not write, I could not read, ceaselessly I went about meeting the passengers[.] It was a strange and interesting voyage; I found out a great deal about the Dutch, and have enough invitations in Holland —if I take them—to last me all summer. I stopped off in this hole to get a good night's sleep with my legs stretched out. I think I feel marvellous. I did little but eat and talk on the boat; my mind was convalescent; my face is red with sunburn—peeling off. Now I am alone in a strange town again, at night, with stillness all around me. I stood on the bridge and watched—the boat-trains roll slowly past towards Paris. All of the people eating stared at me through the glass. They had seen me on the boat. Tomorrow I am going to Paris, but may stop at Amiens. I am beginning to seethe with life and vitality again.

This is an unending and unsatisfactory letter. All of the things I want deeply to say to you, I cannot—I have become terribly secret around the sore spots, and can hardly talk to myself about them.

But I want to say this, dear Aline: I have not and can not forget all the pain I have had because of you. I do not know when we should see each other again, but my heart is bursting with its love for you. I do not know what else I may have said in my letter—I began it weeks ago—but you can always come back to this. I do not know what this will make you feel—whether it will be joy, or triumph or amusement, or scorn, but I shall be proud of my love, no matter what happens or who shall mock me. They can not hurt me now.

I shall be in Paris only a few days, and I do not know where I shall go from there. But I shall get my mail at the American Express Co. I hope you will write me there.

Good bye and God bless you, wherever you are. For me it will never happen again as it did this once: there is no one to equal you, and no one will ever take your place. Tom

Boulogne-Sur-Mer- /
Monday Night / July 9, 1928

There will be little fancy patches in this that may make me squirm ten years from now. But no matter about that—the thing that made me write them will still be there.

After Midnight: I am going for a walk through Boulogne.
I love you, Aline.

54. Karlsbad [5 July 1928]
My dear:

I have expected, at each stopping place, to find word that you had sailed, but no doubt you are finding New York a good place for the early summer.—We left Rapallo about 9 days ago, and went up to the Dolomites, stopped off a while at Milan to see the cathedral. It was a remarkable sight but I didn't care for it very much. Did I send you a card from Pisa? That was so much more beautiful. But then we motored for three days through the most unbelievably gorgeous and thrilling mountains you can imagine. We got a nice little car, almost like a mule, that seemed to know every turn in the road, and a hardy brown peasant for [a] driver, and I assure you that most of the time I expected to go over the edge any minute—all the roads wind along the edge of the mountains, some of the turns too terrific for words, up and up to the most incredible heights, over rocky passes, and then the downward drive! Horrible but so glorious. At times I actually had to hide my face. Terry adores it, no mountain is too steep for her, and I am afraid I was not a very good companion. We often drove with snow beside the road. After climbing very high, the mountains are literally carpeted with the most exquisite flowers, miniatures of the flowers we know, and of the greatest brilliance of color, tiny daisies, cyclamen, primroses and columbine, bluebells and clover, and over all a froth of forget-me-nots, and such sweet smell. It was beyond words—the most exciting country I ever saw, and all I could say was how terrible not to have you with me. That would have been perfect. I speak of you so much, I want to share all of the loveliness with you. I don't even know where you are, or how things are with you. I have worn your letter out, reading it over. I wonder if Mrs. Boyd has done anything about the book. Terry is a lovely travelling companion, she has a fine disposition, and is so smart about everything. She engages our accommodations and takes charge of the finances, and is able to drive a fine bargain with any of the foreign thieves. But she has not been well, seems to be so tired.—I got a terrible sun burn in the mountains. My face all covered with water blisters, and my lips swollen out to 3 times their size (I looked the way you some times make a funny mouth). Had to stay in my room most of 2 days with wet compresses. The driver says it was partly due to the altitude. Balzano, the place that was our starting point, is a charming town in a peaceful vally, with the great stony dolomites all round. The region belonged to Austria before the war, but is now Italian soldiers. Of course every one speaks German, but all the signs are Italian. We drove over some of the rocky passes where they fought, it must have been frightful. I'm afraid I've used up most of my adjectives and have none left for Carlsbad, but same ones would hardly do, I'll try a different set. We've been here three days, and I never saw so many funny people in all of my life together, including the funny ones at Bath. There is every shape, size and nationality (not many Americans) all drinking the waters at prescribed times. The great mineral springs (there must be about 18) are open at certain hours of the day. We go down to begin at 7 A.M., and at that time, you see the entire population circulating round with glasses of water, and there are orchestral concerts to keep you going. I have gone on a cure with Terry, and it is vigorous to say the least. But I will loose [sic] some of my adipose deposit, and you simply couldn't stand the place without. This is our day—We go and drink 4 glasses at the Markt bronnen, using about half an hour, then go up to another spring, the Schlossbrunner, drink 4 more glasses, (takes at least an hour to get down these) dash madly for the toilet then take a walk or sit and read the paper. Then 1 glass of milk, and go to bed from 11 to 3. Then, go down to the springs, repeat the doses, and sit in a beautiful leafy cafe and have another glass of milk, and watch every one else. Take a book along usually. (I've bought all the Tauchnitz edition[1] complete, by now.) At 7, we go to the doctor, he enquires about our symptoms, he hates me, for I have none, we walk a little more, have another glass of milk and go to bed at 8:30. No meals! And the queerest thing is I don't feel hungry. I think we will have an egg tomorrow, or something of the sort.

July 6th

This is tomorrow already, but no egg. I am getting quite lovely, my eyes are so clear, and my face smooth and nice, but a very tired feeling. I write you while we take our morning rest. I never thought the time would come when I should feel like resting, but here it is. The strangest thing is that I don't feel hungry, I suppose drinking the waters does it. The taste isn't bad, one spring is a little sulphurous. —I hope that I'll have some letter from you before I leave here.—I wonder if I wrote you, the day we went to Pisa, we stopped for lunch at a lovely little town on the sea called Lereci, and discovered it was the place where Shelly lived, and was drowned. The Mediterranean looked so serene and blue, it was too ghastly to think any thing so tragic could have happened there. Byron also lived there and wrote a great deal. I am glad Miss Stott was able to help you to clean up. If you are gone, I don't know how I will bear to go down and finish up in the fall. Thank the Lord I have plenty of work, when I come home.—Will you ever know how I love you? I want you to do whatever you think is right for you. I have the utmost faith in you.—

Yours Aline

1. Tauchnitz Latin and English pocket dictionary.

55. [17 July 1928]

My dear:

I wrote you in a sort of frenzy this afternoon, God knows whether I was crazy or not. Ever since I left New York I have been longing for some word from you, and it came like a crash, I could only see you and me in the world. I've been doing my utmost to meet your wish for freedom, but I held the hope that you would care enough to at least put forth some hopefulness for the future. You said you did not know whether you would ever see me again. So I must take it as a decision.—It would seem as though I have written you every thing about my love, yet I want to go on saying the same thing again and again. Today has been a nightmare, the most blinding heat and humidity, and my soul wrenched out of me.

I tell you the truth about my life and you haven't the sense to see it is true. I have always told you the truth. I have literally spoken to no one outside of Terry & Oliver, and occasionally a patient who may be waiting in the doctor's office. Tonight we came home at 8, they went to their room and here I am in mine. I've been looking out the window for an hour, watching heat lightning breaking the sky. Tomorrow will be two weeks since we came. My time has been crowded with thoughts of you and memories, quick pictures of things together, I try my best to push them away. This starvation is a queer thing, in a way it gives me a greater hold upon my self.—There is a magnificent storm breaking, I hope the heat is over. My room has a little balcony looking out over the valley. Some other time I will write more about the place itself. I loathed it at first. Terry is better since she came.—I am going to stop now, the lightning is terrific and I want to put out the light. Good night dearest. God bless you and bring you peace.

My dear,

The terrible heat is over[,] such a relief[.] I see in the papers that it has been very hot all over Europe. I am glad Miss Stott was of some help to you in clearing up. She is a nuisance when she gets going, I always make her keep quiet when I've had enough. I wish you would tell me what to do with your things. I have no room at home for all those books. The manuscripts etc. I can put in the cellar, if they are packed in the baskets. Did you leave all of my letters there? Please write and tell me if you did. I shall never go to the place again to work, only when the time comes to pack up, and maybe even then Stott will do it for me. I shall give her every thing that is there but my drafting table. I am going to try to get an office next to Helen Arthur's, there is a place there about twice the size of our kitchen. I am sending in an application for it. I am so happy that you feel better, and like settling to work. I do hope you aren't going to drink a lot and have rows with people, you waste yourself so that way. Tom when I think of you going with some other woman I am frantic. I have beat my head on the wall, to think of you holding some one else, to think of the way I love you. I think of my head in the fold of your arm, so many times when you were lovely with me—How can you—

I wish you would go to England to work, it is the best place.—I'm sailing home on the Reliance Aug. 15 from Hamburg[,] leave here July 25, in a week. Will be in Vienna about the first. Mails are so uncertain here. I wish I had not come away from home this summer, any thing seems easier than this.—Write to me please dearest [c/o] Thos. Cook in Vienna[.] Aline

56. Paris / Hotel Burgundy / Thursday / July 19, 1928
Dear Aline:

I got your telegram Monday, and your two letters today. I have just sent you a telegram through the messy anarchy of a French post office—which apparently is the only way you can send one, but I hope to God it gets to you tonight. But I suppose you know before I ever send you any sort of message all I can say to you in it—I love you. But the more I say it to you, the more bitter and dejected your answers to me are. Your two letters have excited me very much—I never foresaw that my own would bring back such an answer. I thought in my two letters I had written as simply and plainly as I could, and it seemed to me that you could not miss their meaning. Yet you say that they hold out no hope for us, and call me "poor foolish Tom" (which is accurate enough) for throwing away the best thing I have ever had. For God's sake, don't do or say anything unjustly now that might throw me back into all the complex torture from which I am just beginning to escape. I am trying to see and understand a few things simply once more. Several people have recently reproached me for being too easy, too trusting, too "succulent." In my heart I know this is true, and when I realize I become suspicious of motives. Now why should you twist and misinterpret everything I write to you, and claim to see nothing good or hopeful in it? If I said in my letter that you could no longer hurt me, that was a very foolish thing to say, because I think you will always be able to do that—but on the whole I tried to be honest and exact.

But I want to be honest and exact without bringing back all the bitterness and ugliness—if a little of it gets into my letters, I can not help it. It is too much to expect me to be completely changed—made over to your liking, to believe and think only the things you want me to—and to do all this at once. I am at times like some blind thing upon the floor of the sea feeling its own way along—I have the great impulse of love for you; and I know that is greater than anything else and it would be foolish to deny it.

Aline I'll have to send you another letter in a day or two—I want to get this one off now, bad as it is. I have been sick for several days after having excellent health coming over. The heat here has been terrific—worse than anything I have ever known in New York. At the top of it, another abscessed tooth popped up, and my head about came off. I went to a dentist here; he bored a hole through for drainage. He had to go through the raw tooth; afraid to use novacaine. I am much better now—haven't seen a great deal of Paris, but I am going out today and tomorrow to see some pictures and books. I spend hours looking at the thousands of books, unable it seems to buy a single one.

Paris is a beautiful city, but its effect on me for two or three years has been one of terrible weariness[.] And more and more, it seems to me, has what is grand and high in the place been coated over by what is cheap and trashy—the place in certain quarters looks like an enormous Coney Island. During their holiday (July 14)[1] there was three days of dancing in the streets, parades, shouting. And suddenly I got sick of their immense triviality. The men and women hopping about like squirrels, the chatter, the accordian music, and the miles upon miles of gim cracks, Carnivals, merry go rounds, Ferris Wheels, etc, fed me up. They have no capacity for boredom, no genuine vanity, only an infinite repetitiousness. We must free ourselves from fear —and the fear of provincialism, the desire to be cultured and sophisticated drove thousands of Americans to Paris as it did me. Now I am over that. Wherever I live it will not be here. London is grander, New York is more alive, and in Vienna there is rest. I do not think I have ever met an American who came here to live who got himself a soul by doing it.

Maybe someday it will become a gigantic place maintained solely for tourists—a strong liquor to be taken at great intervals. But I'm going to see some more books and pictures. I've got to make up my mind during the next day or so where I'm going. I want to get to work now. I'll wire you as soon as I decide, or just before I go.

Your cure is Spartan, and sounds marvellous. But I know how you must suffer on such a diet. But I am not glad that it is making you more beautiful; for that has caused me trouble enough already, and I am not glad it makes you look two years younger, because I look ten or fifteen years older than when I met you, and in the true course of things, we should each look our age.

I won't let this letter string itself out indefinitely. Goodbye, my dear, for the present. When you get this you will be almost ready, I suppose, to eat a square meal again. That should be excitement enough.

Aline, the heat and my illness have made it hard for me to be decisive and brief. I cannot tell you at this moment what I shall do, where I shall go. I'll let you know in a few days. But I do love you with all my life and spirit—believe in that and don't twist it into something else. Tom

1. Bastille Day.

57. Carlsbad [Sunday, 22 July 1928]
My Dear—

Your telegram reached me alright and today your lovely letter. Isn't it terrible that you have had another ulcerated tooth, and it must be alarming to put yourself under the care of a French dentist, or have you an American one. Your letter came just as I was on the way out to the springs for my late afternoon waters, in fact the porter ran down the road after me with it. As Terry and Oliver were with me, I did not open it for some time when I could be a little by myself. As you say you wanted to be exact and honest and I think you were to a certain extent. I did not twist your meaning, I only found what I honestly thought you meant. Possibly you forgot some of the things you said, and possibly you did not say some things you meant. I know you love me, and no doubt that should content me. It is a glorious thing. But this knowledge would not be enough for me for we are in a curious place now, my dear, and I must wait. I do earnestly want you to have time to recover yourself and certainly to do your work, and maybe get a clearer view of what there is for you in life, I admit that I am confused. I see no perfect solution, but I know my consuming love for you, and my desire is to be near you and share your thoughts and your life. I have always wanted to be of help to you, and often you have berated me because I seemed to be of no use. But I assure you it was only because what I did seemed no use to you. I tried my best.—I do not know who told you that you are too trusting[;] they certainly have never heard you speak to me.—I wish I understood why it is in every thing that concerns my relations with you, I am sensitized to the utmost. When I see your writing on an envelope I get a physical tingle, and your words affect me as no other words.—Terry has been so nice to me, naturally she could see my state of mind. I had to tell her one day all my terrible pain. All, I could not tell her, but I think she is understand[ing and] certainly sympathetic. I wonder if, when we first knew each other, you could have foreseen this, you would ever have written me that first letter. This much I know that the irrevocable difference in our ages is the only thing that has kept me from you.

Tomorrow I break my fast, and have an egg. It is Sunday, and as we leave Wednesday, the doctor wants me to have a little food. Monday I will have one meal, a piece of chicken and some bread. The cure has been an experience, Spartan indeed. You know how fond I am of food, I am glad to finish, but in a way it has been a great rest. My physical condition was equal to a sort of convalescence. I feel drained and relaxed the way you do after a bad cold and very tired, and the complete lack of responsibility in daily life has been wonderful. Your day mapped out with mathematical precision and no strength or desire to change it, and I sleep a great deal, as much as you do. When I go to bed at 11 A.M., I read about an hour, and then off in a deep sleep until 2 or 3. But I will be glad to see some pictures, and look forward to Nurnberg. And it will be wonderful to see the Breughels again in Vienna, and all the drawings at the Albertina we didn't see there—I read quite a lot from the big poetry book, things I hadn't read before. And as for the rest, I found a whole floor of Edgar Wallace I never had. Now I am at Orley Farm, by Trollope. It is gentle and just about my gait. I wish you could see Carlsbad, it is a fantastic place. Fortunately, we live way up on a hill, away from the town, near the woods. We live in a house that is really not a hotel, very nice big airy rooms and bath rooms, and very clean. There seem to be a number of such places here, where people live who take the cure. The front door is locked and hall lights out at 10 oclock, and utmost quiet. I look out over a lovely green valley. There are literally hundreds of hotels in the place, every one filled up to say nothing of boarding and rooming houses, and not a soul here who isn't taking some sort of cure, going out from the town are lovely woods, with shady mossy walks, and boskey restaurant deep in the trees. We are going to take a little victoria tomorrow and drive to the nicest one for our egg. Some people take a walking cure, miles & miles a day up into the hills, withal you never see any one who looks sick, but a lot of fat ones and grotesques beyond imagination. I've never seen women so beautifully dressed anywhere, the finest from all over the world, and Jews Jews Jews from the richest to the poorest. I hated it at first but now find it interesting.—I hope you will feel like going to England to work, it seems to me the place for it. You are right about Paris, and I know that you will never find any peace there. Oliver has to go to England on business, one of his text books is being published there and he has to go over. He and Terry love each other a great deal and seem to have a fine life together, I think one of the best and happiest married states I have ever seen, in spite of great differences in temperament.—I could go on writing endlessly, I will but no more tonight. Will you do something to make me feel good? Will you write me a letter to the boat when I sail home? The Reliance, Aug 14 from Hamburg. Please write in good time as the mails are so slow in Europe. Or if you are in England to Southampton. Terry has to go to Berlin on Theatre Guild business, so I will be able to see the pictures there, and maybe I can stop at Dresden on the way up. Do you remember, that Mr. Bondy told us the picture gallery at Berlin was so wonderful. Dearest, will you write to me when you can. I am half dead for you. I wish you could see me, my face looks so nice[;] you would adore it. Would you ever have believed it could be done—Yours, I love you forever[.] Aline

58. Carlsbad [Tuesday, 24 July 1928]
My Dear:

I have just finished packing my trunk. We leave tomorrow at 2 P.M. Two days ago I broke my long fast, first had an egg, second a piece of zweiback, and the next day some fricassee of chicken. It tasted good, but it is surprising how little I can eat. About ½ portion of anything fills me up. I feel well, and look wonderful, still rather languid, and suppose that will last until I am on my food again. I wish I could go right to the boat and so home, so does Terry. We aren't up to much travelling and will have to take it slowly. Only I'm hungry for pictures. I never saw the museum in Munich that has all the machines, either. I had hoped to get a letter from you before I left, but it seems not.—I wonder if you saw Mrs. Boyd again, and what you did about Mrs. Resor.[1] I am thankful you tried that, even though you decided against it. Anyway, she said you were fascinating and I think alas yes all too much. You are my love and my best companion and a thorn in my heart, now.—I miss you in my life, you know I think that I was [with] you practically every day last year. I've been in a bad state about you since I left home, better though since your last letter. It was so funny saying goodbye on 40th street, with all the people passing, so different than I thought it would be.

I don't know why but I like best to think of you going to England to work. Better for you than anywhere else, so I feel. But anywhere is as good as anywhere else I guess, so long as you have the book in your head. I am glad you are still good friends with Olin. He is a fine person and very rare, and worth treasuring. Write to me please. I long for you all the time, and long for news from you. What will come from all this pain?—Dearest love[.] Aline

Better write Equitable Trust hereafter, please. I think Vienna about the [5th], c/o Thos Cook. I keep writing the same thing[.]

1. Mrs. Helen Resor was a friend of Mrs. Bernstein's from the J. Walter Thompson Advertising Company. After reading Wolfe's novel, she offered him a job writing advertising copy which he never accepted. She had stipulated that he work a minimum of three years.

59. Paris [Sunday, 24 July 1928]
Dear Aline:

I got another letter from you today by registered mail. They can not come too thick and fast to suit me, but I am excited and distressed by much that you say in them.

In this last letter you had a picture of a heart pierced by seven swords. You saw it somewhere on a priest's surplice. You say your own heart is like that because of me, and one more sword thrust (from me) and you will bleed to death. I think that this is the first time in a letter that you have used your great cleverness of head and hand in a bad way. It was you who first talked to me about being "fancy"—and I think I took your teaching so much to heart that I strive now for absolute plainness[.] If you have not seen from my letters that my love for you dominates every other thing in my life, it has been because you did not want to see.

You know very well that you are in no danger of "bleeding to death" and that you have had a very good time this summer. I wrote you a very long letter a few days after you left New York from which I never received any answer. I did not expect one; I did not believe you would send one. As soon as I wrote you from this side, however, they began to come. I am not reproaching you, my dear, but I do not like to see you go into antics and poses over something that has become to me at least all that my life can hold.

I think you enjoy seeing yourself heroically and tragically, so do I. But this is much too serious a business for me now to enjoy myself in romantic postures. I know how often I've been "snooty" to you; but it is funny now to see you being snooty to me about your letters. You keep asking me if I have them or if I have left them at home. I have a good many of them with me, because I value them and cherish them. You ask me to destroy them. I do not want to, because they are fine and moving letters, written to me at times when our hearts were filled with love and truth, as mine still is.

For the past six or eight years, I have exhausted myself in an effort to know and do everything. The bookstalls along the Seine, the confectioner's stores along the Rue St. Honore, full of preserved fruits and candies and pâtés I could not eat, all the places I had not seen worked me up to a frenzy of despair and hopelessness.

For years I have wasted myself in this way. Now for the first time I am willing to put up boundaries somewhere. I still spend hours before the bookstalls, but I spend more time hunting for one good book than it would take to read a dozen bad ones; I spend most of the time in rejecting the trash. I have a feeling of control and contentment I have never had before. I feel much better because of it.

I must get this letter off. Aline, my heart is full of love for you; you are the only person who has ever possessed my life. I would not do one thing at the present time to cause you any pain, and I have never meant to say or do anything in these letters to cause you any. If there is any power in love to heal and restore, as there is certainly one to forgive, then surely we shall get by all right. You know that you are wrong in finding in my letters that I have given you up or left you:

you must make your peace with yourself on that score, but I shall never give you up out of my heart, because my love will stop only then, when my life stops.

I think I may go to Cologne and down the celebrated Rhine, and then to Munich. I had hoped that if you were at Nurnberg we might not be too far away to see each other. But I want you to enjoy yourself and have a good time. I do not like these places in your letter where you say you go nowhere and see nothing. That is not right, if it is true: surely the good life does not have to be gained except by getting into a nunnery. But I have no doubt your gifted pen gets a little more agile at these places? I am not trying to be mean. I love you, my dear. This would run on interminably if I did not cut it short. Way up on the top floor of the Louvre where few people go, there are the best Degas I've ever seen. Also two grand Cezannes—two men playing cards, and some apples and oranges.[1] Did you ever see them. I went there yesterday.

I wish I could be with you when you escape from starvation. I picture you sitting down at a table groaning with roast goose, sausages, Austrian hams, ponderous cheeses, and cold white wine. Or will you go in for it at once?

I send you all my love, my dear. I know you are beautiful after your cure, since they couldn't destroy in three weeks what had been there before all your life. Tom

1. *The Card Players*, *Still-life*.

60. [Paris, Wednesday, 25 July 1928]

My Dear Aline:

Today I got two or three more letters from you, written at Rapallo, and sent to me from the Harvard Club. Everything you write me excites me; my heart begins to beat louder when I see your pen on an envelope. Your letters are like you with the most astonishing vividness: please thank Terry for her nice little postscript and give her my love.

Where you will get this letter I don't know. I haven't yet decided where to address it—you are through at Karlsbad, you say, July 25th, and you are going on to Vienna. So, perhaps I shall send it there.

I am leaving here tomorrow, I think—for Brussels, I think, and Cologne and the Rhine, and Munchen, I think. But I'll let you know as soon as I do.

I have spent two hours today going up and down the bookstalls on the Seine, and fumbling millions of books, and at length buying one! It is about a man named Julien Benda[1] and his philosophy and writings: he spits on Bergson and is one of the great moderns. It is amazing how much of all that I should care to read and have read already, and what tons and tons of junk there are. It does not do to think too long about it: all those dusty and forgotten books fill me with horror[.]

I went to La Sainte Chapelle today for the first time. My conscience is at rest about it now. It was beautiful and cool, and through a glass I could see the French lawyers in robes and collars walking up and down a long corridor. It made me think of a play by Eugene Brieux[2] and interminable litigation and hairsplitting.

The other night I saw your friends, Alice Lewisohn and her husband, at a restaurant opposite the Luxembourg Gardens. I was the guest of two old maids from New York who teach high school there. Miss Lewisohn's husband has let his hair grow down to his shoulders; he seems to be in training for the part of Jesus Christ at Oberammergau. He stared at me very fiercely and bitterly, and presently they got up and went across the gardens. Her protective coloring is marvellous: she has managed to look like a little French housewife already. But next year, I have no doubt, she will look like a Tyrolese peasant, and the year after a female member of the Sonèt, and the year after like a Thibetan nun. That is the power of the theater.

It continues—hot here, although the terrible heat of a week ago is broken. I have enough of Paris for the present, although I think I have understood the place and seen it in a different color this time. It is not for me—this place. I have never seen anyone who could come here and get more from it than I can, but it is essentially foreign to me. I see it from the outside—it unrolls for me like a great pageant; it is seductive and beautiful, but it will never possess me. The French are the most external people living; I am a secret and lonely person—I need a sense of withdrawal and asylumage that Paris does not give. And I do not think I have ever met an American who seemed to me to have become a better person from being here—there is a great deal that is grand and beautiful here, but the things that seem to control most of them are physical, long eating, drinking, and easy adultery. But life is too stupidly degraded with these things—I am not going to bore myself through the guts and the belly. Also the effort to get at what is good becomes constantly harder—the Louvre is the biggest fraud in the world with perhaps a dozen good pictures in its miles of corridors; the bookstalls have a few good books lost in tons of junk; the whole city is being lost in trash and Rue de Rivoli gimcrackery[.]

Thursday, 3:30 A.M.

Dear Aline:

I have walked this city for 15 hours today and tonight and have come home to get a few hours sleep before I go away. I am going to Brussels today, and possibly from there to Holland. I have left Munich as my address—Amthseches Bayerisches Reiseburo, Promenadsplatz, 16—or some other horrible name close to that. So if you get a chance to write me, send your letters there. I do not know now exactly when I shall be there, but I shall get no more mail until I get there.

I got your long letter today; it gave me the shakes when I saw it as all the others do. The time for your sailing is very close, and you are going to several places—including Vienna—and I shall not be able to see you before you go back. The thought of this makes me sad—what can I say to you? No matter what I have thought or believed, the feeling has become very clear in my mind that it has been a very grand thing for me to have known you. This is not to say that I think of myself as "a lucky fellow." Sometimes I have imagined your friends as saying contemptuously that I was a lucky fellow, and that I should be grateful for any consideration so great a person as yourself might show me. But it is not lucky to sweat blood. And I do not know what it may mean for my life to have known you. I wish I could believe it might mean some sort of triumph or success—some rich deposit that might add to my value and my power. But I neither believe nor disbelieve this. How can I now, right in the thick web of it? The whole engine of my life mounted to its greatest drive and expenditure when we were together, but whether on this account it will hereafter be in a better engine I can not say[.]

But, my dear Aline, there is a conviction of truth beyond proof and reason. When I have been most bitter about you, my bitterness has always been below my admiration about you—that you were burning in all of heaven like my great star. And you have always burned above my life like that great star—all the rest of it has been like a useless shouting below my great and everlasting star.

I think this is the truth of it.

Thursday / July 26

My dear!

I'm off for Brussels in fifteen minutes. It's hot as hell and I'm in a dreadful hurry. I am sending this to Cook's at Vienna—please write me at Munich. God bless you, my dear. I love you with all my life. Have a good time with your companions—but think of me. I love you, my dear.

Will write from Brussels. Tom

1. French philosophical writer and novelist, defender of reason and intellect against romanticism and the cult of emotion.

2. French dramatist whose social comedies were dedicated to the welfare of the poor, women, and children.

61. Brussels / Hotel Des Boulevards / Friday [27 July 1928]
Dear Aline:

I came up here yesterday from Paris—It was all very strange and swift. I came on a fast train in three and a half hours. Then here I was in another country and another city. I sent you a letter five minutes before I left—I hope the hotel people can be trusted to mail it, and that you got it, and this one, in Vienna. I spent twelve or fifteen hours a day out of doors in Paris; I looked at hundreds and thousands of books and bought a few.

I roamed around in a great many places I had not been before. Then I came here.

This city is like Paris in many ways—and tries hard to be. There is an immense fat looking Palace of Justice on a high place overlooking the town, and broad streets, and avenues leading up to it. There are the parks and boulevards and innumerable cafes—all very French. In many respects the place is more luxurious and elegant than Paris. But the people are heavier than the French—they have the Flemish phlegm; they are a rather surly lot, and I feel something ignoble and mean in them as I did about the Czecks. They stay up until all hours, and are very gay—there are hundreds of luxurious wine shops, beautifully decorated with polished wood. People sit in these places and drink champagne at less than fifteen cents a goblet. They have prohibition here too—you have to get along on all sorts of wine, beer and champagne. If you want stronger stuff, you must go to a store and buy at least two quarts. That's the right idea, isn't it?

To prove that I am not yet an old soak I'll tell you that I have not been within miles of being soaked. My customary beverage is beer—I drink six or eight glasses a day. The swelling heat continues. I had hoped it would be better here, but Brussels is as hot as Paris. The country is dry and dusty—there has been no rain for a month: today rain fell for five minutes—I was ready to rush out and worship it, but it stopped. I have been thinking that really good weather is one of the rarest things in the world. Certainly man has not been well adapted to his universe—he has to struggle and suffer most of the time. For weeks now I have seen thousands of people in real distress because of the heat; in winter we are grateful for an occasional day when the sun shines and we do not feel the cold too much—perhaps in a year there are two dozen days when we are at ease with the weather. And if we find so many when we are at ease with the world, our work, and ourselves, we can count ourselves lucky.

I wish I believed in struggle more—in its power to ennoble or strengthen us. But I do not—and I struggle all the time. But I believe that what is at the bottom of my constant torment is a belief that I have always had that men ought to be happy—that there ought to be 200 perfect days instead of 20, and that we ought to get gloriously ahead with our work most of the time, moving with perfect rhythm, and filled with a deep and tranquil joy. People glibly remark that such a life would bore them to death, but they are only being foolish and smart. For my part, I think it would be rich and magnificent. Therefore—to find deep tranquil joy, I keep on cursing, and casting about the world like a madman, still believing in a harbor somewhere, enough rain, enough shine, good men, the good life. Few people could probably give the right answer to this search as well as I could—but I keep on. I have more faith than I had as a child—when I believed that anything strange and rare could happen. I do not think life teaches us anything; it leaves a deposit which becomes a part of us and which we use. But nothing is more false than the belief that the idealist loses his ideals—he becomes more fanatic, and the more mad he sees the world the more does he believe in the Elysean Fields.

I have almost reached the summit of my egotism—I have determined recently that it is not I who am bored, it is the world. Every day now I see a few things which give me a sense of joy and life, but they are sprinkled in among all the stupid weariness of the world.

Saturday

Today, thank God, it rained and rained, and the sky was gloriously grey, and it has made very much more fresh since—if you understand my fluent French idiom. I meant to get this off to you this morning, but I went back to see the pictures and walked all around in the beautiful upper part of town. It is late Saturday night; I am writing this from the veranda of a wine shop—you have never seen such a place as this town. They do not have a single café here and there—there are blocks of them, one right next to the other—all very elegant and very gay. The people dress well—there seems to be no lack of moving around. As I told you the museum is very limited but there are some of the best early Flemish and Dutch pictures I have ever seen—grand things by Memling and Dirk Bouts, and Breughel, and Cranach.[1]

There are some things and places in Belgium I should like to see —Louvain and Antwerp again, and perhaps Ypres. I shall be here in Brussels several more days. I hope this gets to you in Vienna in time for you to write me here. I did not expect any mail here and told them in Paris to send everything on to Munich, but there's an *American Express Co.* office here, and if you get a chance to write, please do. I would not miss any of your letters for a great deal, but if I am not here, it will be sent on to me.

In your letters I think you talk a great deal more of love than I do in mine. I feel that I am always bringing in other things—what I have observed, or felt, or thought, or what has interested me in a great many ways. And when I read the letters over later I am sorry for this; I wish I had talked to you about love more, for I feel that as regards me you are interested in that alone. You know so many people with greater talents and better intelligence than mine; and I know that I can say very little about anything that will be interesting and original to you. Your own feelings towards things are usually softer and finer than mine, and no one knows better than I do how much cleverer you are than me. Yet I bring all sorts of things into my letters because I used always to dream of a life with you in which all this would figure, and even now I am always a little ashamed when I have said again and again that I love you. You can say it, and it is always fresh and interesting when you say it, for you have the power to say it in a thousand ways[.] But I lack that power. I used to feel that love was part of my life—or that very life and all the million things that went boiling through my brain was part of love. I have never been able to cut them apart as you have your life, your many activities, your relations with other people, and your feeling for me. And I think a great deal of our trouble has come from that.

When I got your letter telling me of your plans for the remainder of your vacation and asking me to write you to the boat I was made very sad. I think I had always expected more or less to see you somewhere, and to have a few days with you. It is part of my temper to postpone pain and a final decision as long as possible. With your more practical and decisive nature you have foreseen this, and you have taken things out of my hands here at last. I suppose you are right—we must not see each other now; but I assure you that you can never be more eager to meet again in terms of loving friendship than I am.

I suppose I may never again give my heart away so freely, for we learn caution out of pain and fear; and I can never give away to anyone else what you already have.

I love you, my dear, with all my life and breath and being—my love for you is not washed free from pain, but it is almost washed free from bitterness and rancour. I am wandering alone like a phantom in strange cities; my heart is full of loneliness—in loneliness of soul I walk along the streets, but I think and dream great things, my eyes and face are calm and good; I am beginning again to be the person I can be. God bless you, my dear[.] Tom

1. Wolfe is most probably referring to the Musée des Beaux Arts d'Ixelles, which contains *The Martyrdom of St. Sebastian* by Hans Memling (1440–1494), noted religious painter. Two imposing large panels by Flemish painter Dirk Bouts (1415–75) are also housed here. Cranach, Lucas the Elder (1472–1556), was noted for his early paintings of nudes, which Wolfe greatly admired.

62. [Munich] Hotel Vier Jarelzecten / July 29, 1928

I prevailed upon my friends to come here. Terry & I have a room with bath like a skating rink, for no more than 2 separate ones.

My dear,

I have seen many beautiful things these past three days, and unfortunately without you. I know every thing would be twice as fine if you were sharing it. I mailed you a post card from a town near Nürnberg called Rothenburg. It is the loveliest place you can imagine, one of the few places of its age that seems to be still alive and remarkably intact. Of course, too many shops with picture cards, but the buildings and shape of the town [are] perfect. I heard the finest choral singing there, it so happened that there has been a song fest in Vienna, and the choral society from Wiesbaden was on its way home. They were having a jolly tour back, it seemed, and stopped on the steps of the Rathaus to express themselves. Big pot bellied store keepers, some little thin ones, and a great hulk of a man leading. But it was like a magnificent orchestra, what a superb time they had. Can you imagine the butcher, the baker and candle stick maker from Yonkers getting up and opening their hearts in song! I am sorry we missed the event in Vienna.—I was met in Nürenberg with disturbing news. Theo has sold our house, and I found the sale contract there awaiting my signature. We are practically forced to sell, as a company has bought all the ground from the corner up, and we would be surrounded or embedded in a flat house. I think that we need not move out until May, unless we find a place to live before that. I felt very much broken up, you know I love that house and it will be difficult to find another place with so much room. Well, there are worse things, but every minute I think of another reason for not wanting to go. And can you imagine the task of moving that huge place. What between longing for you and news of the house, I had a bad time for a while, until I got over to see the Dürers and then the house part moved way off to another place but you stayed with me. I kept thinking of this "Then glut thy sorrow on the morning rose."[1] I don't remember the rest of it or the beginning, is it Keats, professor? You know I am a poor scholar, but a fond heart.—Maurice Wertheim's eldest girl Josephine is here, she is waiting for me, we are going to the Pinakothek. I'll write more this afternoon.

—We didn't go there, went to the Deutches Museum instead, the one with all the machinery. It is the most remarkable place I have ever seen, where did they get all the money to do it. And when I saw it I couldn't imagine why they didn't win the war. We went through 115 rooms of the 400, and passed out completely. Phil is lost somewhere, hasn't turned up but we expect him in a day or so. Theo's lawyer who is also my cousin, motored down here from Nürnberg with us. We took several hours to go through what is called the Franconian Alps[,] very gentle and lovely and stopped at Begreuth. A sentimental journey as we did not stay for music. But we were fortunate enough to get into Wagner's house, I could tell you so much better than write you about it. It is a great ugly house, beautiful with comfort and evidences of life, enormous rooms and the heaviest stuffed furniture, I thought I could not be sentimental but found a catch in my throat when I saw his composing desk. The family live there still, his little grandson showed us round. The drive down was lovely, very rich farm country, and so neat. We are waiting here to get in touch with Phil, he is somewhere in the Dolomites, and that will bring us late to Vienna. Tom dear I will not hear from you, and I want to know where you are. It is very hard for me to be in all these places we visited together, the man who is manager here asked for you. I find it irksome to be with people most of the time now, except Terry. Josephine Wertheim has 2 girls with her and a teacher, and they eat with us and it nearly drives me crazy. It takes hours to get a meal ordered, so tonight Terry and I excused ourselves and ate alone, here in the hotel. Let me tell you it is the finest eating in Munich, I am so sorry we never ate here together. We had a trout saute with butter, broiled tomatoes, and a pineapple souffle—and it was the first meal I have enjoyed. I am sure my Carlsbad bloom will wear off before I see you. Please Tom, if you do not receive answers to letters or telegrams it is only because I am not in touch with mail. I will have mail at Vienna and then not until Berlin, a few days before going home. I want to fly, and may be will go from Vienna by plane to Prague if the others want to go there. I hate to go again. It will be a relief to be home again, I have been away long enough, without you. I could stay away with you indefinitely. I am hoping for news that you have started your book. I just figured out with Terry that we will be in Vienna the 3rd or 4th. Instead of the first. If you receive this in time will you telegraph me there, [c/o] Thos. Cook? It would make me feel good to hear so nearly from you, if only one or two words. I love you so, and I am trying my best not to bother you, but also to let you know how dearly [I love you]. You are always with me.

Yours Aline

Terry sends you her best love, and says she is crazy about Germany.

1. Keats, *Ode on Melancholy*, ii, 1.5: "Then glut thy Sorrow on a morning rose."

63. Brussels / Hotel Des Boulevards / Tuesday / July 31, 1928
Dear Aline:

I have sent two long letters—this is the third—and several postal cards to Thomas Cook's in Vienna, but since I do not know when you will be there, the only address I can be sure of is the *Reliance* on August 14. You will certainly find a letter from me there, and perhaps several. I had hoped you would get my letters in time to write or wire me to the American Express Company here in Brussels, but there has been nothing yet. But I still hope to hear from you.

I wanted to go to Vienna too, but I heard there is an enormous Kulturmusikgesellschaftpreiswertgesundheitgemutlichvolkspieler-festung[1] there, as well as certain people I do not want to see again; so I have postponed my going until Schnitzler, Wassermann, and the rest of my compeers come back to town.

Some strange power in Brussels always lures me into rubber-necking buses. The last time I rode out to Waterloo with James Joyce and his family; today I was gnawn with curiosity to see some American tourists on the hoof—I jumped into another just as it started off on a tour of the city. The guide indicated all of the good things—such as the museum where the good paintings are—with a flourish of his hand as we rolled past, and took us to see all the things he thought American tourists would like to see—a piece of concrete where Nurse Cavell[2] was executed, the equestrian statue of King Leopold, the Nigger Torturer, the City Hall—the famous mayor, who defied the Germans and was imprisoned for four years in Germany, came up the stairs bowing to our applause, and the fountain of the Pissing Mannikin, which is the huge national joke here—a little naked boy who squirts water into a basin through his You-Know-What. After having thus seen the treasures of Belgian civilization, we brought up before a lace shop where the women went in and were swindled out of four prices. That's one way of seeing Europe, isn't it? They were a tired and dejected lot, and refused to get out of the bus at half the stops.

I hoped to see parts of the city I had not seen before—and I did. We went through miles of new and ugly suburbs on our way to the armory and shooting range where Cavell was executed, and we came back by a place called "The Crazy Museum" which is the weirdest place you ever saw. It has in it the paintings of a crazy man named Wertz[3]—as a painter he was a tenth rate Rubens, but as a maniac he has a throne of his own. There are forty foot canvases showing a man buried alive trying to force open his coffin; and one called *Hunger* showing an insane mother dismembering her baby and putting the parts in a stew pot.

Wednesday Morning / August 1

Dear Aline

I am finishing this and sending it on to Vienna today. It is the last letter I shall send you there as I can not at all acertain you will receive them. When I write you again I shall send the letter to your ship.

I hope you have had a good and interesting trip and [have] seen a great many of the things you wanted to see. I suppose you are looking forward to your return to New York where you will have several shows to do. You are fortunate in having work which satisfies you so completely, and in which you are so successful.

I have begun to do some work the last few days—I do not know where I shall go from here, but probably to Germany. There are two or three places in Belgium I should like to see—Louvain and Antwerp—which I have already visited—but distances are so short here, I can leave my things in Brussels and get to any of them within an hour or two.

I shall keep on writing to you, and I hope letters from you are accumulating for me in Munich, but I have no idea when I shall get there. I am more or less cut away from the world and hope it will have some medicinal effect on me, and put me to work again.

I am dried up this morning and have no more to say to you. I love you and hope you will find happiness and satisfaction somewhere. I will never forget you, and no one else will hold the place in my life that you have held. Tom

1. A "wholesome, hearty cultural and musical folk festival."

2. Edith Cavell, English nurse who became a popular heroine of World War I and was executed for assisting Allied soldiers in their escape from German-occupied Belgium.

3. Antoine Joseph Wertz (1806–65), an artist of great power and individuality, preoccupied in his paintings with the horrible, the grotesque, and the fantastic. In 1850 the government of Brussels built him a large studio, known as the Musée Wertz, which housed his collected works.

64. Vienna / Hotel Sacher / August 4, 1928

My Dear:

We arrived in Vienna at 10 minutes to six yesterday, and I dashed immediately to Thos. Cook, and there found all your letters and cards. I sent two telegrams, one to Munich and one to Brussels. I don't know whether you want to take a long journey to meet me, in fact I thought you did not want to see me, you said so many times in New York, other wise [I] would have suggested it and made it possible. I wonder if you remember how many times you told me that I must not try to see you this summer. I love you enormously, and think of you many hours during the day and the night. I must send you this letter now, as there is just a small chance of its reaching you in Brussels.—I thought I explained in my letters that we were going various places before coming to Vienna. We stayed 2 days in the mountains, which delayed our coming here until the 3rd—I'm writing you a long letter to Munich[.]

My Dearest love[,] Aline

We go to Prague Tuesday, and from there expect to fly to Berlin. It takes about two hours I think. I've never been up in a plane. Haven't time for Dresden.

65. Vienna / Hotel Sacher / August 6 or 5, 1928

My Dear:

I am afraid that the telegram I sent you to Brussels came too late. If we only had been here on schedule. I would have caught you. I sent you a short note also, which I hope you will get in Munich. But we were delayed waiting for Phil, and then stayed some extra time in the mountains. I wrote you a card each day, it was almost impossible to write letters, as we motored about 8 hrs a day, and I was dead tired in the evening. I must tell you all the lovely places, we first went through the Bavarian Alps, then The Tyrol, (overnight at Innsbruch). Then through the Bechtesfaten region, which is very beautiful and lunched at a place called Königsee, and took a boat round the lake. Unfortunately too many tourists, but fine. Then back into Austria and stopped for tea at Reinhardt's Schloss[1] in Salzburg. It was very entertaining there, the house remarkably grand and theatrical, exquisitely furnished and kept, and the grounds pretty with all sorts of strange fowl, cranes, flamingos etc. Not unlike Schonnbrun,[2] but small delicate and a little more French. Reinhardt was away, but his assistant did the honors and showed us around. We were frightfully dusty and mussed from travel, and I felt like a lump of coal, in the tea room which was painted shell pink with lovely gray green fat German-French furniture and masses of pink poppies all over the room. We had a meagre tea, though, and the Theatre Guild contingent decided to eat on the road thereafter. Then we drove through a glorious region called the Salz Kammer Gut, an extension of the Tyrol, but much more beautiful, with lakes much like our dear English ones where we were so happy. We reached Isch about 9 P.M. and stayed the next day and night. Terry and I were very tired. My eyes were bad from so much dust and wind. It seems that Maurice used to spend his childhood summers there, and caught his first trout. So he went off on a sentimental trip, tracing the streams where he had been with his father, and altogether having a pleasant time. He caught one trout which everyone forgot to eat. The place is charming, so green and sweet. If you have chance you must try that region. Next day, all day on the road and here in Vienna, I was so afraid Cooks would be closed, that I urged the driver on the last ½ hour. I must say that it took me a great while to read your letters, your writing is terrible, and I wanted to get every word. I room with Terry and it is not easy reading them with some one else around. My dear, you always move me and touch me so deeply. I had no idea you wanted to see me this summer. You kept telling me all spring that I must make no attempt to see you, no demands, and that I must not beat you down. I wonder if you forget all these things, even the very last day in New York you told me as much. And then we finally said goodby on 7th Ave and 40th St. So strange. I love you more and more, my longing for you grows. I wonder that the strength of it does not pull you like a magnet. I am beautified by your love, and my hope is that it will bring you back to me. I want you to be not only my friend but my lover, friends cannot stay for hours in each others arms. I have prevailed on my friends to come to the same places where we stayed, you may think that strange but it has satisfied me. They seem to like it, and I feel you, I think something of you has remained in each place. Yesterday morning Phil and I went out together and spent the morning at the big museum. The Breughels are thrilling, and I spent a lot of time with the other pictures. In the afternoon we all took a sightseeing bus, and really saw everything of the outside of the city, for nearly 4 hours. Among other things went to the great suburb called Grisling, which is a mass of wine restaurants, and very pretty, and out to the Vienna Wald. It seems to me we wanted to do that, but never reached it. I have bought two little wooden angels to hang over my bed, Gothic ones, with sweet stupid faces and lovely dresses. They took my last penny and I have to borrow from Maurice till I get back. Terry also is broke, as our cure in Carlsbad was very expensive. I could cable home but do not like to, and our trip has been expensive too. I will be alright when I get home, and if you need something, let me know. I start work immediately for 14th street[3] but they are slow to pay. I have about 3 or 400 in bank in N.Y. left over from The Follies. It seems to me that in every letter I send you a complete schedule of our movements. I wonder if you skip that part. We go from here to Prague, fly from there to Berlin and expect to arrive the 10th and have to go to Hamburg the 12th in order to spend a day there and embark on the 14th. I wish you would tell me where to write you after I leave. And Tom dear, don't be angry, but please settle down and work some where. You have been drifting around. You've been going about now for two full months since school closed, as you say seeking something, which you will never find except in yourself and your work. This is your chance, write your book, pin yourself down to it. I know it makes you angry when I talk to you this way, but it is the only way to do, the longer I live the more I am convinced. You can't go on indefinitely with no obligations. You have freedom from everything for the present and you never know how long that may last.—The world keeps turning, and each turn brings with it another set of circumstances. You have a great gift, for God's sake use it. And you must not write to me again that you think I am more great or clever than you, for that is not true. You have by far the greatest gift, I maybe have more balance and a little wisdom from living.—Write me a lot, my dear, every thing you write is beautiful to me. I am so afraid you may miss me if you come to Berlin. If we can't get rooms at Hotel Adlon I will leave word where we are[,] also telegraph you. If you come inquire very carefully if we are not at that hotel. I am your true love, devoted and true. Aline

I'm going to the Lichtenstein now to see the other Breughels[4]—I'll look at them twice, once for you.

1. Castle of internationally famous Viennese director Max Reinhardt (1873–1943). Reinhardt, one of three founders of the Salzburg Festival, made his home a meeting place for international celebrities, until he was forced to flee to the U.S. in 1938 because of his Jewish heritage.

2. Schönbrunn Palace in Austria, designed by the great Austrian architect von Erlach and noted for its rococo interior decoration.

3. The Civic Repertory Theatre was located at 105 W. 14th Street.

4. The Liechtenstein Museum contains, among other Breughel paintings, *St. John Preaching*, *Dance of Death*, and *The Blind Leading the Blind.*

66. Brussels [9 August 1928]

Dear Aline:

I am beginning this letter to you tonight which I shall add to from time to time, and send to you on the boat at Hamburg. I still remain in Brussels, but I shall probably leave here in a day or so. I may go to Antwerp for a day to see the pictures, stopping off at Malines which is on the way. Then I think I shall go into Germany.

I have had no answer to the three letters and several postcards I sent to Vienna; so I shall not try there again. I hope they are sent on to you before you sail. Also, I hope you feel much better since your

Karlsbad cure, and are beginning to eat heartily again. I not only suffer acutely when I'm unable to eat, but when those who are dear to me are also unable to eat. Your letters from Karlsbad were drenched with so much sweetness and light and with such a sense of spiritual rarification that I can well believe you when you say that after your long fast you felt as if you were floating along. But I suppose a few good smells into the fleshpots since may have materialized you a little and made you a little more like common mortals. It will not do to get too close to heaven right in the rich prime of your life: the world is a very sinful place although you of course have never had a chance of finding this out—and it is just as well to know a little of what's going on. As for me I have known a number of saints, several dozen martyrs, and thousands of honorable men and women, all of them good talkers. But I have become too coarse grained to appreciate this nobility: I go around patiently looking for people with limited vocabularies, very few gestures, and flat monotonous voices, who have no beautiful thoughts of any sort, but who will not chat with you, betray you, or lie to you. Thus far, I have not found many, but China, Russia, India, and the entire continent of Africa remain unvisited.

Cologne

(I have read this last page over and found it bitter. It was foolish of me to have written it, but I assure you that at the time it was written it was more of a general observation than a personal one. These fits come only rarely to me now—*I love you* and I no longer want to say anything to trouble you.)

Several weeks ago I read in the paper that a woman had rushed up to the king of England while he was on horseback in Hyde Park, fell on her knees before him and asked him to do something to relieve the condition of the miners in Wales. The report said that the woman had been placed under arrest and was being examined for insanity. I have been thinking this over for some time now and still I can make nothing out of it. It seems to me to be one of the strangest things I ever read.

I went to Louvain today—it is a town that was completely destroyed by the Germans and has been completely rebuilt, house for house. It is an amazing piece of reconstruction—the houses are new, raw, and ugly—but very solid and prosperous looking. I also went through the new library—the one that has been built with American money, and that has caused so much trouble recently because of the quarrel between Warren, the American architect,[1] and the priests over the disputed inscription—"Destroyed by German fury; rebuilt by American generosity." For my part, I side with the priests. I think the inscription is full of hate and brag; and the building already looks to me as if we have made them pay us penny for penny in advertising our charity. Almost every stone is carved with the name of an American college, university, or society—there is much too much of it. The library itself is a good building—an attempt to imitate the old Flemish, and about as successful, I judge, as our best modern attempts at home to copy the old Revolutionary houses; but the reading and studying arrangements are magnificent—the best I ever saw.

Sunday Night

Dear Aline—

I have at length had enough of Brussels—I have walked and explored for hours today until a great weariness of body and soul has descended on me. But I saw one thing today of enormous interest—the Socialist and Communist parties of Europe are having a convention here during this next week: they had their opening parade today. I read very little of it in the French and Belgian papers—they said as little about it as possible, and one respectable Paris paper—Le Martin—said this morning "about 600" delegates were expected, 600! At one o'clock today people began to line the Boulevards Max and Auspoch; at two o'clock the parade began. In all my life I have never seen a more tremendous or impressive exhibition. The parade marched by in massed groups for more than two hours —there were at least fifty or one hundred thousand marchers, and two or three hundred thousand were looking on. They were here from all countries—big, bullet headed Germans, Czecks, Frenchmen, Dutchmen, Belgians, Flemish-men. And the staging of it made Rheinhardt look childish—it built up to the most thrilling and dramatic climax I have ever seen. The parade started with several workmen carrying enormous banners on horseback; the horses were powerful slowfooted truckhorse[s], and I cannot describe the effect to you of these great laborious animals walking slowly by among massed lines of people. Then came thousands and thousands of people by regiments—young men in gymnastic costumes, little girls in white blouses and blue dresses, little boys with red berets on their heads, miners in wooden shoes and overalls, the Czecks in red blouses—each preceded by his banner. You got an overwhelming sense of organization that began at the cradle and extended to the grave—in addition to the regiments of children, there were feeble old men and women, peasants, laborers, and just the terrible poor. And there were bands and fife and bugle corps by the dozen. The batallions went by singing the Internationale;[2] the crowds at the side cheered, the big bullet headed Germans and the Czecks threw up their arms stiffly and shouted Hock.[3] This went on until I was worn out by the magnitude and number of the thing. Then, after almost two hours had passed there began a spectacle I shall never forget—Advancing down the street was a forest of great banners of red silk—they came eight abreast, and there was over a mile of them. The brilliance and magnificence of this can not be put on paper—it was like a new Crusade, richer and vaster than any of the old ones. That forest of red waving and undulating slowly overpowered everything else—as they began to come by, I could see that each banner was inscribed with a different device—the metal workers of Lille, the students' gymnastic society of Antwerp, the miners of Mons, and so on. The final smashing effect of these banners—their number, and the message they bore of infinite and complex organization—was terrific. You felt that at last all the poor, the weak, the entire under half of the earth had been drawn together in a powerful disciplined organization, and that their power now was irresistible.

Cologne / Thursday Morning

Dear Aline:—

I came up here at night before last after the most weird adventure at dead of night through Northern Belgium in an effort to find a room and a bed to sleep in. I went to Antwerp Monday—I wanted to spend a day there and see the pictures again. When I got there[,] there was not a room to be had in the city. I walked countless miles —down to the docks and through the old narrow streets of the town. Night came on; the streets were swarming with people—all of them, I suppose, with rooms. It began to be a nightmare. I was only thirty five minutes from Brussels, but it was another room. For blocks around the station there were nothing but cafes and hotels; there were dozens of little wine shops and taverns—really brothels—closed in, all full of people. There were enormous dance halls with floor[s] half an acre wide swarming with hundreds of couples—soldiers and his [sic] bags and clerks with their girls. You got in for a franc. There were millions of little shops all crowded with sausages, books, pastries, neckties and so on. And billions of people—as infinite in number as only small quick people with dark skins know how to be. All this I took in and went bedhunting again. Midnight came, the terrible racket in the streets seemed to increase—I had no bed. At twelve forty I clambered into a little train with my baggage and went tearing through the dark of Flanders to the little town of Maelines—half way back to Brussels. I got there at one o'clock and found two thugs with a dilapidated taxi who took me through dark and foul alleys for the next half hour stopping at the most villainous looking places to ask for a room. One or two I refused; several more we could not rouse: we finally drew up near the station again in front of a dirty little drink shop closed for the night. After hammering and pounding we roused a dirty looking man with a smutty beard on the top floor—up four flights of sagging stairs—and put me into a foul room with a bed which stank from its dirty covers. But I was tired and wanted rest—I had walked twenty miles that day—I locked the door and tried it, pulled off my clothes and lay down on top of the bed—I was not going between those leprous sheets. Then the three villains began to talk next door—the man and his two mates, waiters or barmen probably in his cafe. The partition between was like paper; they began to talk in low mutters, then more rapidly and loudly as they grew excited. I heard him say he had asked me 15 francs for the room, and was a great fool not to have asked "the English man" for thirty. Then they began to whisper, then to talk loudly again, then to whisper. Then they became comically quiet; I got my big stick you bought for me in London, and kept it beside me on the bed; I took my number 13 shoe and put it on a chair ready to the other hand. I waited. The lights in the square about the station came through the window at my head and printed the iron grill work of a little false balcony upon the door at my feet. I could see everything very plainly. I lay there quietly and waited. A little after three in the morning they tried it. One of them got very quietly on the floor, which creaked terribly, opened his door, and came outside mine. Then in the light from the square I saw my door knob move very gently. I jumped to the floor with the most blood curdling yell you ever heard, and I let drive for the door with my shoe. It made a terrific noise; I suppose they thought the Huns were upon them again. He was back in his room like a shot again, and they were all talking together in great excitement. To make [assurance?] doubly sure I began to sing and talk loudly to myself, striking against the wall from time to time, with the cane and bursting into sudden fits of insane laughter. Then the little trains began to scream and puff and to slot the funny little freight cars about on the tracks 50 yards away, and a couple of express trains from Brussels roared past, and the square began to fill up with people and wagons, and morning came. I knew I was alright then; so I lay down upon my foul cot and went to sleep. I came back to Brussels at noon, went to Amexco to see if there were any surprise letters or messages, ate, collected the rest of my baggage, and left for Germany at [2:50?]. It seemed when I got here that I have a talent for picking the damndest times and the damndest places. I forgot to tell you that the trouble in Antwerp was caused by a convention of Esperantists[4]—from everywhere! And you never heard such a Babel of Tongues! And here there is an enormous convention of—I believe—The Press. No rooms again; I spent the night with a German worker's family, but this time—you can be sure —between clean sheets. And yesterday morning I was early up to find a hotel room, and a bath, and solidity once more. I found several, and I am established at this place—a modest middle class sort of place, but beautifully clean, and efficient, and orderly. I have a charming room for about $1.50 a day. Why is it—for all the talk of infallible French taste, the German coarseness—that these people at least can furnish a hotel room with wallpaper and bedding that does not look like Suite *A* in a whore house?—

Here I am again among the Heinies. The solidity and heaviness of everything after France and Belgium is startling; these people are very grand and great, and very brutal. I was looking at them last night in a café, while they swilled beer and listened to a ponderous orchestra playing Beethoven. The men have large massive heads, big browed and deep, capable of great creation. And then below all this, the hog jowls; the little beery eyes, the shaven necks, the pendulous bellies. It seems to me one of the most tragic things I have ever seen—this union of the brute and the god. It was not the French, the English, the Americans who brought these people to defeat and ruin—it was themselves: their music and literature shows to what spiritual heights they can go—so much of the rest of it how hopelessly they are wired. I always get frightened about Food when I come here—and you know how great a *scare* that must be. When I watch them at their food—those terrifying and unbelievable dishes—I had one the other night—in which one devours eight portions of different meats and sausages, it seemed to me that they are being devoured by a raving monster—a terrible disease of the gut which will never have enough.

As for Cologne—so much of it is new, solid, heavy. Their new wealth and power shows itself everywhere. I went around in a bus—you can see where my pride's gone—the suburbs are filled with huge brick and stone houses, with lawns and trees, which the guide points out as the homes of Schultz, the banker, Oppenheimer, the chocolate manufacturer; and so on. It is in a startling fashion like America, and these people, in a great number of ways are the people we are most like. I have not been to the exposition—but with German thoroughness they have built huge Austellungen buildings across the Rhine. In the modern manner. I think the cathedral is magnificent—as for me I have never cared so much for the walls and carving of a cathedral as for the *space* it encloses. I understand immaterial architecture better than material. And the space here is glorious—soaring and sombre, and full of noble joy.

My dear, this letter has only things and events in it. I got your telegram before I went to Antwerp; I decided to write you in Berlin, and to send you another letter to the boat which will be more about us. I earnestly wanted to see you this summer, but your plans as you described them before leaving Karlsbad did not permit it, and I knew you were right in saying this was no time for us to see each other again. I have thought about Berlin a great deal, and I have decided not to go there. To see you for three days in a new and strange place before you sailed would be too hard and too unsatisfactory. Its effect on me would be explosive—I am at length achieving a kind of peace and certainty, and I have faith and confidence in a day when we can meet again in terms of loving friendship. I have just finished reading a very terrible and moving book by Octave Mirbeau called *Le Calvaire*—which must have been in a large measure autobiographical. The situation is so shockingly like my own, and the madness and desperation to which it drives the unhappy man so real that I have not yet fully recovered from it. I am sorry that in one place in this letter I had a streak of bitterness. That is almost all gone now, and I believe will go entirely. I would have destroyed that part and rewritten the letter, had it not been that I should have destroyed other things too, and I wanted to get this off to you. But please remember that my total feeling, and my present feeling is one of infinite love. You are beautiful and you are good—no one will ever take the place in my life that you have taken. I want you to be happy in your work that you are going back to, and in any other arrangements you may make for your happiness.

There is not much more that I can say here—I will try to say it more completely and briefly in my letter to the boat. I love you; my life was so torn to pieces because of my feeling that I was losing power for any single act. I know you will hope with me that I succeed in focusing and collecting myself again.

I know you must be rested and strong after this summer—I wish I could be there to see the first beautiful play I know you are going to do.

I shall stay here, I think, only a day or two. If you have time send me a line or two to Thomas Cook and Son. There is no Amexco here. I hope you get this in Berlin. God bless you, Aline. I love you with all my heart. Tom

1. Whitney Warren, of the prestigious New York-based architectural firm of Warren and Wetmore. In addition to membership in several European artistic societies, Warren was a member of the Ecole des Beaux Arts in Paris. He was a hero in World War I, receiving the French military medal in 1918. He was selected in November 1920 to restore Louvain University and in April 1921 announced his plan to restore Louvain Library.

2. Theme song of the International Working Union of Socialist Parties, also known as the Vienna Union. The Internationale was closely associated with the International Federation of Trade Unions. Strongly against fascism, they advocated increasing the power of the working class throughout the world.

3. A cheer or toast.

4. In August 1928, the annual World Esperanto Congress met in Antwerp. Esperanto is an artificial language created by Ludwik Zamenhof in 1887. Still in existence, it was intended for use as an international second language.

67. Praha[1] / Esplanade-Hotel / August 10, 1928
My Dear:

I left Vienna yesterday morning with the same regret we felt last year. It is a lovely city, and every place I went spoke to me of you. I went twice to the big picture gallery and once to the Liechtenstein, which looked finer than before. And there is an exhibition of Dürer drawings at The Albertina that is one of the finest things I ever saw. You must go if for no other reason, although Vienna itself is reason enough. All the same waiters and page boys are at the Sacher, and all remembered me, which is always flattering. Our party were crazy about the hotel, I was afraid it wasn't Ritzy enough for Wertheim, but he liked it best of any hotel he ever lived in. Terry and I had a palatial room with a bath and foyer hall, for less than $6 a day which is very reasonable divided. I missed you all the time. I think of you constantly and share all the beauties with you. In fact it seemed to me as though I was bound to see you there, and looked every where for you. There is no one in the world like you and I adore you.—Prague is a disappointment, don't you think? I dislike it here very much and cannot find a bit of happiness in the city. Do you remember that we were not on good terms when we were here? Maybe that is why I felt so miserable all day, and will be glad when tomorrow comes. We leave at 9:30 to go to the flying field. I am very much excited about going up. The chances are I will be very ill, as it is much rougher than ship travel, all people tell me. I am thinking of course that I may see you in Berlin. I felt sorry that I telegraphed you to come, as I fear you do not want to and it will take you away from the places you want to go. Also I think it will make it very difficult for both of us to meet for so short a time. We are having difficulty reserving rooms there. Maurice even telephoned in his lordly way today.—I know you are sober by the tone of your letters. They are such beautiful letters and give me so much comfort, as well as pain. I have been absolutely sober, two beers in Munich and two cocktails at the Sacher bar is all the drink I've had, and I have no desire for any, also very little desire for food. I eat one good meal a day, usually lunch, and a boiled egg and tea generally for evening meal, occasionally reversed. I think that starvation cure made the stomach smaller: I've put on a little flesh, naturally. It is terrible that you did not see me when I looked so nice. But I still look so much better than I did with my round belly, and my face looks so much smoother and less harassed. But I fear that when I get home to my own table I will begin to eat again. It is difficult to refrain when things are set before you. If we do not meet before I sail, I wonder when we will. I feel sad and blue tonight, I will send a telegram to Munich before sailing. Please dear, where am I to write you? Let me know immediately. Do you know I've written something to you every day, if only a card. I love you so.— Aline

1. Prague.

68. Berlin / Hotel Esplanade [11 August 1928]
My Dear:

We arrived yesterday, could not get rooms at Adlon Hotel, a nasty place anyway, and came here which is lovely.—Your letter came here, I was so afraid you would come to the Adlon and miss me that I bribed every official and flunkey in the place, so when I came in at lunch time I found a boy waiting with your letter. I had been hoping so desperately that you would come although I knew it would be very difficult for both of us, and very disquieting. I am in a constant agony of longing for you, and it seems so strange to me, if you love me so, that you would not take this journey to see me, even if you do not care to see Berlin (a very peculiar reason, isn't it?) I do not seem to be able to put into words the love and longing I have for you. I feel now that I will never be satisfied with this loving friendship you talk so much about. The phrase stings me to helpless anger. I am your true love until I die, how dare you write me to make "other arrangements for my happiness." That is what you wrote. Have you no sense! Ever since you parted from me, you write that you love me, and never once have you said you would come back to me. Except in "loving friendship[.]" Well, once for all, that means nothing and you know it. As you see, I feel bitter, angry and horribly discouraged. This whole summer has been a prolonged agony, except for the times I have been able to lose myself in pictures, and what will be the consequence of it all. God knows I only hope that you will benefit by it. I am also discouraged that you drift so endlessly. How about your work? Wasn't that the idea behind our separation this summer. Tom dear forgive me, but I am so hurt that you didn't come to meet me here, when you could. For heaven's sake do something, you are now in the most precious time of your life, and it seems to me you are doing the same thing you did four years ago, aimlessly wandering. Possibly I am wrong and that sort of thing is necessary to you. I think I know, but must be mistaken.—We came from Prague here by aeroplane yesterday. It was a strange and terrible experience, and I hoped several times the God damn plane would smash and go down. This is not fancy talk as you call it, but the truth. The wind was blowing a gale, and we had what is called a very rough passage. It was terrible, nothing that a ship does in the most violent storm could compare to the plunges and leaps of the plane. The earth was wonderful to look at from above, so perfectly designed. I felt deathly sick but could not vomit, and for the last hour of the ride had a steady sharp pain in my heart and was a beautiful indigo blue color when we landed. Terry fortunately was sea sick all the way, which they say is better for one. However, she couldn't get up today. Phil and Maurice have flown a lot, and there were other passengers in the plane who said it was the worst they had ever known. The strangest thing was that I had no sensation of fear at all. And if it weren't for the awful sickness it must be a marvellous way to travel. I had some tea when we got settled in the hotel, and stayed nearly an hour in a very hot bath, finally got warm, and went to bed. But the bed swayed, and my head nearly cracked all night. No more flying for me for some time.—I wish to God I could sink into some state of insensibility. I don't know what to do if I go on being wracked this way by my feeling. I wish I could be so noble that I would be happy just because you have your freedom, or whatever you choose to call it, and are doing what you please. I'm not that noble, in spite of the Carlsbad cure. As I feel I don't think it is in me to do any more beautiful shows, in spite of your advice. I also do not think it is in me to make another home for my family, and root up my old one. Isn't it funny to have reached my age and be all at sea! And here I go giving advice to you about settling to work. More people than I, have lived through it. Without you I am finished with it.

You must dread getting a letter from me now, they are all so painful, but I guess not so painful as to see me. Do you think you ever will again?—When I think that you are being untrue to me with women, I have murder in my heart.—I am true to you and me and love forever. I went to the museum here for an hour this morning, it is very fine. Some magnificent paintings. My head hurt so from the flight I couldn't stay very long. Fortunately I can get off by myself, occasionally. Phil comes along, when I look at pictures. I am sending you a lovely Egyptian head. Berlin is much lovelier than I had thought, I took a little one horse hack and drove around. I will get up very early tomorrow, as the galleries all close at one o'clock Saturday and 3 other days. The pictures seem to be grand. Will know better tomorrow. I hope you will let me know where to write you, will go on sending mail to Munich till further notice. You will find a great collection from me there. If I feel no happier soon what shall I do? Just go on. Well, my darling an ache only aches the person who has it, I found that out by now. Time is a dream—

I love you[.] Aline

69. Köln / Hotel Terminus / August 11–12, 1928
Dear Aline:

I want to get this letter off tomorrow morning so that it will surely reach your ship before she sails. I got your telegram in answer to my letter this morning; and I was glad to know my long letter had reached you. I do not know how much or how often I have written you this summer—I am afraid I have written too few letters and have tried to say too much in each of them. That is another reason I marvel at *your* letters so, and value them so much. You are brief and complete—just as you are in your beautiful theater work—you know what to leave out, and where to stop. I do not. I want to say everything, to roll all my life up into a ball for you, and to do it all in a page or two. And in my effort to say it in a hundred words I use five thousand. And I never say it—it always gets away from me.

For several years now I have had a recurrent vision which come[s] especially just before I go to sleep. I see the dark forest, and a glimmering form among the trees—I try to fix it, to get its lineaments clearly, but it is gone like smoke. And this thing that escapes me is what we always dream we'll capture. It draws us on, and we are sad because we do not find it.

So what can I say to you before you sail? More than ever before I wish I could be one of the great kings of speech, so that in a hundred words I could wreak out the whole fabric of my heart and life for you. But I can not.

I am a procrastinator and an evader; I hate pain, and I will lie to myself about it, and put it off as long as possible. You face things at the moment more squarely, and you see them more clearly. For me, this is the most poignant and bitterest moment of all. I have never felt so keenly the certainty of our parting as I do now, writing you on the ship that will take you thousands of miles away from me. Even when we left each other in New York, I think I told myself I should see you again in Europe. But even then I think I knew that I shouldn't.

Because, dear Aline, it is not now that I am losing you—that happened a number of months ago, I saw it and knew it when it happened—I was obsessed with the work I was doing, driven on desperately to finish it, and unable to stop and save us both at the time. I was like a man engaged in some violent effort, who is yet conscious of all the sounds and movements around him. I think you must have seen and understood something of the agony of those months—my job to do, the horrible pain lengthening day by day, and no escape—until I roamed the streets of New York by night cursing like a madman, bolstering myself to face them with doses of raw gin, and so far losing myself as to call your house at unexpected times, day and night, in an effort to keep track of you. When I remember all this now I about go blind with the pain of it, and can hardly see to write. In spite of all this, I love you, and I do not know how I can say anything that will make it clear to you. It is not clear to me; I can not explain things in any reasonable way—I can not say much about it even to you, and I can say nothing about it to anyone else. It is almost the only thing that ever happened to me I could not talk about—I hope the time will come when I may. I am not very hopeful, Aline, about the future of my life, our life—of anything, at present. Love made me mad, and brought me down to the level of the beasts. I have a smouldering faith which will not down that somehow or other it may also have power to heal and restore.

The memory of your great beauty and goodness never leaves me and never will. Even when I run into a blind spot, and the world reels and turns black before my eyes at the memory of some terrible moment of shame and evil, my love for you remains. My dear Aline, I am not attacking or accusing you now; I grieve for you as I do [for] myself, and this world's wrong. I see you caught up in the ugly web of life, stained and spattered as we all are by its million evil lusts—worn and jaded and devoured by it, thirsting for a satisfaction we never get. I have thought of you these last few days more and more, and as some moment in the past comes back and burns a hole in my brain, I have caught at my throat with my hand, twisted with a cry in the streets, covered my face and eyes until all the people have stopped to look at me. I will pray for you as I have prayed for myself if it is to nothing but the unliving silence; and I have a sombre but undying faith that we may yet be saved.

The terrible mystery of living has laid its hand upon my heart and I can find no answer. All about me I see the jungle rut and ramp—the little furtive eyes all wet with lust, and the brutes heavy of jowl and gut, and ropy with their sperm.

I see the flower face, the compassionate eyes of love and beauty, the pure untainted loveliness—I see it under the overwhelming shade of darkness: the hairy stench, the thick blunt fingers fumbling at the heart, the foul wet belly.

But I say that a man who has seen the darkness is one who believes most earnestly in the light; and that we who know the living weight of evil—whose dark face is bent above the world—must also believe in the living power of good.

I am going to end this letter now, and try to write you another one tomorrow. I had wanted to write a single and complete letter, but I have run into one of the pain waves again and I can hardly get the words upon the paper. There is no word against you in this letter. I have no word to say against you; my heart is smothering in its love for you. You are the most precious thing in my life, but you are imprisoned in a jungle of thorns, and I cannot come near you without bleeding.

You ask for an address—I think you had better keep the one in Munich: it is, I think, Amtliches Bayerisches Reisebüro Promenade platz, 16.[1] I hope they keep whatever mail may be in wait there for me. I am going up the Rhine from here, and there I think I shall go on to Munich. I may stop at Bonn and Mainz, or Wiesbaden, but if and when my address changes I shall let you know. I hope I shall find mail from you when I get to Munich. I shall try to write you again before your boat sails, talking of practical things—the disposal of my books, mss., etc.

I know that you are eager to get back to New York to begin work on a new play. And I know you have seen many beautiful things this summer, and are rested and restored by your stay at Karlsbad. Whatever you do will be beautiful and fine, because of your great talent, and because you are always learning new things and making yourself richer and better. I am impatient to get whatever letters you may have written me in Munich, but I dread it somewhat too, for fear that they will sadden me, excite me, or tear me apart. Remember that you have many friends who love and admire you; and that you are in their company most of the time. This is a resource that is denied me.

Loneliness hovers over me like a dark cloud—I do not mind it now as I did once; I am in a solitary position for getting my picture of life—but I hope your letters will not make me any sadder than I am.

What can I say at the end? Nothing but what you have heard too many times before. I love you with a single and absolute love that rises above and dominates everything in my life. Tom

1. Official Bavarian State Travel Bureau.

70. Köln / Hotel Terminus [12 August 1928]

Dear Aline:

I seem to be spending most of the time before you leave in writing you letters—I sent one off to your ship this morning, and I want to get this one off tomorrow. It will probably be the last one you will get from me on this side of the ocean. I do not know whether these letters have been of any comfort to you or not. They have not always been cheerful, but they have been full of my love for you, and, I hope they have rung true. My feeling for you rings true, at any rate—that is, there's no doubting or changing it even though it's mixed up with a great deal of torment.

I have stayed here longer than I intended. There is a surprising amount to see here. The place is very much bigger than I expected—

the people here say that it's bigger than Munich and surpassed in size only by Berlin and Hamburg. There are, of course, a great many museums—one for everything, in the German manner. The picture gallery has some fine things: early German pictures, mostly by unknown people, that are beautiful. Those Germans of the 14th century never painted a bad picture. It is largely their contribution, and the wood carvings, that makes this country richer than any I have ever seen. There are some pictures of surpassing beauty by the man who called himself The Master of The Life of Mary.[1] There are also some small but very great pictures by Lucas Cranach; and in the modern sections the usual terrible efforts of the German to be they-don't-know what, but something very smart. But there were two so good that I thought I had made a discovery—one was a young man, and the other was a grand picture of a man and a woman with some children sitting on the grass. When I got up to them I found that Vincent Van Gogh had painted the young man and Picasso the family group.

The most interesting thing here at present to my mind is the enormous exhibition on the other side of the Rhine of the Press. I have been twice, and spent a solid day each time, and I must go again. The place fascinates me, as I know It would you if you could see it. First of all, there are the buildings. You saw something of the new German architecture last year in Munich at the Ausstellung's Park. But that was only a little dribble compared to this. First of all, the *size* of these buildings is stupefying. There is one which makes the Louvre look like a modest family dwelling. Then there is the style. The Germans have mastered a new manner in architecture and they are working in it with absolute precision and certainty. I went to the building today given over to the exhibit of the Soviet Republic. It was marvellous—an enormous and impressive piece of propaganda; and I was terribly sorry you could not see the decoration. And yet it seemed to me these Russians were novices compared with the Germans. All these planes and spirals and cylinders slanting up into the air, slashed with red and black and placarded with statistics were very startling, but there was a great deal of waste and fumbling. And very often they defeated their propaganda purpose: you had to stand on your ear to find out how many peasants bought their own homes in 1928, and get down on your belly while rotating placards told you how many books were printed in White Russia last year compared with the year before the war. The effect of the whole place was uncanny. I staggered out feeling as if I were stepping out of a modern abstract painting called Portrait of Mrs. Schultzberg When Absent From the Drawing Room, which has a piece of cheese in the foreground and a gigantic eye peering through a buzz saw.

Tuesday Morning

Dear Aline:

I spent another tremendous day at the exhibition. I must get this letter off to you today at the latest; so I cannot tell you more about it. Everything that needs to be said about all the newspapers in the world, and about all the allied trades of book printing, advertising, telegraphy, drawing, lettergraphy,—everything that is printed—has been said. The mind reels before this terrible sea of print—a sea for the most part of triviality and sensation with a magnificent organization behind it. I have gone up and down the thousand streets of this town; I have walked the miles of the exhibition; I am about ready to go.

The buildings—even to the Luna Park section—which consists of one enormous beer and wine restaurant after another—as if this gluttonous town did not have enough—are splendid and modern. I marvel more and more at the great power and intelligence of a people who could do this. It is the most tremendous gesture I have ever seen —a sweeping piece of propaganda for the German language and German civilization.

The magnitude of all this does not oppress me as it might have once. There was a time when I was in love with all the beautiful women in the world and desired to have them all. Now it seems that there is only one woman in the world that it is possible for me to love. And just as a limit has been given me here, so a limit is being given me to all other things, and I feel in me the rising of a deep excitement of my spirit. There was a time as you know when I wanted to read all the books on the Seine, to eat all the cakes in the Rue St. Honoré. I do not any more. In a way I feel as if my real education is just beginning—whatever comes to me now must come from within me. It cannot be given to me by anyone else. My whole culture, my whole picture of life has become intensely personal—I walk down the ten thousand streets no longer gorging like an anaconda but seeking out in this wilderness what may have some meaning for me. If I had escaped from the gluttony that was overwhelming me into that lock step that degrades our life so, I should have been still worse off. There is a year when everyone reads Feuchtwanger,[2] or goes to see a Play by O'Neill or O'Casey, or talks about the sculptures of Brancusi.[3] And there are other years belonging to Cocteau, and Andre-Gide, and Hemingway. For this reason I doubt that the "cultivated" person one meets in the great cities, such as New York, has anything approaching the culture that belonged to a stonemason in the middle ages who tucked away in the dark niches of a cathedral his pictures of hell and heaven. Do you remember with what joy we found for ourselves those beautiful pictures that no Baedecker, no

Dial had pointed out for us—how we saw for ourselves Grünewald[4] and Pleydenwarff[5] and Breughel? All life should be like that; but all life is like the Americans massed in a reverential herd before the Mona Lisa, or like the Germans, who fold their hands in instructed raptures before all the Rubenses. But the people who think they are superior to all this, but who go through the same obedient gestures in turn before African sculptures or *San Louis Rey*[6]—are they any better than the other geese? I am building up slowly out of myself a vision of life which shall be as much my own as I can make it—and although the clamour and the shouting about for things alien to my spirit still disconcerts me, I have learned to have faith in my loneliness, knowing that we are all alone and strangers on the earth. It does not matter about being "original" or "unoriginal"—those two words have been responsible for hopeless dishonesty—it does matter about coming to things for yourself. When I think of you—a rich and rare substance, so beautiful and so single among all the people I have known, I wish for this for you as well. You are unhappily situated among the most prominent and prosperous Geese or Geese Drivers: I have been mad so many times to see you in the procession, obediently mouthing the season's jargon, eating the goulosh that began in Moscow and ends in Harlem. Yet I know it cannot hurt you very much, for you were born glorious and exempt from all the weary toil and struggle that marks my effort towards some little wisdom.

I must close this unending letter. Here are a few practical requests: I give you all of my books and manuscripts, or such of them as you will have, and anything else you may find at Eleventh Street. You have often asked me what you could do with them, of what use they would be to you. I do not know; I know you do not want to be encumbered with old junk, but if there is anything you would care to save out of it, take it for yourself. Get Stott to pack up what is left, to burn it, keep it for herself, or donate it to the Soldier's and Sailor's Home. You have left a great deal of your own stuff there—tables and paints and instruments and drawings. Please do not be wasteful about anything, and please try to get all the use you can out of the place until October the first. Please make full and complete use of it—. I only ask you not to do one thing: destroy my books and papers, or give them to the junkman or some charity, but do not let any of your friends or acquaintances use them. Do not let anyone use the cot on which I slept for any purpose, either sitting or lying down, as long as it stays in the room where I slept and where my books are. If it is moved out of that room into one of the others it may be used in any way soever. This is all that I ask, but I pray that any one who violates my wish on this matter may be cursed with a most bitter and bloody grief.—There is one thing more: Mrs. Roberts wrote me a long and beautiful letter which I have put off answering as long as possible because of a question it raises. They are coming to New York very soon—about the beginning of September I think—she and her husband, and her young daughter Margaret, who is going to enter college at Baltimore: I told her about my beautiful place, and when she said they were coming to New York for a few days in September, in a burst of wild sentiment I said it would be a grand thing if they could use my place. She was very eager about it, but I began to regret having spoken almost immediately. I said Stott was going to be there, and that the other person whose place it was even more than mine would have to be consulted. You know how much I like her; but I am uneasy about having her there among my books and papers, and I think I shall write and tell her it's impossible. But I am going to give her your name and address and ask her to call you up. I wonder if you could see her for a few minutes. She is a good and lovely woman, and says that she has loved me like her son. Dear Aline, do with our place what you will, and if *you yourself* would not be uneasy about the Robertses, and it would not be too difficult to ask them to come in. But please try to do your first show there before the lease expires.

It has been almost three years since we met. I have crossed the ocean five or six times during that time, a thousand scenes have passed before my eyes, and how much water and blood has gone below the wood since then only you and I can say. It seems very long to me. How long it must seem to you, who have done so many other things as well, I do not know. We all must mint from life our individual coin. Everything I have said or seen or felt during those three years, have been radiated from you, or have streamed in towards you. You are past any sort of reckoning my great vision. To see you as others see you, to see you as you really may be, I cannot. My glorious and beautiful Aline, who are one immediate youth to me, I love you, I love you. My tender and golden love, you were my other loneliness, the only clasp of hand and heart that I had. I was a stranger, alone and lost in the wilderness, and I found you. We were forsaken and lost, as all men are in ninety countries among the eighteen million people of this earth. My dear, my darling, we were the only lights in that enormous dark. All the pain, all the weariness, all the agony, all that has happened and that has passed between us could not outweigh the miracle and power of love which in a wild and winter place has kept me warm. And now you are going back across the sea into your way, and I am going on somewhere into mine; and which of these is the better way no one can tell. But the terrible width of the sea and the sky that must stretch between us does not frighten me: I told you that you were my great star that burned in all of heaven for me, and no distance can keep you from me, no distance of time or space or circumstance can take you away from me. The halters of earth are broken, and the feet of the wind are shod. My heart, my love is beating for you. God bless you, and keep you, my dear Aline, my one and lovely light in all this dark. Great star, will you burn on for me? Tom

I hope to God this gets to you. It is past two o'clock in Tuesday afternoon. I am leaving here tomorrow I think and may be in Munich next week. Please write me there.

1. This anonymous artist was called "Master of the Death of the Virgin." He flourished in Cologne in the first half of the sixteenth century and died there in 1556. Wolfe is probably referring to *Death of the Virgin*, which is in the Cologne Museum.

2. Lion Feuchtwanger (1884–1958), German novelist and playwright known for his historical romances.

3. Constantin Brancusi (1876–1957), Rumanian pioneer of modern abstract sculpture.

4. Mathias Grünewald (1475–1528), German religious painter.

5. Pleydenwurff was a German painter and one of the early engravers on wood around the end of the fifteenth century. He is said to have executed the cuts for the Nuremberg *Chronicle*, printed in 1493.

6. Thornton Wilder's *The Bridge of San Louis Rey*, which won the Pulitzer prize in 1927.

71. Hamburg / Hotel Atlantic / August 13, 1928

My dear:

As soon as we arrived I went to the Hamburg Am. line to ask for letters, but whatever mail is here was already on the boat so I can't have it till tomorrow. We found much to our disgust that we have a train trip of 2½ hrs. in the morning, beginning at 7:30. I thought the boat left right in front of the hotel, there is plenty of water, all around the city. The city is quite interesting, but I haven't seen much of it. This afternoon we went out to the famous menagerie of Hagenbeck.[1] It is the most amazing place, animals beyond your dreams of strangeness and I am awfully tired today and will welcome the rest on the boat. And heavy hearted as well, I love you and want to be with you and cannot see what to do. I think I should literally have died without the pictures this summer. You will be drowned in my letters and cards when you reach Munich. I wrote a terrible one from Berlin, but Tom dear it couldn't begin to say what I felt. I keep going over the same thing again and again, what new thing can I say? I live back upon times I remember with you, times I remember distinctly that I have looked at you or that you have kissed me. It turns me inside out, I'll ask you no more what you mean to do. My attitude seems always to be the suppliant beauty. Hagenbeck is a great dealer in animals, supplies the zoos all over the world. Maurice bought two black swans and four flamingoes for his country place. They are so beautiful, and we expect to have the flamingoes on board. They are partly a pearly white with soft red orange and pinkish feathers, the wings lined with black, and very very thin red lacquer legs. I am glad to stop travelling. Berlin was so much nicer than I had expected, all Victorian classic, and the most superb museums. You must go if only for those. The paintings are magnificent, and every inch of the Völkerkunde museum also. There is an enormous museum of classic sculpture,[2] a lot of it bad but that is where the lovely Egyptian princess is that I sent you. Isn't she like Edla? I'll write you if possible and mail from England or France on Board. Will you please send the word where to write to you henceforth,—I am so sad that you did not see me before I left. It seems as though you would never make the effort again. I hope all goes well, and that you are working. Tom what more can I say to you! I hate to put the burden of my self and my love and my sadness upon you, but you have to know how it is with me. I love you, Aline

1. Zoological garden at Stellingen, near Hamburg, founded by famous animal trainer Carl Hagenbeck in 1907. In this prototype for future open-air zoos, animals were exhibited in uncovered, barless pits.

2. The Ägyptisches Museum, specializing in Egyptian art and culture from 5000 B.C. to 300 A.D.

72. On Board the Steamer of the Hamburg-America Line / August 14, 1928

My dear:

I found your letter waiting in my cabin when I arrived this morning. I read it immediately, and like all of your letters, [it] filled me with gladness and pain. In this one you gave me more sense of your love for me, and I think that you tried to convey once and for all your meaning, that you have left me. I do not understand your lack of clarity on this, but I read twice that part of your letter, and that is what it seems to mean. As soon as you receive this, will you please pull your mind together and tell me what you mean, instead of digressing. I got your letter at about 10:30 A.M. today, it is now 7 P.M. and I have been thinking of you and what you say, constantly and I can make little of your intention. One thing you seem to be clear about, and that is that at present you are swept with a tremendous feeling for me. But I cannot see what goes with it. You surely have no sense of responsibility towards me. I hardly think that ever enters your mind. You have got to recognize something in this present situation, beyond your own desire for finding yourself or making your own life. It is sad to think that in all your letters you dismiss my condition by saying I will be alright because I have my work to do. I would dearly love to see once that you wished to comfort me and hold me near to you. I want you to do well for yourself, and now instead of working, and using these few precious months, you hang around Europe. I have no doubt that travel is of the utmost value, no one knows better than I do what it means to certain temperaments. But when I think that you might be making something for yourself now, how can I be but angry at your description of spending days trying to get a room. No doubt you will be incensed at me for writing this way, but you need it Tom. You need that advise and much more that I can give you. I am filled with rage to see you doing nothing with your magnificent travel. I still feel that it is magnificent. And you should know by this time that to sit down and spill your book on paper will not do. Do you know what I mean? You will have to work it many times after it is down. In spite of your wish that I write no more letters to sadden you, I must say this, that I am so torn with pain now that I can barely speak. It is a terrible ordeal to have to be with my friends now and were it not for Terry's tact and kindness I could break down some way. She knows my state of mind, but of course I cannot tell her just how things are, and it is hard for her to see why we are parted, possibly forever. At any rate, she was good enough to let me have my room while I read your letter.—Well, it is so and I will never ask any thing of you. If ever I have sinned in my life, I have atoned in suffering. I am so confused, so thrown down and beaten by this feeling that I know nothing to do. I only wish it would extinguish me. I am sending this off at Southampton tomorrow and I hope you will soon be in Munich to get your mail and to stay some where and work. I wonder if you ever wrote to Mrs. Resor, or went to see her. I hope you did not let it go without. As to your things, I will try to have them packed and stored without going down there. If Miss Stott is still alive when the time comes I will ask her to attend to them. I wonder if you packed up the books or if they are on the shelves still. I shall give away every thing that is there as soon as possible. I have not heard further about the terms of sale of our house but we may be able to stay this winter.

Tom I love you beyond anything I thought was in my nature. I wonder if you know what you do.—Take care of yourself, and be faithful to your own goodness, and don't for God's sake waste every thing as you have me— Aline

73. On Board the Steamer of the Hamburg American Line / Wednesday / Aug. 22 1928
My Dear Tom:

I found a letter from you waiting here which I answered, and wonder whether your wireless meant that you had written a second one. If so, it is a pity I missed it, for now I daresay it will be lost. We expect to land tomorrow late in the afternoon. It has been a very long trip across, much too long, nine days, and very rough. It is the roughest crossing I have known at this time of year, and I had to stay in bed four days of it. I got terribly sea sick and couldn't raise my head off the pillow, nor eat any thing but cracked ice. Yesterday was the first real meal I had in five days and I can't say it tasted very good. Unfortunately our cabin is way up front, so we felt every bit of motion. Thank goodness it calmed down yesterday and I got up on deck for some air. Today is glorious, blue sky and dancing water, and the first time the sun is out since we left Southampton. I never had a bout of real sea sickness before[.] It was nearly as bad as the aeroplane.—I am going home with a very heavy heart, with no promise of you in the future & New York will be frightful. I think of you all the time now, and I wonder what has been born of these three years of love together. I packed up my things this morning and did your letters up in a bundle. I was going to throw them into the sea, but then could not bear to part with what your hand had touched. —I can't write any more, my head is no good today. Will look for a letter soon home. As soon as I hear from you again I will write you about how things are with me. I'll probably write as soon as I get home, any way. I can't tell you how wearisome this trip has been. Any way, the rough weather kept me from getting fat: I wish you could see how nice I look.—I'm utterly miserable and unhappy—

Aline

But I love you—

74. Wiesbaden / Hansa Hotel / Monday Night and Finished Tuesday Afternoon / August 27, 1928
My Dear:

When I think about you and talk to you a thousand times, and say a million things to you, and invent a million of your answers, the days go by and I do not write you a letter. The last one I sent by registered mail to America almost two weeks ago, reclaiming it at the post office after I found out that your ship had already sailed from Hamburg. I thought of sending it from Cherbourg, but I wanted to take no more chances; but I did send you a telegram to Southampton which I hope you got.

After I left Cologne I went up the river a short distance to Bonn, a quiet university town, where I stayed a week. It was cheap, the town is off the beaten American tourist route, and I wanted to see something of the kind of Germany that most of the Germans live in. The celebrated part of the Rhine begins above Bonn; I took several little excursions on the boats which go everywhere—to Godesberg, Königswinter and so on. Bonn has one exceptional claim to greatness—Ludwig Beethoven was born there. I went down to the charming little house, now closed in on a narrow and crowded street, but still keeping its garden behind with the neat red borders of geraniums. And in the house itself everything that he used or handled or that belonged to him is meticulously kept. All that music and all that glory was born upstairs in a tiny room so low you have to stoop to enter. And in one case are his earhorns—huge brass things that he used perhaps to catch a little of the magic he created. When I saw them, and remembered his deafness, my mind leaped back to you. And then it occurred to me that there is this *extra* grand thing about deaf people who are grand anyway to begin with, and who have the beautiful and noble souls of artists—I mean Ludwig Beethoven, and Helen Keller, and you, my darling. Because of their deafness they get a kind of magnificent strength and freedom—there is one wonderful picture of the man striding across an uneven field, with a great wrack of stormy clouds behind him, and the wind blowing in his fierce wild hair, and a tempest of music gathering in his terrible stormy face. You see from this very plainly that he is a complete world in himself—he hears nothing around him, and he needs nothing around him. He is strong as a god; he is not weak like most of us, and does not need to lean on the thoughts or writings or sayings of other men. I have often noticed on the faces of deaf people a kind of lovely, *listening* quality—as if they were hearing music somewhere within; and I think it is something like this that gives your own face its indefinable loveliness. I believe that there is a deep and glorious music in the heart of all of us which very few of us come to hear in all the savage jargon of this world. You are strong and beautiful because there is a great deal of it in you, and because you have been able to hear it. For almost two months now I have been going about among strange people, saying very little, seeing and thinking and dreaming a great deal. The music I hear is strange and lonely: that is the music in our hearts, that is the truth about our lives that we forget in all the tumult. We are strangers and exiles here—I feel it now more certainly than ever—and the only home a man ever has on earth, the only moment when he escapes from the prison of loneliness, is when he enters into the heart of another person. In all the enormous darkness between living and dying I see these brave little lights go up—the only hope and reason for it all. Perhaps I have read all the books and seen all the pictures and heard all the clever ones talk to become a child or a fool—but foolishness is not so rare a thing in the world that I need feel conspicuous about it. I believe in love, and in its power to redeem and save our lives. I believe in the loved one, the redeemer and savior.

Tuesday Morning

I am going to get this off to you today; so I shall perhaps not be able to put down all the things here I want to. I left Bonn a few days ago and came on up the river to Mainz. The first part of the trip—as far as Coblenz—was disappointing, although there were occasional patches of interest. But from Coblenz the wonders begin. It is really a fabulous country—a kind of magic landscape in which you seem to have left the real world behind you, and to have entered another where anything may happen. Although the wonderful part of it is only thirty or forty miles long I had a feeling at the end of the day of having gone half around the world. The "Schnelldampfer" took thirteen hours to go 100 miles: there was something grotesque about it, because below all this Lorelei magic, these boats swish up and down loaded with great fat hogs who spend the entire time eating and drinking. The boats are nothing but floating restaurants—the decks are covered with big tables, and the enclosed part below deck is one huge restaurant. And as they pour the Rhine wine down their glass cage, and look at their illustrated maps, and say "Ach! Die Drachenfels! Ach! Die Lorelei!"[1] and so on. You can understand all the fables that have come out of this region once you see it. The river flows and winds through it like a magic thread, everything leads down to the river—the Rhine hills are not so very high; they are really huge masses of rock that rise almost sheer into the air. On the top of one of these rocks, leaning right over the edge will be the ruin of some old castle—sometimes only a wall, an arch, or a tower—sometimes a great fortress. And wherever these rocks are covered by soil, every inch has been used by the wine growers. You can look up the steep side of the hill and see the exact spot where the rock begins and the soil ends. In the thin rocky soil they grow the glorious wine. The vineyards are almost the most wonderful things about the trip. The entire Rhineland is a fabric of terraces—elaborate stonewalls built into the hill every ten feet or so. The effect of this, with the rock above, and the river, and the shade falling into the hollows and gorges, is very much like the effect of a landscape by Cézanne, but much more wonderful. I believe that what the Americans say about the Hudson is true—the river is much grander than the Rhine, and the scenery more spacious. But the thing that makes the Rhine wonderful is the civilization it has carried for centuries, the enormous cultivation of the place now. We have done very little for the Hudson except to decorate it with sugar refineries and oil tanks.

The Rhine also shows *Tourismus* at its most horrible. I shall never forget those long white boats full of great fat people eating and drinking and peering out through the glass with the magic light and shade above[,] and about you there is something grotesque like a nightmare about it. The other day I saw a post card illustrating one of Grimm's fairy tales. There was the magic forest behind, and a little magic stream before: a large fat fellow was lying beside the stream holding out a plate into which several fish were leaping from the stream, while all around him were running fat little pigs and geese with knives and forks stuck in them.

Most of my geography has been discovered in route. I got off at Mainz because the ship ended its day's run there: I had passed Wiesbaden a few miles down the river, and had got *that* straight in my mind—I had never before known where it was. I stayed in Mainz two days. It is a flat hot place, dirty and bristling, and filled with French soldiers. It is a sad thing to see these fellows swagger around, misusing their power over a bigger and stronger people in such a way that the trouble they cause now will fester and not be forgotten. The military has taken over the finest buildings in the town: the officers have a club in a magnificent building with a terrace and garden. I went by one night as a number of them were going in with their women:—there was music and dancing and loud gaiety, and all around the big stolid Germans were going about their business.

Wiesbaden is occupied by the English. You see them Everywhere by the thousands. And at night the terraces of the most fashionable hotels and the Kurhaus are filled with English and French officers, dressed up in their fanciest uniforms, and eating and drinking sumptuously. What is it all about? My respect and liking for the Germans is growing. The swinish, heavy, shaven-headed part of them I can never like, but I have found the poor and humble people very honest and straight forward. And the patience and solidity with which they endure this painful business is remarkable. I wish some Titan would stretch his hand forth out of the stars and pluck off the earth and drop it into the deepest pit in the universe all this crawling lice in uniform. Then we might be able to patch the business up again. Europe is one appalling fabric of hatred—all the papers are full of the Kellogg treaty[2] now. The amazing part of it is not that the nations are searching around for a possible enemy, but that they kept shifting about making and remaking treaties, in an effort to find a friend.

Wiesbaden is beautifully situated on the shoulder of the Rhine hills that begin here. I wish you could have been with me to see these lovely towns the other day—sometimes there was only room for a single line of old gabled houses along the river with an old fortress tottering right over the edge of the cliff above, and all the space in between, from the backdoor to the turret, one beautiful network of terraced vineyard. Then the country widened out a little in late evening, the hills were lower, rounder and less rocky—and nothing but glorious, cold, golden, sparkling *Wine* around the towns of Bingen and Rüdesheim.

The water here comes smoking hot and salty out of the earth, I go to a great boiling pool of it under a big glass cage and drink six or eight at a time. I take it internally, but not externally—I have recovered some of my good Christian prejudices about taking too many baths. The town is a big place—150000 people—without much to see, and very little. Most of the people apparently are seriously taking the cure. There are big solid looking hotels, luxurious shops, a hundred tourist agencies, and streets filled with big solid ugly looking "villas" and houses. It is a town in the German manner—a wide outer boulevard that circles the city with streets running in. It is not very expensive, and very quiet: I have worked ever since I came here, as I did at Bonn: I made a great many notes during the summer in a little book; and I have been writing in the big one for about two weeks. I have written over 100 pages, and my speed is increasing. I am putting it down as fast as I can, and going back over it later. I am going to Frankfurt in a few days and from there to Munich, where I shall stop my travelling for a while. I have had no mail in five weeks—I think of the mail I hope I shall get in Munich with joy, and with hope and fear. I am more thoughtful, calmer, and very much humbler than I have been in a long time. I want to do something with my own life without bothering too much about the other fellow's.—Aline my mind is often tired from the weight of all the people, all the swarming variety, all the innumerable mass of pictures and books it has seen. I am getting a much clearer view of all these things—I no longer want to gorge myself with the universe, but I still get uneasy with it, and am confused by it. But on one thing I have never had a moment's confusion since I met you. In all Europe and in all America I have never seen anyone remotely to compare with you. I can never again for anyone else reproduce the feeling I have had and have for you: I think you know that I am speaking the truth—you have seen me at my best and at my worst, and in your heart I think you know there is not enough life and heart in any living man to distribute *that* energy around promiscuously. In Mainz and in Wiesbaden there are enormous museums—regimented in the German manner, and devoted to the old civilizations that have existed here—the Stone Age, the Bronze Age, the Iron Age, and the Romans.

In Mainz in a stone coffin of the Bronze time, there is the skeleton of a woman, the wife of some old chieftain. Skeletons are not beautiful or romantic things, but I felt no horror when I looked at this one. I saw her again in all her beauty: her small head, her little gleaming teeth, her straight and delicate bones—the hands and feet so small and lovely, and every knucklebone tenderly arranged—you may be sure—by some bullet headed German scientists. And around the small straight bones of her forearm, there was a round heavy bracelet of bronze, and around her neck a heavy bronze ring that made me think at once of the ornaments you wear. As I stood there I felt the eternity of love—the Romans had gone—the Vandals had gone; but there two people had defeated time and death. I felt near to them; I felt my brotherhood and kinship, I thought of you, and I knew then that my love for you was the most enduring thing in my life, and would hover above our bones when the great towers of America are forgotten, and the great chain rusts around your neckbone.

I must send this off at once. I hope there will be a letter from New York when I get to Munich and I shall speak to you then about practical matters. I wrote Mrs. Roberts and asked her to call you up when she came to New York. Stott has the mss. of one copy of my book. It is for you. Please do *not* let Mrs. R. see it. I explained to her the difficulty in the way of coming to Eleventh Street, but asked her to see you and talk to you—which I hope very much you can manage. About letting them stay there you may deal with it now at your own discretion. On no account do it because you think I want it: my mind is undecided and nervous about the matter, and for reasons of sentiment, your decision is at *least as valuable as mine!* Do you understand?—They are not *hard up;* they are in better financial shape than they have ever been—so economy has very *little* to do with it. I hope you have a beautiful show to do. God bless you, my dear. This letter is long and dull, but in it at last can you not see how much I love you? In my letters I shall try to say everything to you without shame or restraint. I'll write again from Munich—perhaps before. Tom

1. The names of famous steep cliffs along the stretch of the Rhine. The Lorelei were named for a legendary maiden who sang and lured passing sailors onto the rocks. Goethe and Heine are among those who have used this famous legend in their works.

2. The Kellogg-Briand Pact, a multilateral agreement attempting to outlaw war, named for U.S. Secretary of State Frank B. Kellogg. Highly unrealistic, this pact sought to settle all disputes by peaceful means but was so open to a variety of interpretations that there was no hope for its success.

75. Frankfurt / Savoy-Hotel / Begun last Saturday—[1 September 1928] and finished today Friday, September 7 [1928]
Dear Aline:

Here I am at another stage of my travels—a very short one, for I came on here from Wiesbaden, which is only thirty miles away, today. It has been over five weeks since I left Paris and since I have had any mail—when one is going about alone it seems much longer. But this is positively my last stop before Munich—long before you get this letter I shall be there, reading a great many stored up letters, most of them, I hope, from one person—the *best writer* I have ever known. I do not know how far away Munich is in miles or kilometers, but I am told it is six or seven hours by a German Schnellzug, which means that it would probably take me all day if I tried to walk there.

Today—or yesterday, because I am writing this well after midnight —was September 1, and there is already a bite of autumn in the air at night. I wonder what it is like in New York—early September can be blazing hot there, but I hope that when this reaches you everything, except your heart, will be cooler. This is the day that the Weintrauben Kur begins at the Kochbrunnen in Wiesbaden. I went for the last time today to get my last internal quota of ten or twelve glasses—and now I know why the girl who fills the glasses laughed so heartily when I drank so much of the stuff—it keeps you going to that Little Place which shall be nameless. What the devil the Weintrauben Kur is I don't know—I've got a little pamphlet telling about it which I must decipher. One end of the long gallery at the Springs was set out with neat little tables and covers—whether one now begins systematically to drink Rhine wine to cure some disease, or drinks something else in order to stop drinking Rhine wine I don't know. But if drinking Rhine wine is a disease it is one of the pleasantest that was ever invented[.]

I have come again to another big German city—one of those places of a half million or so in which this country seems to abound. I hope there are some good pictures here—I believe there are—and I know there is a famous old quarter full of those Elfland houses that Albert Dürer painted—I have already seen great posters announcing a huge exhibition here of old burgher houses. It is apparently scattered about—one part in a famous 16th century house, another part in a 17th century house, furnishings, rooms, decorations, and *costumes* in the Völker Museum. I describe all this hoping it will cause an ache in your Museum-and-antiquity-loving soul.

I got here as it was growing dark tonight—the ride was not interesting; the beautiful Rhine country ends about Wiesbaden, and the trip was through a flat fat looking country full of crops and grapes. I love to come to a strange city along towards darkness—you get an impression, a suggestion of things which is half magic: sometimes it fades completely next day—you see how wrong you were. Again I have walked up and down new streets—great broad solid buildings, and rich shops. Have you ever noticed how all Germany seems to be built in just *two* styles of architecture. There is the lovely Albert Dürer and Nürnberg style—great delicate gables, cross timbers, and lean-over upper stories, and then there is the Kaiser Wilhelm Deutschland Über Alles styles—great Rings, and avenues and boulevards filled with these solid ugly masses—all bulging in front with bays and balconies and round turrets. It is impressively rich, powerful and ugly—it seems to have been done (most of it) between 1880 and 1900, about the time, perhaps, it was becoming evident to them that the rest of the world ought to be colonized and given the advantages of a *real* civilization. That sounds like a malevolent speech full of the spirit that we ought now to put away—but I did not mean it against Germany alone. The way she felt about her excellence and her duty to enforce it on others is only the way England has felt, and the way a great many of us in America are feeling now.

I get very tired taking it in—and I really believe I am taking a great deal in. But I feel like a great blundering child—I am feeling my way along by myself, and what I get is good and lasting, but it does not come in that brilliant and triumphant way I like to think it should. My life has been full of bitter strife and spiritual labor—a great deal of it, you very correctly say, unnecessary—but then things come to me in that way. I should like to be one of these cultivated magnificents you are always meeting in books—these Cyrils, and Hilarys, and Maitlands, and Napiers who divide their lives between Paris, London, Vienna and Rome, and speak twelve languages beautifully and without effort. These bastards were born superior to all the agony and weariness of life; they were cut from their mother's umbilicus prattling epigrams in French. I should like to be like them—but I'm not.

The amazing thing about it—about Europe, about Germany—is how fundamentally alike it is—how much the same. Tonight it came back to me stronger than ever—the thing I believe I wrote you about once before, from Brussels. Here is a great city of a half million people—and the only amusement they have found is—Beer. I'm willing to admit it is a very good amusement—but in three or four thousand years of trying, why haven't people been able to try something else? At first, as in all new cities, I get a sense of oppression[,] confusion and variety—people swarming everywhere, loaded shop windows, trains and cars going by, and a thousand places of amusement. Germany has gone in for Night Life heavily and solidly—all over.

Sunday Night

I've been walking around again today—and tonight I went to one of their Revues. I think they must be the same the world over—they had the Russian fellow in the leopardskin and his lady partner. He remained proudly aloof in one corner of the stage; then she bounded at him and sprang recklessly into his arms. Then he walked slowly across the stage in a dignified manner supporting the small of the lady's back in the palm of his hand. I thought this couple was playing in Paris and New York this week; but I see they have them here.

I am glad you were not here to see the costumes. The Revue claimed to be Viennese; and there was a scene in which one girl walked out dressed like the Stefankirche, another like the Rathaus, and so on. You may not believe it, but it was there, windows, steeples, and all. The intermission was the best of all—I had had nothing to eat; I went out into the promenade and bought a huge sandwich of Blutwurst. After that I had a happy idea—I had some beer. It was a huge circular theater, loaded with people. Where in God's name do they come from? Out of their mother's womb, the Bible says. But it is incredible that their mothers should have so many wombs. There is also here an enormous Schauspielhaus with a bust of Goethe on one side, and what do you suppose on the other? Schiller. And an Operetta Theater that is absolutely modern, and quite handsome—like a beautiful white block of concrete with places to go in and out. When you see it you think you are looking at a model of it—or at its Abstract Idea. The theater is very active in Germany. Kaiser has just written a play about a girl who sees a man next to her in church, and then in one or two other places, and becomes convinced he is her husband. Furthermore, he believes it too. And so do I! for that matter the piece is said to be a masterpiece, and will go where all the masterpieces go—to New York. Also, a piece called Donnerwetter advertising "1000 naked women." Try that out on your *Grand Street Follies.*

Frankfurt / Tuesday

Dear Aline:

I am going on to Munich tomorrow, or, at latest, Thursday. I find it simply impossible to see anything of a city as big as this one in one or two days' time. There are a great many things to see here—a great many things that may not be interesting when I see them, but I want to have a look. The town still seems to me vast in its extent: like the German temperament it sprawls all over creation in a bewildering way—there are only a half million people here, but from what I have seen, there might be five million. There are great broad streets, squares, and places, but I do not know where they lead to or where I am when I get from one to another. The French build a town with a Grand Place, an Arc de Triumphe, and long straight avenues leading up to it beautifully. But that is how the French mind works, and Frankfurt is how the German temperament works. Last night I went to the opera here—do you know that they have an Opera in Wiesbaden which has only 150000 people? And a huge place here, looking exactly like all the other opera houses I have ever seen in Germany. I stood up in the topmost gallery, and paid one mark. The place was jammed with people, and the piece was a Viennese Operetta by Johann Strauss—Die Zigeunerbaron—which means The Gypsy Baron, although I did not know it at the time. One or two of the pieces were very lovely, but a great deal of it was very dull, I thought. A huge fat man played the romantic prince in a fancy uniform and fez, but he had a good voice, as did most of them. And the sets were quite good. There were hundreds of people—on the stage, gypsy maidens, fancy hussars, village people, beggars, thieves, ballets—and they have this thing, I suppose, in every city of any size in Germany. And the people swarm in—they have the greatest hunger for music I have ever seen. I do not think they know or care very much what's what—they like all music that is played as opera, just as they like Rubens. And in their book shops where there are a huge number of translations from other languages, particularly English, there is very little discrimination shown. Galsworthy and Edgar Wallace, and James Oliver Curwood,[1] and Jack London are all mixed in together.

Tuesday Night

After a Long Day's March: I forgot to tell you that I have grown a mustache—all in two weeks time. I was looking at it just now; it covers my upper lip and gives me quite a piratical look. The people in this modest hostlery insist on answering all my questions in French, although I have registered under my proper name and nation. They are not going to be fooled for a minute—after I had spoken to the head porter in English in an effort to prove my respectability, I heard him tell the desk clerk (with a knowing smile) that my English was good, but spoken with a pronounced accent. And I suppose that is very true.

I think you would probably hate the moustache, but I have a lot of fun watching it grow. And it has helped show me how well the world has got to know itself, and what a Great Big Family we are, with airplanes and schnellzugs, and so on. When a German takes a 6 foot 6

American for a Frenchman, or an Italian, or an Englishman—all of which has happened so often that I have become sensitively patriotic, and want to shout out about it—you can see how close we really are to the final union.—Now I'm going to tell you a Great Big One—you won't believe it, but it happens to be true. I made the Rundfahrt of the city today in a big bus: when I got in at the Bahnhof platz at 3:30, it was crowded with large solid Germans—there was one vacant seat, and another opposite in which a gentleman was sitting. He looked up quickly as I came down the aisle, smiled in a nervous sort of way, and said very rapidly in English "Sit down here." I sat down beside him; he pulled up his knees and crowded over against the side of the bus as if he was afraid of me. The man was James Joyce. I think he may have recognized me from the time we went out to Waterloo from Brussels just two years ago this September. He looked much older, he was quite bent, but very elegantly dressed—that is[,] better than he was last time, and instead of the single eyeshade, he wore black glasses in the sunlight; and he had another pair of plain ones for indoors—we went into the Rathaus and Goethe's House: both were fine. In the Rathaus, which is called the Romer, every one had to stick his feet into huge felt slippers before going into the Main Show, which is [in] the huge Kaiser saal. He wandered around by himself peering at things while a German woman gave a long winded lecture to the sight seers; then he got interested in the beautiful polished floors, and went skating up and down in his slippers in a very absent-minded way. We had not said a word to each other; but we kept smiling nervously and insisting by gestures that the other go in first by the door. We left the bus at Goethe's house, and after we came out again into the street he said to me that it was "a fine old house." I said I thought it was one of the finest houses I have ever seen—as it is—and that they were not able to do it [that way] any more. I said I was going back to the Old Town, which is right near the House, and which is as close to Elfland as we'll ever come. He said he thought he'd go "and get lost there for a while"—like a fool, I was too awkward and too shy to ask to go along—I am sure he would have let me: he wanted to be kind and friendly, and it would have been a grand thing for me to have gone with him. But I didn't, and I must wait now for the third time we meet—The Magic Third!—which will be in Dresden or in Heaven. Then I can speak. Joyce carried his right hand in a sling of black ribbon when he sat beside me in the bus, but he took it out when we got out of the bus.

After I left him I walked down one side of the street and he the other, both towards the old town. I peered into windows and looked at him from the corner of my eye; finally I went back to the Market Place, where the Rathaus is, and sat in an old house out of Grimm's fairy tales, where they sell the best Apfel wine and Frankfurters in the world. I had two orders of both. But all the time I kept thinking of James Joyce and the chance I had missed. I am not as certain as I was two years ago, when his son was with him and told me it was he; but the only reason I doubt it now is because twice seems so incredible. You won't believe it was if I tell you one item of his costume—he wore an old French beret—which he pulled off and left on the bus seat when we got out anywhere—but it did not seem out of place. Besides, his *Portrait of the Artist*, Jugendbildnis here—is in a great many of the book windows, and the face of the author, I am sure, is the face of the man I was with today.

I still spend hours at a time gazing into book windows, and looking at books, until I almost think I have photographed in my mind the *names* of all that have been printed. And do you know how many *have* been printed—in this country alone last year? A bookseller in Wiesbaden told me 36000. Of course, I am sure that at least 15000 of these are translations of the works of Galsworthy and Edgar Wallace, and several thousand more are guide books—for they have more guide books and more maps than anyone else in the world—so that only six or eight thousand really great authors are left. But the total is paralyzing—it has two effects on an ambitious and hopeful writer—either to discourage you from ever wanting to write again, or to spur you on to contribute your atom, since there is no reason—so far as I can see—why anyone with ordinary wit and only a little skill should not become one of the immortal annual 36000 if he wishes to. But it takes the wind out of your sails.

Wednesday Evening

My heart and soul has been at war with the German city, and now a kind of peace and certitude has come out of it. Last night when I came in I saw scrawled on a slate in the hotel's lobby a notice in English which said that "members of Tour 105 should be ready by nine o'clock tomorrow morning for the tour of the city, after which lunch will be served. The departure for Cologne will be at 12:30[.]" Thus in 6 days and nights these people traverse the country I have spent a month in:—I talked to two old ladies from Ohio who were on this tour—they were very sweet, and told me all the things they had seen in their ride around town during the morning. One of them kept talking of "Goaty's House," and I wondered what in God's name it was until it occurred to me she meant Goethe's House. I wonder what Goaty would say if he could hear them—he has one of the handsomest and noblest heads I've ever seen, but there doesn't seem to be much humour in it.

Thursday Evening

You once told me that you had been in this part of Germany and that it had been an unhappy time for you. I think you said that you had been here to Frankfurt, and that you remembered very little of interest here. I think you were wrong there, and if you came again you would find a very great deal to interest you. It is one of the most interesting cities I have ever seen, and when I went again to that bewildering jungle of old houses today, and started to go through some of them, I groaned because you could not be here to see it. They are making another of their endless Ausstellungen—first you go to the Historical Museum, which is in an old place, where memorials, paintings, furnishings and costumes of Old Frankfurt families are kept. And now I know where a lot of your pals come from! The Rothschilds started here; and other prominent names are Kahn, and Wertheim and Oppenheimer. Some of the furniture was beautiful—it was a rich Jewish commercial life, and it developed great elegance, simplicity, and comfort. When you have finished with this exhibit you are sent on to some of the famous old houses—there is one that dates from the middle ages—it gets bigger as it goes up, and leans over like a futurist painting of a sky scraper—it is one of the most beautiful places I have ever been in, and they have kept everything—pots, pans, furnishings, books, the kitchen oven, a laboratory full of wonderful old bottles and globes, like the one in Nürnberg. After this there is a fine old house that belonged to a noble family—Litchtenstein House.—I am going to finish this endless letter here. I am going on to Munich tomorrow, but with a feeling that I am leaving undone a great deal that I should have done. I have bought a book full of pictures of Frankfurt and a book about Matthias Grünewald.[2] If you begin to get little packages containing picture books and pictures, add them to your collection and keep them for me. I saw a beautiful book that I wanted to buy for you—a huge book full of the painters and artists of the 20th century—it was the best thing of its sort that I have ever seen, but it cost $12.00. It costs very little to send them—you can send about 12 pounds for a little over a dollar.

This has been a dull letter; I have wanted to tell you too much, and there is no room for it. The deeper, inner things I put in my little book—I have filled one and begun another. But all I can put at the end here is that my life is a prison into which only one person has ever entered. That person is you. If all my life were as certain and direct as it is here, there would be no doubt and no confusion. The world is very strange to me during these days—I have only been alone for two months among strange people, but the kind of aloneness I go in for makes that seem very long, and everything very far away. I carry you around inside me all the time—my own voice sounds strange to me at times, and the whole world unreal. You are my living reality; there is no time and no distance that can take you from me—you are travelling with me everywhere I go.—I lay down and slept for three hours—from eight to eleven, here; because I was up most of last night investigating the Old Town by moonlight. It was magical. This town has not the magnificent unity of Nürnberg; nor the grand quality that Nürnberg has. The Old Town here is a labyrinth of Elfin houses, quainter and more like Grimm than anything you will find elsewhere. I sat in the square before the Römer last night; the moon was blazing down—I was on the terrace of one of these incredible houses, drinking a glass of Rhine wine. When you are tired, you can go to one of these fancy tenements and drink apple wine—cold and heady—and eat hot frankfurters—what else is here? A Volker Museum, that has a magnificent collection of Asian, and Chinese, and African, and Malaysian things. Among other things there is a case full of Japanese dancing dolls, several of whom looked exactly like Miss Trumann[3] of the Neighborhood: it made me think of the Japanese[,] no, I'm sorry, it was Burmese ballet you had there. Also a collection of Chinese actors' costumes, and terrible and beautiful Japanese No masks, and African wooden dolls, and golden brocades from Sumatra, and trinkets and costumes the whole world over—including the millions of spears, swords, daggers, and knives on which the world still exercises most of its artistic talent. Also, a magnificent old church here—their *Dom*, with one of the richest interiors I've ever seen; and Goaty's house and museum; and the picture and sculpture galleries; and the Kunstgewebe which I have not seen—and the Lord knows what else.

Their night life is heavy and brutal—I took it in last night—went to a couple of cabarets and bars and spent $1.25. A very poor and very heavy imitation of Paris—if anything can imitate an imitation. There is an impression of variety everywhere—their life, however, is much more standardized than ours, no matter what they say. All over Germany they are drinking beer and eating great slabs of pork and veal covered with heavy sauces. The markets are filled with the most beautiful green vegetables and fruits—enormous cucumbers, great clusters of grapes, peaches, plums and so on—but you never get them on the menu. I am tired of the heaviness and monotony of the food—tonight I had a beautiful inspiration and ate two soft boiled eggs. I almost wept with joy, recovering one of these simple and magnificent things I had almost forgotten. Then I went to an enormous Bierkeller nearby in the Bahnhofplatz and watched them. This is their *real* night life—Beer. There was an orchestra that made a terrible noise, dressed up in Bavarian costume. The leader grinned and went through antics and the crowd roared with laughter. Someone would bring him a great mug of beer, and his band would play and sing Ein Prosit! Ein Prosit! and the crowd would all join in holding up its glasses. Most of the people were large and heavy[;] they swilled down quarts of beer, the air was heavy and thick, the band banged and shouted, the crowd sang, now a sentimental song, now a smashing beer song—the great tune of Trink Trink, Brüderlein Trink. This is the real Germany—it is impressive and powerful and yet, after a time, I dislike it. Nevertheless, I think this country interests me more than any in Europe—can you explain this enigma?—here is this brutal, beer swilling people, and yet I doubt if there is as much that is spiritually grand in any other people in Europe as in this one. This beer swilling people produced Beethoven and Goethe, the greatest spirit of modern time. And it produced long ago those fairy and enchanted heroes in Nürnberg and here. And at the present time it has such men as Wassermann[4] and Thomas Mann writing for it. Also in its books—particularly in its thousands of art books—magnificent books on Gothic, and the painters, and everything—it far surpasses in delicacy and understanding any other nation. Can you understand it? When I get up from a meal now, I feel that I have eaten something brought dripping to me from the slaughter house. The quantity of meat they consume is enormous—it has almost made a vegetarian of me; I did not know that there was room enough for all Germany to support so many cows and pigs—the air is filled with the death-squeals of butchered swine.

Friday Evening

Well, I've done it; I've devoured the city—almost—enough for this once, and I'm on the way to Munich by tomorrow morning. I will not be sorry to leave here—it is a flat dirty place, full of noise and bustle—but intensely interesting. Today I went to the Kunsthandwerkmuseum—pottery, furnishings, Greek vases and two grand rooms from the old houses; then back to Goethe's House, and the Museum; then to the Sculpture gallery, then back to the picture gallery to see the good pictures once more; then back to the Old Town where I bought views, and a beautiful book about Frankfurt which I am going to send you. Then I sat down and had a final glass of Apple Wine.

Now I am thinking of Munich—my heart begins to pound when I think of the letters I hope are there. Tomorrow is Saturday; I shall therefore not get any mail until Monday—it will then be *seven* weeks since I've heard from anyone. My Dear, the letters I hope to get from you are the ones I really want—I think of them with joy and fear: I love you, whether you do me or not, and there will never be any power of deception or denial in me great enough to say that I don't.

What has happened in *my* world since I dropped out of it, I do not know. It has been only a short time; but I believe it has been a time of spiritual recuperation. I look wild and crazy and ragged, but I believe I am almost as sane as I can hope to be. I get a great draught of strength from looking at Goethe's lonely and tranquil head, and at Beethoven's fierce and all-sufficient one, and from the memory of your beautiful and calm one. I get, you see, a good part of my courage from better and greater people, but that is as it should be. I still have moments of insanity when I rush into a big book shop and call for the name of some book in English which I know they haven't got, or which I invent, insisting that it is in the Tauchnitz edition. Then while they look, I stagger around like a drunk man from one shelf to the other thumbing over countless volumes, leaping from one place to another, until they all begin to follow me around, to keep me from doing damage. And I have other charming little fancies—such as buying out all the sausage shops in Frankfort, together with all the preserved fruits and plum-cakes in Rumpelmayer's here, and bringing it all back to America with me. Sometimes in the old Market place here and in Mainz, or at the fruit stalls, I have grown mad to buy up all the wonderful fruits and vegetables. I have rushed from one stall to another, buying a peach at one, a bunch of grapes at another, and at Mainz, even, a huge cucumber which I began to devour before all the yelling peasant women.

But these fits are rare—I am calmer and more secure, and trying somehow to get at my picture of life. And I think of you and love you, and wonder what you have done, and are doing. And I think of all the pain and trouble, and I am sorry a thousand times over, my dear, for my part in it—but that does no good. A little of it comes back from time to time and I writhe in the streets. I hope this letter may find you happy, or bring to you a little of myself—if you want to have it—and tell you a little of my feeling for you.

I shall write again from Munich—but not a history next time.—Do you know that for one whole day this week I wandered about with my ears stuffed with cotton? I wanted to see what the world seemed like to Beethoven and yourself, and what that strange music on your faces is like. It was wonderful. Do you know that I think about it by hours—deafness—since I left Bonn, and that I have written thousands of words in my book of a person who finally comes into his place in life, and is suddenly and beautifully released from the useless toil and weariness, after an illness has left him partially deaf. It may sound foolish, but it has turned into something exciting and interesting—the whole terrible effort of a person to get close to his own spirit, to find himself among the jargon and roar of modern life, is suddenly resolved; and while people are feeling sorry for him because of his "affliction" his heart is really swelling with a secret and profound joy, because he knows he has found himself at last. On his face that was once so full of torture and struggle, there comes that strange eager listening look that deaf people have—suddenly his life that was frantically without bounds becomes a strong and secret fortress: he begins to build up for himself and out of himself his picture of life. As you know, this is a fiction applied to one of the figures I have written most about—a figure of myself—but I think it is a fiction that may be more real than reality—you yourself know where it came from, and I hope it does not seem cheap or common to you. I would like to tell you more about it—this is not the book; it is only a part of the book—there is lots of story this time and I hope it will be interesting. But I want you to tell me as exactly and clearly as you can what your own partial deafness has been like.

Aline, my dear—I'll go on forever if I don't throttle myself. Take time away from designing, or your other activities to read my letter—it is longwinded and dull, but behind it all is my love for you, more certain and more lasting—no matter what has happened or may happen—than ever. God bless you, my dear. Tom

P.S. I saw a book in France called *Remède A La Vie Moderne*—I wonder if it is as good a remedy as ours.

Also, in a bookshop here and [in] Cologne a book by one Walter Bondy,[5] called *Kang-Hsè*, with a beautiful Chinese pottery doll on the cover. Can it be our friend? Didn't he say he was a specialist in *Kermik*? Do you want the book? Here is *Another*, if you will believe it: I've had nothing to eat today but two soft boiled eggs and coffee which I had at *Wiener Sacher*'s branch here. Now I'm going out to the pig-pens again. I think I shall have a dainty little Vorspeise—say a Schwedish Gobelbissin—this is only a little caviar, a couple of Eggs a la Russe, some sardines, a piece of Bismark herring, a slice of liver wurst, one of ham, and some tomatoes and—Kartoffel. After this, three or four slices of roast pork with mahogony sauce, and side dishes of Rotkohl and Bratkartoffeln.

In spite of their cooking skill—I know stage designers who cook better than the Germans do!

1. Twentieth-century American novelist and author of popular adventure stories set in the Northwest.

2. Mathias Grünewald (1475–1528) was a German religious painter known for his harrowing portrayals of the crucifixion of Christ.

3. Paula Trueman, one of the permanent members of the Neighborhood Players.

4. Jakob Wassermann (1873–1934) was an Austrian novelist who became internationally famous with the publication of *Christian Wahnschaffe* [*The World's Illusion*] in 1919.

5. Wolfe and Mrs. Bernstein had met Bondy on a train while traveling to Prague in 1927.

76. [New York, Early September 1928]

My Dear—

Well, here is the fly back on the fly paper again, very sticky and gluey fly paper and very very warm. You never felt such heat and humidity, and you never saw such dirt and disorder. This city is preposterous, there is not one street left to ride or walk on. It is much worse than when I left, and I am sure the three months were spent by organized labor in either digging up streets or pulling down houses. I have never been so depressed about living here before. Our house is surrounded by radios and phonographs, and from all sides come dreadful screeches. Even Riverside is torn up, as they are covering the rail road tracks and building a new wide drive to accommodate the hordes that grow up here every year. But worse than everything is the dust and dirt.—Yesterday I got the letter you intended for the boat, it was so surprising as I thought you had mailed it and discovered too late that it wouldn't reach. It is a very exciting letter, the most beautiful letter I have ever seen. I imagine that by now you have found the raft of mail I kept pouring onto Munich. I fear that I sent you some very cross letters, but I assure you, no matter what I wrote you did not convey in any way to me half of what I felt, and still do feel. It seemed terrible to me that you would not see me before I left. Well, you didn't, and that's that. I keep looking forward each day, hoping that the next one will bring a little ease to this ache for you, but no use. It has to stop some time. I had a pretty bad time today, for I had to go to 11th street to get out some drawings for the Civic Rep. Theatre. I had expected never to go again, but Miss Stott couldn't find what I wanted. So I put my paints, papers, etc. all out on the table and I am moving them out tomorrow. It was horrible to go there with you gone, and still so much of you there. Don't worry my dear that your bed will be violated. Not your bed nor your love nor my love, so far as I am concerned will ever be violated. But it was just like you to write that way. I am awfully sorry that you offered the place to Mrs. Roberts. I simply cannot put it in order for a visitor, and what is more I cannot send Miss Stott away after we said she could stay there, besides there is only one bed. I will be just as nice as I can be to Mrs. Roberts when she comes, I do hope she lets me know for I should love to see her, and you may rest in the thought that I will do every thing in my power to make her happy here. I felt down there today as though I would lose my mind. It was a bad dream, and I couldn't believe in any thing in the world. Stott has moved her things up there as the house she lived in is to be torn down, and she had notice to leave. So it looks very strange. She has kept every thing neat and clean, and had all my things put away too well. Eva Le G.[1] is giving me part of an office at the theatre to work in for the present and tomorrow my stuff goes over. It is a nasty little place, but any thing is better than the horror of being in our house without you. I am amazed that you do not understand that, you keep telling me you hope I get our money's worth out of it.—I have an enormous amount of work to do for Eva, Bourgeois[2] opens Oct. 1, another Oct. 3, Cherry Orchard[3] Oct. 24 and Peter Pan[4] Nov. 14. A terrible schedule. They have engaged a girl to help me which will be something, and I am fortunate in being so busy. As soon as I get my things moved I expect to do the great marathon of my career. My one hope is that the designing will be alright under such a strain. Now I'll tell you something that made me furious, you still have the type writer down there, how could you not return it. I don't know what to do about it, haven't any idea where it came from. I will try to send a line to Abe at the University, I don't know his address, and I imagine he is not at college now, are they open yet? So will you please write to him immediately to communicate with me or Miss Stott. It is too dishonest to keep a machine like that. I am simply beside myself to know what to do with your baskets and boxes of things. I have to clean every thing out of our house here by degrees. If you had any intention of coming back to America I could keep them a while till we move, but probably the best plan will be to take some place in a warehouse. You tell me with such magnificence to do with them what I please but I have to do all the doing. It seems to me today as though the world was on my shoulders. I have had difficulties to face and things to smooth out and do for my own people since I came home, and I am not yet adjusted to it, besides having to keep myself in hand about our parting. I was enormously lifted by your expression of love in this last letter, but it seems as though your desire is for me to burn on for you, your star, but to burn on at a distance. Tom dear I'll burn on till I burn out, for you and only you.—Edla has not been very well, and my sister looks frightful. Eddy has to have her tonsils out as soon as her play is over, she has had one sore throat after another. I cannot make out what is wrong with Ethel,[5] I think she needs a good rest. She is too conscientious, and works herself to death. This must have been a terrific summer in New York. I think you are wise to have arranged your life so that you can stay away. You say nothing at all of your new book. Maybe when you get to Munich you will work, or maybe you have been working. The printing exhibit must have been marvelous, I wish I could have seen it. But I found glorious things to see in Berlin, and I hope you will go there some time. In spite of the fact that the smarties think it chic to admire African art, it remains grand. And the Chinese things are superb. If only you had been there. I can't talk to anyone about things the way I can talk to you. As soon as I came home I took out my little angel from the closet, my little Eugene, and he stands over there with his arms stretched out to me. Like a damn fool I go and say goodnight to him.—One more thing, Tom, did you ever write Mrs. Resor. If not, do so at once, please, for me. I kept telling her how much you wanted to go into the advertising business —I am not working for Davidows, as they got some one else to take my place. I think they were sensible as I am so uncertain for them. There is rejoicing in my family, they hated me to go there. But the income was good and now I haven't got it. As soon as I finish these 4000 plays I'll have to look out for more theatrical jobs. In a way it is a relief, you know I haven't liked it much myself this past year, the tailors seem to smell worse as the seasons roll on. This is a long and wordy letter, full of complaints and grumblings and I am sorry it isn't happier. Both of my children are lovely, so generous about life and so sweet. I love them so much and I love you so much, and I wish I could unfurl my wings and fly with you there. I begin to feel about New York and theatrical people much the way you do, except for Terry and Phil and Helen & Agnes.

I wish there was some way for me to salute you through the air. I love you forever, and will keep you in the centre of my heart. Aline

Ink is not my medium, so you mustn't mind pencil.

1. Eva Le Gallienne, talented actress, director and producer, was the president and founder of the Civic Repertory Theatre.

2. *Le Bourgeois Gentilhomme* (*The Would-Be Gentleman*) by Molière opened at the Civic Repertory Theatre on 1 October 1928 and ran for thirty-four performances.

3. *The Cherry Orchard* by Chekhov opened at the Civic Repertory Theatre on 15 October 1928 and ran for sixty-three performances.

4. *Peter Pan*, by J. M. Barrie, opened at the Civic Repertory Theatre on 26 November 1928. This was the first revival of the Barrie classic since the 1924–25 season.

5. Ethel Frankau, Mrs. Bernstein's sister.

77. München / Park Hotel / Sunday Night [10 September 1928]
Dear Aline:

I begin one letter to you almost as soon as I have mailed another; but in my mind and heart I am keeping up a kind of permanent communication with you, which seems to be clearer and stronger than it ever was because I have been cut away from all news of you for almost two months. I got here last night, and tomorrow morning I shall go to my mailing address and collect my mail in a bag—at least I hope there is so much of it. All day I have wondered how many letters I would find there from you—and what you would say in them. Have you ever in your life gone about the world for two months by yourself—speaking to no one you knew, living completely in a world of strangers? I think people should be compelled to do it—two months is a very short time, but very few people get even this privacy and asylumage for their spirits. I wonder if you came here to this noble city again after you left Karlsbad—I have gone about today to the places I remembered so well—they all flash back in your mind with a mass detail you had forgotten. It is a grand and beautiful city, one of the few I have ever seen that lived up to its legend. I believe there are few places in the world that are so marked with something that endures and that can be felt nowhere else. You were right when you said that this would be a good place to live. There is something here that you do not get tired of—I don't mean only the beer. And you can distinguish this city by very little that is quaint and pretty—as you can Venice with the canals and grandiose palaces, and Frankfurt with the Old Town[.]

Monday Morning—
or Rather / 1:30 afternoon

My Dear:

I have spent all the time since 10:30 reading your letters—I found over 40 letters and post cards at the Travel Bureau, and do you know what I read first? First your last and latest letter written to me from New York a few days after you got home. This put to rest my fears about earthquakes, strokes of lightning, or building collapses. Then I spent two and a half hours more reading your letters and post cards. I shall go back and read them over and over again, but I should think this is a fair average of the time my heart—my inner self—gives to the world, and the time it gives to you—15 minutes to fire, famine, and slaughter and the 1800 million people of the earth, and 2½ hours to you. My hand is trembling so—and not with any calculated theatrical quiver either!—that I can barely write you, and I know I cannot finish this now—I want my mind to settle down from all its boiling anarchy that these many letters of yours have brought to it. I shall probably never be calm enough to answer them one by one—it has just occurred to me that we are like two terribly excited people who speak by turns in a wild rush without paying any attention to what the other one has said. But how I wish I had *your* gift for expression, my darling. My letters seem poor enough things after I have read yours—there was one today that had been sent on from the Harvard Club at the first of your journey: it described your trip up through the mountains of Northern Italy and said your little car was like a little mule. I am going out to eat lunch—and to reflect—and I shall try to answer this when I am quieter.

One thing I'll answer now—not only that my whole heart and my whole life is utterly possessed by love for you—it would be foolish and affected for you to pretend not to know this now—but that I am not irresponsible as you would have me, or lacking in any desire to see you again. Your letters say these things and cry out against me so often for saying what I have not said that I wonder if you have not simply adopted this method of getting rid of me. If you have, in the name of God change it for a better and more decent one—don't say that I shot myself, but that you were through with me and you shot me. No one will do anything to you for it; some people may even be grateful to you.—Before I go out to lunch let me say this: I have just counted your letters—I had 14 of them including two that had been sent on from the Harvard Club. This means about 12 letters since I left Paris 7 weeks ago. There is a total of 61 pages; I have not written you so often, but in my last letter from Frankfurt there were 30 or 35 pages written upon big sheets of hotel stationery. I have really written you far more than you have written me—your letters are fine because you do everything easily, but they are obviously written in great haste. Thus, I doubt if writing them would average over 30 minutes apiece—if so much—and you have spent just six hours of the last two months in writing to me, no matter how much you say you have spent in thinking of me. Also when my letters are long, you show by your answers that you have not read them fully and completely—they have bored you, you have glanced at them. That's all.

To say that I am utterly depressed by what you so grandly call "my work" would simply be the most enormous understatement—I have no hope and no feeling left for it at all. In one of your letters you say that you "still" believe in my "great talent." OW! Did someone put you up to using "still," or did some flash of devilish cleverness show it to you. You could not have found a better word that could sting better. Do you know what my mind supplied? (in parenthesis)? Still (in spite of—); still (no matter what other people say); still (although you are thus far a total failure); still (because it makes me feel so noble and grand to keep on saying I believe in you when no one else does)—Well, if you believe in my "great talent," my dear, it's no more than I do. The truth of the matter is that print is one of the easiest and cheapest things in the world—there are over 30000 books printed every year in Germany alone, and in the whole of Europe and America there must be easily 100,000. Well I have never succeeded in becoming one of this immortal horde. There are hundreds of thousands of books and magazines and newspapers being printed, and I have never had talent enough to get a single thing printed. I have dreamed of doing something good and fine, and I have never succeeded in interesting anybody enough in anything I ever wrote to run it through one of the printing presses which are belching millions of tons of print into the world every month. It should be one of the simplest and easiest things in the world to get something printed—but I have never been good enough even for this. If you knew the loathing I feel for my scribbling, the horror and hatred I have of all the lies that have been told me, you would not tell me more lies about my talent. I have been nothing but a word scribbler: you attack me in one of your letters saying that if I want to succeed I'll have to work, and write and rewrite several times. You know that this is twaddle; you know that as far as work is concerned I sat up night after night for 18 months until the sight of my left eye is blurred and defective—there are days at a time when I can barely use it at all. There are very few books that have the labor and the sweat lavished on them that I put on mine, which was dismissed by the publisher with a few contemptuous words—And besides, even if it were true that I might be clever enough to crawl into this army of book and story writers—most of whom have absolutely no talent and yet have more than I have—I say, even if I could do this, how much heart and soul do you think is left in me for trying after five years of being kicked in the face? Now for God's sake don't talk any more canting twaddle about not quitting, rising again to continue the struggle, and so on [. . . .]

78. [New York, Early October 1928]
My Dear:

I have had two weeks of the most gruelling work of my entire professional life. Yesterday I had dress rehearsal of Bourgeois, and today of the Bernard play, and [I am] trying to get Cherry Orchard finished for next week. I am a wreck and I don't know what for. It certainly isn't "Art." And then we finally got moved out of 11th Street. I don't think I could have done it without Stott. All your books and manuscripts are packed in cases and put across the way at that forwarding company. I have the receipt, and don't know whether to send it to you or not. Do you want it? I will put it into an envelope with your name on it in my desk until I hear from you. It was a heartbreaking business. For a moment I hated you for causing me such terrible pain. It was the first time I had such a feeling and it frightened me. —I had been hoping and hoping that something would come to keep us together, but when finally your things went it seemed inevitable, the end of things. I sent the few pieces of furniture to Miss Stott.—

Your very long letter from Frankfurt came a week ago. It was so bulky that it was detained at the customs branch of the post office and I had to open it there to show there was nothing dutiable to conceal. It was an interesting letter, and as always I am warmed by your words of love. I hardly know how to tell you the way it affects me, it is as though you pressed your hand upon a bad wound within me. You have possibly by now waded through the accumulated mail awaiting you in Munich. I trust it was all kept there for you. I should love to know if it will have any effect upon you similar to your letters upon me.—My work at the 14th St. theatre is too hard, and as soon as I finish the present group of plays I intend to leave. I don't know whether it is the work or my intense emotional depression, but I'm worn out, which doesn't seem right after three months' vacation. I am going to try to build a house in the country for my family.—I am glad you are enjoying your travels so much, and it is only right that you should do so when it means so much to you. I had hoped that you would work, but I guess you can't unless you feel like it. Or maybe you are working. If so, for God's sake make it short. I wonder if you really put cotton in your ears for any length of time. I always claimed that deafness had its compensations. I can't write any more now, my eyes hurt. I'll write more after the opening. This business of moving out of 11th St. had distressed me beyond words. I hope that the benefit to you will somehow make an even balance. I love you so and will be faithful to you forever. God bless you. Aline

I am faithful to much more than you, faithful to my whole idea and the way I love you. Do you deserve it?

79. Munich / Thursday / October 4 [1928][1]
Dear Aline:

I got your cable today—I was very pleased and glad to know you had remembered me on my birthday which I had about forgotten. But I am sorry I did not find a letter from you as well—it has been six weeks or more since you got home, and during that time I think I have had only three letters from you. This would be often enough if your letters were of any length, but they have been scarcely more than notes—little dashes that you wrote down and sent off in five minutes. This is one reason why I have not written you since coming to Munich—my own letters were not so numerous but they were ten or twenty times as long as yours—it may be childish, but it seemed only right to me that you should catch up.

Today is the first time that I have been for mail since Saturday. I went to the hospital Monday and got out this afternoon. I had a mild concussion of the brain, four scalp wounds, and a broken nose. My head has healed up beautifully, and my nose is mending rapidly, although I may lose the little loop in it that you were the first—and the last!—to admire. I am shaven as bald as a priest—in fact with my scarred head, and the little stubble of black hair that has already begun to come up I look like a dissolute priest.

What happened I am too giddy to tell you about tonight. I shall begin the story, and try to finish it tomorrow. I had been in Munich three weeks—during that time I had led a sober and industrious life—as I have since coming abroad. It is now the season here of the Oktoberfest. What the Oktoberfest is I did not know until a week or two ago when it began. I had heard of it from everyone—I thought of it as a place where all Bavarian peasant people come and dance old ritualistic dances, and sell their wares, and so on. But when I went for the first time I found to my disappointment only a kind of Coney Island—merry go rounds, gimcracks of all sorts, innumerable sausage shops, places where whole oxen were roasting on the spit, and enormous beer halls. But why in Munich—where there are a thousand beer drinking places—should there be a special fair for beer. I soon found out. The Oktober beer is twice as strong as the ordinary beer—it is thirteen percent—the peasants come in and go to it for two weeks. The Fair takes place in the Theresien Fields which are on the outskirts of town just before the Austellungs Park, where you and I went two or three times. I went out to see the show two or three times—these beer halls are immense and appalling—four or five thousand people can be seated in one of them at a time—there is hardly room to breathe, to mingle. A Bavarian band of forty pieces blares out horrible noise, and all the time hundreds of people who can not find a seat go shuffling endlessly up and down and around the place. The noise is terrific, you can cut the air with a knife—and in these places you come to the heart of Germany—not the heart of its poets and scholars but to its real beat. It is one enormous belly. They eat and drink and breathe themselves into a state of bestial stupefication—the place becomes one howling roaring beast, and when the band plays one of their drinking songs, they get up by tables all over the place, and stand on chairs swaying back and forth with arms linked, in living rings. The effect of these heavy living circles in this great smoky hall of beer is uncanny—there is something super-natural about it. You feel that within these circles is somehow the magic, the essence of the race—the nature of the beast that makes him so different from the other beasts a few miles over the borders.

Friday Afternoon [5 October]

To continue. I went back to the hospital today to have my head dressed and bound. My wounds have healed splendidly—there is only one at the back of my head that needs a dressing. I shall go only one more time—on Monday—after that the doctors are done with me, and the rest is up to my new growth of hair, and the good will of my nose. I have bought a little black cap that fits snug over my head—it is the thing the students wear after they have had their duels, and it makes people stare and whisper, and waiters ask me very respectfully if I've had a sword fight. When I tell them it's nothing more gentlemanly than a brawl at the Oktoberfest they are visibly disappointed.

This is what happened: I had gone to the Fair two or three times, once with a German who lives here in the pension where I am staying, once with an old woman, an American—whose husband was an artist and with whom she lived here for fifteen years during the palmy days.[2] Now she is alone; she goes all about the world in tramp steamers—she has just come here from a trip around the world—and she has only one remaining tie on earth—her affection for the villages in Oberammergau. She has written two books about the Passion Play, and is at work on a third. But she has a conviction she is going to die, and when she went out there last weekend, she tried to get me to come with her. She wants me to write the book. When I refused to go, she was bitterly chagrined and left me in a huff. I should probably have kept out of trouble if I had gone out and stayed with Jesus—one Anton Lang.[3] That is where she was. But I didn't want to get tied up any farther with an old cracked woman who thinks that the whole universe spends ten years in getting ready for the play in this village. And in this I believe I was right.

The Oktoberfest, and those roamy smoky halls, with that enormous weight of people, with those old swaying rings that had in them so much that was unfathomable and of the essence of life, drew me back with a kind of terrible fascination—(Copyright secured here!)—I know what you are saying at this point with a wrinkle of your own—I hope!—unbroken nose. You are saying, 'O yes, I know what drew the bum back with a terrible fascination! It was that 13% Oktober beer!' But you are wrong here. If you drink enough of the regular six or eight or nine Munchener, it will probably have the desired [effect]. But I have told you all the truth of my alcoholic life here—there has been no drunkenness until the Oktoberfest.

There is an American Church in Munich. It is not really a church—it is two or three big rooms rented in a big building in the Salvatorplatz—a place hard to find, but just off the Promenadeplatz. They have six or eight thousand books there—most of it junk contributed by tourists. But you can go there in the afternoons for tea—if you are lonely you can find other Americans there. There are a good number of old fraus who live in Germany—who have lived here the best part of a lifetime—some with German husbands, some with American, and some just those innumerable old spinsterly women from Georgia, Indiana, Kansas, New England who infest this continent—have lived here for years. Why? Where in God's name do they *get here* from? What drives them here alone, un-manned? At any rate, these old dames have their circles and their guilds and their gossip, just as they would in an American town. They give teas to welcome the minister's wife back from America, and teas to the minister and so on. The minister is a heavy high character, mushy sort of man, always groaning that he has a cold or an ache, or can not walk far. He is bored to death, hates it here, has learned no German in two years—it all comes out in every mouthful. Why he stays I don't know[.] Another misfit. But I became the wild haired boy with the minister and the gabbing old dames[.] I dropped in every day or so and Sunday, I blasted myself from bed and appeared in time for the man's sermon. This is the first time I've been to church in six, eight or ten years. The man talked about temptation, and all I can gather is that "he was agin it." It was a pitiful, wandering piece of nonsence, but I listened solemnly, nodding my head from time to time. After it was over he waddled down on me in his splendid robes and said how gratifying it was to have "a man of my intelligence" in church.

There was a young American there with his wife and another woman—his wife's friend. He had come here to study painting. The other woman who is a sort of slut from Mount Vernon—married to some dupe at home—had spied me out, and got the man to ask the minister to introduce them. This he did benevolently—I was delighted to talk to these people; they asked about rooms, life in Munich, Galleries, and so on. I told them all I could, and suggested that they go to hear the music which is played every Sunday by a military band in the Odeonsplatz. I took them across to it. But there was no music on this Sunday; there was instead a parade of a famous old regiment into the Hofgarten. After we had looked at this for a time—the crowd was very thick—they suggested that I come home to their rooms for luncheon. They were living there on things they bought outside. I went along very glad of their company. Then I told them about the Oktoberfest and suggested that they go there with me during the afternoon, as the good museums were closed. So we went out together; the weather was bad, it began to rain. There was a great mass of people at the Fair—peasant people in their wonderful costumes staring at all the machines and gim cracks. I took them through several beer halls, but we could find no seats. Finally, after the rain had stopped we managed to get in at a table some people were leaving. We ordered beer and Schweinswurst—the slut began to wink and flirt with numerous people at other tables. I speak of her bitterly, because as she sat their [sic] by me, leaning her slut's body against me, and being "cute"—which is to say nasty—I thought of you, and of how I looked to find part of you in all women, and of what a poor slimy thing I had there by me. Yet, you must not blame me—there was no evil in anything I had done, and I was beginning to desire only to get rid of these ugly people, who were full of quotations from the American Mercury. And do not think I received my injuries in defending the slut. I think I should not have raised a finger in her defense, if some of the men had assaulted her. But my injuries did come in a way from my desire to be rid of these people—I was nauseated by them, I wanted to be alone. I think they saw this, they suggested we all go home and eat together. I refused, and said I would stay there at the Fair. So they paid their share, and went away out of all the roar and savagery of the place. When they had gone I drank two more liters of the dark Oktober beer, singing and swaying with the people at the table. Then I got up and went to still another place, where I drank another, and just before closing time—they close at 10:30 there at the Fair, because the beer is too strong, and the peasants get drunk and would stay forever—just before closing time I went to another great hall and had a final beer. The place was closing for the night—all over the parties were breaking up—there were vacant tables here and there, the Bavarian band was packing up its instruments and leaving. I talked to the people at my table, drank my beer, and got up to go. I had had seven or eight liters—this would mean almost a quart of alcohol. I was quite drunk from the beer. I started down one of the aisles towards a side entrance. There I met several men—and perhaps a woman, although I did not see her until later. They were standing up by their table in the aisle, singing perhaps one of their beer songs before going away. They spoke to me—I was too drunk to understand what they said, but I am sure it was friendly enough. What happened from now on I will describe as clearly as I can remember, although there are lapses and gaps in my remembrance. One of them, it seems to me, grasped me by the arm—I moved away, he held on, and although I was not angry, but rather in an excess of exuberance, I knocked him over a table. Then I rushed out of the place exultantly, feeling like a child who has thrown a stone through a window. Unhappily I could not run fast—I had drunk too much and was wearing my coat. Outside it was raining hard; I found myself in an enclosure behind some of the fair buildings—I had come out of a side entrance. I heard shouts and cries behind me, and turning, I saw several men running down upon me. One of them was carrying one of the fold-up chairs of the beer hall—it is made of iron and wood. I saw that he intended to hit me with this, and I remember that this angered me. I stopped and turned and in that horrible slippery mudhole I had a bloody fight with these people. I remember the thing now with horror as a kind of hell of slippery mud, and blood, and darkness, with the rain falling upon us several maniacs who were trying to kill. At that time I was too wild, too insane to be afraid, but I seemed to be drowning in mud—it was really the blood that came pouring from my head into my eyes—and there was *always*, *always* alive in me one bright living spark of sanity and consciousness. This place in my brain and my heart kept crying out for you—it kept crying out *Aline*, *Aline*; not for your help and guidance, but because it seemed to me I was lost; and I thought with pity and horror of all the sea between us—first of the actual Atlantic between us (drowning in mud and blood I seemed to hear the sound of each separate wave that lengthened out from Europe to America)—and then of a greater sea of fate and chance which had separated us—here I saw myself drowning in hell a bloody snarling beast, and you, all glorious, at the other end of the universe, unable to redeem me.

I was drowning in oceans of mud, choking, smothering. I felt the heavy bodies on top of me, snarling, grunting, smashing at my face and body. I rose up under them as if coming out of some horrible quicksand—Then my feet slipped again in the mud, and I went down again into the bottomless mud. I felt the mud beneath me, but what was really blinding and choking me was the torrent of blood that streamed from gashes in my head. I did not know I bled.

Somehow—I do not know how it came about—I was on my feet again, and moving towards the dark forms that swept in towards me. When I was beneath them in the mud, it seemed as if all the roaming mob of that hall had piled upon me, but there were probably not more than three. From this time on I remember fighting with only two men, and later there was a woman who clawed my face. The smaller figure—the smaller man—rushed towards me, and I struck it with my fist. It went diving away into the mud, and this fellow I remember no more until I saw him later in the police station. Then as I turned toward the larger figure I saw the heavy fist swing towards me. It was a great, clumsy, lumbering blow that a boy might have avoided, but I was too drunk either to avoid blows or to notice them. I saw it coming; it struck me full on the side of the nose; I was turned half around by it, and felt the numb scrunch of broken cartilage. Then I struck at this figure and missed it—it must have been six feet away—struck again and knocked it into the mud. It rose, we struggled together in the slime, I was choking in blood and cared for nothing now but to end it finally—to kill this other thing or be killed. So with all my strength I threw it to the earth: I could not see, but I fastened my fingers and hand in its eyes and face—it was choking me, but presently it stopped. I was going to hold until I felt no life there in the mud below me. The woman was now on my back, screaming, beating me over the head, gouging at my face and eyes. She was screaming out "Leave my man alone!" ("Lassen Mir den Mann stehen"—as I remember). Some people came and pulled me from him—the man and woman screamed and jabbered at me, but I could not make out what they said, except her cry of "Leave my man alone," which I remember touched me deeply because I saw you standing there in her, as indeed I sometimes see you in all women. These people went away—where or how I don't know—but I saw them later in the police station, so I judge they had gone there. And now—very foolishly perhaps—I went searching around in the mud for my hat—my old rag of a hat which had been lost, and which I was determined to find before leaving. Some German people gathered around me yelling and gesticulating and one man kept crying "Ein Arzt! Ein Arzt!" ("A Doctor! A Doctor!") I felt my head all wet, but thought it was the rain, until I put my hand there and brought it away all bloody. At this moment, three or four policemen rushed up, seized me, and hustled me off to the station. First they took me to the police surgeons—I was taken into a room with a white hard light. The woman was lying on a table with wheels below it. The light fell upon her face—her eyes were closed. I think this is the most horrible moment of my life—how far away I felt from you then I can never put into words. I thought she was dead, and that I would never be able to remember how it happened. The surgeons made me sit down in a chair while they dressed my head wounds. Then one of them looked at my nose, and said it was broken, and that I must go the next day to a doctor. When I got up and looked around the woman and the wheeled table was gone—I am writing this Saturday (six days later); if she were dead surely by this time I would know.

Tuesday Evening [9 October]

Dear Aline—

I went down to Oberammergau Sunday and returned here last night. Saturday morning I received a card from the old woman saying that players from a neighboring village—Garmisch-Partenkirchen—were giving a play in Oberammergau on Sunday Evening, and that if I was interested I might come. Sunday morning when I awoke I thought of it in bed: suddenly I decided to go—the Sunday before I had gotten into trouble at the Oktoberfest, this Sunday I would go and talk with Jesus. I got up, put my pyjamas in a valise, and went to the station. It rained, hard spouty rain, all the way down into the mountains. They were grand and lonely; I was terribly depressed, a wound in my head had broken open and was beginning to hurt. The little fourth class train was mixed in with freight cars and went rattling and jolting along. It was the first day that I had felt any pronounced letdown from my injuries, but I was almost exhausted in body and mind. When I got to Oberammergau it was raining; a little old German, who had lived in Africa and written a book about it, had come down on the train with me—he was going to the same hotel where the old woman was staying and offered to show me the way. When I got to the Alte Post I found the old woman in her room pecking away at her typewriter. She peered at me crazily with her old weak eyes—she did not recognize me for a moment. Then I told her what had happened—she was divided between kindness and moral preachments and vindictiveness—if I had come with her I should not have gotten into trouble; she had had a "premonition"—(just like my mother)—when she had left me and so on.

This is only [the] first half of [the] letter. I am sending [the] other half in another envelope.

This is the Second Part of the Letter

My head was hurting where a wound had broken open and festered—we went down stairs looking for the doctor who comes every Sunday afternoon to play cards with some friends. His name is Anton Lang—he is the one who plays Pilate, the Christus is also Anton Lang. The little eating and drinking room of the Inn was filled with the simple Passion Players all swilling down beer. The weather was raw and chill—all the flies in the world had crawled in on the table cloths to die. I sat down on a bench with my back against the tile oven Christ had made and waited for Pilate to come in. Presently he came in, but refused to have anything to do with me until he had played his game. He is the great man of the village. He played cards all afternoon while I dozed by the oven and tried to keep the flies out of my beer. Then at dark I walked home with him to his house—he lives in a marvelous old place, with a great overhanging roof, and the most elaborate Baroque—The place is a Baroque place, by the way. The inside of the village church is one great mass of baroque, the little figures that the woodcarvers make—woodcarving is the principal industry in the village—are almost all baroque, and from the pictures I have seen and the looks of the players, the Passion Play itself is baroque. That night I went to the theater with the old woman. The play was called very aptly *Schuldig*—which means Guilty. I had expected to see a folk play, but this was a modern or semi-modern thing—a kind of German Galsworthy about a man who has been imprisoned for 20 years for a crime of which he is innocent, and who then goes out and finds the man who committed the crime along with his wife, and kills him—and thus becomes *Guilty*.[4] The players were like Little Theatre players throughout the universe, the settings were like Litl. Th. sets, and everything was played in a thick grey gloom. With my head you can imagine how cheerful I felt.

The next day the old lady took me around to see some of her friends—the ex Mary Magdolane, who is a widow trying to make ends meet, the Herod, and just before I left at night the Christus—Anton Lang. He is a potter, and lives in a big house—he seems to have done very well with it, and the old woman says he is well off, but always pretending to be hard up. He married a very shrewd woman—the daughter of the village blacksmith—she saw the advertising value of being Christus, and she has made the most of it. We waited for him in a living room—one of his children, a little boy, was fooling with a toy on the floor, carving a piece of wood for it with great skill. Christus kept us waiting some time—we had been to see him once or twice before; I think he feels his importance somewhat, and is bored by this old cracked woman who has known him since he was a child. I think she knows that, and it has made her bitter—she talks again and again of how beautiful he was as a child and a young man—she brought him up to Munich on a visit just after he had played the part for the first time, when he was twenty two or three—she keeps talking about him as he was then. "Anybody would have loved him to death," she said. I think she is in love with him; she is for some reason very bitter against his wife, and claims she has coarsened him. And I think it is still hard for her to distinguish between God and the man who plays the part of God—this man keeps changing back and forth in her mind from the human to the divine. He came into the room after we had waited some time—he was like some business man, polite but serious, who lets you know his time is not to be wasted. He still wears his long Christlike hair—but I forgot all about this, he was so worldly. He had on a working smock, he said he had been "baking" all day—he had a large order from America which must go off in a hurry.

Saturday Night [13 October]

My Dear:

I got a letter from you today—my first one in two weeks—if you could have seen me tear open the envelope and begin to eat the words one by one I am sure you would have spent an extra five minutes and written a little more. It is only your third or fourth to me since you went back to America, and they have all been beautiful flashes of lightning—you could not write anything that wasn't alive and beautiful, but I wish the fireworks were a little longer. Of my own 60 or 70 or 80 or 90 pages from Frankfurt you say it was "very interesting." Tell me—where did you learn to squash people so thoroughly? I cursed because you had to go to the Customs to fetch the thing away—I do not believe you have read it. Your letter would have shown some instance of it—some responsiveness—but there was none. You have often said boastingly that you did not have much sense. I believe this is true—I believe actually and literally that you have not got much sense—but you have something else that supplants it ten times over. I think of your beautiful low forehead—your face has a sort of radiance that is not a brain-radiance so much as a spirit-radiance. I have some sense—a little, whether you believe it or not—and the proof of it is: look at the mess I have made of things. Haven't you ever noticed that people with lots of sense nearly always make a mess of their lives? In your letter today you said that when you moved my books you hated me. You said it was the first time you had ever felt this way and that it frightened you. Perhaps you don't realize that this last has become almost a stock phrase in your letters. You have hated me for the first time several times, and been frightened by the feeling several times. I do not think you know how much bitterness your letters show. Your declaration of love glares out angrily at me from over a wall. But let me tell you this:—I know that I deserve it all, and more. I know to the very bottom of the cup how badly I have acted, and my heart is simply dead with such despair that I can hardly lift my tongue to speak. I feel as I felt that night when I was drowning in the mud at the Oktoberfest—I did not care for my body's loss, but I felt my soul lost in the mud beyond salvation, and there was no power of hope left in me to cry out. At the end of your letter you say you are faithful to me and that you love me, and you ask me then if I deserve it. No, I do not. I once had the love of a beautiful and elegant woman and I sit here now writing to you—and if you could see me!—a brute with a shaven head with a long raw scar on it, and a bloody eye, and a broken nose. But this is not the first uneven match that was ever mated—you are not the only unhappy sister; you have had company.

I have lost all impulse—I am a bat staggering about blind in the universe. I must come to an end, a limit; I must end this letter—and I do not know how to. I am leaving here Monday—leave Monday I must—for Austria, Salzburg, then Vienna, I think. I seem to be only a wretched atom wandering about on the Bavarian plateau—it seems vast, I am lost. Munich is not large, it seems at times vast to me. The distances terrify me. Up and down, up and down, I pace along the Ludwigstrasse before those huge Teutonic-Italian buildings which dwarf and tire me. The royal library is 142 of my long paces[;] that must be almost, if not quite, 500 feet. I have been inside of it—miles of waste space—but huge long [wings?] piled high with books. My heart sickened. How many? I asked one attendant. He said 500,000. I was grateful and gave him a coin. The next one said 750000. Still, this was not bad. A third said over 4,000,000[.] I almost screamed at him that he was wrong, and rushed away. My eyes grow blind staring at the barbaric script in the bookwindows. Thousands, millions of books on every triviality, and then thousands and millions on how to build airplanes, steam engines, copper mines. I have gone through hundreds of rooms in the German museum—and still I have not seen the end.

Sunday Morning [14 October]

I do not think I have told you what happened to me after the police doctors had looked at my wounds and dressed them that night at the Oktoberfest, or how I found doctors to look after me, and so on. From the doctors I was taken before the police next door where they asked me many questions which I did not answer. They also had two of the other men there, looking very bloody, also—and perhaps others I did not see. Then they let me go, when they could get nothing out of me—I had lost my hat, and was one mass of mud and blood: it was raining hard and wet—a young man I did not know went along with me, and when I asked him what he wanted, he said he "had no role to play." We got a street car and came back to the centre of town where I got off and shook him—at the Odeonsplatz. That day at lunch with the three people who had gone to the Fair with me I had met a young American doctor who had come here for special study. Now I was going back to their place to get his address. I found the married pair in bed, and the other woman out with the doctor. They stood around and gasped and looked scared—the woman made me a cup of tea—in a few minutes the woman and the doctor came back. He gave me the address of another American doctor who was working in a famous clinic here, and told me to see him the first thing the next morning. Then he and the woman walked most of the way home with me although I did not need this help. The next morning I got a taxi and drove through town to the clinic. My appearance almost caused an earthquake in the pension and people in the streets stared at me. I had been directed to Dr. Von Mueller's clinic—and Dr. Von Mueller is one of the greatest doctors in the world. His picture was in all the papers the other day—on his 70th birthday. His clinic is in the hospital near the Sendlingerthorplatz—I found the great man in the office, and when I asked for his American assistant—Dr. Du Bois, whose name I had been given—I was told he was at home, and that I should go there. I felt low spirited and was on the point of asking old Von Mueller himself to look at my head (which would have been a great breach), when in came this man Du Bois. The name is French, but you never saw anyone more prim and professorily American. He was very tidy and dull looking, with winking eyeglasses, and a dry prim careful voice. I felt done for. I told him what had happened and where I was hurt, and he listened carefully, and then said in his precise careful way that we ought perhaps-ah-to see what can be-ah-done for you. By this time I thought I was dead.—But here let me tell you the truth about this man. Dr. Du Bois, who is, I found later, a professor in the Cornell Medical School (hence the professorily manner)—he is one of the grandest and kindest people I have ever met.—In his dry prim way he showed me for days the most amazing kindness—and then refused to accept anything for his services, although he had come to my pension with me in a taxi, to help me pack, when the German doctor said I had to come to the hospital, and had gone back with me, and had visited me once or twice a day, and brought me books, during the time I was there in the hospital. At any rate—he asked the great Von Mueller first of all where we should go across the street to the Surgical Building and see the great Lexer, who is the best head surgeon in Germany.

Salzburg / Monday Night
[15 October]

My Dear—

I held my breath until I got over the blessed border today—I have escaped. Tonight—in spite of a desperate cold that is making me blind—I feel that life from now on is going to be freer and happier and wiser—and although I've had this silly feeling before, I believe somehow it's going to be true. Munich almost killed me. It scarred my head and broke my nose, and last of all smote me in ten wretched seconds with a deadly cold which burned like fire along the membranes of my nostrils, and then made a sour lump in my throat.—Munich almost killed me—but in five weeks it gave me more of human experiences than most people get in five years.—The old woman—the old woman who had only Oberammergau to live for, who was living only to write a final book about the Passion Play—hunted me up again yesterday (Sunday). She had done nothing for days but follow the flight of the Zeppelin—all Germany has been talking of nothing else for days—as I write this tonight in Salzburg no word yet has come that the Zeppelin has landed—a thousand reports, true or false, have come—but nothing that will give these people hope. I feel sorry for the Germans, I hope their Zeppelin gets there—somehow there is an enormous national eagerness and hope

—as if the success of this thing is going to make everything all right with America, with the world.

The old woman lived only two or three doors from me in the Theresienstrasse—likewise in a pension—a great cold house, full of decaying and elegant furniture—tattered tapestries—that is run by a Frau Oberst—an old woman who is an army major's widow. The old woman came back from Oberammergau a day or two after I did, and came to see me several times in my pension, but I was out scouring Munich and its interminable museums. I went to see her two or three days ago—I found her in the living room of the pension with the radio phones fastened to her ears, and a look of crazy pleasure in her face. She asked me where I'd been, and I said the German museum—she had never heard of the place although she'd lived here ten or fifteen years—Here's something more exciting than all the museums in the world, she said, and she began to babble and stammer about the Zeppelin—as if no one had ever heard about it before. She had brought me a number of pictures from Oberammergau—Christ had sent me two pictures with his name scrawled below.—I paid her for the pictures. I knew she had very little money, for I had been told in the American Church that she had spoken of buying a place for the rest of her life in the Old People's Home at Oberammergau (you have to pay for it). Then I said, God bless you; this has been a very strange thing, and I shall never forget you. She insisted on kissing me and said she felt like a mother to me. She begged me not to get into any more trouble—and then asked angrily if I had. She said I had been broadcast over the radio the night before—my heart began to thump wildly, and she said she had caught the words an Amerikaner "Verbrecher" (that's German for criminal) so and so metres tall. The poor old thing had been so shocked and impressed by my story of the Oktoberfest and my difficulties with the police since that she had [. . . .]

1. In the upper right hand corner of page one was written: "Saturday, Oct. 20—Vienna. I got here yesterday. Feeling much better now. Writing you more."

2. Louise Parks Richards was the widow of a painter who had studied at the Royal Academy in Munich. She had seen the Oberammergau Passion Players perform for the first time in 1890, and was consumed with interest about them ever since. In 1910 she had published her first book, *Oberammergau–Its Passion Play and Players: A 20th Century Pilgrimage to a Modern Jerusalem and a New Gethsemane* (Munich: Piloty & Loehle).

3. The actor from the village who performed the parts of both Pilate and Christ.

4. It was primarily for the purpose of seeing this play that Wolfe had traveled to Oberammergau.

80. [New York] Oct. 16, 1928
My Dear:
Madeleine Boyd just telephoned me that Scribners are much interested in the book. She sails for Europe tomorrow and will communicate with you. I hope you are still in Munich. I haven't heard from you for nearly 4 weeks and feel terrible about it. Either you are ill or don't care, or I don't know what, and it makes me feel awful. I have been worked to death, no one can go on doing the amount that I do, and survive. But it helps dull the edge of my loss of you. I am so excited about the book, she seemed to think they are likely to use it, and I hope you will come back if necessary. I know of nothing that will make me happier than to have the book published, unless it will be to have it a best seller. My heart just leaped at the message from Mrs. Boyd. Wait in Munich until you hear further. I am sending you a cable today, maybe it will cheer you up. I have now had three plays produced since my return. The Cherry Orchard last night, and it was a great success. But it has been a superhuman task. The Grand St. Follies opened in Philadelphia and also seems a hit. I went to bed today thinking nothing in the world would ever make me feel good, and then came Madeleine's message and it woke me up a lot, and I will hold my thumbs.

It is just as well you are not here, because you hate me so when I work hard. I look very well, though and seem to retain my Carlsbad figure, gained about 3 pounds. I'm going up to Westport with Lilly for a couple of days to breathe some air, and think a little for a change. But I find most of my thoughts seem to turn to you. The way I love you keeps burning. I cannot change a particle.—I am awfully bored with my work, and everyone I talk to bores me. Quite a new state of affairs for me. The only thing I have liked is the play of The Cherry Orchard. What I did for it is nothing, but the play itself so grand. Nazimova[1] is swell in it. It is fine to have a work so beautiful and great before my eyes, so hard not to be side tracked and lowered by all the trash abounding in this land of liberty. But I never will be, and my love and respect for the glories is steadfast as my feeling for you. I will not admit of the poor and flashy.—This is a terrible place to live, and half my effort goes to fighting it.—My dearest love, please write to me— Aline

1. Alla Nazimova played the part of Madame Ranevsky in *The Cherry Orchard.*

81. Salzburg / Hotel zur Traube / Thursday [18 October 1928][1]
This has got to be the last section of this crazy letter. I hope you don't have to go to the Customs House for this; it's not worth it. But my head is at length clear, and I have a wild feeling of victory—as if

I'd beaten the fires of darkness, and so on. Of course it's silly—but too much happened to me in too short a time. I got over the border into Austria Monday fairly choking for air. For two of the last three days I've been in bed here at this little hotel. My eyes were streaming; my nostrils were stopped, my lungs were clogged, I had a cough that tore the lung and the blood out of me, and a fever. But I knew that I could beat down now anything that tried to stop me—I dosed myself terribly with aspirin and soda: today the thing is definitely better, and I'm going on to Vienna first thing tomorrow morning. I've been out today—went up on an exceedingly high mountain—by way of elevator—to see the city. Went to City Museum, and Mozart's Birth House.—That's all the sightseeing I've done here.—If I come to the important things [in so fast?] a manner it's because my wits were addled, perhaps, and I've not been able to get it all done at one time —I couldn't go on the other night—I was too dead and feverish— The old woman is dead, that was what I was about to tell you, but couldn't. She came to see me that day to warn me that the police were on the track—fanatical as I am I knew that story was wrong because they had been there three times asking their meticulous questions, and it was all over. But she had heard the two words—Amerikaner Verbrecher on the radio and her old mind leaped to me at once. Sunday night I went to the theater in Munich—I came home after eating about one o'clock and after a time got in between the damnable damp cold sheets. I came here at two o'clock Monday— left Mun. that time. At midday Monday I came back to my pension to pack—she lived only three doors away at another. I went in to see her and to say good bye. Mary Magdalene—I had met her a week before in Oberammergau—was there with her father—the old man who played Judas two or three times, but is now too old. He was a devoted friend of old lady Richards; she talked to me about him and said "she loved him to death," and what an artist he was, and how comic. He is a little old peasant with a wrinkled comical face, shrewd and sly, but good, and a stringy beard. He cried when I met him there at the Pension—they are going to take her back to Oberammergau and bury her there—in the Catholic churchyard, with all the Langs and the rest of them. One of the Langs named his child after her—the only Catholic child (she told me a hundred times) to be christened a Protestant—they allowed her to take part in the ceremony. The child is dead and is buried in the village churchyard; she will be buried there too—she is still a Protestant—died one— although she said a thousand times she was going to become a Catholic before she died. The Pension people said they had tried to get me at 11:30 the night before, but that I was not home. The old woman had been sitting in the cold living room downstairs at 10:30 with the radio phones over her head, waiting for the next report of the Zeppelin which was to come at that time. A young German in the Pension was with her—he had a pair of phones over his ears. As the report began to come over, she seemed to faint on the sofa. They revived her; she seemed to be all right. A little later she went up to her room, and a few minutes later one of the maids heard something strike the floor. They went in and found her with a great bruise on her head where she had fallen and struck her head against the little night cabinet by her bed. She was alive, but she never recovered consciousness after this. They called her doctor—an old German she had known since the old days in Munich—he said she had been tubercular then, and had had a bad heart for [ten?] years or more. She told me she was 74 years old but she was 78—that was how old she was, and her papers proved it. The Oberammergau people were weeping as if they remembered her as she used to be. When I was there a week or two ago they were patient, but gave the impression of being bothered with her—she had grown old and childish, and they did not have time for her as they once did. I asked them if I could go back with them for the funeral—they told me it wasn't necessary and seemed not to want me—my wild appearance—(and I was choking with cold)—perhaps frightened them off.

I cannot say any more to you about it now—I've only put it down here. I do not know that I feel anything at all except a sort of relief. I am not hard, I am not cruel—I have a kind of joy that old lady Richards is out of it, and another kind of joy that I'm out of it across the border. Do not hate me for talking like this—what I really feel must come out later. I did no harm to this old lady: I have harmed no one except myself and you—I think maybe I brought a little happiness and content into her life.

The whole thing—meeting the old woman when I was terribly lonely, the companionship of two queer birds, her anger at me when I refused to go to Oberammergau, my brawl at the Oktoberfest, my hospital experience, my visit to Oberammergau, and finally the death of the old lady Richards makes a very strange story. I don't know what it means—I shall write you more about it later.

My Dear don't think me hard—I am glad the old lady is dead. I was here to see and know about it—I'll tell you all about it some day.

I'm glad I'm alive. I've meant to lead a good life, and I've led a bad and wasteful one. But out of all this waste and sin I believe—in spite of all logic—that some beauty will come. I love you, and as long as I love you beyond myself—as long as I could think of you then while I wallowed a beast in the mud, and believed myself to be near death—as long as you came to me then—then all is not lost, all good in me is not dead.

I'll write you a clearer letter from Vienna. I'm all right now. I've beaten death, I've beaten Germany (I'll explain that *insanity* later), I've learned something.

The Herr Geheimrat, I believe, has made a bad job of the nose. It looks to me hopelessly crooked, although people in Munich insisted it looked all right. My hair is cut in a wooly nigger fuzz, and my scars shine through the brush.

I love you, my dear. That's the only hope for me. I'm not as crazy as this letter sounds. Only I had to put things down. Tom

P. S. What I am wondering all the time now is whether a lovely woman can love a brute with a broken nose. The accursed weather of Munich cannot be described. Snow fell there the other day—mid October! And God! how I come to hate the leaden sky, the wet thin sunshine—But the Magic that is around Salzburg—all white and lovely!

1. At the top of the page Wolfe wrote: "All of this part of the letter. The first part I am sending in another envelope big enough to hold it."

82. New York / October 18, 1928
SCRIBNER INTERESTED BOOK WRITING DEAREST LOVE = ALINE

83. [New York] October 18, 1928
My Dear Tom:

I sent you a cable concerning your book two days ago, but unfortunately it was returned to me, I enclose notice from Western Union. I have not heard from you since you arrived in Munich. I presume all my letters were too wearisome for you. I hardly know what to do, as the Scribner people are anxious to talk to you and it seems too good a chance to miss. I write you still to Munich, as I know of no other address and apparently you do not care to keep me informed. I hope you are alright in health.—Abe Smith called me up yesterday, he is going abroad and wanted your address and as I had not yet heard that you had left Munich I gave him that. He wanted to see me to ask my advice about travelling etc. but I was so weary I couldn't talk to him. I was going to Westport for a couple of days, but decided to stay home and rest instead.—We are going to build a small house on our piece of ground up in Kensico, and that will just about take my last ounce. My dear, I always want to write how much I love you, but what use is it? Aline

84. New York / October 20, 1928
SCRIBNER INTERESTED BOOK DEAREST LOVE = ALINE

85. Vienna / October 23, 1928[1]
Dear Aline:

I have been here four or five days—I sent my long letter in two sections a day or so after I got here. I hope both parts arrive at the same time and that you are able to read them—I know it will be a job (to read it) as the writing is a wild scrawl, and very soiled and crumpled. But it is a good description of myself at the time I wrote it. I have not been a frequent correspondent the last five or six weeks, but you have been about as infrequent, and very very scanty. I got a strange and troublesome letter from Miss Stott today—full of hints and forebodings, and undesired compassionateness. I had sooner have no letters at all than this kind at the present time—I have lost all capacity and desire for work—the kind of work I thought I wanted to do. I circle and twist about all day in the labyrinthine streets—so strange and narrow and crooked—of the old City here, taking down the names of the books on display in the bookshop windows—scrawling, scribbling insanely the names of the books other people have written, and unable to continue with one I had begun for myself. I have no confidence and no hope. The huge vomit of print that inundated that world has sickened me and killed—for the time at least—all my creative energy. Only my mind seems to stay alive—my heart is leaden and hopeless—but my mind keeps working like some animal trying to find its way out of a maze. I do not think much of my ugly face with its broken crooked nose or my ugly head with its fuzz of hair and the great lurid scar from which no hair will grow—I will not care much about this if only my heart and my soul will come alive again.—For so complete an Egoist I find myself in a strange fix—at least I suppose I am an Egoist, because many people have accused me of it, although the accusation has always seemed to me a silly one—such as—Why are you always you and not I, or the Rest of Us?

1. This is apparently an unsent fragment that Wolfe left unsigned.

86. [New York, Late October 1928]
My Dear Tom:

I was in a great state of worry over not hearing from you for so long and today received an alarming post card saying you have been in a hospital in Munich with a broken nose etc. The lower half of the writing I could not make out very well, as the pencil was somewhat rubbed out. I cabled you twice this week, both cables returned saying you were not in Munich. So the moment your card came I wired you. You must write one telegraph immediately to Madeleine Boyd, I will enclose her Paris address. Scribner's want to see you about your book. I am so excited, and wonder how the new one is coming on. I was in a bad state of worry over you. You really should be a little more thoughtful of me, if you care at all. How on earth did you ever have such an accident. I imagine the most terrible things, and hope you are writing me. But I am afraid it had to do with liquor. I make out from your card something about sailing home. Did it never occur to you that I might worry, not hearing from you in 4 weeks? I was on the point of telegraphing your sister. I do not know whether Olin is sending you money or not, and wonder whether your finances have anything to do with your coming back to America. I do not flatter myself that I have any thing to do with it, you told me before you left that Olin promised to help you out. I was paid yesterday by the theatre, and have $750. I will send you some if you need it to come home, $500. I have no more, and God knows I've worked hard for that. If I live through *Peter Pan* it will be only because I am a super woman in physical endurance. I hate the play, it is an awful piece of junk. My designing will probably be poor on it. I have been thinking of you so much that I expect you to materialize before me some day, and I wonder what it will be like to see you again, whether even you intend to see me. Will you ever kiss me. I thought surely you would stay a long time in Munich and write, but I might have known you would not do what I expected. Anyway, you have had a long vacation and should feel strong and rested. I envy you the extraordinary quality you have of detachment from responsibility. I know it is an attribute of genius. Maybe it is the genius I envy you, for I know I have it not. But I think you hardly take the proper responsibility toward yourself. I am here preaching tonight and better stop. My whole career or profession, or what ever you call it, has resolved into two aching legs and a bad head. But I look well, some of my Carlsbad cure is still with me. I'd like to go there and do look after yourself,

Love, Aline

Madeleine Boyd
c/o W. A. Bradley
5 Rue St. Louis en L I'le
Paris

87. Vienna / Thursday Night / October 25[1] 1928
Dear Aline:

I'm going to try a *short* letter to you to see how it goes. I sent off my last huge scrawl in two installments a day or so after I got here, and I hope you got both parts together, and were able to read the contents—as ugly and sordid as they were. It has been a matter of

3½ months since I landed this time upon this land of Europe—and what have I to show for it? Some 30000 or 40000 words actually written, some three or four books full of notes—which I may use, a half fair-to-middling reading knowledge of the German language although I still speak very badly, a heart full of hopelessness, a broken nose that is taking a crooked twist across my face, a criminal stubble of hair upon my head, and a large white scar on which no hair will grow—and a great, grand, unfading love for you, my darling, which seems to be the only beautiful and redeeming thing in my life, and which is so much better than the rest of me that I cannot believe it belongs to me, or is a part of me. A year ago when I saw that your feeling for me was dying, and that your affections were finding a place elsewhere, I went about like a wild animal, seeking for some relief and escape. I have never found it; I no longer have the same furiousness, but I have a much deeper grief, and there is a feeling of distance that I can not bridge over. It is not the number of miles between Vienna and New York—that is not much—but it is a distance of loss and spirit. Your beautiful face comes to me as a kind of light—I can remember it only as a flower, and a radiance, and the corners of the mouth.

I circle the maze of the Old Town here like a maniac, taking down the names of hundreds of books in the windows—trying to dig out of all the nightmare horror of dust and forgetfulness and junk with which Europe is weighted down, something that may have a little beauty, a little wisdom for me. This terrible vomit of print that covers the earth has paralyzed me with its stench of hopelessness—I can not lift my head above the waves of futility and dullness—I have no hope, no confidence, no belief in my ability to rise above the level of even the worst of it. Impulse is killed in me, life is dead—for I am sure so much of this—most of it!—was begun hopefully, was thought good by its perpetrators, found praisers. And to think that this world is full of people who say this and that confidently, who write criticisms, and talk confidently of literature and art, who peck around in the huge mess with a feeling of complacency and pleasure —I can not follow them, understand them.

My cold is better, but still hangs on. All of the Wiener Wald is growing yellow; I went through Grinzing the other day, and the peaches were in among the grapes, and the branches of pine hung out before the wine shops, where the new wine is drunk, and on the Kobenzl hill, and on the lovely hills around, all of the Wiener Wald was turning yellow and today at Schonbrunn, the paths and lanes going from the palace to the carriage house—where we were—were covered with yellow leaves. The sun was thin and red, the ghost of the moon was already over Vienna—and Vienna has reached its autumn too. This life, the glorious city is in its yellow leaf. I am going to Budapest, then back here, then to Florence, Rome and Naples, and then home. I am going to work and try to make some money. God bless you, my dear. I hope you write [to] me. Tom

1. Wolfe included a question mark in parentheses after the number 25.

88. Vienna / Sunday Night / October 27 [1928][1]
My dear Aline:

In several of your letters you have begged me to make use of "this precious time"—not to waste it—to make something of my life here while I have the chance. Every one of these words stabs me—I know how right you are, and how little I have made of my chances—how I have wasted everything most precious—paramountly yourself—and made a wreck of everything I wanted to make beautiful. I do not know the reason for it. It seems to me that the people who lose all reason in this world are the people who try most desperately to find it. I know I have always been after the reason of things—I am now more than ever—and my brain is weary and wants rest, and can not get it. It is like something that hunts round and round inside an iron cylinder trying to find some way out when there is none.

My dear—if only I had a little of your calm certitude, your wisdom, your beautiful vision; or if only I had some of the false certitude of other people—of men who believe only in the bank business, or furniture, or automobiles; or of others who believe that no painting is good that is not like the Picasso's, or no writing that is not like Gertrude Stein's or Dickens or Perandello's. I am going through a horrible struggle of the spirit, and unless I find some way out I am done for. It is not new—it has gone on now for several years. You have seen it, and I do not think you have ever understood it very well, for in your own work you have been so certain: you have so fine a talent and you have found the thing you like best and for a while you are best fitted. Dear happy Aline—you were right about me. I'm a Bum—but I've always wanted to be something better. I am not lost yet, there is still hope and life in me, and with God's help, and my own, and above all, almost, I hope, with *yours*, I'm going to pull out of it. My dear, will you save these letters that I have written you. They have been poor jumbled letters, but outside of my notes, they give the only fairly consecutive account of my life for the last four months. Please save the last one about the Oktoberfest—it is a broken mumbling sort of nightmare, but I put down without any literary varnish some of the things that were happening at the time. I have not yet been able to see the whole thing clearly—I don't know what it means—but I believe there may be a strange and moving

Vienna — Sunday Night Oct 27

My Dear Aline: In several of your letters you have begged me to make use of "this precious time" — not to waste it — to make something of my life now while I have the chance. Every one of these words stabs me — I know how right you are, and how little I have made of my chances — how I have wasted everything most precious — paramountly yourself — and made a wreck of everything I wanted to make beautiful. I do not know the reason for it. It seems to me the people who lose all reason in this world are the people who try most desperately to find it. I know I have always been after the reason of things — I am now more than ever — and my brain is weary and wants rest, and can not get it. It is like something that hunts round and round inside an iron cylinder trying to find some way out when there is none.

Thomas Wolfe to Aline Bernstein, 27 October 1928 (By permission of the Houghton Library, Harvard University)

story in it—in my strange relation with that poor cracked old woman who had dropped in on Munich from a trip around the world on tramp steamers picked up here and there—and who talked of Sumatra—she went there because she liked the name—and in all the rest of it: how I got my head and nose broken, and went to Oberammergau, and had Pilate dress it, and met Judas and his daughter Mary, and the businesslike Christ—and then the end of it all. What does it mean? Out of my folly, and my marred face, and scarred head —out of all my crazy bestial foolishness I want to get something now that will perhaps pay a little for it. But do you know I do not feel that the thing has coarsened me? I have a pretty low opinion of myself at present, but I have a better feeling towards the world. I found almost unbelievable goodness and kindness behind the dry prim manner of the Cornell Professor-Doctor. And the old woman! She was cracked like myself but she wanted to help—my impulse as I lay in bed that Sunday morning to go to Oberammergau is one of the strangest things that ever happened to me. And the people in the hospital—I never told you about that part of it. I was there only three days—and I wanted to go sooner—but it was a strange experience for me. Do you know what I shall never forget about it?—the place of course is Catholic—all Bavaria is Catholic—and over the door of my room there was a big modern crucified Christ. All the nurses are nuns—I shall never forget them: they are really beautiful and innocent people, my dear,—and the expression of their faces made me think of you. They have none of your worldly experience, they were really little children—little girls—but there is also something about you that has always made me think of a little girl. Do you remember one night when I had a bad tooth, and you and Stott were there, and the old girl went rambling on about how she first met you, and how small and dainty, and like a gay girl you were. You began to cry—we all feel like that when someone tells of a time that is irrevocably past—but I did not have to use any imagination to see you dainty and small and childlike again, because all of these things are yours, and you will never lose them. So it was with these Nurse-Nuns—they brought me food eight times a day—huge meals with beer, two breakfasts, one with sausage, and so on, and always with this childlike eager smile on their face. And once in the hallway I got to talking with another patient who had cut through a ligament in his hand fooling with an automobile. He had been in America and was eager to try out his English. He asked me how I had got the cuts on my head, and I told him at the Oktoberfest. Two of the nuns were there, and when they heard me say Oktoberfest they began to smile and giggle at each other like little girls[.] They were so innocent of the world that to them it was a sort of joke, a kind of fable—I was a gay fellow who had got drunk and been in a fracas—they did not know that it was not my head or my nose, but my heart that was all bloody with it. As a matter of fact I had practically no physical pain at all, save when Geheimrat Lexer cleaned my wounds the first time, and later from a cut in the back of the head which the great man's eagle eye missed entirely for two or three days until it began to fester. Isn't it a colossal comedy, or tragedy—this Doctor business? They study so hard, they pretend to know so much, they really know so little. As for the great Lexer I don't know whether to curse or bless his memory. He did not do a damn thing after the first day, when he looked at the scalp and probed and cleaned, and pressed his fat fingers down hard. As for the nose, he did nothing. He said "Es steht gut"—Let it stand, and instructed his young assistant to stick wadding soaked in iodine up my nostrils, that was all that was ever done—I had [to] breathe through my mouth two or three days. Now my nose looks crooked to me—it seems to twist around to the right—we never notice these things before, and we can never remember later what we looked like. Dubois soothes my fears by saying I was probably paying the Great Lexer to do nothing—that an inferior surgeon might have twisted the organ all out of shape with screws and clamps, and so on. Neither did he sew up the big scar on my head, although Dubois told me that is what *he* would have done. The scar is perfectly healed now, but white and hairless among my black kinky head. The Great Lexer thought he was hell. They acted—the nuns and young doctors—as if he were God Almighty: they breathed out the magic sounds of "Herr Geheimrat," as if saying an incantation. I was very meek and chastened for a day or two—he treated me like dirt and I took it all because I felt so guilty—until I found the place on the back of my head that he had missed entirely. It had begun to hurt like hell during the night, and they had told me it was the bandage. Of course only a part of my head was shaved at the time—the other place was still lost in the bushes. When he came pounding into the room the next morning, looking like a butcher in his white gown, and grunted at me in his usual surly fashion, I was no longer meek. I ripped the whole damned badge from my head and pointed a quivering finger at the place he had not seen. "Was ist?" he said, looking startled, and in a choking voice I said "You didn't see this, did you, Herr Geheimrat?" He was very much taken down, and got out of the room in a hurry, followed by his worshipping assistants. As he went out he muttered that my hair was too long, and I must have it all shaved off. So Johann the attendant came in limping—(to shave *all* my head)[.] Herr Geheimrat also limped, and I knew I was prancing around in fury, hating them because they all seemed to limp. But when he went over my head this time he did it carefully. The festered place healed slowly—it is all right now, but there is a hard scab, or tissue, or lump that won't come off. The first day in the hospital they almost drove me crazy. When I got up the morning after with dried blood all over my face, and my head in its bloody bandage, I was not nervous, but depressed. But the doctors did what Oktoberfest, and all the blood and the police had failed to do—they got on my nerves. They say nothing, or only enough to let you suspect the worst. Dubois cautioned me because I went rushing up and down stairs at the pension and hospital, and tried to help me in and out of the cab. Then when the Geheimrat got busy on me in the awful white room full of glass cases and instruments, and a sister laying out the tools and cutting bandages, and told me furthermore to lay down on that terrible table—then I began to cave in. I am sorry to admit this, but I said to Dubois like a little frightened child, "They're not going to put me to sleep, are they?" and the man said no with a gentleness and mercy I shall never forget. I was glad this man of my own race was there with me—as I lay there on the table, he put one hand across my knee, reassuring me by his grasp as if I were a child. This man, my dear, with the winking eyeglasses has a very noble and beautiful spirit. As a matter of fact, all Geheimrat wanted was to look at my nose—he got me down there for that, it did not hurt, but the old hog might have told me that before. Their method the first day was to kill all hopefulness in me—even Dubois shared dutifully in this. Perhaps, they said, things would go well, but there was always "the danger of infection setting in." I thought by their manner that my skull was fractured and that they were keeping it from me—I asked Dubois, and he somewhat unwillingly admitted that my skull was not fractured, but then added: of course, the nose is part of the skull. You can imagine how cheerful this made me feel. The next morning, a police investigator in a cutaway coat came in on me without warning and asked 15000 questions. He was very courteous, but his manner was ominous, I thought, and he put everything down meticulously. By this time I felt that I had killed two or three people and would be placed under arrest the moment I was able to leave the hospital. Craftily I asked for some newspapers to read, and Johann brought me several—all several days old. This confused me—I knew that it was all up with me, and that if I should attempt to sneak out, I would be met down the hall by a police guard. Finally, about eleven o'clock, one of the nuns brought in a large visiting card and asked if I would see the Protestant minister. The place is Catholic, but they apparently do what they can to save the damned as well. I said that I would, now convinced that death was immanent and that the man was coming in to give me a few last words of spiritual comfort. He came in, all dressed up in a frock coat, with a bible under his arm—a little ninny man with a mustache, looking as Lutheran as God. He talked to me a few moments gently, asked who my nearest living relatives were, and then rising, said in a sephulchral voice: "Has the Herr a wish?" I knew that what he meant was "before you die," but I said feebly I should like some newspapers. I thought I would work him and read of my crime in this way. "Something to read!" he cried at once, went out, and came back in a minute or so with a Stack full of horrible

German Protestant church tracts, meant to save the depraved—some such title as "Light and Life," etc.

By this time, Johann came in and said I must come into the operating room for "Verbindung" (Binding—but it sounded worse)[.] He helped me gently out of bed and took me down the hall to the awful white room with all the tools, and the Sister cutting bandages, and the young assistant. The young assistant rips the bandage from my head with one movement, the big wound has already begun to heal. Herr Geheimrat comes pounding in his butcher's frock for thirty seconds—takes one look at my nose, then at my head, and says gutterally as if pronouncing some almost unthinkable wisdom "Dies ist gut, aber das ist besser."[2] You can hear the sister and the young assistant draw in their breaths rapturously as if the consummation of all things has been reached. Then Geheimrat fires ten seconds of gutteral instruction at the assistant, and goes pounding out again at his limping gait, to give some other poor devil 40 seconds of his precious time, or to lecture to the medical students for three hours—I am told he talks that long.

As for myself, in spite of all that had happened that morning to upset me, I felt greatly reassured by this exhibition, and congratulated myself on having this great man for my doctor. I felt naturally that a man who could take one look and say "This is good but that is better," with such authority was almost beyond the possibility of error. But during the night the other wound began to hurt, and in the morning I found it, and lost all deference for the great Lexer. He could say "This is good but that is better," but his penetrating eye missed entirely a raw and festering wound. The man never had a civil or decent word to say to me the whole time—he grunted, and I felt my guilt. When Dubois brought me to him the first day, he was all dressed up like a stockbroker in striped pants and a cutaway, with a fat cigar between his fat fingers. He was the picture of heavy prosperity—he grunted out, looking at my bloody face and bandages: How did this happen? and when Dubois coughed and ahemed and said the young man had been to the Oktoberfest he snorted and said "Natürlich!"—leaving the rest unsaid, but easy to supply. I do not think he is a bad fellow, they say he is a great surgeon, but I remember him without great affection.

My room was large and comfortable, my bed was one of these things with which the Germans torture themselves—four thick hard mattresses, and a dozen enormous and not very soft pillows that break your body in two half way up. The room looked out on a garden with a high wall around it—all of the leaves were growing yellow and falling; I could see the nuns walking about two by two, and convalescents with their wives, and wheel chairs. At night I could hear the noises of the Oktoberfest—not very far away—the merry go rounds, the tootings, the gimcracks, and later people coming home tipsy—singing and shouting.

The rest of the story—the essential part I think you already know —I have been very lengthy, because I wanted to tell it all to you. But all of it I can't tell now until I see you again.

I passed my birthday in the hospital—wondering if you had written or cabled me on that day. And my mind kept going on and on, and back and forth, over the whole sorry mess.

Wednesday Night [31 October]

Tonight I went to the Theater to see a Russian actress—I suppose she is—named Orska. She was playing three one acts—one by Strindberg in which one woman does all the talking, and the other says nothing, until she drives the talking lady mad. It was very jolly. Then there was a comedy by Molnar[3]—and last, the Big Show—what do you suppose: *The Old Lady Shows Her Medals*—by Barrie.[4] This is the big hit of the evening: I couldn't help thinking that in America Strindberg would probably be the hit and Barrie would come in for a hard panning, and much sarcasm. These poor people are fed up with blood and hunger, and they want a good juicy tear in the eye:—on the other hand we are all about 22 years old in America (which is a *grand* thing for us!) but we simply must suffer, mustn't we, when we put a good and serious American writer, without being Strindberg-y on the one hand, and a cheap lying Saturday Evening Posty knave on the other. I have had my nose broken and my head scarred, and I'm not much to look at—in addition I'm a gloomy fellow, and something of a nuerot—but the damned Yankee optimism is in my blood. Optimism for what I don't know, for certainly my prospects at present are not very bright—but I keep believing things are going to be better. I have had it demonstrated to me a thousand times that the European mind does not work in this way. Shall we go here? Shall we go there? Shall we do this? Shall we do that? Why not? It is indifferent and un-hopeful—it is no paradox that for this reason it gets an enjoyment we can't get at present: if the moment is agreeable and pleasant, it enjoys it. I have really learned something, seen something—a good deal—but my mind keeps asking me what I am going to do with it. What are we in America going to do with Europe and with what we learn from Europe? How are we going to use it? We have got to make something out of what we have. I feel it is wrong to go on writing books and plays about American subjects using ideas and methods that we get abroad. On the other hand I think it is wrong to do what Anderson did—even when he wrote such grand stories—that is, to make a virtue of being ignorant and crude and simple. This is good perhaps for a starter, but we will get tired of it in a hurry, because it becomes a literary fashion and has no relation to our real life. We are not so damned crude as we boast—we have tremendous industrial and mechanical sophistication, and to write about ourselves as if we are a lot of simple and superstitious peasants of the Protestant faith is ridiculous.

I am going to Budapest tomorrow or Friday and shall stay there four or five days. Then I am coming back here and going to stay where I shall get a ship for New York. It is the farthest away from home I have ever been; I think of the Hungarians as being a strange—almost Oriental—race. But I am quite excited about the city, and what I shall find there—Everyone who has ever been there has spoken of its beauty. I wonder if there are good pictures there, and if I can get along with German there. I hate to lead the life of the hotel tourist, who is nursed along certain main highways like a child, and is told everything by a guide with a memorized spiel in English or French. But I will never succumb to this. I have gone to many new places here in Vienna—I will tell you about them when I come home. I still think this is a beautiful and charming place—it has a flavor no other place I have ever seen has—but there is a sadness and hope lessens here that during that glorious summer weather of our stay here I did not see. There are many more people here now—the streets are crowded with people, the opera is in full blast, the theaters are going—but it is sad. I know 1001 sadnesses about this place, but this also I must tell to you later. I will say this: I cannot think of any place that has more charm and interest than the streets of the Old City here. The Old City is that part bounded by the big fashionable Rings—you know—the one where the opera is. There is none of the quaintness of old Frankfurt, but you will fill yourself suddenly in a narrow old street, with those magnificent old houses in the light beautiful Baroque style.

Thursday

Your own hard work makes me envious and sorrowful. I am coming back and taking hold of something; I want to work at it as hard as I can. I wish I could have seen your *Hedda Gabler*—but the Repertory Theatre will probably continue to do it throughout the season, and I can see it when I come back.—My dear Aline, these letters have not been very cheerful, but have you noticed how full of love for you they are. I think my only touch of bitterness was when I felt you were not writing enough. Well, God knows, I've written too much—I'm putting an arbitrary end on this one now. I'm going to see the magnificent Breughels this afternoon, and also one or two by another great painter named Packer.[5] I am bringing a lot about him home. God bless you and keep you. I should like to see your face again. Tom

1. Although Wolfe wrote "October 27," he apparently misdated the letter for Sunday was 28 October.
2. "This is good, but that is better."
3. Ferenc Molnar (1878–1934) was a Hungarian novelist and dramatist.
4. Strindberg's "Die Stärkere" ["The Stronger Woman"], Molnar's "Stilleben" ["Still Life"], and Barrie's "Die Medaillen der alten Frau" ["The Old Lady Shows Her Medals"], were presented at Die Wiener Kammerspiele that Wednesday evening.
5. Michael Packer (1435–98) was a Tyrolese painter and wood carver.

89. [Vienna, 29 October 1928]

Dear Aline:

This unspeakable, dismal, lousy hotel where I stay at night—and at no other time—insists on charging me for cheap writing paper—and I am driven to this extreme in my emergency, for I won't pay for what ought to be given.[1] I went to see the glorious pictures today—at least that's one thing that pays us back for all the tawdry junk we have to wade through. The pictures in the big gallery here are even better than I thought—and aren't the Breughels glorious? Did you ever know anything to equal them? And do you ever hear any one speak of them? There are some very fine pictures there by Teniers—and Holbein. Teniers was a very fine painter, in spite of the fact that we get tired of him from seeing him everywhere—but just think of the difference between Teniers and Breughel! What is it? Teniers

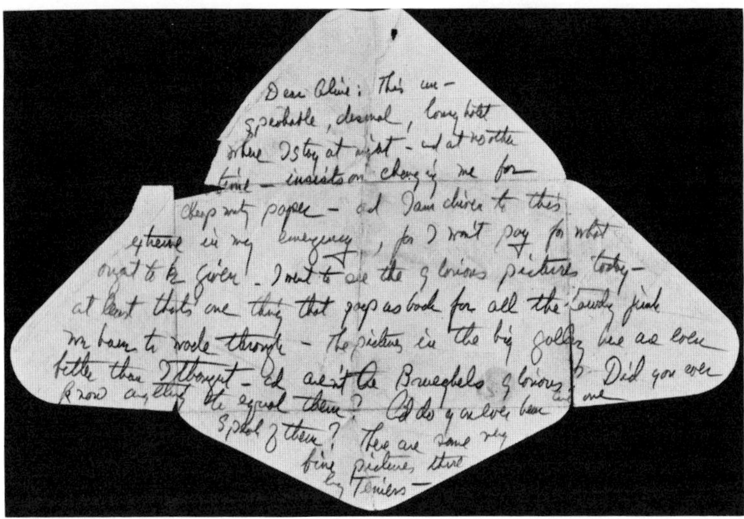

Dear Aline: This unspeakable, dismal, lousy hotel where I stay at night – and at no other time – insists on charging me for cheap writing paper – and I am driven to this extreme in my emergency, for I won't pay for what ought to be given. I went to see the glorious pictures today – at least that's one thing that pays us back for all the tawdry junk we have to wade through – The pictures in the big gallery here are even better than I thought – and aren't the Breughels glorious? Did you ever know anything to equal them? And do you ever hear any one speak of them? There are some very fine pictures there by Teniers –

Thomas Wolfe to Aline Bernstein, 29 October 1928 (By permission of the Houghton Library, Harvard University)

was a fine skilled artist, full of strength and originality—but he never did anything to touch that glorious picture of a peasant wedding or banquet.[2] You know the one?—two men are carrying on a big board platters of some strange food—all rich yellow globes? And one man, a musician, is standing up behind the guests with his bagpipe—Everything that Breughel has touched—even this peasant scene—has over it a strange super-natural power of imagination. I realized today more than ever before that these pictures are not to be seen—they are to be studied. It is simply terrific what he has put into these pictures. Each one, like the going up of Christ to Calvary, and the Carnival and Lent, and the Tower of Babylon are cosmic spectacles. There are a thousand stories in each one, and as you begin to examine them, you see that each story is touched with this super-human penetration—this un-earthly quality. I believe the reason we have felt Peter Breughel is one of the greatest painters that ever lived is the reason an art critic and aesthete will never accept—will accept only as a mark of a painter's inferiority—namely, Breughel was probably the greatest storyteller and dramatist who ever used paint. I think he is one of the greatest story tellers and dramatists that ever lived—and he has brought over into paint a talent that is incredibly like the one Rabelais used in writing.

1. Wolfe wrote this letter on four ripped-open envelopes.

2. Breughel's "Peasant Wedding." The Albertina Gallery also has "Christ Carrying the Cross," "Fight between Carnival and Lent," and "The Tower of Babel," which Wolfe also mentions.

90. [Vienna] Monday Night [29 October 1928][1]

Dear Aline—

I got two more of your blessed letters tonight and a cable about Scribners. In my present state Scribners does not make even a dull echo in me—I have seen so much print that I feel it is criminal to add to it. Perhaps you can help me to get back a little vanity, a little self-belief, a little boastfulness. God knows we all ought to have some, and all my egoism has plunged downwards and left me stuck in the mud. But every word in your letters I love and cherish—My dear, I am coming back to America, and get some kind of paying work, and then perhaps, if you want it, we can have some kind of life together again. Everything I write you runs on into words—I am going to be definite for once now: I love you dearly, I have acted badly while wanting to act well, I want to redeem myself, I want to see you again, I want to try to act fairly and humanly towards you from now on, I want to go to work. I am coming back to America next month—one week in Budapest, two weeks in Italy, and home if possible from Naples. I will be an ugly sight with my clipped hair and scar, but I wish I were as certain of everything in my life growing better as I am of this.

—I went to the Albertina today—surely of all places on earth this is one of the most beautiful[. . . .]

1. This is apparently an unsent fragment.

91. Vienna / Tuesday Night / October 30 [1928]

My Dear—

Thank God I have recovered my paper out of the depths of my travelling book-case—paper in Vienna seems to be a kind of precious gold leaf, and is doled out at high prices a sheet at a time. Also, I have found a pencil I can write with—the fountain pen with which I started so nobly lies buried somewhere in the mud or dust of the Oktoberfest. Today I got a letter from Mrs. Boyd—on her way to Paris—saying a Mr. So-and-So was interested in my book.[1] She gave me her Paris address, and I answered her at once from Cook's. She said she hoped I would not do anything with it except through her —a very gratifying apprehension—and I told her in my letter that she could depend on me to stick closer than glue if anything came of it in any way through her efforts. She also said she hoped my new book was almost finished—and my heart began to throb up and down like a sore tooth. I have made thousands of notes, and written scenes here and there, and gone and investigated and explored all over. I hope that my awful habit of poking my nose into dark corners will not get that Very Sensitive Flower broken again. Darling Aline—I love and adore you, and I would give my crooked nose and my weak eye for a little of your strength and ability. You love the theater, and the theater is a beautiful and marvelous thing—so grand, and yet, when all is said and done, so limited. Don't bristle up at the word limited. It is a beautiful word—we can do nothing until we know our limits—I have never found mine, I don't know what they are—and at present I am spiritually a grovelling worm wondering why some useful catastrophe can not erase this constructive-less, atom-less, light-less, nothing-less life. In my torment the theatre here is cake and pudding to me—in one place *Faust*, in another Somerset Maugham's *Finden Sie Das Constanz*[2] does something or other? in another an English mystery play, Nord Express 133; in another The Old Lady Shows Her Medals by Barrie in German alone with a one act by Strindberg, and one by Molnar; in another a dull operetta by Lehar; in that work,—as I may have told you I am in the tragic position of the Egoist who has absolutely no faith left in his own ability, —The best thing left in me is my love for you, and a genuine object worship for a beautiful work that has been touched with the light of genius. Quite often I am intelligent enough to recognize such a thing when I see it. But these things are not very numerous when compared with oceans of junk. And I realize furthermore that most of the people who have made a great report in the world have been fools and asses with a perfectly preposterous belief in themselves. Who else but a great simpleton could have devoted years of his life reading nothing but Dumas—yet that is what Tolstoy did and he is worshipped by millions of people today[. . . .]

1. Madeleine Boyd, Wolfe's agent, had written on 15 October, but her letter did not catch up with him until the thirtieth. She had written: "This is what had happened, Covici-Friede read the book, and although struck by the excellence of some passages would not undertake publication. Mr. Maxwell Perkins was next, he is very much interested, would like to see you to talk things over, now where am I to get you?"

2. *The Constant Wife.*

92. [Vienna, 1 November 1928]

Dear Aline:

About the only thing I want to write during these days is a letter to you—and I want to write that all the time now. It is my only way at the moment of talking to the only person I care about talking to—my being-alone-ness has become a kind of terrible joke. I have somehow lost all power of breaking my own silence. The Viennese are a friendly—a gemütlich people; and I am sure I would have no difficulty in talking to them—and I do occasionally and often, whenever I meet them, and particularly in the coffee houses which are their home. But it is not real talk—it is a kind of foolish babble—"Vienna pleases you?—Yes, it is very schön, and the people very agreeable. Have you been here long? Two weeks already, and I bleib here perhaps a week longer. But meanwhile I go to Budapest? Do you know Budapest? It is very schön. I've heard—and so on." Meanwhile, my heart and soul and brain leans over the cornice and leers down on this foolishness like the gargoyles of Notre Dame. I live in a strange world—I will brood for an hour over a map of Vienna that I carry in my pocket, studying the vast cobweb of streets. Then suddenly I will rush into the Ring, seize a taxi, and yell out some address in the outer rim of town that the driver has never heard of. He has to study my map—we go out and out, across the great outer girdle—today it was a great bare spot on the map marked Sportplatz. When we got there, it was a huge field with a fence around it and turfed banks, which is used as a football field. All around the places were shabby buildings with small shops downstairs and people leaning out of windows above. The man was surprised and looked back at me to see if a mistake had been made. But I jumped out and paid him, and ran around the corner of the fence till he had gone. Then I walked on and on, straight up the long sloping street that seemed to reach the Magic Mountains—the soft hills of the Wiener Wald looming against the horizon. It was All Saints Day—most of the shops were closed and the people were out in force. They were almost all walking in the same direction as I was—towards the Magic Mountains. The shutters were down on most of the little shops, and everything had a strange quietness, it seemed to me. It was amazingly like a dream I used to have of a dark street, and dark shuttered houses. There was only one bit of light and sound in the street that came from a carnival. I was in this carnival riding the merry-go-round, surrounded by noise and lights and many people. Then it seemed that I was looking through the bars of a bright wooden gate into the dark street (from the carnival). In this street, there was no sound, no vehicles, no traffic except a great crowd of people all walking silently and steadily in the same direction. They did not speak with one another, they turned their faces neither to right nor left,—not even as they tramped past the gate of the carnival and the white light fell over them. I knew that in the white light the faces of these people looked thin and ghastly—sallow and damned; and what their march meant, and all that silence I could not say, but I felt that death and doom and the end of all things was there in that place; but whether it was I who was dead in that carnival, or these strange phantom shapes from whom I was cut off, I could not say either.—This dream came back to me today as I walked up that long street with the people all tramping steadily towards the country—and strangely enough, when I got into the outskirts of the city, and the buildings were uneven and scattered about with much open ground—ugly and messy as the outskirts of great cities are—I began to come on shabby little carnivals—only a little merry-go-round and a few swings, grinding out old Schubert and Strauss tunes incessantly. Then I went on and on, the hills were very close and beautiful now—I was on their fringes, and I could see the edges of Vienna right and left, vast and smoky and roughly circular. I came to a place where there was a whole colony of stucco homes, all alike, all ugly, with gardens behind, and trying to look like the Austrian equivalent for an American suburban stucco "English" cottage. I sometimes think that the enormous difference we think we see between Europe and America is not as deep as we believe—when you see these cottages all alike it is not hard to imagine an Austrian Arnold Bennett or Sinclair Lewis writing a book about the people in them. The things you and I have liked best in Europe—the grand pictures, the buildings, and so on, belong mostly to an order of things that has gone—the world—the world that has to eat and drink and labor is probably being "Americanized." At least, they groan about it, and deprecate it—but I think they earnestly want it for themselves. To be "Americanized" is simply to be industrialized in the most complete and serviceable fashion—America is the apex of the present industrial civilization, but that is the only civilization the modern world has got. The European who carries a really good load of hate against America, nearly always hates because America is rich and Europe is poor; because America is strong and Europe is weak. But the European does not always put it so honestly—he salves his pride by picturing himself as a lover of the good and beautiful, a defender and patron of the arts, and a despiser of filthy money, while the American cares for nothing else but money, and so on. A great fat boy in one of the big beer houses in the Neuhauser street in Munich one night poured all this into my ear while he swilled down liters of beer and gorged himself with the fourteen different meats and sausages of a delicatessen Aufschnitt. There is not a picture or a book in the world for which he would not have foregone a liter of his beer.

Budapest, Thursday /
November 8, 1928

Dear Aline:

I have been here since last Friday night, and I have already heard of Hoover's election. The news seems to be authentic, and his election to be overwhelming. This only makes me sorrier than ever that Smith didn't get it. Why is it that the good people, the right people are so often the underdogs? From this great distance it looked as if the whole nation had gone mad in an effort to strangle the man. Now, what are they going to do with him? His intelligence for government will be wasted while small incompetent people thrive in great jobs. And now that it's over the people who voted against him because he is a Catholic will insist that this had nothing to do with it. The only American paper I get to read over here is the Paris New York Herald, and this filthy little sheet, together with all the filthy little people who write letters to it, has nearly convinced me that most of the good Americans have stayed at home. We are a people who ought not to live out of our country too long—the attempt to make Europeans of ourselves succeeds in producing loose and abortionate idiots. But America is also a very difficult country for many people to live in, unless one can with a great hurrah join in the rush to elect the Hoovers and Coolidges. And think where you find yourself in this rush? With the Ku Klux Klan, and the Anti Saloon League, and Senator Heflin,[1] and John Roach Straton,[2] and the Methodist Church, and the Rockefellers. My part of America is not with this. It is somewhere perhaps with the part that voted for Smith—and he got beaten four to one.

But I am coming home. I am an American and I must try to take hold somewhere. I am not burning with indignation or revolt, or anything. I am tired of struggle and should like to fall in step if only I knew how. But how? I have no genuine conviction that any other nation is closer in its spirit than we are, that any other nation cares more for the good and the beautiful than it does for money. They are all, so far as I can see, an ugly, grasping, greedy lot—if anything a great deal grosser in their desires than we are—and their cry against us comes from a dirty money-envy and money-hatred, and from nothing better. This goes for everyone I have seen this time except the Austrians; and the Austrians are a gentle indifferent lot, who want to dream—who live in a world of images. So much has been taken from them that they have no hope of ever getting back to any kind of strength or splendor. Therefore, they dream—and decay.

I am a citizen of the most powerful and the most interesting nation of modern times—and I wish to God I knew how to make something of it.—

(Evening)

I have just come in after walking miles and miles through this city. You must come here—you must come here in the summer. Then I think you will get all its splendor. It is one of the ugliest places I have ever seen—and also one of the most beautiful. The buildings are very very ugly, with rare exceptions. They look as if they had been built by French architects with German blood in their veins. They are big solid ugly buildings coming from 1880 or so down to the present. They have meaningless bumps and balconies and protuberances—they are of grey plastery looking stone or dull brick. But at night along the river it is a magic sight. The Danube is a grand stream, like the Hudson, and it sweeps between Buda and Pest with a grand curve. I am living in Pest, which is by far the greatest part of the place. But Buda is by far the most beautiful. Buda is on a series of lovely hills which begin just across the river. One hill is a great fortress, on another a huge palace—bigger than the one at Vienna—where Maria Theresa[3] or Franz Joseph[4] and the rest of them got crowned kings and queens of Hungary, and then, of course, lived in them no more. And then on other hills and hollows are houses—not very pretty houses (I saw them the other day). They are little, plastery villas and stucco cottages, and grey ugly apartment houses. But at night the lights bright and clear upon the hills, give the whole place a fairyland effect. You have heard that it is beautiful, and it is—but the beauty is almost entirely in its situation.—The Viennese people say that these people are barbarians, and they are right. This is what you want to come here to see. It is unmistakable, and it makes this place interesting. I have been to the picture gallery, and most of it is second and third rate Titians and Luini's[5] and so on. There are some good pictures, too—The best Greco I have ever seen, and some fine Goyas, and a few good ones by Cranach. But there's nothing that would justify your coming all the way across Europe to see. So it is with most of their public buildings and monuments. There's a great house of Parliament of which they are immensely proud, and insist that you must see. It was built in the 1890's, and you can imagine a little what it's like. But it's right on the River—on the Pest side—and in the evening sun it seems to rise and float upon the water. As it gets dark the great dome and spires melt into the light, and it undergoes this fairy transformation that all things along this magnificent river seem to take on of evenings. I am sure they thought they were following the English houses of Parliament—what with the river and all. But you look at the domes and spires of this place from a distance and you see the domes and minarets of Turkey all over the place. And when you go into the place—there you begin to find the East. They have an Upper and a Lower House,—just as we have, with a great dome in between.

Friday Night

(I'll finish telling you about Parliament[.]) But the decoration is Oriental—heavy barbaric patterns with gold and stripes and mosaic work. They love deep red plush and even cover the railings of stairs with thick red folds of it. They love red carpets and marble columns of rich hues—the Senate houses in the parliament are round with great Turkish balconies above for diplomats and journalists and above that another balcony with Turkish designs in marble.

Friday November 9

I have bought you the most magnificent book today. It is the best book they have on costumes and designs and peasant houses—it has everything in it, and it is all pictures. There is an index—(in simple Hungarian which you, as a cultured person, will decipher instantly)—and then 250 or more magnificent plates. It is one of those completely satisfying books that seems to annihilate all the bad ones. You feel that if there were only a few thousand books like this in the world, we could make a huge bonfire of all the rest. It has everything in it—people, costumes, houses, doors, furniture, pots, pans—everything is beautiful and clearly and simply produced—the photographs are excellent and the designs splendid. For God's sake, get somebody at once to do a Hungarian play for you—with this book you would have all the other designers in New York going crazy with envy and despair. I have just been feeding my eyes on its savage colors again—I know you will like it. It is a new book—published only a month or so ago. Also I am sending you a little photo which was made by an Australian lassie who is doing the universe with her equally dull parents. This was made in a Hungarian village two or three hours from here—it was made, of course, on Sunday when the people get all dressed up. She showed me this and I liked it—the design showed up so clear and good that I thought it might interest you. I asked her to have another one made, and tonight when I came in I found it in my box, together with several small coins, and a note saying she owed them to me. The coins are driving me crazy—I have no recollection of a debt; the hotel is full of crazy women. In my box were two more letters from two more mad harpies. If I appear to boast, leave me my little bit of triumph. I have not often been so honored lately by ladies of un-commercial design. There is a poor gray haired half-cracked woman here who is an interior decorator in New York, but gave up her business in New York, and is wandering about Europe trying to get some kind of peace, apparently, for her damned soul. According to her story, which is so woven in with a thousand sicknesses of the soul, she had one love affair late in her spinsterhood. The man jilted her in Spain and married someone else. She is crazy and sick; but then I need not be particular for so am I. She it was who introduced me first to herself, then to the Austrians, and to a couple of Hungarian young women, very nice and charming, whom she met on the train coming from Vienna. She seems to have a great knack at meeting people—there is a very interesting and intelligent woman lost in her; but she also has some of the unpleasant qualities of her race—which is also yours. Her poor tortured face is fixed with a smile of strained and Christlike sweetness, which finally annoyed me past endurance. I went to some museums with her—she had some very sensible things to say about the buildings and shops here—but a day was enough. She flows with oily tortured sweetness. She flows all over you. If I dropped a box of matches, she wrung her hands and begged me to forgive her. I think she is really in this condition. And she flowed all over me in the street—I would go into the gutters, I would flatten myself against walls, if we were standing still I would back away instantly, in great comic semi circles—but always that woman would be upon me, with her milky tortured smile, and her heavy soft body pressing against me.

Saturday Night November 10

My harem has deserted me today—without saying good bye or anything. I suppose my manner got so cold and haughty. Why is it? After weeks of being alone I get simply starved to talk to people. I am excited, thrilled, grateful for their companionship. The whole world throws off its leaden color. Life becomes good and happy again. Then—at the end of a day's time, these same people drive me frantic. I wonder how I could ever have been such a fool as to let myself in for it. I become nervous, my fingers twitch, I rub my fuzzy head and finger my scar constantly—everything they say annoys me, and makes me impatient to get away. I will do anything at this point to be alone again—and I say things that offend and anger them. Then I go through a second torture for having said them. I told the New York woman finally after I had almost [backed into] half the buildings and walls in Budapest and backed all around in the most obvious circle[,] please, for God's dear sake, to walk on her own side of the pavement—that I was being driven crazy by her constant leaning against me. She said that she was honestly not conscious of it—told me several life stories, all horribly confused, said she was a child, and a virgin at 40 or more, and innocent of the ways of the world, and so on. Only wanted to help me; do whatever would please me. This syrupy Christliness with the child business annoyed me still more—I think she believes these fables herself, because they excuse her. I finally got away definitely the other night when I was to go out to drink with her and the Hungarian girl. Didn't see her again, but she left a little Hungarian dictionary in my desk as a gift for me, with a saintly note around it. I answered very pleasantly thanking her, and last night there was a bottle of Eau de Cologne tied with red ribbon. Also the Australian girl's snapshot of the peasants and 50 filler (½ a pago—9 cents, which drives me mad because I do not know the reason), and a note in German from the Hungarian girl telling me where I could find a good costume and picture books. They are all gone now—New York and Australia—and the Hungarian girl I shall not look up. It is shocking how many of us are sick and groping.

I am going to Mezö-Kövesd—the little village—at 7 o'clock tomorrow morning. I must get up at six, and as it is now past two, I am not going to bed at all. I'm simply going to lie down with my clothes on—the hotel people have instructions to get me up at all costs. I shall get out there by 9:30 or ten and come back early in the afternoon. I am intensely interested in seeing the place—country and city in this land are sharply divided. In Budapest people are proud of being like Europeans—they live the life of Europeans, and are proud of their streets, their buildings, their Parliament, their trainways, their coffee houses—"better than Vienna." This is too bad—they suffer by comparison as all imitators suffer. Their imitation is young and obvious—so much of it is like a Cannibal Nigger smoking a cigar and wearing the stovepipe hat of the missionary he has just eaten. If you were here your trained eye would see all this in a hundred places. For example, tonight I passed by a place that sold nothing but lighting fixtures. It is a place which no description can describe—which no one can believe until he sees it. From the ceiling hung by a hundred chains a nightmare jungle of glass. Great festoons and fountains of crystals, some colored, some clear, all meaningless, all bewildering. It looked like a Victorian ballroom in the hands of the Turks. At another shop for kitchen fixtures, there was a huge gas range of white enamel, all painted over with designs and peasant covers. The pots and pans were of the hard raw colors they like, and there were hundreds of little brass designs, which could be bought separately, and which apparently serve no purpose since to be nailed to the wall wherever the aesthetic fancy directs.

Monday Evening /
November 12

My Dear—

If all the rest of my journey has been waste, and if I have done very little for myself with it, I think what I have seen these last two days might almost make up for it—not for what I may get from it, but for the news that I can now pass on to you. When you come to Europe again—when you cross the Atlantic again, you must also cross a good part of Europe and come to Hungary. Here in Budapest you must use the services of two or three intelligent Hungarians who speak English—I can give you their names and addresses. Unfortunately I did not have these people with me, and many things I saw I can only describe without knowing exactly what they mean—although my mind deciphered most things, and I found today on consulting an Hungarian here that most of my guesses were correct. Yesterday morning at six o'clock I got up here—with the aid of the hotel staff—and went to the East Station. At seven o'clock I left the station on an express train bound for the village of Mezö-Kövesd, about 100 miles away. Away *where* I do not yet know, for I had failed to look the place up on the map before I started and I have been so charmed by my fancies that I have not dared to do so since. It could not have been Westward toward Vienna, for I came that way; I do not think it could have been Northward, for the Czeck borders are only 25 miles away from Budapest. I do not think it could have been Southward across the great plain—the Alföld that extends to Jugo-Slavia, for although I rode across a vast and dreary plain, and found this town planted in the mud of the plain, I could see a low range of hills away in the distance. My belief now is that I was on the Bucharest express—for a ticket man in the station asked if I was going there—and that Mezö-Kövsd is eastward or southeastward from Budapest. It was a grey wet foggy day of the sort that seems to afflict all Europe from England to Hungary—and farther perhaps—at this time of year. And the landscape was wearily depressing. For a while after leaving Budapest, there were low hills and rolling dismal looking country—possibly everything looks dismal now. Then, for the greater part of the journey there was a vast muddy plain stretching away infinitely until it was lost in the steam and haze of the horizon. This great plain is one vast farm—the land is striped with bands of plowed field and bands of green unplowed field[6]—and these long bands stretch straight away as far as the eye can travel. This also adds to the impression of hopelessness.

Tuesday Evening / November 13

Dear Aline:

I'm going back to Vienna tomorrow, and then to Italy, and then home. I shall not stay in Italy, although I should like to see something in Florence and Rome if I could. I have seen enough—all that I can hold at present. I am at times flattened out by the tremendousness of my ignorance; but other people are also ignorant—and I have the same chance to learn as other people. What I really feel, however, is not so much my ignorance, as the overwhelming ocean of junk one has to wade through in this world before he comes to something good. It is not that Art is long, but that Junk is unending. My dear, my heart lifts up at one thought—I should like to see your face, all wreathed in flowerlike smiles and loveliness—I must finish telling you about Mezö-Kövesd, for that is one of the good things. I got there a little before ten o'clock—the train stopped at a dreary station surrounded by the vast muddy fields. At first I did not know where the village was—there seemed to be scattered houses away in the distance—I walked away from the station around a huge field of mud. A great many of the young men of the village were assembled on this field; there were bugle calls and they were lining up in military formations—from little boys to young fellows 18 to 20. The rain had collected in pools all over the place and big fat ducks and geese were everywhere—in the muddy streets the fields and the yards of all the houses. I was terribly depressed. I wondered what I had come for—the place seemed so barren, so lost, that I thought Russia must be like this. But I heard a churchbell ringing away in the distance; and women, dressed up in these amazing costumes, began to hurry along, coming from the little white houses that bordered the road. Finally I came up to what seemed a main street—it was another mudhole, but it seemed originally to have been paved. I turned off to the left—in the wrong direction, away from the main part of town, and I walked straight along this street for a good distance until suddenly the last white house of the village ended, and the great wet fields began, with the muddy road running straight into eternity. I realized that most of the people I had seen were going in the opposite direction. I turned and went back as fast as I could—all the people stared and whispered and frowned and snickered—little children in their strange costumes giggled at me—any one of these people would have stopped the traffic in New York—the children found me strange and comic, yet the men with their embroidered aprons and their ridiculous derby hats stuck straight off of their heads, and the women in their bewildering costumes, did not seem at all strange to the children. Presently I saw the church ahead of me, and began to pass the little shops of the village. It is a very sinful place—everything was open and doing business—I suppose the people work during the week, and that Sunday is their best day for selling and trading. The street opened into a kind of square before the church—it was obvious that this was the centre of the town. There was a brisk business going on in the market place among the fruit and vegetable peddlars, and dozens of men hung around in groups, loafing and gossiping as they do in our own small towns. I made straight for the church, after having provided the whole market place with a new subject for gossip—I went into the church and found it crowded. In the cold little vestibule outside the doors several old women were crowded muttering responses to the service, or kneeling on the dirty concrete near the doors. I went into the church and stood near the doors. A priest in gorgeous robes was making his sermon—the church was crowded—all of the aisles and bare space, as well as the seats, were filled with people. In one solid section of the pews sat all the married women, with black conical shaped bonnets, and sober costumes. The old men, the chief men of the place, I suppose, sat in another part wearing those wonderful robes which are among the few beautiful things I have seen in Hungary—for what I have seen here seems to be wild and strange, for the most part, rather than beautiful. I have pictures of this wonderful robe in the great book I have bought for you—it is a garment in which every man looks like an emperor. It is a great block of thick stiff white wool or felt with short sleeves, although most of the old men wear it as a cape. It sits upon the shoulders of a peasant in the most regal and splendid way—it can be embroidered along the edges and the two arms and shoulders in a way that suits their barbaric fancy—and some of the decorations were magnificent. Most of the old fellows wear a kind of turban—very handsome—of fuzzy black wool, with this robe, and of course the stiff high boots that nearly all the men wear. And God! but they're dirty—after church I looked at some of the old fellows—some with the faces, moustaches, slant eyes, of the East, and their beards were stiff and caked with dirt. The young unmarried women are together in all their splendor in another part of the church, and I suppose the young men elsewhere

—although most of the young brides were loafing around in the market place outside. The priest finished his sermon and left his cage in the wall; then the long Catholic ritual before the altars began. The people knew the order perfectly, they listened faithfully, made all the responses, began to sing from time to time, then listened again while the priest sang out Latin in a high voice—what he said was indistinguishable, and seemed calculated only to make a weird reverberation in the church. Old women remained on their knees on the hard cold floor during the entire service—there were wretches there in filthy rags—over the whole place there was a close warm odor of hay and manure—the place had an unmistakable smell of a stable. Nowhere have I ever seen the simple animal nature of men so plainly as in this church—I kept thinking of this as they all stood there with their smell of the stable hearing of their kinship to God. When it was over they all streamed out slowly—and immediately two men in blue uniforms outside the church began to beat rapidly upon small drums. The crowd split in two and gathered in two great circles around the drummers. Then when all was quiet, the drummer put aside his drum, pulled a slip of paper from his jacket, and began to read rapidly. The old fellows in the woolen robes stood around looking wise and puffing thoughtfully at their funny pipes. The announcement, I learned later and guessed then, is a kind of weekly official journal—probably with decrees, laws, tax announcements, and so on. When the reading of this was over the two crowds broke away and streamed rapidly down the street—probably to gossip or to eat, or to their homes. But I began to look for a restaurant. I had been warned that it was hopeless—that I had better take a few sandwiches along, because I could not eat the food I might find there. But so much preparation is not in me—there was a place on the square marked Etterem—that means Restaurant—and I went in. I am sure it is the Swell Place of the town, for none of the gorgeous peasants were there; but a dirty fat waiter with a dirty stiff white shirt and greasy black hair. Also several of the town Dandies—they must be all over Europe, just as Maupassant put them in his French country towns—a man with spats, and a Hungarian-English tailor, and a sensual barbered face with pointed mustaches—and a luscious smile showing his old-pearl teeth—I'm sure he went to Budapest often and was a great Rounder. There were several of this kind there—one came in with a bald knobby head, a golf suit of loud checks, stockings to match, spats, and elegant brown shoes you could see your face in. He was the damndest looking monkey I've seen. A young fellow was drawing their caricatures at a pago—17 or 18 cents—apiece. They all gathered around, looked knowing, said it was very good, ordered their own portrait, and roared with laughter when they saw the result. Then they took the drawing all over the place showing it to their friends. I had him draw me—perhaps I will send you the result. I recognize myself, but it is as if I have been in hell for several years. He seized very cleverly on the salient things for exaggeration—my pointed nose, which apparently I have not yet lost, and the heavy overhang of my underlip.—I thought I would eat something, but an unfortunate visit to the urinal destroyed my hunger—I ordered a bottle of beer knowing they could not do anything to this. Then I left the place and began to explore the village. I walked out by the church along the muddy main street or road in a direction opposite the one I had just taken. I went straight on past the cemetery, past the little white houses, until I came again, abruptly as before, to the open country. Nothing but the land—the vast muddy land stretching away to nowhere. There were hills over to my left. But I was terribly depressed—the barrenness, the greyness and monotony of this life frightened me. It seemed to me that the life of people in a Middle Western village must be gay compared to the life here—and I still think it may be. And the road stretched straight away until it too was lost in the fog and steam of the horizon. I turned around and walked back towards the church. But instead of going the whole way, I turned off the main road, and went down a muddy road to the right. Here was the main body of the village which I had not before suspected spread out behind the church. It is one of the strangest places I was ever in. All of the streets that I had seen heretofore running off the main one had been straight muddy alleys with the little white houses punctually spaced along the road. This straightness, and the feeling of open space, with the awful unending land all around had depressed me. Back in this part, however, I immediately became more cheerful. The muddy little roads that serve as streets wound and twisted about and met each other in a labyrinthine pattern. The little white houses were covered with roofs of dry reeds bound together, and of the thickness of a foot. On these reeds patches of green moss were growing. The houses were one story, with perhaps a half story attic above—this upper part was often of wood with carved designs on it. The end of the house faced the street; the doorway, with a very narrow wooden perch that ran the whole length of the house faced the side yard—this mudhole was full of quacking geese and at the back there was always what seemed at first to be several stacks of beautifully ricked hay—mellow and odorous. Then I discovered that these were not haystacks at all; but that they cover their pig pens and barns with hay—the pigs were rooting and grunting in the slime. In the middle of the muddy street people were drawing water from a well—these wells are as familiar in Hungary as that strange [dance?] in the pictures of Peter Breughel—I mean the wheel on top of a pole. The well is a bucket attached to a long pole which swings up and down, by weights and balances, I suppose. Back in this part, as I say, I lost a great deal of my depression. Although the streets were mudholes and the geese and swine were quacking and grunting everywhere, the little white houses with their thick walls and small windows, on which moisture was gathering showing warmth therein, and the reed roof, and above all, I believe, the mellow sweet hay covering over the barn and sty, shut out the awful emptiness of the plain all around, and gave a close warm look to things. They were huddled together here with their pigs and geese, but I felt that they must get a great satisfaction out of the elaborate ritual and convention of their lives—how elaborate it is I did not then know, nor do I yet know fully. My train back to Budapest—the only one before night—passed at 2:30—it was not 1:30; I found the Turkish spire of the church above the houses and made my way towards it, knowing the public square was there. When I came into the square again, I saw one of the most extraordinary spectacles I have ever seen—it is as bright and strange and wonderful to me now as it was the moment I saw it. When I had left the restaurant an hour or so before[,] the square had been deserted. Now it was crowded with hundreds of people—some standing, others walking back and forth. But what caught you immediately was that these people were not mixed into the great shuttle of a crowd—they were divided into groups and companies with military formality—the blazing color and pageantry, all regimented, made me think of one of the old pictures of a battle, in which you see the companies all drawn up in blocks upon a plain outside a city. The young men in groups of twenty or thirty were stationed at various places around the square; the married women elsewhere; the older men still elsewhere; and the young girls, themselves in groups of twenty or thirty[,] marched back and forth and around and up and down. Of course this explosion of color that simply turned that grey day into a pageant came mostly from the girls. I can't go on to describe the costumes—for they were infinitely varied—the one uniform detail came in the wonderful shawls they wore over all the rest of the bewildering business. These shawls were of some delicate material—silk probably—with a great variety of patterns around the neck. Then they were fringed with a great thick border of woolen thread—this was a solid color and was either a brilliant yellow, or crimson, or red. Curiously enough, those groups with red, and so on, seemed to keep together. As to the rest of it—you can see it better than I can—the long pleated skirts, covered with strange designs—the skirts are one thick mass of ruffles, and when the girls walk, the skirts billow and undulate and show inches of thickness where they are kicked up by the feet. Over this they wear the apron—similar if not exactly the same as that worn by the young men—and I am told the apron on the young man is a sign of bachelorhood. It is black or blue—this apron—but it has across it a strip of embroidered flower and leaf work, which is sometimes over half its length. As the girls go up and down in groups, the young men stand together, or march off in columns of twos—they all grin and snicker among themselves, but they act otherwise as if the other is not there. I did not find this funny. I did not find it naive and delightfully childlike. I had a feeling of terrible disgust and revulsion against this elaborate and evil ritual. These great swathings of pleats and ruffles and shawls which concealed the bodily lines of the girls were only foils to the evil searching curiosity of the young men, whose talk—I will bet my nose, because I was born a villager myself—was mainly of breasts and fornication. The huge sexual rituals of society are weakened and dispersed in great cities because they exist mainly through close observation. And they are all-powerful in the village for this reason—if you try to break a custom you will very likely break your heart as well. It is for this reason that I believe in cities more than in villages—I think there is greater good in them, and higher life, and a greater spiritual freedom. I am simple enough to understand the village—that is what I felt at Mezö-Kövesd the other day—there was an evil and barbaric complexity about this that I loathed. But I recognized it as one of the most remarkable things I have ever seen. The thing that brings *wonder* is not the *strange* thing alone—it is the touch of the familiar with the strange thing—that is what makes it strange. And all the time I was feeling the strangeness of this parade the other day, I was simply being pounded all the time by its fundamental likeness to *all* village life. When I was a college boy in the South, the young men used to go to a neighboring town on Sundays—a town where there were two or three girls' schools. The young men would line up in groups outside the church, where the girls attended, and wait for them to come out. Then they would snicker and talk among themselves, as would the girls. But they would not speak. Later in the day, or in the evening perhaps they would go courting. And in Asheville, and in all American small towns the young bucks line up before the drug store, or the post office, and watch the girls go by. I looked at this parade in Mezö-Kövesd as long as I dared—I will never forget those blocks and company formations, with the Virgins marching up and down with rhythmically billowing skirts. Of course, I harmonized with this scene about as well as would a Chinaman at a meeting of the Ku Klux Klan, and I got many unfriendly glances; but my curiosity was stronger than modesty or good manners—I took it all in gaping. Then I had to run for my train and just got in—sleeping as well as I could most of the way back across that dreary musty plain upon the hard bench of a third class carriage. I got back to Budapest a little after four—but darkness had come; the streets were swarming with messy noisy crowds, and at one place they were fighting to get into a movie where Charlie Chaplin was playing; at another they blocked traffic before a newspaper office listening to football results; all of the coffeehouses were jammed. My guess that the city and the country here in Hungary are absolutely divided is right—in America, the small town people dress and act and look much the same as the city people. I went to a restaurant, got what scraps they had—I was much too early for a Buda Pestian dinner—and went to the hotel where I slept twelve or fourteen hours.

The next morning I got up and asked where they kept the peasant costumes and furniture. The place is barely referred to in the guide book—they use their space rather on their House of Parliament, their Art Museum—full of Italian, Dutch, Spanish and German paintings and horrible "modern" junk of the modern Hungarians—I mean so-and-so dying at the feet of Emperor So-and-So, and oleo-margarine, nudes, and so on, and Munkacsy[7] and Laszlo[8]—in fact, they exploit their second-rate things (their "European" part) and say very little of what they should be most proud of. At any rate, I found this place—The Ethnographical Museum—far out at the edge of the city, housed in a great white building. This is the second fine thing I have found here—but this is so good that it would be worth *your* coming across Europe to see it. It is a place that has been divinely created for you—I was at once enormously excited and terribly disappointed because you could not be here. The Museum is devoted to their Folk Culture—it has not perhaps the enormous variety of the museums we saw in Munich in Nürnberg. I mean the Bavarian National and the Germanic—but it is all grist for your mill. The things are beautifully mounted, and it has astonishing unity—since, it seems to me, almost the entire culture of these people belongs to the land. It is first of all the most magnificent costume museum I have ever seen—every kind and variety of peasant costume in all the different parts of Hungary, from the great woolen coats to shawls, jackets, boots, jewelry, whips—and then the peasant furniture—fine and strange, and infinitely superior to the horrible junk the curlyed Budapester furnishes his house with—all of this is intelligently and clearly displayed. Then there are their family implements, their cooking and baking things, their pottery—everything. This covers one enormous floor. Upstairs you have the cultures of other lands—not so elaborate, but very interesting. There were a few very beautiful Chinese and Indian things, but what interested me most were the costumes of the Baltic and near-Asiatic peoples. You can almost follow the trail of the East beginning in Hungary, and continuing through Albania, Montenegro, Bosnia, and so on to the Orient—you see the jewels become heavy and Eastern, the women's dresses bagging into Trousers, the barbaric decorativeness of everything. Then there are also the Eskimos, the Mongols, the Slavs, the Arabs, the tribe peoples. All of this is very interesting—but the thing you must see is the Hungarian Folk Culture.

My dear, I have written these last pages Wednesday night. About a thousand and one other things—the theatre, gypsy music, Hungarian literature—O yes, O yes, they have a literature—Hungarian food (which is very good as well as full of all kinds of colors—I must tell you later. The people here have been very kind to me—they want to do all they can to interest the world in their cause; and of course they have been murderously treated. They had 20000000 people before the war; now they have 7000000. Over two thirds of their country has been given to the Czecks, the Rumanians, and the Jugo-Slavians. How they can continue to exist they do not know. They despise the people who now have most of their wealth and land—the Rumanian, Czecks and so on. They call them peasants and barbarians and speak of themselves proudly as "a highly cultivated people." And the Austrians speak of the Hungarians as barbarians! So it goes! What do we know? We say the world is a small place—but the fact is, it is much too large a place. What does the man in Nebraska know, or care, about this people or their troubles? Yet they have an extensive literature, a great capital, a history thousands of years old, and the honor of saving Europe twice against the Turks who came storming up out of the East. They were themselves a Nomad Eastern people who settled upon these plains many hundreds of years ago—and now their young village men wear embroidered aprons, and the old men great coats of white wool, and the young girls are swaddled in elaborate costumes—every stitch, every pattern, every design of which has some meaning.

And here in Budapest the Singer Sewing Machine has agencies, and Cadillac and Chrysler; and the people read Jokai and Herczeg Ferenc and Biro Lajos and Molnar Ferenc and Lewis Sinclair and Wallace Edgar and Bennett Arnold and Takats Sandor,[9] and a whole raft of other Hungarian writers. But what do they know about this in Newark; or what do they know about Newark here.

What's it all mean? I think I have found a little meaning, a base of culture and understanding that is universal. Some day I shall try to tell you what it is.

Goodbye and God bless you for the present. I try to put down everything and I can not put down a tenth of what I want to say. Where are you? How are you? Have you ever really lived at all, and shall I ever find you again? My dear, in all this wilderness you are the only sure thing—and I do not even know now whether I can ever find you as I believe in you in any other place than in my own heart.

I am going back to Vienna tomorrow. Then I want to get to the sea and to a ship again. I seem so far away from it now that I can hardly believe I shall ever find it.

God bless you. I send you the only part of me that has kept all its life and glory—my love. Tom

This hotel, by the way, is on the river, with a view of glorious Buda. It is splendor for me but I have only paid a little over a dollar for my room.

1. James Thomas Heflin, member of the United States Senate from 1921 to 1931, whose advocacy of white supremacy and anti-Catholicism and whose refusal to support Al Smith in the 1928 presidential election laid the groundwork for his defeat in 1931.

2. American Baptist clergyman and reformer, who as pastor of the Calvary Baptist Church in New York (1918–29) crusaded against dancing, cabarets, atheism, prizefighting, and liquor.

3. Empress Maria Theresa (1717–80) was the Queen of Hungary and wife of the Holy Roman Emperor, Francis I.

4. Franz Joseph, or Francis I (1768–1835), Emperor of Austria, was the last of the Holy Roman Emperors after Napoleon dictated the dissolution of the Empire upon Austria's defeat in 1805.

5. Bernadino Luini (1480/90–1532), a Milanese religious painter noted primarily for his Madonnas and his unusual frescos that contain many secular elements.

6. Wolfe divided his letter here and labeled it "Second Part of Letter," in order to place each half in a separate envelope because of its great bulk.

7. Michael Munkacsy (Leib), (1844–1900). Noted Hungarian religious painter who received, among other honors, the Medal of Honor and the Cross of the Legion of Honor. He is thought by many to be undeserving of these awards.

8. Philip Alexius de Lazlo (1869–1937). Hungarian born, naturalized British portrait painter, internationally famous for his portraits of famous men, among them Theodore Roosevelt and Woodrow Wilson.

9. The Hungarians listed names in reverse order; Wolfe is imitating the practice. Mór Jókai (1825–1904), Hungarian editor and writer of historical romances; Ferenc Herczeg (1863–1954), conservative novelist and playwright; Lajos Biró (1856–1931), playwright who wrote sympathetically of the lower-middle class; Ferenc Molnar (1878–1952), playwright and novelist, most famous of the Hungarian writers, whose works were translated into English in 1927; Sandor Takáts (1860–1932), cultural historian specializing in sixteenth- and seventeenth-century studies.

93. [New York] 333 West Seventy Seventh Street / Nov 8, 1928

My dear:

A few days ago I wrote to you and I wonder how much of what I thought I put down, really got to you. My heart was full, and so often I have nothing new to say that my very words must seem old and threadbare. I wish I could put my pencil in some flavor, cinnamon and fragrant things and so add something new to my constantly repeated idea, my always present love for you.—Do you ever see an American paper? There has been terrible excitement over the election and Smith's defeat is the triumph of bigotry and money grubbing. He made the most sensationally popular campaign[;] his personal triumph seemed immense, and then he was beaten by this great majority. They won't have a Catholic, for some reason I do not pretend to understand. The great American people prefer their drink illicit. Maybe there are enough people who really believe and practice prohibition but I have heard of few. Big business is relieved, there were 5,000,000 shares of stock bought on the exchange today. We went to a party at Mr. Goodman's[1] election night and had champagne, which I enjoyed. But I've lost my taste for strong drink. Also for light conversation. I find I can't talk to any one any more, unless about books or pictures. I'm a heavy one, and remember how I used to be able to rattle on by the hour, if any one would listen. I think I could talk to you three days running non stop either for rest or food. There is little to relate but much to talk about when there are two together. I wonder if you will let me know when you come back, whether you want me to meet you at the dock. This has been a beautiful autumn, warm and cool together, and the leaves staying a long time on the trees, very golden. I went up yesterday to our estate, as we call it. It is heavenly. Did I tell you there is a fine old apple orchard, and the lakes stretching out, and a lovely view? Unfortunately we can't swim in the lake as it is part of the N.Y. City water supply and it would never do to flavor their drink. It seems like a gigantic task to build a house, I wonder if I'll ever finish it. It means no more travel for some time. Teddy and Edla are both crazy about it and I am sure I'll like it when it's done and it will be beautiful.—I have a little breathing space now, three or four days and really took a walk today. My scenery comes in next week, and dress rehearsals start, so I'm enjoying the fresh air. Every couple I see walking together is a stab in my heart. I have really tried to be good and do the best I could for everybody, all my life, and now, here I am, caught in this merciless trap. Is it circumstance, or my own nature that is torturing me? I have given up hope of any help from you, I have cried out to you often enough. My only salvation will be to press my pain in upon myself until it no longer hurts.—

I wish you could have some clothes made for yourself, 2 suits and an overcoat. If you intend to come back to America, it will be wise, you know how hard it is and how expensive to buy clothes here. I would telegraph some money if I knew where you would be at a certain time. I hope your wounds are healed. I am sick to think of it all, where are you now this minute—

Dearest—Aline

1. Phillip Goodman, theatrical producer.

94. Budapest / Saturday / November 10, 1928
Dear Aline:

The little photograph[1] was made last Sunday by an Australian girl in the little Hungarian Village of Mezö-Kövesd. The people get all dressed up like this on Sunday—this is a man and his little boy, and it seemed so good and clear that I asked the girl to have another made for me, so that I could send it to you.—I am going to this village tomorrow. The other picture was given to me today by a woman who runs a peasant costume shop. It is a good shop and full of real things—barbaric and savage. She gave me the picture—which represents a peasant and his bride in their wedding costume—when I told her I had a friend who would come to see her some day and buy out her whole shop.

I am writing you a great long letter about this place, and all that has happened to me. I have found two or three more excellent places in which to get a cracked head and a broken nose—only I am going to use the *other* side next time. I have bought you the most magnificent book—costumes, people, furniture, pots and pans, drawings photographs—all wonderfully clear and exact. You can not have it—it is only a month old, and the best they have. I am coming home; I am going to try to get hold of something, and to do something with my life. I love you with all my heart, and with all my life—I suppose you are out courting again, but will you let *me* call on you?

God bless you, my dear. This is the East—this is the meeting here of Europe and the East. I am going back to Vienna next week. But I'll send my long letter from here. Tom

I look like hell—but I love you.

1. Photograph included.

95. [New York, 10 November 1928]
My Dear:

I had a shortish pale violet letter from you today. It disturbed me terribly, for in it you said that a year ago you knew my love for you was waning and my affections were placed elsewhere. That is the sort of nonsense that makes life so terrible for you and me. You take some glimmer of an idea, a false one at that, and enlarge and embroider upon it until it fills all the space in your cranium. You know perfectly well that my love for you has never abated, and my affections have never left you nor lighted upon anyone else. I can see you working yourself into a frenzy over an entirely false premise. How often I have lived through that very thing with you. I believe that every scene we had together last year was based upon some such thing. You know—I have always loved you and never changed, and you know that it was you that went away, so please, no more self delusion. I feel so badly that your dear head is damaged. I can't believe that you look different. Your hair will grow alright, I am sure. But I hate to think of the difference in your nose. Do you think you caught the terrible cold the night of your brawl? The Great Brawl we'll call it. Vienna must be divine in the autumn. Isn't all the wine district lovely, and Kobenzl? Today, Edla and I went out and for seven hours looked for an apartment to fit our family. We could find only 2 with enough bedrooms and those were only to be had at fabulous rentals. It is the most disheartening business. You never saw any thing so dreary as the succession of apartments, one precisely like another. Ugly and pretentious. It was like heaven coming back to this old house, that has been warmed with our life all these years. What is the matter with this country, people put up with all sorts of inconveniences and ugliness. Just imagine how we could live in Munich for what it costs us here. And I am sure there must be pleasant enough people, they are surely not all the beer swilling variety. There must be fine thoughtful people, where else do their good writers come from, Thomas Mann & Wassermann etc.—I wonder if you have heard from Madeleine B. yet. I'm wild to know the details of Scribner & the book, and I can't find anything out here. And you don't tell me anything about your new one except the number of words you have written, which I do not understand. Also, you say you are coming back and earn some money. There seems to be plenty in New York, but what to do? Are you teaching again? If so, Oliver (Terry's Husband) says you can earn 4 times as much in the public schools (high schools) than you can at the university. I know I can't earn enough in the theatre, and if I need money, must go into the dress designing again. But hope never to do that.—I saw Melville Cane[1] a while ago, and told him Scribner likes your book. He was delighted and told me he thought you one of the most remarkable people he ever met.—I'm just finishing Virginia Woolf's book *Orlando*. It is remarkable, a curious tale, not really a tale. I can't tell you about it, you must read it when you come back. I wonder when that will be. I suppose your Italian trip will spin out, I can picture your inveterate lingering in Italy. Florence will offer you such different flavors. Phil tells me the best and cheapest clothes are to be had there. Why not get yourself some? Also it is a great place for hats. I seem to remember a hat market near the Uffizi.[2] I hope you will see the Roman theatre at Fiesole, it is so lovely. I wish I could be with you there, or any where for that matter.—I am going up to Minna's for a week after P. Pan opens. My body longs more and more for the country. Minna goes to England in December. She is in terrible shape and should get away. Almost melancholia. Edla is here another week and then goes on the road again, as long as the show holds good. She is livelier than ever, and is so happy about having a home in the country. Good night dearest God bless you.—Faithful, loving,

Yours
Aline

(I wrote you only yesterday. My head is so tired from our day's hunting.) This is a very stupid letter. It means that you must never think I have stopped loving you for a second.

1. Melville Cane was an eminent attorney. A writer himself, he specialized in contracts for theatrical and literary clients. Wolfe had met him through Mrs. Bernstein. He eventually reviewed Wolfe's contract with Scribner's before Wolfe signed it.

2. The Uffizi Museum in Florence which Wolfe later visited on 7 December. For a list of the paintings that impressed him, see *Notebooks*, 1:266–67.

96. Budapest / Thursday / November 15 [1928]

Dear Aline:

I know you would be grateful if I wrote you only short letters for a time. Yesterday I sent off to you two great hulking envelopes—the parts of a single letter which I could not cram into one packet. And now I am at it again—but this time only a page or two.

Today has been of a thick grey drizzly streaming dampness that I do not believe we can ever duplicate in America. I went to the Museum a final time to see a few of the good pictures—I am sending you a picture of the Greco. I have been prowling around all afternoon in unexplored parts of the city—in the narrow side and back streets that are not in the guidebooks. In one place I found a great church with two domed Turkish looking towers. I entered reverently with my hat off—immediately half a dozen men spoke to me in a shocked excited jargon. I put on my hat. I was in a Synagogue. If you had been here I would not have made the mistake. But the interior of the synagogue was vast and high—better, I thought than the crowded, dark, bewildering Baroque churches. There seemed to be some room left in the world that was not taken up by things. All day long something that Emerson wrote has been going through my head. He said that "Things are in the saddle and they are beginning to ride us."[1] I have never known very well what that meant until recently. In these little side streets were small messy crowded shops, with loaded windows—windows packed with cheap clothing, beads and bracelets, poisonous looking sausages, shoes—and antiques. I think that in this wilderness of things nothing has so depressed me than these thousand antique shops that are scattered all over Europe. I remember them by the dozens in Brussels, in Cologne, in Frankfurt, in Munich, Vienna, here. Is there no end to it—these dusty dark little holes with the dirty old canvasses of dirty near "old masters" stacked against the walls—with 19th century prints of a dashing cavalier trying to seduce a lady who wards him off with her coy plump arms —a canopy bed in the background—with baroque Jesuses on the cross, old daggers, old pistols, old chests and chairs, pottery and painted glass—I say is there no end to it.

I went to another museum today—and found in it room after room of furniture, pictures, old books, armor, rugs, and peasant clothes—all[,] the man said, to be sold at auction next Sunday. And when this auction is over the place will promptly be filled with another—with genuine hand-wrought things, with old treasures, and so on. In the London and Paris papers there are day after day reports of auctions in the big auction rooms—day after day reports of the sale of drawings by Titian, a head by Greuze, a pastoral allegory by Botticelli. And the art critic reviews the exhibitions of five new artists daily—all are "charming," "significant," "magnificent flesh tint," "one of the few artists living who"—

More than ever I am convinced that the good things are good—but I am sure the perpetrators of most of this rubbish thought it was good as well, and now it lays mouldering in dirty little antiquariats, deader than the buried dust of the poor devil who made it. My head and all the hopefulness of my heart are paralyzed—it seems almost criminal to add anything to this great dusty weight of things that loads the spirit down.—If I could be one of these people with magic in their touch and the glow of life and truth in their creation, but I do not feel it now, do not believe it.—The sight of all work—the uselessness of nearly all work—saddens me with the almost entire uselessness of my own life at present. Today in the city park near the museum, I saw peasants working in the drizzle. They were dressed in sopping bundles of rags, they stood ankle deep in the gluey black mud, and they went back and forth with a few futile little spadefuls of dirt in primitive little wheelbarrows. Their labor was so futile, so silly—yet they were at work at something and I was not. As I watched these men, for the first time I had a genuine admiration for mockery. I longed to see a great steam shovel at work there, biting huge lumps of dirt away—getting ahead, doing whatever it had to do in a fifteenth of the time of these wet wretched men. I cried out at the cheapness and waste of life—of the waste of my own: yet, there are many other people even less worthy than I am who are the lords of creation. I should like to forget about it—to go out and listen to the gypsy music and drink Tokay wine. Yet what I call my brain keeps going like forty devil blacksmiths—I must find work that I believe in, and then I must believe in my own excellence and importance as a kind of modern Christ. I would ten thousand times rather write Advice To The Lovelorn for W. R. Hearst than be guilty of such slop as *The Sorrows of Young Werther*—yet it created the reputation of Goethe, and hundreds of young men all over Europe wept buckets of tears and shot themselves because of it. Bernard Shaw knows no poetry, no literature, no history—he read a few books and tracts on socialism forty years ago; but he will express his opinion on a thousand subjects he knows nothing about, not only assured of his own infallibility, but hailed by millions of adorers as the great prophet of the age.—Most of them have been asses who thought they were God Almighty—I am only an ass who doesn't think so.—And yet I brood over all the huge grey wilderness of life, not like a God, but like a Tenth or a Hundredth God—as I write this my brain keeps toiling over this big slimy drizzly city, trying to get a picture—a single instantaneous picture—of the whole monster that I have pieced out so painfully, street by street, turn by turn, bit by bit. In the Andraecy as they are sitting in their coffeehouses, reading incessantly their newspapers—the Az Est[,] the Pesti Hirlap, a dozen others, none of which I can understand.[2] The lights are gleaming in ten thousand little houses and villas on the hill around Buda. The trams crawl over the great bridges; in dirty little saloons the poorer people are playing cards and drinking some strong wine—downstairs here in the Hungaria, the most famous gypsy band in the world is playing—the swells come here to dine. People are crowding and thrusting to see Charlie Chaplin, Milton Sills, Greta Garbo—elsewhere there's an opera and Hungarian musical comedies with Hungarian-American Jazz. Elsewhere they are playing Oscar Wilde and Moliere, and so on.—The shutters are down on most of the shops with their paralyzing display of things—but they have been left up on most of the bookshops; and tonight at midnight and later, I shall make my rounds, seeing what there is on display that I must know about to add to the depth and ranges of my soul—Surely for all my toil and trouble there must be some reward—surely there is some sureness, some fixity somewhere. I do not care about my broken nose, or my scarred head, so long as I can add something good to my spirit—but whether I can or not, I have no way of knowing.

My dear, I believe in this: I believe that I shall see you once more and hear your voice. Here is what I want you to do: In a blank book write down under the heading 'A List of The Things That Are Good'

—all the good things that you can remember. I will do the same, although I have begun badly under the Ironic Title of Triumphs of European Culture,—a list which starts, I believe, with The Risidenz In Munich, and goes all the way through the paintings of Salvator Rosa[3] to the Place Pigalle, Paintings of the Modern Hungarian School, Excursions on The Rhine, The Confessions of Alfred The Masseur (To Be Had Along The Seine), Manchester and Leeds, The Daily Mail and The London Times, and the Cafe New York in Budapest. This is only a small part of the whole.[4]

Good night, my dear, and God bless you. Perhaps there *is a little gold in the mud in which I'm covered*. We'll see. Tom

I bought you another glorious *book today*!

1. This line is from Emerson's poem "Ode to Channing." The correct quotation is from the seventh stanza:

> The merchant serves the purse,
> The eater serves his meat;
> 'Tis the day of the chattel,
> Web to weave, and corn to grind;
> Things are in the saddle,
> And ride mankind.

2. *Az Est* [*The Evening*] and *Pesti Hirlap* were the two most popular papers in Budapest in the twenties. The *Az Est* was founded as an evening paper and later became a sensationalistic paper published in the afternoon. *Pesti Hirlap* was an afternoon paper.

3. Italian painter (1615–73) noted for the philosophical and personal quality of his landscapes. Wolfe is using his name satirically.

4. Wolfe's complete list, entitled "Triumphs of Modern European Civilization," can be found in the *Notebooks*, 1:224–26.

97. [Italy, 17 November 1928]
Dear Aline:

I came here from Budapest last night, and went for my mail to Cook's this morning. I found two letters from you—that makes exactly two in two weeks—although, I am very happy to say, one of them was longer than are your usual ones. I am sorry to see how the snake of concealment has crept into your letters—they gave me no picture of your life—they still speak, but without great convincingness, of your love and fidelity to me, etc. of how you climb the stairs at Le Gull's four times a day, etc.—Nevertheless, I love you dearly, as I always have—of the weakness of the flesh I know something myself, and have no right to do anything more then pray[. . . .]

98. Vienna / Saturday / November 17, 1928
Dear Aline:

I came here from Budapest last night. Today at Cook's I found two letters from you. Also news from home, and a letter from a Mr. Peters (I believe) at Scribner's. His letter had words of praise and admiration—with reservations indicated—and he would like to see me.

I am going from here to Italy within a week, and from Naples home. I should then get home in December.—I am sorry if the long smudgy letters have distressed you. You say the part about Oberammergau is a good story. I hope so. I would like to get something out of it.—As you indicate in your letter, the part about the old lady dying is a lie. I was still too shaky when I told my lie to make it convincing. This was in Salzburg. Unhappily my nose and head are not lies—but very ugly realities—I should like to know what it is that made you doubt it—because in this way I might be able to find the strange gap which separates the real from the imagined. I still have confidence in my power to lie, but I lose that confidence when I write to you—I think I have never told you an important lie without soon after giving you the truth; but I have usually felt you know the truth anyway. I do not know why the death of the old woman should seem a story. Death would now be a natural circumstance—she must be past 75. Perhaps there is a belief in us all that sudden death is unnatural and melodramatic.—I also wanted very much to finish her in my experience just as I had the other people. There was no artifice about the rest of it—I scrawled down every day or so what was happening to me. It was all true up to Oberammergau (*as well as, I mean*) and the radio, and the Zeppelin.

Budapest and the Hungarians grew with me from first to last. I think they have made very little that is beautiful—but much that is interesting. I found them extraordinarily kind and eager—the hotel people not only gave me a room for a very little, but went to unlimited pains in directing and helping me.—Vienna is lighter, more elegant, very poor and shabby, decayed,—I am in a temper over the *shabbiness* of so many things—the damned cheap envelopes that tear and won't seal properly, the lead pencils that break every time you whittle—the damned cheap flimsiness of so many of the simplest things. But then these people are terribly put to it, and must pick and scrape.—Today—November European weather—grey dismal, thick and heavy. No wonder they get ahead so slowly. And everywhere! Everywhere! The interminable coffee-house—they are doped, and their dreams are such poor ones—to sit in the coffee house, and dream and dream—what? To read perhaps one of the thousands of little want ads—soliciting for prostitution, worded with preposterous elegance—and to dream it may be true! "Elegant and beautiful young widow, aged 32, from fine old family, with assured income of 600 shillings a month desires honorable companionship with young professional man—law or medicine preferred. Exchange of letters and photographs desired with meeting in coffeehouse as a result. Only the highest references considered. Address PXZ Kleine Anzeiger 426 etc[.]" I have made this up myself, but it is typical of hundreds. Today or tomorrow is the hundredth Schubert anniversary—his picture [is] on sale everywhere here, and they are remembering him in a hundred ways—Auctions, statues, concerts, church masses, etc. As for me—I have conflicting moods about music—but most of the time I think they are a lousy lot. And actors and actresses too! To think that there are men like James Joyce going blind, and scraping along, and jeered and whistled at by the fools in the saddle, while they crowd down front, rip off their pearls, throw their roses, twitter, sob, ooze sperm and pull up their skirts for some stinking Jew that plays a fiddle! And bitches like Bernhardt and Duse content to rant around in twaddle by Sardou or D'Annunzio[1]—your Nation and New Republic crowd will grovel in Ecstacy—and throw mud and sneers at a man with the tremendous capacity of H. G. Wells.

You once said that my taste in other things seemed good, and in music cheap—that I was always humming Celeste Aida or Samson and Delilah, and so on. You wrong me. I hate Aida now, but S & D isn't half bad.—But as for most music, good or bad—I am no longer sure that any of it—the grand opera—grand composer kind—is good. What are we to say of Wagner when, if the truth is known, all that he does with most of the people who scream for him, is to create an erotic emotion, and make them do something unpleasant in their panties. If you don't believe it, go and look at the Jews with eyeglasses and little moustaches at a New York concert, or at the Germans in any opera house in Germany.—I am unfair, but I began to doubt last time in Munich. His great friend, lover, mistress and patron was the crazy man who almost wrecked the country with his extravagance—I mean Ludwig II,[2] of Bavaria. The peasants will even now lynch you if you hint that this imbecile was insane—yet he had them bring snow from the Alps in July in order that he might go sledding, and all manner of abominable foolishness which he had got from reading about Marie Antoinette and Louis—At eighteen he wrote love letters to Wagner—they are the letters of a love-sick woman; later, he kept Wagner by him in the Residency until he caused the revolution and Wag. was banished to Switzerland. Then he would ride over the borders at night to see his darling. Wagner boasted about his conquest like a proud whore—of the two he was the most contemptible, for the other was mad. No matter. Mean men have been great geniuses—that I know—but here is Ludwig II, still celebrated by the Germans as "the great art lover," "the artist soul," and so on. Well, you have seen the Residency, haven't you? He is responsible for those rooms which [are] all gold gingerbread and gold tapestry. He is responsible for the 20 and 30 foot canvasses of the Nibelungenlied[3] also his coach, in the Terman Museum, that our Barocks by Barocks[4] you ever saw.—Here, and in a thousand other ways, he showed himself not the artist, but merely the criminal vulgarian, laying his dirty waste in order to carry out some form of nauseous magnificence.—Yet or *Thus*—he loved Wagner and all his works! That is why I wonder about Wagner! I myself get spermy at places in Tristan—but it is not Wagner himself[,] perhaps only an enormous piece of Baroque.

Well, more of this when I see you, my dear! I don't know why I should have suddenly got so bitter about music. Perhaps it is because I feel more and more the disproportions of things—the enormous weight of junk, the comparatively few beautiful and enduring things! But this I feel more than ever—those few good things are worth almost any agony—even my own!—they are worth finding, worshipping, living and dying for! God bless you, my dear—

****

Tom *****

*****

I.L.Y.S.O.S.I.L.Y.S.O.S.I.L.Y.M.D.M.D.M.D.

1. Gabriele D'Annunzio (1863–1938). Prolific Italian poet, novelist, and playwright. His work was often criticized as being derivative of current literary styles. Wolfe had never forgiven Sardou for having criticized Mrs. Bernstein's designs during staging of *The Lion Tamer* in 1926.

2. Ludwig II (1845–86), known as "mad Ludwig," was Bavaria's eccentric king from 1884 to 1886. Although he was a fervent admirer of Wagner, he was forced to expel him from Munich after a little over a year because of strong public outcry. The king was obsessed with the arts and concerned himself in later years almost exclusively with grandiose architecture. His most fantastic creation, Neuschwanstein, was a fairy-tale castle decorated with scenes from Wagner's romantic operas.

3. *The Nibelungenlied* [*Song of the Niebelungs*] is the most famous Epic saga about the origin of the Germans. It was passed down orally until the thirteenth century, when the tales were written down by monks. Wagner's famous *Ring Cycle* is based upon this series of tales.

4. Baroque.

99. [Vienna] Sunday / November 18, 1928

Dear Aline:

Today was Winter as it ought to be. It was bright and sharp, and tonight the stars are out and the wind is howling hard. I went down to the Donau Canal this morning—the faded dingy looking buildings of Vienna were all splendid in the sun, the water was light and sparkling, and the hills of the Wiener Wald beyond the river looked about close enough to throw a rock at. All the people were out—it takes only a little to make them gay. There is something very brave and high about this place—the people are idealists and dreamers, and this part of them has triumphed over all the terrible reality of their present life. Do you remember how glorious Vienna seemed to me that first time? And how happy? We had all that golden weather, and everything I saw was touched with magic—the wide blue sky of middle Europe, and the wonderful parks and gardens, where you could eat under the trees and hear the Wiener music. And the thousands of people on the banks of the river, all in swimming or lying in the sun, all brown and blond like Marie Jeritza.[1]—It is not like that now.

Sunday / November 25

This is the next Sunday—About the only time I have spent in the hotel this week has been sleeping time. I have discovered many new and interesting things—the Old City of this place is a fabulous cobweb of beautiful hidden places—of grand old palaces, marvelous churches, little secreted streets that are full of romance. But it is sad, sad. They have had so much taken from them that there is absolutely no hope left in them—in a thousand new ways I have seen their sweetness and charm. This has been Schubert week—he died one hundred years ago, and the ceremonies in his honor this past week have been endless. I have attended three or four of them—my old fatal weakness of having a hundred desires and only one body, one active pair of legs, and one brain has kept me from seeing *all* the things and being in all the places. But I stood in a huge crowd last Sunday wondering what it was all about—finally the crowd dispersed having seen no more than I had. I walked up the street and found a new memorial which had been unveiled in his honor that afternoon—a statue, and as foolish and meaningless as most statues are—a naked lady sitting down a la Rodin with her head bent over. The relation of all this to Schubert's music failed to pierce my dull hide, but all the people stood there patiently, full of their devotion. Their devotion to him is astounding—his picture is everywhere, books about him are everywhere, he has been sung, played, memorialized in churches, opera, concert houses and public places all this week—and always to great crowds. I think Schubert has become a great symbol to these people, standing for all that was best and greatest in "the good old time." He is Vienna incarnated—the thousand pictures of him showing him playing his pieces in warm looking 1825 drawing rooms, with lovely women and intelligent sensitive looking men around him; they show him walking through the rich old streets of the town with his friends; or sitting at a table in the court of a wine tavern in Grinzing composing a song, while young people make love at nearby tables, and so on. Schubert stands for what was fine and affectionate and tender in the life of Vienna—the people know this and he is rooted in their hearts forever. Last Sunday after dark I went to the Rathaus. A huge crowd of people was gathered outside, the great Vienna Men's Chorus was assembled on the steps, singing his songs. Most of the people were poor, shabbily dressed, but with that elegance and delicacy that I have never found in comparable degree elsewhere—and as the great choir sang his songs, a strange and radiant tenderness shone in the faces of all these poor people—this is the only place where I have ever seen the religious emotion. What it is I do not know, but I know it comes only with pain and hardship and poverty, and that in America we do not know what it is, and should not. This music in the open air at night was glorious—the great men's chorus is a marvelous instrument, the director plays on it as on a great organ. Its single great voice whispered against the Rathaus, then it would rise like a wind, and be given back again. The Rathaus was all lighted in and out among its Gothic traceries and the effect was very beautiful—like illuminated lace. Later I went to hear this same chorus in the big concert hall—they sang a dozen of Schubert's songs. The music was simple and tender and grand: in addition, he had sense enough—which is rare in a musician—to choose great poetry for his songs. Two or three of the songs were written by Goethe and one of them is the most beautiful lyrics I have ever read. Here it is:—

Nur wer die Sehnsucht kennt,
Weiss, was ich leide!
Allein und abgetrennt,
Von aller Freude
Seh' ich an's Firmament
Nach jener Seite
Ach, der mich liebt und kennt,
  Ist in der Weite:
Es schwindelt mir, es brennt
  Mein Eingerweide.
Nur wer die Sehnsucht kennt
  Weiss, was ich leide![2]

It is all lovely but the part "Ach, der mich liebt und kennt—Ist in der Weite" touched me most of all. Are you able to translate it?

Monday

Last night I went to see Faust at the Burgtheater here. The play began at 7 o'clock and continued past eleven with only one short pause. I must add it to one of the good things for which we can forgive the rest of the life. I had a copy of the text, but in the darkness I could not follow it. But I understood 2/3 of the German, and the course of the play is well known to everyone. I can not speak of its philosophy or the greatness of its poetry—but I can say that as entertainment it is magnificent. Four hours of it—and I was never bored! Your heart lifts up at all the weary dust—you feel yourself a god because another man was great enough to create all this. Faust's own problem touches me more than Hamlet's—his problem is mine, it is the problem of modern life. He wants to know everything, to be a God—and he is caught in the terrible net of human incapacity. The acting was magnificent—the man who played Mephistopheles was a great actor, and the mechanism of the great stage was grand and interesting. I will tell you about all this when I see you.

Wednesday Night / November 28

Last night also I saw Georg Kaiser's *Oktobertag*. I do not know if it has been done, or is being done in a New York theatre, but if it hasn't why don't you speak to Miss Le Gallienne about it.[3] I bought the play in Munich and had read it before I saw it. Both in the book and on the stage it seemed to me a very real and moving play—modern in spirit, but with no eccentricity in the unity or production. Kaiser is the best of their Expressionist writers; but this has none of the expressionist foolishness to it. The structure, the dialogue, the whole action is set forth very briefly and simply—it is astonishing to find such a spare form in a German thing. I am bringing the play home and will tell you about it.

Today I received 350 dollars by cable from you. I cabled the other day and said I would need 250. This is very generous of you—I do not think I have been extravagant, but I had only 180 dollars of my own left. I have bought an overcoat and books here—I think I will let Cook make my route for me to Naples—I hate to do this, but my time is limited, and I might waste both the time and money if I tried to do it myself now. Cook's gave me an estimate that was complete down to what I should have for breakfast, and which would lead me aboard the boat, there—says their estimate—"our responsibility ends." The whole thing, for a little over two weeks, including railway fare, hotels, bus rides, excursions, and all my meals, was about $115 —to Naples. This seems to me fair enough, since Naples is a long way off. There is a boat sailing about Dec 12; but I shall have to hustle now—as I will not have my full two weeks. I shall have to stop overnight in Venice—and I want to divide most of my time thereafter between Florence and Rome, with a final day or so at Naples. I am simply ramping and chafing to get to work again—I have books and books of notes: I have all my head can hold at present. I have got to get some of it out of me or I shall burst. I have explored and explored in this marvelous town—I love the place and its people; but I can do no more at present.—I have conflicting periods of despair and hopefulness—I want to bring the whole place back with me to America—all its works and all its people—I am crushed by my little knowledge one moment, and weighted down by all I have seen and known the next.—But I am badly in need of people to talk to again: I have tried to devour too much of the world by myself, and I feel like a man who is out in mid-ocean in a row-boat. But I do know this—however many things and books and people there may be in the world, no one has exactly the same picture of life as I have, no one can make the same kind of picture as I can—whether it be bad or good. And I have not lost all hope yet that it will not be ordinary—that somehow, it will be saved from the sickening mediocrity of almost everything.—You say that my mind is duped by its fantasies—but you can have no idea how insanely literal it can be. When I see ecstatic tourists wandering around in a bazaar, seeing in every Viennese a sensitive lover of beauty, art, and music, my literal mind gets busy. I know what hundreds of thousands of them are doing—I have a good guess into what hundreds of thousands of them were thinking. Most of them work, and wish they didn't have to. Their work is no more romantic than it is in America —not so much so, because in America a man works with the hope of getting rich, but here only with the hope of getting fed and clothed. When their work is over they go to a coffee house, where they meet their girl or wife or mistress. They talk with animation, but what they have to say is rarely interesting. They drink coffee, and read newspapers incessantly. I know what is in the newspapers, Crime, politics, Poincaré,[4] the Rhine, Graf Zeppelin, sport, the theater, today's radio, etc. They have some magnificent museums which they rarely visit, and many of which are closed in the winter. They flock to the movies, as our people do, and see the cheapest sort of American films. And at the present time *Chicago* and *Burlesque* are both playing here.—I think the main difference is this, and that this is what people really mean when they talk about Europe's "art and culture." In America we feel uncomfortable if we are doing any kind of work that does not bring us money—even if a person has enough of his own to live on comfortably he must always be doing something else. An American with an assured income of $200 a month would probably try by extra work to make it $400. But I am sure most Viennese with even $100 a month would quit their jobs in store and office and spend the rest of their lives with pretty girls in coffee-houses. In America we very properly abominate "loafing," but we are not always sure what loafing is. I am sure that a good deal of the cultivation in the world may come from an appearance of loafing, and that most creation comes that way—that is to say when a man's body is indolent and lazy but his mind fiercely and mercilessly at work.

The other day I went back again to see the great pictures in the Kunsthistorisches Museum—we do not visit museums on working days in America because we feel we should be at work. I think there is that fundamental difference between Europe and America—we have an entirely different value of time. I know you used to storm at me because I took so much time in dawdling, but I assure you I am a brisk go-getter compared to these people. Time means nothing to them, and your heart aches when you think how large a part of their lives is spent in coffee houses reading newspapers. An American would not stand for this—he would not "waste his time so." Yet, the lives of the commuters seem even more dreadful to me—I have known dozens in New York who told me they spend three hours a day coming and going from work on a train. Thus, it may be true that the atmosphere in Europe is better for work in the arts. But why is this: as you know modern architecture all over Europe is for the most part hideously ugly while trying to be very beautiful. The buildings have heavy meaningless decorations, hideous statues, and a dull and uninspired heaviness over all—Budapest is a terrible example of what I mean; and any German city.—The astonishing fact is this—that so much of what modern Europe has done with an eye to beauty is very ugly, and so much of what America has done with an eye to its commerce is very beautiful.

November 29

*This is Thursday morning, and I am going to get this letter off to you without more delay. I wish our old garret on 8th street was free—when I come back I am going to see Scribner's and Mrs. Resor at once, and see what I can do. I have not yet asked Olin Dows to help me, but he has often said he would, and if I get into a tight fix I may call on him.—I am sure I can make some money, if I can only get where the money is. I have even thought of trying to get work taking rich Americans through Europe in summer—I know enough about various countries and their languages now to give them ten times as much as they would get on one of the regular tours. You are not right when you say I have no sense of responsibility—but I have no sense of what is going to happen to me in the future. At any rate I lived in a garret once and was not unhappy there; I am willing to work; and I have not yet lost all hope entirely. I do not know what your relation to me will now be, but I have always loved you, and it seems to be the one fixed thing in my life. I will not tell fairy stories to both of us now, nor believe that a leopard can change his spots—but I do hope that a little knowledge and wisdom comes with all the struggle and waste, and that a head with a scar on it may be a little better than one without a scar.

If Cook's can only get me to Naples in time for the boat I shall be home shortly before Christmas; a thousand wonderful things I can not tell you now. But I hope it can all come out when I get back—All I see now is the magical towers of New York, made by money and power. I even have a sense of power and pride because my country is so young and strong. I want to become part of it, to make use of it in my life.—I wonder if we do see things better when we are far away from them—from here I see only the glorious elements of America, the great towers, the wealth, the hope, the opportunity, the possibility of everything happening. But deeper in my Soul is the remembrance of other things, the horrible fatal things that sicken me when I'm there—the bigotry, the hypocrisy, the intolerance, the Ku Kluxers, the politicians—the cruelty and evil cynicism of the men in power.

But I hope that among the 15000000 people who voted for Al Smith there is a new America—the kind of place that I see from this old decaying city. I understand that many of these people came from the immigrants and the sons of immigrants. Do you remember when I first saw you on the boat you wore a scarf round your head and said you were an immigrant? So am I. Perhaps this is the party and the America we both belong to.

God bless you, my dear. I will not add more now—I am not as stupid as my letter, for the thousand things I want to say are stopped in me from sheer number and weight and weariness. I love you with all my life—I have written you a poem, but it is not finished yet.

Tom

1. Austrian-American soprano. She was a member of the Vienna State Opera from 1912 to 1935 and also sang at the New York Metropolitan Opera House from 1921 to 1932.

2. Ms. Cohan's translation of this poem reads:

Only he who knows longing
Understands what I suffer!
Alone and separated from all joy,
I look into the firmament
   from every angle.
Ah, he who loves and knows me
   is far away.
I'm dizzy, my insides burn.
Only he who knows longing,
Understands what I suffer.

3. This play was finally performed in London in 1939.

4. Raymond Poincaré (1860–1934), controversial French premier from 1922 to

1924, who was forced to resign and was later reinstated in 1926. He retired from office in 1929.

100. [New York] 333 West Seventy Seventh Street
[21 November 1928]
My dear:

In all the letters I've had from you, you never mentioned whether you were stunned by the amount of mail from me that must have awaited you in Munich. There must have been a ton, I wonder if they all reached you. I know that for some time I wrote you every day, either letter or card. No wonder you drank so much at the Octoberfest.—My work has become a Frankenstein, a monster that rides me day and night. I want to be rid of it. Do you remember how at one time I worried that I would not have enough to do? I literally haven't time to wash my hair. Last spring the Guild did this play of Sil-Vara,[1] which I designed, and now it is coming again, and I have to redesign the set, as they are doing a new version and need a different layout. I could kill them for doing it now. It opens in Boston Dec 18th or 20th. Edla is on the road, and will be in Chicago on her birthday, Dec 3rd and I am going out to see her. I miss her so, the house is dead without her. She enjoys being away, she has not travelled much, and I am glad she has a good time. Agnes Morgan & Helen Arthur are with them. I wonder when you will be home again, and where this letter will reach you. I am tempted to write to Amexco Florence but your movements are so uncertain and no doubt Buda Pesth will have a great lure for you. Now I am about to go off on a terrible lecture to you. I gather from your last letter that you have done very little on your new book. I read it over again and that is the sense I get. It is a cruel thing you are doing to yourself. If you cared nothing about recognition and success I could more easily understand your goings on. Possibly I have no wisdom, and what you are doing is for the best. But some day if ever you mean to succeed, you will have to forego your indulgence of the moment. I get so sore when I think of your great strength and talent spending itself to your detriment. I have the utmost faith in your genius[;] if I had only half of it I could rise to great heights. Believe me dear that to see you succeed and reach greatness in your writing will be the greatest happiness I could know. I wish I could take your hand and go beside you step by step. My love for you is so great. But you told me last year that I was no good for you, that I never did anything but cause you pain. I am afraid you love me better in your letters than in life. I love you every way. I long so to see you that I can't help but hope you will materialize from the air. And I am disturbed and very nervous and worried, what it will be like when you do come back. I feel that I could talk to you forever. I want to get some rest before you come home. I think you have had a grand vacation. This time, maybe you have more writing done than you have led me to believe. If only I could transfer my capacity for work to you, we would be a great team. God bless you dear, I love you forever[.] Aline

I keep every thing you write to me.—I am so disappointed that Mrs. Roberts never came.

1. On 31 December 1928, *Caprice*, a play by Sil-Vara was produced at the Guild Theatre. It ran for 183 performances.

101. [New York] Nov 22 [1928]
My dear:

I am in the midst of a dress rehearsal.—Hence writing in my note book. I mailed a letter to you last night and this morning received one from Budapest, from you. I am, naturally[,] awfully excited about your coming home. I am yours forever. Of course I have never been courting as you call it, how many times need I tell you that no one exists for me, in my heart but you. My inner life is lived with you. I don't know what you want but I am here for you. You write now that you are coming back to make something of your life, you said you were going away to make something of your life. The thing to do is to do it, and no one can do it but yourself. There are plenty of places in the world to get your head cracked and your nose broken if that is what you are after, but why? isn't once enough or did you like the way it tasted. As soon as you come back we will sum up what you want and what you can do, and for once in your life make a plan and see where you stand. You are too good to waste. We will hold together.—I thought you would come back to see the Scribner people sooner than this. If they want your book you will have a big work to do on it.—I must get away to see Edla for her birthday. I had thought of going for New Year, but maybe you will be home by then. —We are working on the house in the country, it will be a fine place to spend my old age. My bones ache for the country. My heart and soul ache for you.

Dearest—Aline

102. [Vienna] Thursday / November 29, 1928
Dear Aline:

In my last letter which I sent off to you this morning I believe I threatened to send you a poem. Here it is—I have decided there is no use in trying to polish the unpolishable; so I send it to you almost as it was at first[.] It is not much of a poem, but it may show you a little of what I have been feeling here recently. In the first act of Faust as they play it here he goes up out of his old Gothic chamber on to the roof of his house where he looks through a glass at the stars, falling prostrate at length at his inability to go further than he has. I think this scene—and of course the whole play of Faust with its statement of my *own* trouble—worked on me unconsciously and resulted in the poem. I hope you are able to read it—the last lines in particular are for you alone. You will see that I do not agree with Robert Browning about stars and their heart-opening habits; but if his eminent Shade is troubled he has the satisfaction of knowing that although my lines may have more truth, his have certainly more beauty.—I read a piece in a Wiener newspaper yesterday about the American writer, Thornton Wilder. He said that he had come to Vienna to see the Breughels in the picture gallery—I naturally feel that you and I have observed Breughel and that Wilder has heard of him through us. But I have two or three more aces up my sleeve which I shall produce at the proper time. One of these is Michael Packer—one of the greatest artists that ever lived. There are some pictures of his in the big museum here, and I am bringing you a book and some of his pictures. What I cannot bring you home is the infinite charm and wealth of this marvelous town. This inner city is a labyrinth of wonderful things—little streets that are so completely hidden that the average passer by never finds them, magnificent old buildings and places which take you into courts, where there are little communities of shops and cafés you have never suspected—and marvelous churches, a few lovely gothic ones, and some very rich—and I must admit—very fine Barock ones.—I went to a fascinating place yesterday—a huge building in a narrow little street that you have to hunt for. The building is called the Dorotheum—it was probably once an immense private palace—now it has been made into a gigantic auction house. I climbed from floor to floor, from one enormous room to another —in a dozen places auction sales were going on. The rooms were crowded with shabby looking people who were obviously habituees —they sat on benches or around a railed enclosure and made bids. There were three auctioneers in each room—and things were sold with amazing speed.—Here again you feel the terrible weight of all the old things in the world—old furniture, old clothes, horrible old pictures; all the accumulated junk that weights us down, sent here for auction. The poor people, of course, have the fatal weakness of poor people everywhere—of accumulating junk because it is cheap. It makes the heart heavy to see them spend their money on things they don't need—a surveyor's trident—gone for 6 shillings to a poor old woman; opera glasses that won't see, stereoscopes that won't work—all of these are snapped up by poor people, and you understand why any quack can sell his salve at any street corner. I know now where the street-walkers of this city get their fur coats—that decay and elegance comes from the auction rooms. Everything, everything is here—and everybody. A great many of the people are swarthy and dirty looking Jews—I judge they are in the second-hand business and come here to buy their stock. There is a marvelous little old street here called the Jews' Street—hundreds of years they have been there—and they stand before their little shops in droves, and almost drag you in. You never saw such gusto, even on the East Side—

(Friday) [30 November]

Today I went to the Academy of Fine Arts—where the students paint. We were there together once—but I had forgotten the pictures. There are some good ones there, but no great ones. Most of them are small canvasses; and I feel I do not understand pictures that are too small. And I hate pictures that are 40 feet high and fifty broad—Rubens and Veronese,[1] etc. The right size is the size of the painters we like[,] Breughel and Packer and Cranach and Dürer and Grünewald. I bought you a magnificent cookbook this afternoon—remember the man who gave his wife a washtub for Christmas. But it is a fine book and tells you to the dekagram just how much of everything you must use. I love you and I wish I could bring you something wonderful. I am bursting with the things I have learned, including German literature, but I also grovel beneath my miserable ignorance. What do I know of those great German authors Wells and Dreiser and Galsworthy and Sinclair, and Herr Oskar Wilde (Veelde—they call him). And the young writers Wilder and Julien Green[2] and Judge Ben Lindsey.[3] The windows are filled with their works. It is perfectly true that I feel bewildered at times when I look at these familiar names. To see ten solid sets of Shakespeare in a window with his name staring at you in this Gothic script almost makes you forget he is one of ours—and the Germans, I think, have forgotten it entirely. They make whatever they think they should admire their own—at the Royal Theater here they play Shakespeare—different plays—two or three times a week and Shaw once or twice. What is left goes to "Goaty" and several dull dogs named Grillparzer and Hebbel and Schiller and Kleist[4] (who was an interesting man). Shakespeare has done much harm, but his greatest crime resulted in half the German classics—the Kotzebues[5] and Grillparzers and Schillers, and so on (this is hyperbole)—I have found this out, and you don't know how happy it makes me. They are devouring the world with their travel books—their books on chemistry, mining, oleo margerine, gout, diabetes, flying, architecture, strength and beauty, advertising and so on—but we have them beat all hollow in story telling. There are countless editions of famous stories—and literally nine out of ten are French, English, Russian, Scandinavian, and American translations.

I am going tonight to a play called *Ida Popper's Karriere*—and I fear the worst. The piece was written about 1904. *Chicago*[6] went on the other night and is apparently a hit here—it confirms their worst suspicions about us. And over in the Prater Street where I saw Strindberg[7] last week they are doing a piece by that other great German dramatist—Elmer Rice. The piece is called Ist (or *Was*) Robert Parker Schuldig? (*On Trial*) 1914—They are playing old American movies all over town, "Die" Boheme at the opera, and Kapitän Brassbands Verkehrung[8] at the Royal Theater. So you see how I am soaking up German culture—But they have no Breughel at home, and no magical old streets, and no people so lovely and so decayed as these.

Cook's has got hold of me—thank God! I'm coming home on a boat going either Dec 12 or Dec 20 from Naples. Sending my books to ship either at Trieste or Genoa—depends on which I take but I think the last one, as time is too short, I want to see pictures in Florence and get a suit of clothes. Leaving here Tuesday morning. Will cut this short now—God bless you, dearest. Hope you can read my poem. Tom

(I am filling notebook after notebook)[.] Written Friday
This is my poem. Don't know what to call it. It is for you.

Who only has seen a star
  Never has known it.
  So near to the eye, but far—
Too far to own it.
Who made us stars has given
  Only the seeing—
Only the sight of heaven
  Far from our being
Only the frustrate brain
  The loaded heart,
Only the toil, the pain,
  The fruitless part.
Only the flaming wish,
  And health to fan it.
A spirit too great for the flesh,
And too small for a planet
  Too great for its little cage,
  Too small for a star,
The grand heart beats hope into cinders, youth into age,
Waging vain war.

Searching till it goes blind
  The barren quarries;
Eating the Earth to find
  What a Star is.
We who are men are greater than men
  And less than our spirit.
Climbing half-heavenward, falling to earth again
We starve in the jungle and die in the plain
Seeing heaven, but too weak to near it.

If Starmaker made the man,
  He made him small;
Puny in reach and span,
  Thirsty for all.
Little of skull and bone,
An exile, a stranger, alone
With a vision too great for him,
And wisdom too late for him,
And the bed that's in wait for him
  Under a stone.
—That it [sic] his hell,
Not that he fell;
But that, like a god half arisen,
He can look upon stars from his pain
And find no help for his pain
But death in the jungle, the wind and the rain.
Who only has seen a star
  Never has known it.
All that *I* know of a certain star
  Is—it is far.
I do not own it.

(End)

1. Italian painter (1528–88) known for his huge ceiling paintings and altarpieces.

2. French novelist (1900–?) of American parentage, who won immediate recognition with his first novel *Mont-Anère* [*Avarice House*] in 1926, relating the story of the house of his aunt in Virginia. His second novel, *Adrienne Mesurat* [*The Closed Garden*] (1927) was eventually selected by the Book-Of-The-Month Club.

3. Benjamin B. Lindsey (1869–1943) lawyer, judge, writer. A full-fledged progressive, Lindsey expressed his views against the privileged in *The Beast* (1910), *The Rise of Plutocracy in Colorado* (1908), and *The Companionate Marriage* (1927).

4. Franz Grillparzer (1791–1872) was the first Austrian writer to achieve an international reputation and was very popular in his homeland. Friedrich Hebbel (1813–63) wrote historical tragedies that concerned themselves with the new moral values inherent in the process of change. Friederich von Schiller (1759–1805) was noted for his classical dramas; and his great historical drama *Wallenstein* (1800) was inspired by the Thirty Years War. Henrich von Kleist (1777–1811) was complex and tor-

mented throughout his lifetime; his dramas bear witness to not only his own struggles but the problems of his age.

5. August von Kotzebue (1761–1819), prolific dramatist and politician, who wrote some two hundred plays and librettos, many of which were set to music by such artists as Beethoven, Schubert, and von Weber.

6. A popular satirical comedy by Maurine Watkins, which opened on Broadway at the Music Box Theatre in December 1926.

7. Wolfe had gone to see Strindberg's great play *Der Vater* on Friday, 23 November.

8. *Captain Brassbound's Conversion* by George Bernard Shaw.

1929–1930: The Long, Bitter War of Separation

The year 1929 was momentous for Thomas Wolfe. His meeting with Maxwell Perkins had been a success, and on 9 January he wrote in his notebook, "On this day I got [a] letter from Scribner's confirming their acceptance of my book." Underneath he inscribed the names "Thomas Wolfe" and "Aline Bernstein." Yet the rift between the two lovers was growing wider. With the advent of Maxwell Perkins, Scribner's warm and supportive senior editor, Thomas Wolfe had found a new hero. Increasingly, during the spring nights Perkins took Mrs. Bernstein's place, as the two men poured over the immense manuscript, making revisions and cutting from its great bulk. By December, Perkins's influence had become so great that Wolfe, at his suggestion and without telling Mrs. Bernstein, had applied for a Guggenheim fellowship, which would enable him to write abroad in isolation and with financial security.

Throughout the winter of 1929–30, Wolfe grew increasingly restless and his diatribes against Mrs. Bernstein grew more violent and abusive. In March he informed her that he had been awarded the Guggenheim fellowship and planned to leave for Europe on 10 May. She felt betrayed, for she was willing to support him while he wrote as she had done in the past. After a few short communications from Paris, he broke off all correspondence even though Mrs. Bernstein maintained a steady stream of letters and cables begging for some response. After traveling for the summer in Switzerland, France, and Germany, Wolfe settled in London to write. Ironically, it was during this period that he began developing one of his most successful and sympathetic characters, that of Esther Jack, which was based on Aline Bernstein, a character that would appear as the heroine of his later fiction.

103. New York / Harvard Club / Tuesday / July 9, 1929
Dear Aline:

I shall attend to everything before I leave. If you are going to Boston Sunday, I think I shall take the boat up Saturday night from here—or perhaps I may come Saturday or Sunday by train. I'll come to the hotel at once. The last four or five days have been regular steam-blanket New York heat—it is so bad that one forgets about it, or refuses to believe it when it is over—men go about in shirt-sleeves that are plastered to their skins.

I came down from Rhinebeck early Monday morning with Olin. It was hot there, but very lovely. It's the most beautiful place I ever saw but a little dead. We had some terrible arguments. I suppose it is wrong to say one cannot believe in the Astors and enter the kingdom of heaven—but I think it is true—I don't even believe one can go to hell by believing in them. One gets what he deserves—if he believes in the Astors it ends up by the Astors believing in him. O. talked to me a great deal about "good form" the "right thing to do," and called a lot of things "incredibly cheap and vulgar." He told me that his late grandfather—the gentleman of the old school whose memory he worships—had said that Rousseau was nothing but a "cad" for writing about people he had known, and I replied that Rousseau would no doubt be greatly hurt if he had heard his grandfather say this. I also told him that to call everything one disliked "incredibly cheap and vulgar" was not the proper way for people who had profited from Boss Tweed's swindling to approach life—or for anyone else—and that one did not excuse one's self from caddishness by calling other people cads.

I think this is his trouble—the thing he really thinks important is to do nothing that would seem ill bred or offensive to the Astors. This feeling is far deeper than his feeling for painting—although he works very hard and earnestly.

Sargent, Whistler, Shaw, drawing-room socialism, boiled vegetables, and all the rest of it.

He's a fine fellow, and good and true at heart. I like him and respect him so much, and hate to see him so full of feeling for fake traditions and false cultures, and so empty of feeling for real ones.

We went to the concert at the Lewisohn[1] stadium tonight—they played very beautiful music—the audience was a fine one, and it was calm and peaceful out in the open. I am going out with some people at Scribners tomorrow night—the new proof is coming in fast and the book will be published in October. I am still very glad about it, but want to finish a new one—the only ambition, I think now, that is worth while is to *want* to do nothing, and to have money to do it. The literary life here from what I can make out is nasty and trivial—I put blood and sweat into my book, and I will be hated by some people, denounced by the old fellows, and sneered and mocked at by the young ones—the rich snobs will believe what is fashionable, as usual, and the cliques and politicians will yell and jeer.

I am glad to know you are enjoying your visit with your friend, and surprised to hear it is so quiet. Do not become too bucolic—I suppose some of the simple pleasures may still be enjoyed in Northampton as well as any place. At any rate, God bless you, and furthermore I shall see you in Boston Sunday. I feel well in spite of the heat which I hate. There is a vast suffering all over New York, and I like them all better. I noticed today how much gentler and nicer their faces are now that they are feeling pain. In weather like this we suddenly remember how hard life is, and how much we have to struggle for so little. Yet I am full of hope and expectancy. It is better to be this way than Brooks—although we are both wrong. At Olin's I read Defoe, Smollet, Dickens, and the poems of Swift. All are very good, although Swift was not a poet. He was Swift. In Smollet there was a scene where two men had a duel by smoking assafoedita in a little closet. One of them finally vomited in the other's face—this ended the duel. It was a very good scene, well written.[2]

Good bye, my dear. My shirt is sticking to my belly. I am looking forward to the trip with hope and joy.

With all my love, Tom

I have found a good dedication for you[3] and I shall leave it with them before I go. You have never cared for what I write but I think I shall write one book someday that you will like—that will be *your* book and your dedication. I love you and can't help it. I hope it is cool where you are—I wish I worked "in a nice cool sewer."

1. Leonard, Julius, and Adolph Lewisohn, who had made their fortunes in copper and lead, turned in later life to acts of philanthropy. Adolph was the major philanthropist of the family. His best-known gift was the six-thousand-seat stadium that he donated to City College of New York in 1915. He stipulated in his will that the college allow it to be used for concerts in the summer at inexpensive rates. His brother Leonard was the father of Alice and Irene, founders of the Neighborhood Playhouse.

2. This episode is from *The Adventures of Ferdinand Count Fathom*, chapter 41. The information was tracked down by the kind efforts of Dr. Pamela Miller, assistant professor of English at Pennsylvania State University, and by Hazel McCutcheon, head librarian at Pennsylvania State University, Ogontz Campus.

3. Wolfe selected lines from Donne's *A Valedictorian: Of My Name in the Window* to accompany the dedication "To A.B." He underscored these lines in his copy of Donne's *Complete Poetry* which Mrs. Bernstein had given him:

Then, as all soules bee
Emparadis'd in you (in whom alone
I understand, and grow and see,)
The rafters of my body, bone
Being still with you, the Muscle, Sinew, and Veine,
Which file this house, will come again?

By July, Wolfe was ready to begin correcting the galley proofs of his book. He rented a cottage for two weeks at Ocean Point, Boothbay Harbor, Maine, for this purpose, and Mrs. Bernstein joined him there. In August, he made a brief trip to Canada.

104. Quebec / Hotel St-Roch / Sunday / August 4, 1929
Dear Aline:

I came here this morning on the boat from Montreal. It rained all the way down and all this morning as well. Now it is grey and cold, with a wind blowing—like early November. I am glad I made this trip—I feel very much better than when I left New York, and I am eager to get back to finish the proofs. I send Mr. Wheelock[1] all the galleys I had left from Boston and convinced him from Montreal Thursday to send me new galleys by Saturday. I got a wire yesterday saying he got my telegram "just too late" to send galleys by Saturday—why, I don't know, since it was sent in plenty of time—perhaps he was not there to get it. In his telegram he said he had all the galleys for the book now—I wrote him (since letter would get there Monday same as wire) and told him I'd be home Wednesday, and to hold them. I'm excited to see them and to finish, so that I can get started on a new one.

I have done some writing since leaving you and have even made a little sketch which I thought I might possibly sell to Scribners in view of their recent difficulty with the Boston Censors. I called it L—ve in B—ston and it is written mainly in dialogue like the following:

"I l—ve you," he said. "Let's get m—ried." "I am very sleepy; I am going to b—d," she said. "O let me l—y my head upon your b—som." "Where were you b—rn?" she asked. He k—ssed h—r p—sionately. They had three ch—dren, the youngest was only a b—by. The policeman drew his p—stol, etc.

I was glad to get your wire and to know you got home safely, although if you did it in seven hours, it may not have been so very safe. I hope the weather has turned cooler in New York, but I know from the papers you have been having very hot days. But the worst should be over now. The whole country is burnt up—coming up on the train we lived in a cloud of dust from beginning to end.

I will tell you more about Quebec when I see you.—I think you know fairly well what Montreal is like—it's 4/5 imitation British—but the beer and ale are splendidly real. You won't believe it, but I have yet to take my first drink—of whiskey. To get it, and other strong beverages, one must go to a government liquor store. There, arrangements are very simple—one can buy only one (or two) bottles at a time—if one wants more he goes out, closes the door, and comes back in again immediately—and he can keep coming back as long as he's able to walk. The ale and beer is sold to you all over town in "taverns"—these are really very cheerful and very continental little cafes. They are very much like places one sees in France, and it seems to me better than most English pubs. Ordering beer costs ten cents a glass—but ice cold lager costs fifteen a bottle, and very strong ale

Thomas Wolfe in 1929 (From a copy in the North Carolina Collection, UNC Library, Chapel Hill)

twenty to twenty five a bottle. I have drunk a good deal of wine since coming here—it seems to me I have had a bottle every meal—but I am glad my money was spent that way: I regret very little of the money I have ever spent for wine, when it is gone it is completely gone, but I always have the warmest and most satisfactory feeling both before and after that there is no better way of spending money.

The food is not as good as it should be, although I have had good meals in French restaurants here and in Quebec. The truth of the matter is that Canada is a province—it gets its news, its customs, and its manners from other parts of the world—New York and London. The country is vast and rich, and I believe very beautiful—but there are only a few million people, not enough yet to till the soil. I had never been able before to visualize the people—now I know why. There is nothing to remember about them—I know that in a very short time most of the faces I remember from Montreal will vanish from my memory. This is not true of certain faces one has seen in New York, Paris, or London. The situation of Quebec is very beautiful—the town is built around an old town which is on a steep hill. From the top one overlooks the St. Laurence—a very noble river—from an eminence very similar to the Palisades. The fields and hills are greener and fresher than at home, and as one looks away into the country one does get an impression of being abroad—it made me think somehow of coming up to Cherbourg on a ship—you know how it looks. But the old houses and "places of interest" do not look very interesting—you would hardly think them worthy of notice in France—what gives them their interest is that they are here in America. I confess that means little to me—it is like Dr. Johnson on the dog that walks on its hind legs—"the wonder is not that he does it well, but that he does it at all."[2]

But the way the people have kept on being French is remarkable and interesting. I have been watching them and talking to them to-day—when they talk English at all, they talk it very badly, and many of them can't talk it at all. This is the first French trait, for the English and Germans usually manage to learn the language after the first 50 or 100 years, unless they own the country as they do here. I went into the "Taverne" here at the hotel to-day—it seems to be one of the chief drinking places of the townsfolk here. I could not make myself understood either in English or French—all I wanted was a bottle of ale—finally I had to get it by pointing. They speak a terrible dialect which only a real Frenchman, perhaps, could understand, and I think "he" would have much trouble. They are of a coarser and rougher grain than the real French—the climate, the vast wild land, etc., has done this—but they are still French to the bone. The "Taverne" was roaring with sound, they shouted, talked with their fingers, hands, and faces.

Tuesday morning / August 6

My dear. I am going to finish this with a few lines—I am leaving here to-day by whatever is the best way, and I shall probably see you before you get this letter. But I want to send it because I think I have written you on every trip I've ever made. I wired you for $75 when I got here Sunday and it came yesterday together with a telegram from you. I am terribly eager and nervous to get back and get to work. It would be unfair to say Quebec has been a disappointment—the site is grand, all the people, language, and customs etc. are French, I have done the round of sightseeing now—but from our point of view there is not a great deal of interest. The houses, I think, are decidedly ugly, and, I am not greatly interested in historical places unless they are associated with some beautiful and interesting object. I have not found any pictures here—there is an enormous hotel run by the Canadian Pacific railroad called Chateau Frontenac—I ate there and saw enough of *that.* It seems years since we ate together at *15th* street. I am anxious to get back to see if it is really true. You've no idea how attractive my drive down there looks to me from here—I get quite warm thinking about it.—It is very cold here, grey, chilly, late October weather.

I am enclosing a check for $75. I love you and hope you are the same. Tom

Are you working on a new show yet? Are you tired of me and do you want to see me as I want to see you? I love you and send you a thousand xxxxxxxx[.]

1. John Hall Wheelock was a senior editor at Scribners. He and his close friend Maxwell Perkins worked with Wolfe throughout the summer on the proofs of *LHA*. It was not until 29 August that the final galleys were completed.

2. "Sir, a woman preaching is like a dog's walking on his hind legs. It is not done well; but you are surprised to find that it is done at all." Boswell, *Life of Johnson*, 31 July 1763.

In September, Wolfe returned briefly to Asheville. He had intended to warn his family about the content of his upcoming book, but he could not. It was his last trip home for seven and a half years. The Bernsteins moved from their brownstone to a new and luxurious apartment at 270 Park Avenue. On 18 October 1929, Look Homeward, Angel *was published.*

As 1930 began, Scribner's offered to subsidize Wolfe so that he could give up his time-consuming teaching job and concentrate solely on writing. Accepting this advance on his second novel, Wolfe resigned from N.Y.U. and accepted the Scribner money from February to June. In the meantime, the relationship between Wolfe and Mrs. Bernstein became increasingly unstable, and he prepared to go abroad on his Guggenheim fellowship alone. Mrs. Bernstein had begun spending weekends with her family at her newly completed retreat in Armonk, N.Y.

105. Armonk [N.Y., Spring 1930]
My dear—

I hope you will find it in your heart to forgive me. But since you have turned me away from your love I seem to have lost all control of myself. I know you will say you still love me, and want me to be your dear friend. Try to bear in mind that it is you who are turning from me and not I who go from you. My love swells up and crowds my body and my mind grows desperate with it. I know you are so tired[;] you will write the best book as soon as you are quiet. Try to bear with me till you go, Tom. You must know this much about people, that a relation such as ours can't be wiped away with words. You are a great person, and just walking out of this does nothing good. You have always talked to me of faithfulness and fidelity. You have always said that I would leave you and stop caring for you first. Well, it's the other way isn't it. I know I have been pretty trying just now, but it's only since this has happened. I mean since you tell me you will leave me. Try to bring what goodness and greatness you have to bear upon helping me just now. I hold you in such high and glorious love. Maybe some miracle will happen. Knowing you these years has been a miracle. I can't put you out from the inmost part of me.

I will do the best I can to be good before you go, and put no more enemy into my mouth. Never lost myself that way before. But never before have lost you. Aline

106. New York / Harvard Club / Sunday / April 27, 1930
Dear Aline:

Here is what I've done about going away. I have taken passage on *The Volendam* on May 10, and I have begun to pack up my books. A friend is coming to help me with packing tomorrow. I am sorry my sailing has been put off but it is less than two weeks off and that is not very long. The dentist told me the work on my teeth is quite serious—he is treating a diseased tooth and said it would be very bad to go before he finished.

As it is I shall go with only part of the work done.

Please get a rest, and I will try to rest my head—when I am through packing and have everything ready I will call you and we can talk together.

I send you my dearest love: you are tired and need a good rest; I hope you are getting it[.] I feel tired and ill, and I do not want to talk to people now, but I am going to be all right, and so are you. I send you my love and kindest wishes[.] Tom

107. Aboard the Volendam / Saturday / May 17, 1930
Dear Aline:

The ship gets into Plymouth tomorrow and I thought I had better get this letter off to you before the mails close. This voyage has been very slow and tranquil: we have had generally good weather, although yesterday was a little rough—fog and slate sky and a sinister oily sea that rolled the ship about. I thought it was English weather, but today is bright and sparkling and already I have seen the gulls from land flying about. We have also begun to pass other boats—we are near land and I am excited at the prospect of seeing it—it always touches me very deeply to see it after being out on this vast desert of water for several days.

I have done absolutely nothing on this boat except sleep, eat, or prowl restlessly from one end of the ship to the other. The people are very quiet and stodgy—my Dutch people who go often on business. Many business people who travel back and forth a great deal, and other people going back to see the old folks at home[.] There are no tourist parties and very few young people[.]

The trip has done me a great deal of good—I have lots of energy, I feel rested, and I will be glad to get off at Boulogne Monday morning. Ten days is a little too long. I am getting off early Monday morning and going immediately to Paris—I will write you a day or two after I get there. I carry away the most vivid meaning of New York, of the ship's sailing and of you. Although I am about 2000 miles away as I write this it is all very near and real. I am impatient about my new book. I keep making notes—but I want to get at it[.] Your cablegram came right after dinner one night—I trembled when I opened it. Perhaps I will not cable you very often, because I think it is a bad habit to get into unless there's some positive need. I think I have told you most of the news of the voyage which is practically—nothing! I know this is a dull letter, but the ship destroys in us the power of concentration—there is always the hum and tremble of the engines, the roll and rock, and the creaking of the woodwork within like old leather. I wish I could tell you the look and color of the sea which has never twice been the same, or a couple of great sunsets, or the moon making great pools of light on the water. We are getting far north almost to the end of England—it is six o'clock, the sun is still high, the days are getting longer.

I love no one in the world but you and there will never be anyone that I can love like you. I hope and pray that I can do a fine piece of work, and I desire your happiness and well being at all times. Please write me your plans and tell me what you are doing. Will you go by Fifteenth Street and see if there is any mail: also see if you can leave instructions for having mail forwarded to me. Could you also go by the Corn Exchange Bank at Seventh Avenue & 14th St. and find out the amount of my balance. Also ask if the Frank Tours Check for $141 has been paid, and let me know how much is left.

You are the real manager of my affairs, and if Mrs. Boyd acts badly I feel better to think that you are there to help me.[1]

God bless you, and I hope this finds you in good health and spirits. I send you again my dearest love[.] Tom

There are a family of the Jewiest-Jews on this boat—their name is Kahn, the father is a doctor. There is also a daughter and a mama. They are going to Rapallo to visit *Max Beerbohm*! Mrs. Kahn's sister is Beerbohm's wife! What do you know about that!!!

1. Wolfe never cared much for Madeleine Boyd. Two years later, his suspicions of her were confirmed when it became apparent that she had not forwarded an advance royalty payment of $250 from the German publishers of *Look Homeward, Angel.*

108. Paris / Hotel Mondial / Tuesday / May 20, 1930
Dear Aline:

I got here yesterday, and I found several letters from people and a cable from you at The Guaranty Trust Co. this morning. I also got a cable when I landed from the boat at Boulogne yesterday. Two or three words from you of any sort give me a much greater thrill than a letter from any one else: I am writing this late at night—I have been busy all day and absolutely alone: the truth is that I am pretty blue tonight and miss you as I knew I would. You remember the clipping from the poet Horace that you tacked up in my place on 15th Street: "You can change your skies but not your soul."[1] That is profoundly true and my soul has been generally full of tumult and unrest. Pray for me to do a good and beautiful piece of work: that is the only way to find any sort of peace[.]

Paris is quite beautiful now but somewhat cold. The country was very lovely yesterday coming up from Boulogne: their spring here is somewhat later than ours, the fruit trees were in bloom, and the trees and fields were a beautiful tender green. Yesterday was a beautiful sparkling day; today was grey and raining. Late last night in the terrace of L'Ecrevisse: I was all alone there, I had a bottle of Nuits and a Chateaubriand with pommes souffles[.] It was delicious, and all the time I kept thinking of you. Today I had lunch at Weber's—I had les oeufs Weber. I can't go anywhere without being reminded of you[.]

Paris is strange to me as a dream. You come back to it and it is just as you left it—as if it had existed only in your mind. The French to me are like people from another planet: they are just what you imagined them to be; when you close your eyes and think of them in New York they are the same: the little nervous taxis with their honking New Year's horns still get you crazy in the streets; the big green houses with people lying over the back, and all the people swarming along the street, talking with their hands, sitting in front of cafes talking a blue streak, usually about nothing. I listen, and it is the same as always—their talk is full of figures—"cinquante quatre," "soixante sept," etc. They never tire, I marvel at the sugars and juices in them which keeps up their incessant energy.

I am staying for a few days in what is for me a new part of Paris. This is a little hotel right off the Grand Boulevards and a noisy all-night street, full of cafes and Cabarets called the Rue Faubourg du Montmarte. It sounds very noisy but this is really one of the quietest places I have found in Paris—it is a "cité": i.e. a group of old buildings having its own street and entrance[.] There are gates and arches at each end of the street: at night the gates are shut, and if you are out you ring a bell and an old man lets you in. An old Austrian on the boat told me about the place—it has little barber shops, cafes, jewellers etc., and is a little world of its own. My hotel is just behind the Palace Music Hall where Raquel Meller[2] plays—I went to hear her last night: she is a very lovely woman and a good artist. The show of course is rotten, but curiously they seem to have got tired of nakedness—during the time I stayed there was not even a remotely naked chorus girl.

I found a letter from Mr. Darrow[3] enclosing dental bills from my two dentists. Dr. Babbit[4] demands $285 (for seeing me five times), and his assistant, Muller, who did most of the work, demands $240. This is a total of $525 and they will play hell getting it, with the $60 which the toothpuller charged for butchering me, this makes almost $600; so you see the "plenty of money" you say I have will not last very long at this rate. Melville Cane[5] also sent me a bill for $40.00 for the little conversation we had that afternoon, and for "drawing up will"—this after I had seen him in a restaurant and he had asked me to "come to see him before I left" etc. I suppose you are right in saying I should not be suspicious of people, but trust them, but I have found many people in New York who would cheerfully swindle the person they met at dinner the night before. Here in Paris the people are petty cheats—they will do you out of a few francs in taxi fares, hotel bills, etc.: in New York, they simply charge you five times too much—this is cheating too, but it is also American business, and the rich people don't protest.

Most people who know you have had a book published think you have made a great fortune—my dentists knew about it and thought this, including that horrible old woman they were always whispering and conspiring with outside. I asked Mr. Darrow to talk to Scribner's lawyer: I am sure they can't touch my Guggenheim money: the rest of my money is in Mr. Darrow's care—if we can protect that they can either take what I am willing to give—$200—or nothing at all[.] Babbitt saw me four times in all—the other man worked hard for two weeks from April 25 to May 9—of course they would have glib reasons for their huge bill, but the plain truth is it is not worth it, nor one half it, and they know it. Don't you think it rather nauseating when the blood-suckers rush in upon a person trying to make a start, and to live in the most difficult way—by creating something. This is all for the present. Write me as soon as you can; I will keep you informed about my movements. I hope this finds you well and happy, and in the country. I send you my dearest love. This is another day in Paris, I am going out to lunch presently—the day looks cool and beautiful.

Love, Tom

I bought books to write in yesterday.

1. The full quotation from Horace is: "They change their sky, not their soul, who run across the sea." *Epistles*, xi, 27.

2. Raquel Meller was the star of the Palace Music Hall and later performed with the Folies-Bergère.

3. Whitney Darrow was Scribner's business manager.

4. Dr. Babbitt had previously been the Bernstein's family dentist. It was on Mrs. Bernstein's recommendation that Wolfe had gone to him for dental work.

5. Wolfe's lawyer, an old friend of the Bernstein family. Although Wolfe rants against him here, Cane was quite fair with Wolfe and tolerant of his excesses. He was his legal advisor until Wolfe's death, revising and rewriting his wills.

109. Armonk, N. Y. / May 23[,] 1930

My dear—

When you have this letter it will surely be nearly four weeks since you have left, and you promised me that when four weeks had gone by, you would settle down seriously to write, whether you feel so inclined or not. I looked carefully in the papers to see any record of the Volendam reaching its destination, but couldn't find any. No doubt it arrived, otherwise that would have been news. I hope you would cable me but none has reached my so far. I have been writing the events of my life for you, but find it very hard to make it simple. I keep putting down all kinds of extraneous things, first thing you know it will turn into a novel and then I'll have to use it myself. It goes slowly and I tear up a great deal of what I write because I find myself going off into descriptions of things we had to eat (showing the influence of Thomas Wolfe, early period), also I keep remembering all our servant girls, who seemed to play an important part in my childhood. Long long into the night I lay awake trying to think how best to tell my story.[1] Only it is reversed, I get sleepy about

10 o'clock or somewhat later, go to bed and wake up about four A.M. It is now ten minutes to five. That makes my day very long. I have been busy getting the place in order and now I am nearly done and very tired of it. I go to market every day, market at Pleasantville which is a little nearer than White Plains, and not so crowded. The entire mode of my life has changed since leaving New York. You know how many people were always around in the theatre and at home, now I literally see no one all day long until the family come home about 6:30. Edla has a job with a small stock company near here, and is working and studying, I must say I find it lonely. Helen Arthur and Agnes[2] are at Pleasantville but I have only seen them once in this week or ten days since we are here. I sit a great deal and look at the landscape, and wish that I could become part of it, and no longer be Aline. The only thing that seems to afford me any delight is watch the things come up in the garden. They are very young, little fuzz like a three day's beard, and like the beard each day they grow a little bit, but very slowly.

I miss you, and feel as though there must be some way to break through this awful distance and be near you. If it works with the radio why not I. Only I feel I should not be welcome. I go through enough torture a day to last a lifetime. If only some change would come upon me, something would open up and show me how to become this calm and loving friend you want. I am nothing but a desperate ache, and surely there must be something else to my life than that. I can't paint or draw, only write this little story for you. I really feel as though I have lived enough. I am afraid that it has been a mistake for me to come here now, but I seem to have been caught in this house. I ought to have some diversion. I see no way of getting off for any time at all. Business downtown is terrible again, and money scarcer than ever. As soon as I feel a little better I am going the round of managers and try to get work to do. So many start up in August. Hard work would be the only thing for my mind I guess, if I have no hope. I can't help but write to you this way. I wish I could be noble and grand and say I am glad you have gone and hope you are having a lovely time and don't worry about me old dear I'm alright. Well, I can't and that isn't how I feel. You said so often that I'd be alright, it was such a nice idea, well, I'm not alright, never further from it. Tom if you'll only work and not drink all over Europe there will be at least some justification for your desertion of me. Will you write and tell me about it, tell me that you have started. Not just little scraps when you come home late at night, but real hours of steady work. Please, make a schedule and stick to it. You are blessed with genius. I love you forever[.] Aline

1. Wolfe was preoccupied for several months with collecting and recording in his notebooks material about Mrs. Bernstein's childhood. He copied this sentence into his notebook and later used it with slight variation as the thematic opening statement of *The Good Child's River*.

2. Agnes Morgan.

110. Paris / Hotel Burgendy / Saturday / May 24, 1930

Dear Aline:

It seems very hard to realize that it is only two weeks since I left New York. I have not done much in the way of going about, but the confusion and energy of the world about you is so tremendous that you don't need to go about much: it wears you out looking at it.

Emily[1] wrote me to the Guarantee Trust Co. I sent her a note, and she was here on the phone, with a letter and finally with her maid this morning. She asked me to come to lunch and I went. Now I must go again to lunch tomorrow with her and Mr. Griffes[2] (you remember him), and she is calling up bookstores, literary friends, etc. to cart me around next week. Furthermore she is not doing it out of love and friendship—she knew I was trying to get away from all that, and she is taking advantage of the fact that being alone all of a sudden is like being doused in freezing water: it is very hard for me being alone now, and I shall not try to lie about it. I would be grateful for companionship from almost anyone now, but I had rather stay alone and have fits of depression than be dragged around again: I shall not see her any more after lunch tomorrow.

It is my own fault—I should not have answered her note, but I got a warm and happy feeling when she wrote me; I was grateful and felt that I had a friend near at hand. You say I condemn people, but I think there is a good deal of charity in me: what I think now is that nobody is bad, but that only a very few people are good. The people who are good invariably have something in them on which they can rely—when they have nothing in them on which to rely, and go hanging about from place to place relying on things and people, they are no good. That is the trouble with Emily.

Monday Night / May 26

I saw Emily yesterday—Mr. Griffes had us to lunch: she came by and got me at the hotel, then drove me to the Crillon where Griffes stayed; we had a cocktail, then we all went to L'Ecrevisse for lunch. Previously Emily called me up; she was in a hysterical condition and asked me what to do, that Raymonde had disappeared, that she had not seen him since 3:30 A.M., etc. As it was only about mid-day it seemed to me she had no cause for alarm, and I got quite angry because I had to listen to this rot, and listen to some more of these histories that I thought I was leaving behind in New York. I forgot to tell you that this Raymonde is a young man she has picked up over here and is now supporting—he wears riding boots and trousers and a creamy white shirt which he wears open at the throat. He has black sheiky hair plastered down with 8 ounces of vaseline: he is like a bad edition of the late Rudolfo Valentino, and he can stand on his hands, and cut flips, and pick your pocket without your knowing it. He also jumps from one airplane to another, so he says, and hangs down by one foot: he can also do the hoochy-koochy and sing American nigger songs in French. Emily said he was "a genius" and that we both had much in common, and that we were both to be brothers. This was during luncheon: I got violently sick, and could eat no more, and had to rush into the restaurant to vomit. I was supposed to go back to her place last night for dinner with her, the sheik, and two or three of her other friends, but I did not go, and I sent no message. I hope this ends it, and I think it ought. Emily explained to me that she had had a terrible night the night before and had got very sick—she said she had been smoking opium: I suppose she wants me to try it with her, since I think she has some silly idea in her head she is a terrible "destructer-ess" who wrecks men's lives, etc.: I don't think she's ever going to wreck anything, not even herself.

There's nothing to wreck—she'll be hanging around this way 20 years from now, trying to fill up her own emptiness with other folks' richness; she will have to hire gigolos in earnest then—she will keep coming to Europe, and that will be all there is to it. [. . . .]

1. Emily Davis Vanderbilt Thayer was a friend whom Mrs. Bernstein first met on her European trip in 1928. Mrs. Thayer came to represent for Wolfe that which was outwardly attractive and inwardly tragic and corrupt in eastern society. He patterned the character of Amy Carlton after her in "The Party at Jack's." She was also satirically portrayed as Amy Van Leer, a hollow, greedy young woman, in some of his early drafts of "The October Fair."

2. Perhaps Wolfe was referring to Charles Griffes, who wrote "Tone Pictures" and "The White Peacock," which were produced on Broadway in 1927.

111. Armonk, N. Y. / June 2, 1930

My Dear—

I had two letters from you within just a few days of each other, and they are a great comfort to me. You seem so much more quiet and so eager to work. I am sure that the voyage helped to soothe your troubled nerves, and the removal of immediate responsibilities is wonderful, at least so I have always found it to be on the ship. Those last days, in fact the last weeks, were mad and tumultuous. But quiet and beautiful and serene as it is here, I would gladly go back to any sort of time to be near you. If you find so many places that remind you of me and our times together let me tell you that every thing I see that is lovely reminds me of you, for you are every thing that is beautiful for me. I should not say reminds me, because you are always with me. I will tell you what I do. It has been very cold until today, so cold that we needed a fire all the time, and today is suddenly one of those steaming hot days, purely American. My old Aunt is here and needs much attention. I am up very early, awake around 5:30[,] sometimes sooner. I read, and have my coffee about 7:30[.] Teddy leaves then for his train. Rest of the family go at 8:15. Then I dress and go down & confer with the Swiss Queen of the Kitchen. I go off to market about 4 times a week to Pleasantville. I have found the only thing that in any way eases my mind and heart, that is working out of doors. I cut grass, pull up weeds, rake, carry stones and do a job that I never had imagined could exist, called edging. It means cutting grass along the edges of places where the lawn mower doesn't reach. It is done with an agonizing implement that breaks your hand in two, and requires a great deal of back breaking. On the other hand it is impossible to think of anything else during the process. I lunch about 1 o'clock, I've done a great deal in the house as well. Edla and I have waxed and polished all the floors till you can see your face in them. Also, I am making curtains for some of the rooms. And we are all in bed by 9:30[,] sometimes sooner. The Goodmans have been here for dinner, and Ann spent the last weekend with us. They are soon going abroad. It is really country life. I spend an hour or so before dinner watering everything. I have had to go to town once a week to see the doctor. I am going tomorrow, and will go down to your bank and find out about the amount of your deposit and the Frank Tours check. I think your dentist bill is outrageous. I told Babbit at the time that you were a young man starting to make your way. Do you think I should do anything about it? Do you know you must have left some of your last letter out as there was no ending to it. You know my dear that I will always look after every thing for you, there is nothing dearer to me than you and your welfare. I wish there was more that I really could do, all that seems possible now is just to think of you, and keep my mind upon your new work. This complete change in my life, so sudden, to be without you and to find myself so removed from everything, it is strange and frightening. I am so blue every night, and wish that I were one of those people blessed with ability to sleep.—I am writing my story for you, once tore it all up and started fresh. I want to make it so plain that it will never pass for what you might call writing. One day last week Emily cabled asking where you were, but I did not answer for I thought you would like better to be left alone. I will write some day and give her your banking address. Anyway, I shouldn't be surprised if you had met her, people always see each other in Paris. Clara Weiss sailed last week, I had dinner with her before she left. I told her that if she met you to tell you how much I love you. I have read a lot in the Home Book of Verse, and find that pain and sadness are no new thing. But who has ever written yet of the glory that we have known? No one, but you will. You will show them all something new. I have as great a faith in you as I have great love for you. My love for you is spread to every furthest reach of my being.—I thought I would paint at once after coming here, but feel unable to. My mind will not, I can't think of any sort of work that will make me go inward just now. The outside work is best. All art seems like a terrible pain. I still have to see the doctor every week. I've had two bad spells since I came here, but altogether I'm better. I wish I could get well of it[,] or something. The most awful part of it is that I lose consciousness at times and it frightens me to think that can ever happen. I am really afraid at night. You know my room is at the end of a wing. I have the police dog sleep at the door leading out on to the little flight of steps. The only trouble is that if I move in my sleep or reach for a drink of water he behaves like a watch dog and makes a racket. But it is quite a nice feeling to have him here.

I expect Eva here on Friday to spend a day or so. She is playing for some benefit in the neighborhood. I believe Mary Benson will come also. It will be nice. Edla's stock company opens this week. I don't think it will be a great success. Can't imagine people going to a theatre in the country. It is a very pretty theatre, built for some community purpose or other. I miss her when she goes off. All the cold weather we had, I wore the green suit I wore while we travelled in England. It seemed to embrace me. And while I was doing the grass cutting it made me think of my barbering on your head. I shall take this letter to New York tomorrow to mail. Will you please hereafter address letters to Mrs. Aline Bernstein, Whipporwill Road, Armonk N. Y. Letters forwarded from 270 are uncertain. I expect we will be here surely until Sept. 15. I hope you will not mind if I send you a cable once in a while. I enjoy being able to communicate with you quickly. This writing seems to me a cold way to do, not to you though, you who can write so. I wish I could put more of me into writing, all that I can do when I speak to you. The living spark of actual physical presence. We used to have jokes together, we can't do that in letters. I can't kiss you in a letter and I can't hold your hand in a letter[;] neither can I rub your back. I'll go crazy—good night my dearest. If you take yourself away from me, you must work well to make up for it. Write and tell me how much you do. Will you keep a schedule of 5 hours a day? It is a good plan. I wish I knew if the book is still selling.—You may not be my lover but I am yours. How can I show you—I am your lover while I live.—What use on earth am I any more. It seems as though I have done all there is for me to do. I don't know. God bless you Tom, keep well and write the most beautiful book in the world— Aline

I forgot to tell you something interesting: Do you remember about an old lady named Smith who lived near us and died? Well her sister has come to live there, a quiet gray haired spinster. I have spoken to her several times over the fence. She called on me this afternoon. I asked her where she lived before she came here, and she said Europe for 30 years. She was in the U. S.-Secret service. Strangest thing I ever knew, I could have sworn she was either pure country spinster or minister's wife. I'm going over and see her soon and try to get her to talk to me. What lives people lead. What I don't understand is how she has preserved her appearance. You know what a keen eye I have, well she is to me absolutely unnoticeable.

112. Armonk, N.Y. / June 16 1930
My dear—

I want to communicate with you all the time, I would write to you oftener but there is so little variation to my theme and you so often have complained of the old phrases. Unfortunately my expression is limited and my feeling unchanged. My life goes on here so much the same every day, the only event worth recording is that I went to Smith College with Eva last week while she took a degree of Dr. of Humane Letters. Did you ever hear of that? I don't know what it means. We stayed overnight at Minna's, and it was not a success, they didn't seem to get on together at all and I was glad when it was over. I never went to a college commencement before, and I was very much impressed with all the people on the platform with their varied gowns. I had always thought gowns were all alike, and never so surprised as when Mr. Wilson[1] marched in done up in scarlet silk faced with blue broadcloth, with a rakish Tam-O-Shanta of black velvet, University of Edinburgh costume. And there were two antique females from London University dressed like Beef Eaters. It was one of those terribly hot days we seem so fond of here, and the parents sweated and smelled and we were chained to our seats while a man from Harvard called Hocking[2] talked for 1¼ hours about the Arteries of Education. It was really an imposition, but then I couldn't hear all he said. There was a great deal of emotion and sentiment in the air and that made it hotter and I think the faces of most educators about us [as] ugly as any thing in the world. And yet it is such a wonderful thing to study and to know. I have told you how often I miss it. The mental discipline that is, the ability to learn and study is what impresses me.

Eva looked so pretty and young seated there, and when she came up to get her hood she was so applauded it was just like a first night and she bowed like an actress and altogether seemed a great hit. I was glad to be at home again. I continue to work a great deal on the ground, I weed the garden and cut grass a good part of each day. Yesterday I tried to paint but it was no go, couldn't do it at all but I believe that if I worked every day I could make something. It takes so many years and such steady application I fear I could not do any thing if I keep up my stage work. That I have to do to earn something. We are dead broke, have you read at all about the financial situation here. The new tariff bill has put every thing to ruin, I think it a disgraceful attitude for this country to take. Of course I know nothing at all about the ultimate effect on business, I have no knowledge, but there have been a series of crashes similar to those of last fall. How the men stand it is beyond my comprehension. Theo comes home day after day literally speechless. What a way to live.—

My one fear is that we are going to lose our place here, I don't see how we can possibly hold on to it, only I also don't know who will buy it. I[t] looks beautiful now, I have worked hard to make it lovely. What for[,] God only knows. We really should live here all of next winter, but it would be almost impossible for me to work and commute, as my hours in this theatre business are uncertain. If I didn't work I would go crazy. I am lonely so much. All the family go to bed very early, Edla is off acting and you know how little I sleep. The nights are the worst to live through. I believe that this is the unhappiest time of my life. I have come to a place of utter hopelessness. My desire to go on with life is practically nil. Possibly this illness of mine[3] has something to do with it. I am better than I was but do not seem to get well.

My sister goes abroad in another week. She is going to travel with Emily for a while, I wonder if you will see her. I haven't heard from you for so long, not since the card I had from you both. I wish you would write to me. Surely it would be possible, if you only knew what it means to me. I get so frightened about you, and my head spins with awful possibilities. But I hope there will not be another head splitting and nose breaking, and I hope the book is keeping your writing hand busy. I read a great deal at night. The Home book of Verse is wonderful but unwieldy. It hurts my hand to hold it. I got mad at the "Ode to Melancholy," such sentimental nonsense to think we can glut our sorrow on the morning rose. I used to think it was fine until I had this real sorrow. Now the rose I want to trample in the ground with my sorrow. I want them all to wither. If only you would assure me of your work and your good living. God knows you could find no fault with mine. I don't even take a drink any more, except occasionally before supper.

For a while after you left, when I was first here alone, I drank a lot but it only made me feel sick and was no good at all, and it was horrid.—I wish I knew something else to do. I envy people with some sort of faith. I wish I could believe in the vengeful God of my Jewish fathers. What sort of people can come of the sick belly wash you Christians were brought up on. I know this will make you laugh, but really Tom the more I see of people the worse I think Christians are.—I love you with every fibre of my being, and I hate myself with the same intensity. I want to do away with so weak and miserable a soul. If I have not the strength to help my self, I know well there is no one who will do it. I love you[.] Aline

1. Edmund Wilson, critic and man of letters, had just published *Axel's Castle*, his study of the symbolist writers of the twentieth century.

2. William Ernest Hocking (1873–1966) was a Professor of Philosophy at Harvard from 1914 until 1943.

3. For further information on Mrs. Bernstein's illness, see her March and April 1931 letters.

113. Armonk, N.Y. / July 5th, 1930

My dear:

It is so long since I have heard from you, I am worried and angry. I sent you a cable this week, but no answer to that. I imagine all sorts of things to be the cause, but what can I do? The last word I had from you was a line on a post card written with Emily, which said you were writing to me. Yesterday I heard of you in a round about way, through Mary Benson. Mr. Griffiths told her he has seen you in Paris, and Mary told Irene who came here and told me. Isn't that a sad way to get news of one I love so dearly?—My letters I know have been sad and monotonous, I have started to write to you several times but there is nothing but the old story to tell.—I wonder if you have written and your letter is lost! I had lunch with Melville Cane one day last week. I was in New York arranging about the sub lease of our apartment. He was the only person to whom I could speak, for I wanted to speak of you. He says you are the white hope of the literary world. I could not give him any news of you. I told him how we have cared for each other and how things are now. He agreed with me that life is not worth this agony.—I had a fine piece of work offered to me last week by a new producer, but I am not well enough to take it. I never felt sick like this before. I try to do a little designing on next year's Civic theatre work but it doesn't go at all.

Tom Beer[1] has been over to see me several times. He brought some beautiful old wine. He is a great deal better and is now working on his new book. For the first time in my life some one wanted to know what I did in my head when I designed. I told him so many things about my working out of character and color together. They have invited me to Nantucket for August but I will not go. I may go up to the Simonsons' for a few days. Tom was anxious to know about you and if you are working. He also is crazy about Mr. Perkins, but says Mrs. P. is horrid. A social snob etc etc, and crazy for money. Aren't women awful? Only the men are noble and good.—

My sister sailed last Monday. I wonder if you will see her, as she will probably be with Emily a great deal.—I have been writing my story for you and nearly finished it. It was a painful operation for me, and I hope will be of service to you. I want you to let me know if you really want it before I send it on, as no one else in the world must see it, you must promise to return it to me, as I know your careless habit and would be angry to have your new friends see it. My hope is that you are well and working. I stay a great deal under the trees in the orchard and look so hard at a leaf or blade of grass, and think that surely a wish so strong as mine must make you materialize. I have to close my eyes to see your face, and sink back into times that are gone. If I could only start living backwards again, like a motor can be reversed. I'd go back to the time we met on the boat and then turn it off. I love you forever. Aline

1. Brother of Mrs. Bernstein's close friend Alice Beer, who gained fame through his literary history of the 1890s, *The Mauve Decade* (1926), and his biography, *Stephen Crane* (1923). He was the model for Stephen Hook in *The Web and the Rock*.

114. Armonk, N.Y. [July 1930]

My dear—

Rita Vail[1] came up here for dinner last night and told me she had seen you in Paris, in fact you had taken her out for a day somewhere. I also had a cable from Emily saying she did not know your whereabouts but you are working hard. If she doesn't know where you are how does she know you are working? At any rate it was kind of her to answer. Thank God you are alright. Suddenly and for no reason that I know, you have cut off all communication with me. The effect on me is terrible, possibly I am crazy, for it is not sane for one human being to be so sensitive to another. A course so wantonly cruel is not sane, either. I can't do anything, I can do nothing but think about you. I dread to wake up in the morning, the day is just a horrid pain to be got through.—Have you no imagination, don't you know by this time what you are doing, or do you know and is that what you want.

I have never done you any harm. My love and my entire will have always been directed to what was best for you, within my knowledge. I ask you to write to me and let me know what this is about. This is the way things were when you left. You told me you no longer loved me in anything but friendship and you demanded the same of me. Of course I can't change my feeling on your demand, but I had hoped that we would be those two loving friends. I can't help loving you with all the intensity of my soul.

I believe that you are doing something in your behavior to me that you don't understand. I think that you have no conception of what it means, otherwise how could you eat your food or sleep or work when you know what you are causing these thousands of miles away. Fortunately I am by myself all day long. I have wild dreams of coming to find you. I telephoned to two of my friends yesterday and was promised enough money.—Possibly you do not read my letters. Anything is possible. Possibly some miracle will happen. Aline

1. A friend of Mrs. Bernstein and Emily Davies. On Sunday, 6 July, Wolfe wrote in his notebook: "Meeting the pretty Jewess Rita Vale at 3 o'clock—more later." He did not mention her again.

115. Armonk, N.Y. [25 July 1930]
My dear—

I am cabling you today, for God's sake what is the matter with you. I am nearly mad with worry about you. If this silence of yours is only an idea, what is the idea. Surely nothing that you gain can be worth what you are inflicting on me. If I do not hear soon will try to come over to find you.—Have you been consulting new acquaintances on how to treat old friends[.] I love you[.] Aline

On 1 August, Wolfe wrote in his notebook: "On Monday—*July 28 I sent* Aline Bernstein, *my former mistress, a cablegram, in response to repeated letters and cablegrams of* hers, *in the last cablegram of which she* said *"Are you all right: Answer at once, otherwise I am sailing to find you at once"–I had not written this woman since 2 or 3 days after my arrival in France but in answer to these threatening letters & cables I sent the following message: Aline Bernstein, Armonk, New York–Am Well living Montreux–Tom Wolfe"–I had no answer during interim but today Mr. Horace Coon (O quite by accident of course, showed up)–This woman, of course, is behind it: she wrecked me, maddened me, and betrayed my love constantly, but she will not leave me alone now. I hope the whore dies immediately and horribly, I would rejoice at news of this vile woman's death.*"

116. Geneva / Grand Hotel Bellevue / August 12, 1930
Dear Aline:

I cabled you this afternoon and said that I would write, but I am unable to say very much to you. I have tried to write you, but the letter I started had too much bitterness in it about our life together, and about your friends, so I destroyed it. I no longer want to say these things to you because they do no good, most of them have been said before.

We have known each other for five years, I can never forget you, and I know that nothing else to equal my feeling for you in intensity and passion will ever happen to me. But we are now at the end of the rope. My life has been smashed by this thing, but I am going to see if I can get on my feet again. There is just one thing ahead of me:—work. It remains to be seen if I still have it in me to do it. If I have not, then I am lost.

You have your work, you have your children, you have your friends and family. If you feel the agony about me that you say you feel in your letters and cables, I can only say that you should give yourself completely to those things that you have. A letter as short as this one is bound to seem harsh and brutal, but you know what I feel and that I gave everything in me to my love for you [. . . .][1]

Helburns, Simonsons, Moellers, etc.—and the Davies and Curtess and Frankau outfits. I hold you responsible not only for your own life, but also for the life of your friends—you can no longer back out of responsibility for them, for you are part of their lives, and they are part of yours—it is no longer possible to believe that these people can be your closest friends, and that you knew nothing of their filthiness, or have never been touched by it: you forbade me to see a few people I knew in New York who were my true friends: you telephoned them to stay away from me, you called them foul names, one by one you have taken them from me during the last five years, and (after I had had a little success *but not before*) you have delivered me over to be exploited, betrayed, and lied about by the people you know. I will tell you who some of those people are:

1. Miss Emily Davies taker of drugs, opiumate, and lover of gigolos, black and white: this lady is a purely literary product—out of Mr. Arlen and Mr. Huxley and Mr. Hemingway, and all the other people who have created these beautiful [. . . .]

1. The following section of this letter, written on the same hotel stationery, is perhaps a section of the draft that Wolfe told Mrs. Bernstein he had destroyed.

After this final attempt at communication, Wolfe abruptly discontinued any correspondence with Mrs. Bernstein for the remainder of the Guggenheim year.

117. [New York, Late Summer 1930]

This is what you wrote to me in your book.[1] Does this look as though I had ruined your work! Do you choose to forget how I helped[;] [I have only had] your interest in my heart. If you had not turned away from me as you did, I firmly believe you would be on the way to greater glory. You still can be. I know now that your love could not match mine, but since your love is gone you at least need not revile me. It is no use to put upon me your own disability. If your "friends" whoever they may be think that I have hurt you, it is because they know less than half truths. I have been the truest friend of your life, and I have for you a love that is inconceivable to such thin gentiles. It's greatest flaw is its intensity and magnitude. My love can see your worth as an artist, where your friends are sicklied over with the pale cast of half baked pseudo-psychology.[2] Today, now, is the turning point of your life, you can take the hard road, the beautiful road, the road the great men of art have worn with their feet, or you can stroll down the easy path with all the little people. If you are my Tom, the great man who has lived in my mind, you will gather yourself together. It is inconceivable that you can waste yourself.

So far as your family is concerned, they let you starve, materially and spiritually. You are under no obligation to them, and you have told me you had no love for them at all. There is money enough in the world for you. You cannot go back, you must go on, it is only possible if you will shake off the small considerations. Why I cling to you so, God only knows, but you are made of stuff so glorious, so terrible, and if I let you go you will be lost. Aline

To Aline Bernstein[:]

On my 29th birthday, I present her with this, the first copy of my first book. This book was written because of her and was dedicated to her. At a time when my life seemed desolate, and when I had little faith in myself, I met her. She brought me friendship, material and spiritual relief, and love such as I had never had before. I hope therefore that readers of my book will find at least part of it worthy of such a woman.—

Signed
Thomas Wolfe

1. Mrs. Bernstein copied the dedication by Wolfe and included it as the final part of her letter.

2. This is an allusion to Hamlet's famous "To be, or not to be" soliloquy.

On 14 August, in his notebook Wolfe wrote the draft of a cable that he most likely did not send, to Theodore Bernstein, Hirsch, Lilienthal Brokers, New York: ORDER YOUR WIFE TO SEND ME NO MORE LETTERS OR CABLES. THOMAS WOLFE

118. Armonk, N.Y. [August 1930]
My dear,

It is a week since your cable. I have waited hoping to have some letter from you. I am relieved that you are well, but wicked enough to have had some secret hope that it was not your intention to treat me so but some circumstance—I fear that you do not even read my letters now.

I stayed by you through your hard days, years, and now when I am down and you are secure, and I beg you for a little comfort, you won't even write me a word.—You must never revile people again, when your own performance is so base. How can you ever escape the evil of your own action to me, your best friend. In your last letter you sent me all your love. I want to believe it, I want still to think you are good. This is a tragedy you are making, and you or I or both of us will go down with it. I have had to refuse work because my mind can't do it and God knows I need the money, I am stony broke. You are now even with whatever ill you think life has done you. You have done so much to this life of mine. Just because you take this ruthless way. And you know that I love you too dearly to harm you. But some day your friend Mr. Perkins when he suffers at your hand the way I do now, will find you out. If you can hurt a dear friend once, you will do it again. Tom all I ask of you is to be my dear friend as you said you would. Surely that can't interfere with writing this new book of yours.

I am bound to you heart and soul forever[.] Aline

119. Armonk, N.Y. / Aug. 18 1930
My dear—

I want to write you a such a beautiful letter, if only I could say all I feel and not make you angry. It seems that my great sin is that I care for you too much. Your cable was such a great relief to me that it is almost a shock. You know here they do not deliver telegrams, they call you on the telephone. Yours came at midnight and the bell woke me up as it did so often when you were in New York. It was so funny to hear the nasal telephone girl say I love you. These past weeks have been a nightmare[;] every thing I saw and heard and thought were charged with pain, really as things become charged with electricity. There is a silly song this year, "What is this thing called love"—Well, I should like to know, for it has taken possession of me. I love you beyond my power of expression, and I will never change. When you say, let us both help, I can't help but feel that the way I am to help (the way you want me to help) is to cut myself off from you.

A friend of mine sent me the enclosed ad, from a London paper.[1] Isn't it wonderful beyond our dreams. Do you know all about it? Will you tell me more. Thank God you are working on the new one, I have not a doubt that you will be the greatest and most famous novelist of our time. But I love my dear Tom that I have loved all these years. Do you remember one day when we were at Ambleside and Terry and Phil came and we spent the day together, and when they left, you actually wept, for you said my friends would take me from you? That time came upon me again when I read these things. I can't assume a nobility that will make me say, Go your way if that is what you want.—I am ignoble enough to love you so that life is misery for me unless it is joined to you in some way. If it were not this question of time, the years between us, I know we could have a magnificent life together.

Have you read in the papers about the terrific heat and drought —The heat was the worst I have ever felt, just couldn't get away from it, day in and day out. Our grass [was] so burnt it looked like a shredded wheat biscuit. Thank God it ended a few days ago. Every one in the city looks half dead. It was just as hot here, but about midnight would grow a little fresher.—We expect to stay here until the middle of September, and then I don't know. We will probably go to a hotel for a while.

Business conditions are frightful, we are dead broke and so are a great many others. We really have to sell this place but there is no one to buy it. I am going to New York today to try and find a place to live, and arrange about packing up the flat. I must also find a place to work. I think I can get a small office in the place where Helen Arthur has hers, for less rent than a studio and I can have her telephone. Every one is pessimistic, and the only good thing I have heard is about your book. I wonder when you are going to England. What a grand time it will be for you. I always think a success in England tastes better than any place else. I am part of the book too, and wish I could taste a little of it with you.—Any sort of trip beyond a suburban train ticket is as impossible as the crown jewels of England.—

I have to start work for Eva this week. I had another piece of work but was unable to take it. I will have to do less this year I am afraid, and 14th St. is going to try to pay me a little better. It looks as though I would have to live on my earnings. I remember a line, As You Like It I think,—"Time hath, my lord, a wallet at his back"—I don't know the rest.[2]—I will never again cry out because you love me not enough.—I know it cannot be controlled, for I would, if I could, temper my own feeling to something more suitable to daily life. I wonder if you miss me. Did we ever really sit and talk together—Please my dear, don't do this to me again. It isn't that you have no time. Tell me how things are with you. Remember that I have been at the lowest place my life has ever reached and I am your best friend, and I am always your greatest lover. Aline

1. *Look Homeward, Angel* had just been published in England.
2. Shakespeare, *Troilus and Cressida*, I, iii, 145–50.

> Time hath my lord, a wallet at his back,
> Wherein he puts alms for oblivion,
> A great-sized monster of ingratitudes:
> Those scraps are good deeds past; which are devour'd
> As fast as they are made, forgot as soon
> As done.

120. Armonk, N.Y. / August 26, 1930

This is a short note, but I have sat over it more than an hour trying to think of something to say that isn't about I love you.

My Dear—

I enclose a clipping from today's Sunday Times book review.[1] So I see it is all the success that the London papers said. It makes me so happy, now you have what you have always longed for, fame, and it looks to me like financial success also. I wonder if you will soon be going to England. What a glorious time you will have, I'm sure they will be mad about you. I am starving for a letter, it is so horrible just to read about you in the papers, and hear about you through others. When I see your name in print, suddenly it is like the impact of a physical blow.—

Terry has been here for a visit of two days, she has just come home from Europe. I was so glad to see her, she was a great comfort to me. I hope that when your promised letter comes there will be something about October Fair. I should love to know how far along it is and whether you will come back to America to have it typed. I imagine that it will sell itself very well, even before people know how good it is. I wish that I could write only of happiness and happy events to you. You and your success are the happiest things I know and the only things to record. I am hoping every day for a letter and some word from you to make things brighter. I can't look into the future, for I want no future in which you are not.—I must stop before I make you angry again. But how can I ever make you know how I love you and how black is the cloud in which I am.

My letters must be so horrid for you to read, and I often think that maybe you do not read them. It seems to me three years since you have left. God bless you my dear[.] Good night.—Then, as all my soules bee, Emparadis'd in you in whom alone I understand and grow and see—[2] Aline

1. The article reads as follows: "'Look Homeward, Angel,' Thomas Wolfe's first novel, has received an unusual reception in England, where it is published by Heineman. According to the reports, 1,000 copies are being sold every four days. The reviews have been enthusiastic, The London Times going so far as to say, 'If Mr. Wolfe can be wasted, there is no hope for our day.' Mr. Wolfe is at present abroad on a Guggenheim scholarship. He is at work on a second novel, 'October Fair.'"

2. These lines from Donne's *A Valediction: Of My Name in the Window* are from those Wolfe selected as part of the dedication to Aline Bernstein for *Look Homeward, Angel.*

121. Armonk, N.Y. / Westchester Co. [Late September 1930]

My dear—

I hope that wherever you may be this note will reach you on your birthday or before it. I send it off in good season. My head is filled with wishes for your success, and my heart is filled to overflowing with love for you. Aline

This is a drop of blood from the middle finger of my right hand. I opened it with a needle.

122. LONDON / DECEMBER 22, 1930

I LOVE YOU DEARLY AND HAVE TRIED TO DO WHAT SEEMED BEST DONT TALK OF HARD YEARS NONE HARDER THAN THIS YOUR DENTISTS GOT PART OF MY MONEY FOR RUINOUS WORK AND I HAVE SENT FAMILY REST THEY ARE LIVING IN WANT AND MUST HAVE IT NOT FILTHY DENTISTS BUT MONEY NOTHING CAN ALWAYS MAKE IT IF GIVEN CHANCE TO WORK AND LIVE IN OWN COUNTRY YOUR FRIENDS HELPED.

1931–1932: The Final Break

Mrs. Bernstein's onslaught of letters and cables during his absence had driven Wolfe into a frenzy of desperation and despair. He attempted to answer her in January but was once more unable or unwilling to begin communications with her. He continued to write furiously, developing not only the character of Esther Jack but also characters suggested by Mrs. Bernstein's family, most notably her actor father. He also began developing the character of the semi-autobiographical figure, David Hawke, who was to appear several years later as "Monk" Webber in The Web and the Rock. *On 26 February, he sailed home aboard the* Europa *and arrived home on 4 March. Subsequently he settled in a basement apartment in Brooklyn, at 40 Veranda Place, to continue writing.*

When Mrs. Bernstein read of his return, she, already troubled by attacks of vertigo because of a circulatory disorder, became ill and had to be hospitalized. Wolfe was deeply disturbed by her illness and, although he refused at first to give her his address, was supportive during her convalescence. During the summer months, they met regularly on Thursdays. During these meetings, she began pouring out her childhood recollections to him, and in his absence, writing out sketches about her early years for him. The more she wrote, the more her own love of writing blossomed. Wolfe used these sketches for "The Good Child's River," his primary literary effort at that time.

Throughout the summer and fall, Wolfe became increasingly anxious about his inability to tie together the various pieces of writing he had begun. He became increasingly hostile to Mrs. Bernstein and her ever-constant declarations of devotion. His mother's visit in January provided the perfect opportunity for the final break with Mrs. Bernstein.

123. [New York, January 1931]
My dear—

I have written two letters to you and destroyed them. This—I love you with a great love, beyond your understanding. I try to stretch my own understanding to include the fact that you have abandoned me but it seems more than I can.—What [would] life be if Tom is false and bad to me— Aline

124. [London, January 1931]
Aline:

I got your note today. If you wrote me two letters and destroyed them, I understand that: I tried to write you this summer but could not—I had said everything a thousand times before. But for nine months now you have sent me first letters, then cables saying that you could not go on living, that I was killing you and was I ready to take the responsibility. I did not think you would carry out these threats and injure yourself, but I thought that they meant you were in the greatest distress and suffering, and I was always afraid that some terrible calamity might occur. I would get sick as I went for the mail—if there was no news it was bad. Then, after one of those terrible cables when I was afraid to pick up a paper for fear of reading of some tragedy, I read that you had made a great success in the theatre. As recently as the first of the year you sent me cables saying you were desperate, why had I deserted you, your pain was too great to bear, you could not go on living, everybody, your family included, knew how you loved me. Ten days later your sister wrote me and came to see me here in London. She said you had never been happier, healthier, more successful and contented in your life than this year. Another person, a man who is your own relative, told me at Christmas that he had seen you at one of the New York wild parties a few weeks before. Other people have told me about your new and old love affairs. Yet, for nine months, while you are rich, successful, and in full pursuit of sensuality, you write me letters and cables which have destroyed my work, my peace, and health. You have driven me from France to Switzerland to Germany to England, and now you are driving me from here. The horrible pain and suffering these messages have caused me is past belief—they have made me so ill I have vomited and had to stay in bed for two days.

125. New York / Doctors Hospital [March 1931]
My dear Tom—

I've been ill and suddenly read the news of your arrival in the paper. It knocked me flat and I am up here with 2 nurses. Apparently to love you as I do is an insanity—I am having a great fight in my self. The way I love you will never stop, but I know now that you will no longer have me nor hold me dear. It is impossible for me to cope with every day life for a little while. You know not what you do. I will try to go on without making any effort to see you, no matter what. But I want you to know that the love for you that burns in me is stronger than you seem to know.—There is one favor I am asking, will you let me see your book before it is published. I believe you owe me that. If you are in doubt ask Mr. Perkins and show him what

I have written you.—I have no doubt that you are doing what is best for yourself, and I trust that I may see the light to put myself aside for you. It seems to me that if only I could see you once or even hear you speak.—I am making a great effort to get myself together and get away from here next week and lose myself in some work. But your soul is within me. Aline

126. New York / March, 1931
Dear Aline:

I found your letter at the Harvard Club last night—it was the first news I had had about your illness; I called up the hospital at once and asked about you. Then I wrote this letter which I was going to send by a Western Union messenger, but it was too late, and I was excited, and I thought of our friend Abe Smith—I wanted him to bring it to you himself and to talk to you, and to tell you the things I have told him; we called up your doctor and he has promised to let Abe see you tonight. I have written this by way of explanation.

Now, about your letter: I want to say this first of all as a first answer to everything—Aline, I love you more dearly than anyone or anything in the world, I will love you all my life, and it will never change—there are many people in this world who hate life and love barrenness and they would mock at such a statement—but it is true, and the way I feel about you will never change. If your present trouble and illness is in any way due to me, I want to tell you that I would rather shed my own blood than cause you any pain. Your letters and cables to me abroad have caused me the most horrible pain and worry of my life. I did not answer them because I could not answer them—I tried to answer them, but I could not, I have said all I could say, by word and letter, thousands of times, and there was nothing more to say, and when I tried to write you, I could not; but if you have any doubt as to the way I felt I hope that you may someday talk to some of the people who saw me during that year abroad, and they will tell you I have told the truth. Then your sister came to see me in London in January, and she said you had never been healthier, happier, more full of joy and contentment and success in your life than you have been in this last year. I then asked your sister why, if this was true, you had sent me these terrible messages saying that you were desperate, and that I was responsible. Your sister then said that you were an emotional and impulsive woman who might think she believed a message like this during the few minutes it takes to send one, but that you then promptly forgot it, and were happy and full of health again. I thought if this was true it was the hardest thing I have been asked to believe about someone I loved as dearly as I love you—I mean, if you were well and happy, and sent me, a young man living alone in a foreign country among strangers, and trying to get on with my work, without much money or friends—messages like these, which wrecked all peace and calm in me, it was a bad thing for you, a rich, talented, beautiful and successful woman to do—but if you were in this distress, your sister was wrong, and I am sorry. You cabled me that everyone, including your family, knew you loved me, and of your trouble, but your sister denied knowing anything about this. Aline, I tell you this because I love you, and because this thing is fundamental—Everyone must be straight and honest and there must be no tricks, or lies, or concealments or evasions from anyone; that is what makes all the rotten trouble. I love you beyond anything in the world, and no matter how cruel and bad you think I have been, I have been all right: I have been driven into a frenzy by this thing, but I went away out of my own country and endured a horror of homesickness and loneliness for a year just to set this thing right;—and if we are both wise and strong and decent now it *will* be all right.

Aline, you must hate death and lies and poison in the people about you, and you must love life. You are beautiful and you love life more than anyone I have ever known. You are the most beautiful and glorious person I have ever known, and this is the person that must now speak, and act, and live. I have loved you and given the best years of my life to you—do not wantonly and cruelly try to destroy me now: no one can hurt me in myself. I am now good and strong, but they can hurt me by attacking me through something outside of me in which my love is fixed—this is the cheap little New York-gossip method, but it is not your method because you are a great woman. Aline, be my friend, as I am yours; love me dearly, as I love you; be sane and honest and strong, as I have tried to make myself alone in exile; and be beautiful and lovely and good as you alone on this whole earth can be. Aline, I have fought it out in blood and agony and loneliness and exile—and I am a young man, and if I do not work and create now, I will die. Aline, surely you, with your great wisdom, talent, beauty, and character can be as wise as I am about it—I need your help, and I need your friendship, and I need your love and belief—but the time of madness, darkness, passion is over, we can never relive that, we can never live through it again. Can you love me as I love you?—I cannot tell you how I love you but I know that the thought and meaning of you is like a bullet through my brain. The sneering life-hating part of the earth, the desolate and empty fools, deny and hate the possibility of such love, but desperse them and tell them that they lie—I will love you, by God, as long as I live, and it will never change. But *do not* misunderstand me, or try to break me with threats, or make me begin something that is ended—that is the way of madness and death, I will never yield, I will endure loneliness and physical death before I do.

Aline, do you understand what I am saying plainly to you here? Will you be my friend and love me as my friend? If so, tell your friends and tell your family and tell the earth without fear or evasion that you love me, and that I love you, but that we are not physical lovers. Let us no longer have any tricks or evasions, I am ashamed of nothing, and tricks and concealments drive me mad.

Finally, I want to say this: I could never write a word about you or about my love for you in print that was not full of that love I bear you—no matter what bitter things we have said, I remember what was glorious magnificent and lovely, and I remember all that was beautiful and grand in you: all of my hope now and for the future is that I can wreak out of pain, hunger, and love a living memorial for you: I can not think of other men, or reputation, I am living alone with little money, and have forgotten the literary world—but if ever I put down what is in my heart, what I have known and felt, and the glory and magnificence I have known through you—then men all over this earth will be moved by it, and will know that it is true. I shall never do anything that concerns you in any way, never write a word that may concern you, without your seeing it, and your decision in it will be in all ways final. I am an honest man; I have been through hell because of you. Now be a living strength and joy to me —be life, and not death—whether I ever see you again depends now on you, I ask only for what we two with all our goodness, strength, courage, and character can do. I have made myself brave and good —I lived alone in darkness and misery for a year, but I worked like hell, and I am proud of myself for doing it, for it took guts, and I would work when my fingers trembled so I could hardly hold the pencil. Now we must live, not die—the time of darkness and madness is over, I have done my part, now you must do yours: if you want ever to see me again you must be wise and good, and you are wise and good. I do not come to the hospital, for I am afraid it will excite you, I am living far away in the foreign quarter of Brooklyn, because it is quiet and cheap, but if you will be quiet and strong, as you are, and wanted someday to see me, then some day we can meet calmly and like loving friends before the world. Surely you must know and see and understand what I have written here—it is dashed down in a few minutes, but my heart is in it. As for me, I shall love you all the days of my life and when I die, if they cut me open they will find one name written on my brain and on my heart. It will be yours. I have spoken the living truth here, and I sign my name for anyone to see. Tom Wolfe

127. New York / Doctors Hospital [March 1931]
My Dear Tom—

I want to send you a word before leaving the hospital.—There can be no extravagant language between us. Even the word love cannot make my meaning, but know by now what it is. Your letter, and Abe, literally saved my life. It is hard to believe that that Jewish face could take on the light of heaven, but it did[,] for it was a symbol of you. I am making every effort to get well. If my legs hold out I'm going on the road with my show, Terry will look after me and I think it will help tide over the time. You are right when you say to wait a little while until we see each other. I'm glad Abe is typing the new book and I know it will be greater than the last. We will make a great friendship from this tie that binds us.—Unfortunately the nurse lost a telephone number Abe left with her. Will you let me know at Hotel Wyndham 42 N. 58th St. how to communicate with you, as I do not know how often you come to the [Harvard] Club.—I want to see you if you will, as soon as I come back. Still very tired.

Yours Aline

128. Brooklyn, N.Y. / March 29, 1931

DEAR ALINE HOPE THIS FINDS YOU COMPLETELY WELL AND SHOW SUCCESS WILL WRITE YOU TOMORROW OR MONDAY HAVE BEEN WORKING HARD WITH ABE GETTING STORY[1] READY TO SHOW PERKINS I MUST COME THROUGH NOW OR EVERYTHING IS LOST HELP ME BY BEING HEALTHY AND HAPPY AND MY DEAR FRIEND LOVE

TOM

1. The story referred to is "In the Park," which deals with Esther and her father and their first automobile ride through Central Park. Wolfe submitted this story to *Scribner's Magazine*. It was rejected, however, and was not published until June 1935 in *Harper's Bazaar*.

129. [New York, April 1931][1]
My Dear Tom:

. . . Dr. Taylor finds some trouble with my blood circulation, in spite of the fact that he is a gland specialist, and that is what causes these strange turns. This year it is worse because of my great sorrow and the stress of my feeling. It got so bad that I began to lose consciousness, I fainted dead in Carnegie Hall at a concert about 2 months ago, and once more while I was working on the stage. Also once last week, in a shop. About six weeks ago I began this trouble with my upper frontal sinus, and it is the most hellish pain, outside of disprized love, that I know. I was in bed about two weeks or so, and had gone out to work not more than 2 or three days, when I read that thing in the paper. The world went round in the opposite direction, and I was carted off to hospital. Dr. Taylor has known all year what was making me feel so dreadful. But this time, my heart nearly burst. If ever we talk together again, I will tell you about that day, or try to write you in detail about it.—This is enough. I will write you [ ] I still have to have these treatments for sinus, they hurt so terribly I can scarcely stand it and I am never without a headache unless I take medicine.—I do not understand what you mean when you said that Scribners were done with you. You have the best books in you that they ever published in their career, and the only object of my living will be to help you to get them out. I could go on writing more to you all day, which seldom happens, but I am afraid to weary you.—Despite all the world I love you and will never change, and if you can't understand it, it is because you will not. Let me now be your dear and loving friend. My mind is here and all I have is yours. Aline

1. I have omitted the first part of this letter, much of which was illegible. The final section is of great significance, since it explains the nature of Mrs. Bernstein's illness. For some time scholars believed that she had attempted suicide at this time, a theory that her letter disproves.

130. [Armonk, N.Y., April 1931]
Dear Tom—

I want you to know that I understand perfectly what you said to me on the telephone. What you want to say is that you no longer have sexual love for me. That is what I take it you mean when you say physical.—Now let me tell you this, that I no longer desire sexual love with you or any one on earth, but my love for you is physical so long as I long to be near you, to share some of your life, to sit beside you, to see you. My love for you cannot change at your command, any more than the sea stopped its tide for the king.[1] You are angry with me because I remain as I was while you have changed.—This is the reason I want to talk to you now, I want to see you in this new way, it is the only thing on earth can help me. You fill my mind, but only as Tom I have always known, Tom who said he would never change, at Chartres, in England where you cried one day when you thought I might leave you. Tom[,] of our life together I beg you to let me see you this new way. I cannot blame you for doing what you have done for yourself, but some things you could have spared me. I have never lived through any thing so horrible as reading in the newspaper that you were here. My life then reached a point where it was utterly unbearable, but you sent me a letter and message and pulled me back into something I do not understand. I believe that you are one of the greatest writers alive and I know you will go on to more success and always more beautiful writing. I think you do not yet know how to work, or rather that certain elements in your temperament are always making work difficult for you. I know so well what you need, and wish I could take out of my self all there is good and give it to you. But don't worry about your writing. Do you try to work on a schedule as you did before? I am sorry your people are in such a bad way.—We all seem to be this year, it is a disastrous year financially.—We try but cannot sell this place, no one seems to have money to buy it. It is far too expensive for us to run. We do all the house work, no servants now. I hope your mother has enough to live on. But all of this business is nothing. The stars have gone wrong in their courses. Life that I loved so has turned on me. Each day is a burning unit that I have to go through. I used to see such beautiful things all the time. My dear Tom I will try with all my might to make my self quiet to talk to you. There must be some way in life to meet, if only I could find some magic that would unite our love and friendship. I honestly thought we had it, but I find I was wrong. I tried to work last week but I was worn out. I'll try again tomorrow. I can't live through the days without. I seem to function more or less mechanically, the jobs I have are not hard but I have been ill a long time before this last part. I know this is a serious and difficult time for you. We have lived through hard times together. I hardly know if I have wisdom, as you say. I only know that when I follow my instinct it is right, and my feeling is very strong that we will do better to see each other. I will try with all my will to be quiet. You are woven into my soul. I must see you and talk to you in this new aspect. Surely you can spare a couple of hours for your friend. Take courage, it will be better so. God bless you[.] Aline

1. King Canute (c. 995–1035) commanded the sea to halt to prove his power.

131. BROOKLYN, N.Y. / APRIL 9, 1931

RETURNED WASHINGTON TONIGHT FOUND YOUR LETTER SAW MOTHER AND SISTER WASHINGTON MOTHER COMING HERE NEXT WEEK FOR FEW DAYS PERHAPS YOU TALK TO HER WILL HELP YOU ALL I CAN YOU MUST HELP ME HAD NOTHING TO DO WITH NAME IN PAPER WHEN I CAME BACK YOU SHOULD NOT BLAME ME YOUR LETTER FINE YOU MUST TRY TO LIVE UP TO IT TRUTH AND FACT YOU CAN NOT BLAME ME NOW FOR NOT BELIEVING EVERYTHING AT SIGHT YOU MUST SEE I HAVE TAKEN SOME LITTLE DOSES FROM YOU AT YOUR FRIENDS WE MUST GET THIS STRAIGHT FIRST IF YOU DO WHAT YOU SAY IN LETTER EVERYTHING WILL BE ALL RIGHT TIRED I MUST GET SOME REST TO THINK THINGS OVER YOU MUST PUT HYSTERIA AND COERSION ASIDE IT DOES IRREPARABLE HARM THINK WE CAN GET SOMEWHERE NOW I SEND YOU MY LOVE WHICH DOES NOT CHANGE

TOM

132. Armonk, N.Y. / May 1931

My Dear Tom.—

You nearly had me on your hands last night, something was wrong with the subway train, and I came to the Grand Central Station 2 minutes before train time. Fortunately I had a ticket, and just made it. When I arrived at White Plains station no car was there to meet me, I tried to raise the house on the telephone but no one heard. So a kind policeman routed out a taxi to take me home. Almost like the story.[1] I was terribly tired and excited, what you read to me of the book is the finest thing I have ever known.

The gardener had fallen asleep and didn't wake up till 6 A.M.—He was terribly cut up about it. What you read to me was so grand, so valuable so beautiful, that I feel my life is not lost if it can make the stuff for you to work with. I have so much more to tell you. You are writing a book that no one has approached, and I am telling you what no one has told before. I know that how I love you is beyond my own power to express.—I know that you are of the great people of the world,—and I know I am of the great people of the world, for not age time abuse nor scoriation of the heart can change my love. I can stand upon the heights with you, and I can bear all pain if I can serve you. There is no greater love than mine, married or unmarried, I defy you to match it.—Truth love constancy, play that upon your instrument and see what noble tunes come from it. Truth love betrayal and desertion make an ugly sound. My feet are in the right path. I walk towards you as into the sun. I can stand the terrible light of the sun in my eyes, if it is your light. When I see you again I must tell you what I think you have learned from me.—I am in my heart your eternal love, but as you wish it your friend and companion.

Aline
Scherezade

Tell your paramour that the present point of view of the young people is *too* tawlerant.

I am coming to you Thursday. I have to come in Saturday to a special meeting, but I think that is the time you set aside for someone else.

1. Wolfe makes use of this incident in chapter 49 of *The Web and the Rock*.

133. Armonk / May 30, 1931

With thee conversing I forget all time
All seasons and their change,—all please alike.
Sweet is the breath of morn, her rising sweet,
With charm of earliest birds; pleasant the sun
When first on this delightful earth he spreads

His orient beams on herbs true, fruit and flower,
Glistening with dew; fragrant the fertile earth
After soft showers; and sweet the coming on
Of grateful evening mild, then silent night
With this her solemn bird, and this fair moon.
And these the gems of heaven, her starry train.
But neither breath of morn when she ascends
With charm of earliest birds, or rising sun
On this delightful land, nor herb, fruit, flower,
Glistning with dew, nor fragrant showers.
Nor grateful evening mild, nor silent night
With this her solemn bird, nor walk by moon
Or glittering starlight, without thee is sweet.

Paradise Lost!
[Eve to Adam, Book IV, II, 639–56]

This is Decoration day, so I send you this beautiful decoration. There is nothing beautiful comes within my sight that I do not share with you. I went to White Plains this morning to see the parade, do you have one in Brooklyn? Spent the rest of the day trying to write my article. It is the hardest piece of work I ever attempted. I could write much, but not the sort of thing they want. It is not easy to write a personal story. I am enjoying the Trollop autobiography enormously. Wasn't his boyhood incredible.—Hasn't it been hot, I hope you haven't been too uncomfortable. The days on this sunny hill have been fierce, but the nights are cooler. I hate these holidays, the only place I can go to be alone is an attic. I fixed up for a work room, under the roof, and it is very warm. But I can look over the orchard and lake. Undoubtedly the pleasantest day in the country is Monday. When I come in Wednesday I will bring what I have written and maybe you will help me on the worst spots. I do need the money so badly I hope the heat hasn't held you up on your work. The more you tell me about it, the more wonderful it seems, and I feel now that some of it, however small, will rest upon me. I live with you constantly, and want nothing more in life than your companionship. You said to me last week, that you thought it might have been better if I had died last winter. Maybe so, for I do not want to burden you with myself. You are looking so wonderful, and seem happy with all your new friends and apparently you have plenty of people to love you. Your writing is growing and I know will be a great thing. I am filled with loving pride when you say I can be of help to you. My visit with you was lovely, next time I will cook again, if you say that is how I can prove my love. Meanwhile, when I cannot cook for you, think of me as your devoted loving friend. Aline

I left my brown silk handkerchief in your pajama pocket, that I was wearing. Please do not send to laundry.—

134. Armonk, N.Y. [June 1931]
Dear Tom:

I meant to ask you yesterday, did you cash Madeleine Boyd's check. If not I advise you to do so at once as she will no doubt draw it out for her own purpose. This has been done by unscrupulous people, and I hate to see you lose money. Possibly I am doing her an injustice, but you might as well be on the safe side. It seems cooler this morning. Yesterday was horrible, I worked on "He,"[1] until after seven, and took a 7:40 train home. The station and train were red hot, like a bake oven. My feet and legs hurt so that I felt I had waded in weariness, like mud. I felt as though I was pulling the train all the way to White Plains. It is so hard for me to travel this way every day. —I trust the indisposition in your tender place has been soothed by the zinc ointment. If you will keep it powdered and dry [in] this hot weather it will not trouble you. I love to hear your voice, and what can be better than having it come as a surprise in the night. I must have been in a very deep sleep and it took me a while to collect myself.—I love you so much Tom, but want nothing but the prize of your loving friendship. I want to establish no physical relation with you, and I want you to understand that. I do not want to lose you from my life. We can make so much that is fine together. I have asked at the Astor hotel if I can go into 218 W. 45th. They will let me know next week.—We will take a trip backwards and maybe find some ghosts. Maybe Nana and Daddy will be there and you can see if they fit [in]to what I have told you. Time backwards maybe is a dream. God bless you, I wish you could have more jolly times, but you will, and this hard time is making the way for it.—I am sure this book will be so beautiful, so grand, and what is more will be such a surprise and revelation to every body.—

Your dear old friend
Aline

1. A comedy by Alfred Savoir, which opened at the Guild Theatre on 21 September 1931 and ran for forty performances.

135. Armonk [N.Y., June 1931]
My dear Tom:

I am sorry that you think I tried to encroach upon your time. I really needed help with my writing, and thought you could spare me an hour as I have to send the article out to Philadelphia by the middle of the week. I worked very hard trying to paragraph it, but

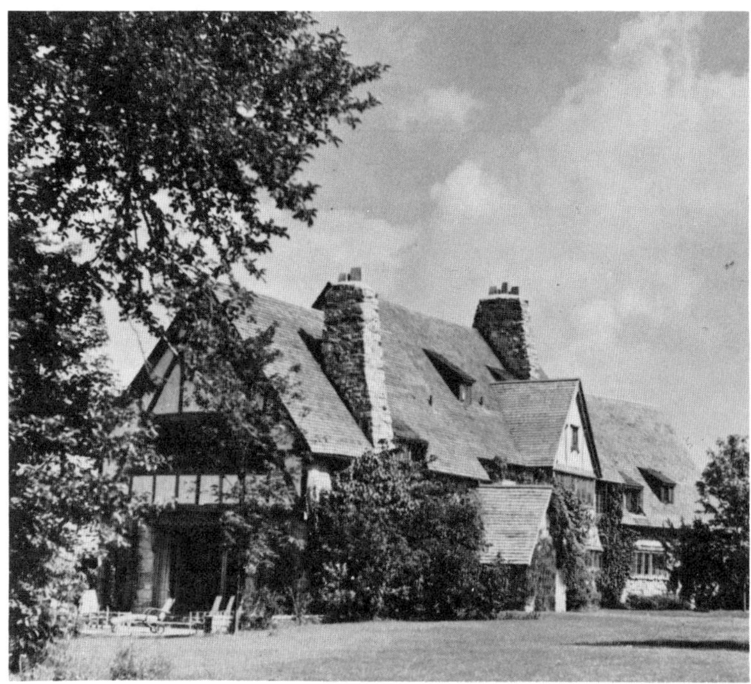

The house at Armonk, circa 1934 (Courtesy of Edla Cusick)

couldn't do it very well. I am taking it to White Plains this morning to be typed, and will send it with a note asking to have it run without any paragraphs, if they will, as that seems to be the only way I can do it myself. No doubt I will get it back with corrections. They have to have all their material well in advance. I am not trying to see you more than once a week, this was just a favor I was asking and I would rather send the stuff in this way than lose my long visit with you Thursday. Maybe they won't like it any way, but I hope so. I think it is interesting, and will bring a copy of it with me Thursday. You know I am your friend and I want the book to go on with no interruptions, and I hope you will go on as you seem to be doing. I shall urge you on, and worry you to work, and give you every thing there is within me. Now I will tell you something pleasant, yesterday about noon time my friend Mrs. Meyer asked me to come to see her, as she wanted me to listen to some music they think of using in the County Centre. I was introduced to the French Ambassador, Claudel[1] and his daughter. I was talking with M. Claudel, about his plays etc. and books in general, and he told me the finest book from America is *Look Homeward, Angel.* I swelled with pride, and I know it will make you feel good, I do not think you have reached the point of satiety—Isn't this accident to Eva too horrible.[2] I spent all Saturday at the hospital and will be over there every minute I can spare. Eva has been burned beyond recognition. On Saturday I could not find a trace left of her appearance. The doctors say her face will recover with practically no scars, but the hands are in serious condition. Miss Hutchinson was badly burned also, but not so bad as Eva, except for one hand which is horribly mutilated. Eva is in a constant state of extreme pain. The whole thing is too horrible. I am sick with it, Eva a woman always so ready with her mind and two poor hands to help every one.—I wish I was back again, a little girl in a cloud, but also I am glad I am this Aline, to know you and have your friendship.

I have remembered a tea party that Nana had,[3] to tell you about on Thursday. Maybe there will be vegetables to bring in, some little onions, any way. They will do instead of the pansies, pansies, for thoughts.

Yours
Aline

You tell me to be good, how can I be better than the best for you. You have conquered me entirely, but you cannot make me do one faithless thing, not with all your jealousy and all the boasting of your own promiscuity.

1. Paul Louis Charles Claudel (1868–1955) was the French ambassador to the United States from 1927 to 1933. A noted poet and playwright, he explored in his dramas the relationship between man, the universe, and the divine. His 1929 play, *Le Soulier de Satin (The Satin Slipper)* was considered by many to be his greatest play. In January 1931, he had presented the Legion of Honor Cross to Charles Lindbergh for his New York to Paris flight. He was an extremely popular diplomat.

2. On 13 June 1931, a water heater exploded at the home of Eva Le Gallienne. She was hospitalized until 12 July 1931.

3. This material later became chapter three of *The Journey Down*, "Nana's Party."

136. Armonk, N.Y. / Tuesday morning [June 1931]

Mr. & Mrs. Heinrich Heine of
Armonk are making beer, it
stinks, but they say it
will be good in 6 weeks.

My dear Tom—

I am glad you found the specs, thank you for letting me know. They cost $18 and I would have had to get a new pair as the ones I have are not much good. Hasn't the heat been fierce? I am thankful for this hill, although it was just as hot here, the sun beating and baking the house. Only I hate the hill because it is far from you. Even if I lived on the next block, I daresay you would keep me just as far.

Thank God it is cooler and you can work. I am trying to do over certain parts of my article to suit a gent named Shuler, on the Ladies H. J. It is getting me so nervous. I wish I had never started with it. I take hours to do a few sentences, because first I don't know how to write, second I have to think of how to please some one else. They wrote me a very agreeable letter, and said the article would be fine if I would do what they want, and they are anxious to get it soon, also not to be discouraged.[1] They want anecdotes of Viki Baum and Susan Glaspel,[2] I haven't any. I hope they read what I am as transcribed by my friend Thomas Wolfe. But he will not write what I am, I fear. I am coming on Thursday, I hope you will sleep some in the night, so we can talk all day and evening. I will tell you about when Daddy was a cop and lots of other things. I hope to bring some green peas from the garden. You are the inmost drop in my heart, I am your faithful and always loving but dethroned and deposed concubine,

Scheherezade Bernstein

I'll have to find a 1002nd tale. Egypt maybe.

1. Although Mrs. Bernstein worked on this article over most of the summer, there is no record that it was ever published.

2. Apparently Mrs. Bernstein had met both of these authors in her capacity as stage and costume designer. Vicki Baum (1888–1960) was the author of *Grand Hotel.* In 1931 she traveled from her native Australia to see the play performed and remained in America, writing scenarios for the movies. *Grand Hotel* was to become known as one of Mrs. Bernstein's scenic triumphs. Susan Glaspel was an American novelist and dramatist (1882–1948) and winner of the Pulitzer Prize in 1931 for her play *Alison's House,* supposedly loosely based upon the life of Emily Dickinson. Mrs. Bernstein designed both the scenery and costumes for this play.

137. [New York, August 1931][1]

I cannot sleep, this is what I think, there is nothing in life that cannot be made beautiful. Years ago I bought a jar on Allen street, because it had a good shape. I paid 65 cents for it. I scraped and polished it, and found it was made of copper with circles worked all round the bowl. It comes from somewhere in the east. I had it made into a lamp and every night when I put on the lights, its surface gives me back fires. It gives me this because I knew and recognized its beauty under the grime of its wandering. Last Saturday when it was so ghastly hot I went to market early, to White Plains. The roads here about are all being repaired. It was so hot the men worked with only pants, no shirts at all. One big man breaking stones [was] nearly as big as you are. I did not see his face, his back might almost have been yours, but nothing on God's earth would make me touch man's flesh that is not you. I thought if I put my hand upon a back, the tissue skin muscle is the same as yours, but nothing but you is you. So I am convinced that we are not nature's fools. We have soul, I review my life for you, and find I have come to a time so like the sadness of my childhood. I know now what I only feared then. If I show you this it is only so much stuff for you to use. You can't look into my heart. You have not the proper light to see. Time is not a dream, time has brought you to touch upon my life and now is moving you past in a widening arc. But what of time and me, I stay fixed in my circle like the planets.

Any plausible female will do for you, to spend the night or the day, or to lie with. Only Tom will do for me. Since you left me I passed through fire and hell, maybe before I am through even jealousy will be burned from me. Only loving pity will be left for you who do not see. You said I am maudlin, if that is what I am, you will live to see the day when you will stand ashamed at your use of such a word. It is true I am maudlin, only because of the strength of a love that confuses my mind. You would put upon my love the ugliness of your desertion and a fidelity, but that does not change my undying fire —Your book will be so great that possibly the sum of my entire life will be nothing compared to it. So something beautiful may come of this constant misery I live.

1. Both letter 137 and 138 contain neither salutation nor signature. They were written by Mrs. Bernstein on a small note tablet.

138. [New York, August 1931]

It pulls me from my sleep it takes me from every thing I want to do or think it must be the terrible thing I knew would happen some day, the thing that frightened me when I was a little girl. Tom is glad and proud that he doesn't care any more, he says he doesn't know why I feel so terrible—chemical change—it is you who go through a chemical change. I am constant, the same, unchanging and you cannot bear to see that, I must be a pain for you to look at with my constancy. I must be a horror so stale and ugly, when I cry. You are right about that; how can I learn to keep from crying. It must be such a bore, you said it makes you weary. There must be some way to stop myself. I feel badly that you have to suffer from the heat. I hate you to live in a place that is not large and fine, I wish you had this big place to live in, and all the country to look at. Tom is so great, but he loves to hurt me. He has no idea what I feel like; he says only men know other's feelings. That is false. You don't know my feelings. You laugh at me, you have no idea how you pierce me. How unpleasant for you to see me still in this love. But over the deep woman's love for Tom, I have the friend's love, your friend, your admirer and your helper. I will see the big book grow from the depths of your mind, I can see you look inward for it. If I could only talk to you as my thoughts run, but you always set up a barrier of distrust between us. That does not change me, it only keeps you from what is good. Where did you get this evil thing.—Horrible years keep my life apart from yours. No solution, no reason, only love dead on one side, your side, alive on my side. But friends love alive for both thank God. I set my will in my mind to make you work. Your satisfaction will come through that, only that, then rest for a while.[. . . .]

139. Armonk [N.Y.] September 5, 1931
My dear Tom—

Will it be alright if I visit with you this week Wednesday or Friday instead of Thursday. Theo has invited his two partners for dinner Thursday night, as that was the only time they could both come.[1] I am sure you will not mind, and I will telephone Tuesday when I come to town. This is Saturday, and after I come back from marketing I am going to Westport to have lunch and spend the rest of the day with Lilly. I am going to pickle a mackerel some day soon and bring it in to you for lunch, a toothsome and palatable morsel, it will shoot cool little silver wires to your brain, and stir up words to put on paper.—I have heard of a great collection of prints and photographs of New York City that belongs to the new Museum of the City of N.Y. I will inquire about them and arrange to have you see them. Maybe you will find a picture with Nana walking down the street, in her tight fitting princess dress. She used to say the dressmaker broke her thumbs smoothing out the wrinkles.—My cousin Grace Permezel is here for a visit. I found her here when I got home yesterday afternoon. She told me an awfully funny story about Aunt Gert, which I will tell you next visit. I am relieved about you now, a little, since I see you are set to work again. I know that in your inmost place you hold the spark of your genius. That will never go out. I wish you were happier in your life, you can be and must be. I wish I could contribute to it, but apparently it is not in the nature of things that I can, but I will stand beside you, above you, below you, to hold you to your work. You have now a great collection of my wishes, but you will only be [fulfilled] through your success and well being. Mr. Einstein's Time has caught me in a grip of steel, and you miss no chance to tighten the screws. But my soul is free to love you as I will.—I have been reading an interesting book called Men of Art by Thomas Craven.[2] It fixes what I have always said, that Art alone lies like a golden [thread?] through life. Everything else goes by. Of course he is concerned only with painting and sculpture, but we know writing and poetry. Your gold is added to the treasure that exists, and I see the wonderful store you have to contribute.—I have a desire to go to see pictures. I haven't been away for so long. But I will do nothing until the book is ready. I love you forever[.] Aline

1. Theodore Bernstein was a stockbroker in the firm of Hirsch, Lilienthal in New York. Wolfe was preoccupied during this period with discovering Mr. Bernstein's past history. Notebook entries in 1931 indicate that Wolfe had followed Bernstein's rise from clerk to broker to member of the firm.

2. Thomas Craven (1889–1969), noted art historian and newspaperman. *Men of Art* (1931) concentrates on painting in the Western world, from Giotto to contemporary French modernism and North American mural art.

140. New York / Hotel Elysee [November 1931]

Dear Tom:

I am sending my writing to you in two envelopes,[1] the paper was too thick to go in one, will you let me know if you receive them. These things are written entirely for you, and I trust you will not leave them strewn about for your landlady and visitors to see. I am sorry I did not do better with the last one, later I will write it again and put in things I did not have the heart to write. I am sure you will recognize everything, even the day itself. There are times now when I feel I cannot contain my love, it drives me wild. And all to no purpose, for with your help we can just as well find some peace and pleasure in each other. I have told you again and again that I do not wish the sexual relationship,—I signed a contract yesterday with Gilbert Miller for a play that opens in 2½ weeks. I will have to work like the devil to finish it. Will you let me know when we may dine together, I will make no engagements this week except Thursday, when we all go to the Goodman's. I prefer to come and cook dinner with you. I love you in every way, and if you will try to control your bitterness against me, we can still win out to a beautiful condition. You must work and fulfill your own self. Aline

I am taking material to work in the country. We have no visitors, but the two days in my own home are pleasant to me. I cook for the family.

1. Mrs. Bernstein sent Wolfe a sketch called "Love in Europe," which eventually became the second chapter of her book *The Journey Down*. She also included sketches about her Aunt Nana, later to be found in *An Actor's Daughter*, and the sketch "Mr. Froelich," which became part of her 1933 book, *Three Blue Suits*. Wolfe did not respond in any way to having received this material until the following winter.

141. New York / Hotel Elysee [December 1931]

Dear Tom:

I am happy and excited about your piece of writing.[1] If you feel you can make it better, all right, but I think it is magnificent the way it stands and I could wait no longer than Monday to give it to Mr. Perkins. I have pride in it beyond any pride I ever felt over my own work. I love and admire and revere your great gift. If only you would let me stand by you and help a little with your life and its turmoil. Why won't you take all that is fine I have to offer and not make needless agony. We could go beautifully and peacefully in friendship. I still smart under the way you hurt and insulted me, before the woman you had with you. It was unfair to all that is high within you. You rail against me and use the scourge of your tongue, when you yourself are guilty of such cruelty. You go to Harlem and go with a colored woman, you cannot hold faith with me. But I love and adore you, and the essence of my being is yours. If you will listen, to me some day, you will hear the voice of your friend and your angel.

Aline

1. Mrs. Bernstein is referring to Wolfe's short novel, "A Portrait of Bascom Hawke."

142. New York / Hotel Elysee [December 1931]

Dear Tom:

I telephoned Dr. Kramer today, and will go to see him. It seems that I had better not start treatments until I am finished this long lot of work I am doing, so that I may come in regularly. I have been feeling a lot better but today had a bad spell of pain for a few hours. I write every evening, and some day will have a long story for you. As things look now, I believe I will be in Washington for Christmas, no doubt working all day. Will you give me Mabel's address and telephone, I will invite her to the opening of the play.[1] Don't you think she will like that? I trust you will feel like dining with me some night before I go. You treat me as though I had been bad, offensive in some way. The way I love you is a precious and beautiful thing, and should not be treated so. How often in life do you think this occurs? An artist should be able to handle life as well as work.—I am out buying furniture curtains and props all day on my shows.—I leave about nine A.M. and get home around six.—What I would really like to do is to cook and sew for you. I had a dream I want to talk to you about. I can't find my [show?] lines *anywhere*. Bartlet or the Home book of verse, but I didn't make them up—Tom, I love you, and I wish you loved me.—Since you don't we have a sad tale, a miserable tragedy, for nothing else matters to me. Your 5 yr. marriage idea is alright, it is as long as you can hold out with someone of inferior attraction. I'd try three, say one yr. 6 mos.—I love you any way, and be damned to you. Aline

1. In his notebook entry for January 1, 1932, Wolfe wrote, "Mama is in Washington with Mabel—Aline went to see them both." *Notebook*, 2:569.

143. New York / Hotel Elysee / 60 East 54th Street [December 1931]
Dear Tom—

I do not understand your excitement about my calling you today, you told me last time we spoke together that it was alright, in fact you said a telephone conversation could be alright. Also I do not understand why you belabored me because Olin called you after I did. As to my answering my own telephone, that is quite natural as it is in my own room, and every one else happened to be in their own rooms, and it would be peculiar if other people came way across to answer my telephone, considering I was right there. As to your holiday dinners, I cooked Christmas dinner for you in 11th St. The following year you were on the steamer arriving in N. Y. The day before New Year's day, two years ago you ate with us at 270 Park Ave and last year you were abroad. Try not to be so cross with me, try to remember that I love you and you are putting me out of your life. As to promises, you promised to telephone me last week, and did not. Why can't you be friendly with me. I could be so jolly and happy and comfortable.—I can't fight the strange phantoms of your brain, I am strong in the knowledge of my faith to you, in you, and my love that nothing can turn back.— Aline

When Mrs. Bernstein called at the Brooklyn apartment while Mrs. Wolfe was there, a bitter fight ensued. Wolfe confronted Mrs. Bernstein about Mrs. Boyd's mishandling of his finances and blamed Mrs. Bernstein for having recommended her in the first place. Finally, Wolfe and his mother humiliated Mrs. Bernstein and put her bodily out of the apartment. This was to be the last direct encounter between the two for several years. Mrs. Bernstein had indeed been correct when she wrote at the end of her January 1932 letter to Wolfe, "I love you forever, and now we drop into a great unknown pool, seperate."

144. [New York, January 1932]
Dear Tom—

Here is still another letter to add to the collection. I did my best with Mrs. Boyd, and I believe you will get some results from her.[1] There were hard words between us, which rounded up my day nicely. My advice to you in the Boyd matter is this, when you have the money, write to her, a short note, and say you consider your business relations closed. She told me she wanted it to end, but may sing a different tune if it was a question of taking in percentage. We live in a crazy world, here it is a sin, in the eyes of ninety-nine people out of a hundred, that I love you. But money grabbing is not such a sin.

Speculating in real estate is noble and fitting, but love is wrong. It is not so wrong as hate. I had five one hundred dollar bills in my purse yesterday, which you asked me to bring you Monday morning. When I left you today, I took one out and threw it over the Brooklyn Bridge, I thought if they cannot understand how I love you, here is something to appease the Gods your people worship. I am sorry for what happened, and realize what a great mistake I made in coming over to see you, I hardly realized when I went that your mother would be there. I was so grieved and amazed with what had happened about your story, and worried about your state of mind, and afraid you would do something to destroy your script. My devotion to you is unalterable, all the platitudes in the world cannot turn my love into an ignoble thing. I will stand one against the world, and I must stand that way without even your hand. If ever you need a friend you need one now, and here you have thrown me out and allowed your mother to insult me, to call my love licentious. Her love for you was noble when she deprived you of your rest to make a few pennies. When she made you wear tight shoes to save the pennies for new ones. You all have learned that pennies, even grown to dollar size, can melt away, disappear even under the eyes of avarice. But love, my love, is great, radiant, lasting. It is not a sin, it is a glory, and those who say it is sin, are degrading themselves. I am ashamed that I lost control of my self, but I am not ashamed that I love you. You must admit it was a terrible ordeal for one to have the two of you battled against me, it would not have happened if we had been left alone. How can she know how close our love had been. But believe me she can understand $750 a week. Love is dirty, money is clean and beautiful. There's a measuring stick for you, and put a notch in it part way up, that's the place to throw out the friend, no use any more. That's the Asheville code, and look at the town, its the greatest cleanest most beautiful, happiest in all this broad land, its citizens prosper, its artists are encouraged and supported, its wives stick by its husbands, except in one instance where a wife walked out on her family in order to make herself some money. But that one doesn't count, because of its noble motive. The next four days I am going to throw a hundred dollar bill over the bridge into the river, just to show God I don't come from Asheville. I assure you we need the money, too. Tell me also, why are they so proud of Pride. The bible teaches otherwise.—Tom, I hope you will let me know the outcome of your talk with Perkins[,] also about Mrs. Boyd. You promised to let me know what you are going to do. Do you know it was only Monday that you were so sweet and friendly with me. I have tried for hours to see things as you would have me, but I cannot believe I have ruined your life and work. For while we were really together you wrote your beautiful book. I believe you have written a beautiful thing again, and all the Scribners alive or dead will not convince me otherwise. Again and again, I know you to be a great artist, and again I love you and will be your true friend despite your family and its ghosts. After you and your mother threw me into the street I still love you and I am faithful to the highest emotion a human being can know. I love you without hope, without hope even of any understanding from you, I love you knowing that my beautiful soul is twisted by your mouths, by the horrid cruel phrases of your mother and yourself. I was a fool to let you both torture me into losing my control. But I was bared to the quick, I have carried this pain of my rejected love since you went, and it is wearing down all of my resistance. It is useless to ask you for love or your favorite word friendship. Tom dear if only I could live backward from now on, to see where my fault with you has lain. I wish that some day there would enter your mind some sense of the value of what I give you, I wish for you every thing to make you happier. Aline

1. Early in January Wolfe received a letter from a German publisher alluding to a contract that had been sent to him one year earlier. Mrs. Boyd had sold the rights to *Look Homeward, Angel* and had kept the advance payment. According to Andrew Turnbull, Wolfe had confronted Mrs. Bernstein with this information in front of his mother, blaming her for having recommended Mrs. Boyd in the first place. Apparently she had called Mrs. Boyd and argued with her upon leaving Wolfe's apartment. Soon after, Wolfe fired Mrs. Boyd, after an emotional encounter with her in Maxwell Perkins's office.

145. [New York] Jan. 14 1932
Dear Tom:

I wrote a letter which I am sorry I mailed to you, but I was so filled with bitterness and hurt at you and your mother, and I am filled with disappointment in myself that I have not shown strength enough nor had the power to hold your love and friendship. One thing I know, I am not the evil person you both believe me to be, and you will live to learn how rare love is. I have literally given you my soul, and if I am not to be utterly destroyed I must take it back.

I maintain that neither you nor your mother have any understanding of my self, of the freedom I demand for my mind and my life. I will not be bound in thought nor behavior by any thing I do not choose my self. I have lived a fine life, I have held to the performance of my duties at home, and if I have not lived sexually with the man I married, it is no bodies' business but ours, certainly not your mother's. I have retained purity in the practice of my work, I have been an uncompromising artist in a world that is full of compromise and ugliness. When we met and loved each other, I gave you the whole strength and beauty of my free soul and free mind. I made a terrible mistake when I did not come to live with you at the time you asked me and the secrecy of our life was bad for us both. So far as I am concerned that has been the one blot upon my own behavior towards you. I seem to have failed to make upon you the impression of my reality. My love will never alter, even though yours has gone. I will always be your help and comfort when you need it. I have concluded that it is time we see each other no more. I have fought against this so long, and now I know I will have to withdraw myself the outgoing love which you are unable to take. I wish I could find an open place in your mind where I could lay all this I have written. I love you forever, and now we drop into a great unknown pool, seperate.— Aline

146. [New York, Winter 1932][1]

Here are a few questions I want you to help me to answer. I have a wonderful memory for anything that interests me[,] and for 40 or 50000 words I have made a woman called Esther Jacobs talk magnificently. But you have done your share in sinking the ship this last year or two—now try to do something to save it. Some of the questions below you can certainly answer and some you will be tempted to falsify in order to put yourself in a romantic and favorable light. —I say this because no woman who has ever put anything down in writing or print—that I know of—has ever been able to tell the truth about certain things: now if you come square with this you will glorify yourself forever, and you will be the crown and jewel of your sex. If you can't do this, *don't answer those questions* where you will be tempted to lie. But please go ahead and answer all the questions you can as well and truthfully as you can. Just write it out as simply as you can for me—your literary style is a damned sight better than mine judging from the effect anything you write me has on me—but just set this down as simply and plainly as possible—I know how you talk, every tone in your voice, etc.

1. You used to say "Nobody ever asks me what *goes on inside me when I design*—the thing that happens. It is the most beautiful and exciting thing but no one has ever tried to find out about it"—Well, what goes on, and what happens. Try to tell me something about it as simply and vividly as you can. What goes on, what happens, what do you see, what do you get out of it? (There's no reason why you shouldn't try to answer this one.)

2. There were many things and objects that interested and excited you: one was the window of a hardware store, another the elevated structure, another the instruments and materials you worked with —your T squares, slide-rules, etc.—Name as many more of these

objects as you can, also things that appeal to your senses—make it as full and rich as you can. You can answer this one.
3. Tell me something about clothes—I don't mean how they are made, but how you feel about them—people are like the clothes they wear, you say—give me concrete examples: i.e., the old women in Boston who had a thousand little ornaments, lace, plumes, head junk—what does it mean, why do they do it, what sort of people wear these things. Give me other examples, too,—men, women, young and old people. Tell me how you feel about theatre costume—no technical stuff, but why you think and feel Hamlet should wear this and Mercutio that. You can do this.
4. What was it like when you had that hard time in childbirth—W. End Avenue, hot as hell outside, and you kept saying "Who would fardels bear"—Try to remember it as well as you can, tell me about it. *You can do this.*
5. Describe the sensation of sexual intercourse and female orgasm as well as you can. Do this as honestly as you can or not at all—it reflects no discredit on you. But try to tell me if you can.
6. With how many different people in your entire life have you had sexual intercourse—counting everyone, even those you *were with only one time.* If you can't get at an exact number, give me an approximate number, if you can't do this, say so. But either answer the question truthfully or not at all, and don't think I'm trying to catch you up: I'll not condemn you or be bitter about this now, that's all over—but I want to find out things that few men ever find out. Now, be honest, be mum, and trust me to be your friend.
7. With how many men have you had protracted sex relations—I mean more than once, many times, over a period of months or years? What kind of men were they, how many were younger than you, and how much younger were they? I'm not trying to find out names—give me some idea what the men were like. How often would you see them, in what sort of places. How long had you been married before you started with the first of these men. Also, did you know two or more of them at the same time, did you have relations with two or more at the same time, during one affair, or when one affair was breaking up, etc. Again, be honest or mum.
8. Why did you paint these pictures that you used to have at your house? I mean the queer flowers, landscapes and designs. You told me you admire the work of Georgia O'Keefe—the flower painter (I think that's her name). Her flowers are often an expression of sexual desire. Were your flowers and pictures like that.
9. When you have sexual intercourse with one man do you ever think of another one, one you have also had s. i. with, or one you have de-

sired. Do you compare the respective physical merits of your lovers, or have you ever done this—the size of their genital organs, their ability to give you pleasure or "satisfaction," etc.
10. Do you ever masturbate now, and did you masturbate after your marriage when thinking of a lover, or when desiring someone?
11. I have a much clearer idea what your life was like when you were a child than after your marriage. You were married when you were 18, I think, and for the next twenty years or more, until I met you there are big dark spaces of mystery. You had two children during this time, your son was sick for a year or two, you went abroad several times—how many?—you painted, you worked at the Neighborhood Playhouse. Is your husband the father of both the children?—is he Edla's father?—had you begun to have lovers between the first and second child, how long after the birth of the child was it that you began a resumed sexual relations with lovers? You have told me that George Bellows[2] was your lover—for how long was he your lover? Why did he stop being your lover? Why did you love him to begin with? Did you feel grief when he died? What sort of man was he? Tell me why you thought he died because he could not be a great artist. Give me some idea of it. Why did you tell me the name of George Bellows and not the name of any other lovers? Was it because he was the most celebrated man who had ever been your lover? When you loved him were you promiscuous? Was he promiscuous? Were you unfaithful to each other?

How have you managed to lead this life for so many years without your husband suspecting it? Does your husband get a feeling of pride and satisfaction when your lover is a well known person? Are you ever alone with your husband, are you both afraid to be alone together, do you ever talk honestly about these things together? [. . . .]

1. Wolfe did not send this fragment to Mrs. Bernstein. The punctuation and capitalization in this letter is extremely irregular. To prevent a series of annoying corrections, therefore, the editor has chosen to leave this item uncorrected.

2. George Bellows (1882–1925) prominent landscape and portrait painter who met Mrs. Bernstein while both were students of Robert Henri at the New York School of Art. Bellows was handsome, charming, and gregarious, participating fully in the art life of the early twentieth century. It is understandable that Mrs. Bernstein would have been attracted to him.

147. [New York, Winter 1932]

Dear Aline:

I've been working hard—so hard that at night I haven't any strength for anything but sitting around in a kind of apathy and going at length for something to eat. The typist comes at two, sometimes at one, and works as long as I can hold out—until 6 or 7 or 8.

During the last three weeks I have written the complete story of a man's life[1]—50000 words—the most work I've ever done in so short a space—and alas! There are *ten* other men's lives yet to be written (Not so long as the first, I hope: I've already finished two of them)—and that is only a section of a book which itself will be only a section of an enormous book. I think my 50000 word story is very good and I also sold another one to Scribner's mag. which Perkins says is grand—it is called *The Web of Earth*[2]—isn't that a good title? It's about an old woman—she starts out to tell a little story and weaves it back and forth until she's told everything—it's a grand piece of work and there was never anything like it: they won't be able to laugh that one off. I think I may be all right now—I've got my self confidence back which I had lost completely—and I have never worked so hard in my life. I have been pretty close to complete ruination but I may pull out yet. I think I'll have a book of 200 or 300,000 words in 3 mos. more—if I do they may be able to publish by autumn.[3] But if I don't finish the book this year I'm done forever —I'll never be able to work again. Max has told me that if I do the job he will leave his work for six mos[.] and go all over the country with me in a Ford. He is also terribly tired and has had a bad year—his eldest daughter has been having fainting spells with convulsions and no one can find out what's wrong with her. Max is a grand man, the best I ever knew, and as complete an individual as ever lived.

I have not written you about your pieces before because I have been too tired at night to read them. I have read nothing. But tonight I did read them and they are very fine. The one about Nana's Party is grand and you ought to get it published.[4] So is the other one,[5] although I gather there is more to follow—*The Three Blue Suits*. I shall keep them and treasure them, or do whatever you want me to do with them, but I can't use them. I tried to write a piece about you once, but, as you know, it turned out to be no good. Maybe I'll try it again someday, but not for many years. I can't do it now, what I write about it seems to have no reality. I wrote a piece about my mother and Max said it is the best thing I have ever done, I did one about you and failed. My mother's visit here literally saved my life. I got back to the earth again, and to a sense of reality and having roots. That's what started me off on this great burst of work—Max says I'm having the biggest wave of creative activity he ever saw, and I hope to God nothing is done now to destroy it. From now on I shall put nothing on paper but what I have seen or known—my vision of life. That's all there is to write about. I guess that Froelich in your study is really your husband but you ought to tell about yourself too. You make Mrs. Froelich out to be a fat, bedamned Jewess and that certainly does not fit you very well. You make everything very vivid and wonderfully real, but Froelich seems to me to lead a horrible life. I think you have told the truth about it, but I can not understand anyone who is willing to live such a life. I understand a great deal—I understand almost every kind of horror—but I don't understand a life that has no roots, no earth, nothing you could get your teeth in. Froelich is a sensualist but he is not a good sensualist. His horrible mistress with her blonde hair and her $2000 bills that she thinks of when she lets him kiss her is not worth sleeping with—I can no longer get an erection over such a woman. The horrible apt house in which he lives on Beekman Place with the talking flunkies and the imported English butler is not good sensuality. I am an [sic] alert and I am also a sensualist, but if I wanted to be only a sensualist I could beat Froelich hands down. I would not live in an apt house, neither would I have an imported Eng Butler, neither would I be always "saturnally perfect" and fix my tie, neither would I sleep with a bitch with an enamelled face and a [?] inside—they, too, are not good to sleep with, they do not give satisfaction [. . . .]

1. Portion of "K 19" entitled "The Man on the Wheel," which further developed the fictional character of Robert Weaver.

2. "The Web of Earth" appeared in *Scribner's Magazine* in August.

3. Scribner's planned to publish "K 19" in the fall, but Perkins later changed his mind.

4. Mrs. Bernstein later published the material about Nana's party in *An Actor's Daughter* (New York: Alfred A. Knopf, 1941).

5. "Mr. Froelich," the sketch that Mrs. Bernstein had sent to Wolfe, was later published along with two other sketches, "Eugene," and "Herbert Wilson," as *Three Blue Suits* (New York: Equinox House, 1933).

148. New York / Hotel Elysee / March 22, 1932

Dear Tom:

I am so moved by anything connected with you that seeing the poster in Scribners' window[1] broke through the work I had built since our last meeting. I have used every bit of my strength to hold out against communicating with you. You had promised me so many times that you would let me hear from you, and that you would not again do what you did last year. I am glad that you are peaceful and able to write again, and will fulfill all the greatness within you, and all of the beauty and power of your writing. It is beyond my understanding to know how you could behave to me as you do, just as it is beyond you to understand the greatness and glory of my love for you. It will never stop, if only my heart would crack and end the torture of each day that I have to live in separation from you. I doubt if the sum of all your suffering can equal that of my life since you quarrelled with me this last time. I would have been so contented with some evidence of your friendship. It cannot cost you too much to write a note to me, even once in a great while. Will you do this for me. How can you find your own peace, built only on your betrayal of me, on the terrible pain of me that you loved so much. There must be some sane base for us both to rest. I am trying so hard to find reason in this, reason in love like mine for you, in the beauty I have found in life every day. Why have I been given my quick understanding if only to come to such a pass as this, ability to do and see all but the one great value of my life, to retain your loving friendship, to keep my soul close to yours.— Aline

1. Apparently Scribner's was advertising "A Portrait of Bascom Hawke," which appeared in *Scribner's Magazine* the following month.

149. Armonk, N.Y. [April 1932]

Dear Tom:

I was excited and happy for you when I read about your having the Scribner prize money.[1] It must be fine for you to feel that you can do as you please for a year at least, rest or work and help your family a little. I read it shortly after I mailed a letter to you yesterday. It is fine to get a prize, I never got one myself, it must make you feel good. But don't forget the things I wrote you yesterday, look at yourself well, and think of your writing not as a prize winner, but as pure and clear creation. I know, I have always told you that you would take your place among the greatest. But this is one of the few things I know for sure, an artist is no greater than himself. Your work is only a projection of yourself, you have the power to a great degree to put this thing forth.

I have a pencil, a sheet of paper on hand to write with, one upon the other, a heart filled with love, understanding and complete fidelity, and I cannot put that forth for you to see. I love you and feel pity for you. Aline

1. "A Portrait of Bascom Hawke" was published in *Scribner's Magazine* in April 1932 and tied for the Short Novel Prize with John Hermann's "The Big Short Trip." Wolfe and Hermann divided the $5,000 prize money. The judges of the contest were Burton Rascoe, William Soskin, and Edmund Wilson.

150. New York / Hotel Elysee [June 1932]

Dear Tom:

You said you would telephone me this week, and tell me what you mean to do. I want to assure you that if you stay here I will do nothing to disturb you. Will you be generous and let me know whether you are going on with your work and what you will do. I am going through such a special hell. I have tried to arrange to go to Russia, but at the last minute Terry cannot leave, and going alone is hard because of my deafness. I have a terrible battle to fight, for I carry with me not only the loss of your friendship, but the horrid knowledge of your hatred and disbelief. If there is any way in which I can prove my love and devotion to you, no matter what the means, will you tell me. The only thing I can do that gives me the slightest relief is to write. I know that I am no writer, but some day you may read what I have to say. Your success and your welfare are always foremost with me, and your companionship, even in these last months when you have hated me so, was the greatest delight my life has ever known. Please be generous in this also, remember how you have abused me and accused me of things that were not so, and make allowance for its effect on me emotionally. It would be easy for us each to make a perfect case against the other. You are a great person in your soul, and I love you forever. Aline

151. [New York, June 1932]
To
Theodore Bernstein, Jr.:[1]

—I have this to say to you: if you are a man with a shred of pride or decency left in you you will see to it that your mother no longer disgraces herself and her family by wilfully running after and doing the utmost in her power to wreck the life of someone twenty five years younger than she is. I here and now demand, having exhausted every other means long ago, that you see to it that your mother no longer tries to see me or communicate with me in any way[.]

1. Wolfe wrote this note to Theodore Bernstein, Mrs. Bernstein's son, on the back of her June 1932 letter, and apparently decided against sending it.

152. [New York] 11/16/32
My Dear Tom:

It is so long since I have written to you, I wrote for your birth day but did not send the letter, I sent you a telegram instead, and since then I decided how silly for me to go on sending you any communication at all; but for some time past I have felt the need more and more strong to send some word to you. I miss you terribly, I live with you every minute of my life, and I love you as always. How are you to know that unless I tell you, you have been so insensitive to any of my real love.—For a short time, not more than a few days in the early autumn, I knew peace, it was as though my love gathered itself together, separated from all the pain and terror of these two years, and rested within my centre, like a ball of crystal. But whatever that was, shattered itself, and there is no peace for me again. If I knew that you were better for your deed, I would be happier. I have abiding faith in you, and my faith in you as artist cannot be separated from my faith in you as a human being, for the two in my mind are one. I believe that some day you will redeem yourself to me, your friend. I have been working again but soon will be finished. We really live in the country, but stay a few days a week here in this hotel, as it is difficult to work from there. I have been writing a great deal myself, I have written about our life together as truthfully as lies within my knowledge. I trust that some day you will read it. I sent you a part I called Love in Europe, I sent it to Scribner's and trust you received it. Tom, the weight of the knowledge of your hatred weighs me way down. Some day if ever you feel changed, will you send me some word to help me. There is so much cruelty that is unnecessary, so much bitter pain in life that could be cleaned away. For a long time I have felt the tug of my soul toward you as though you must be ill or in trouble, and it has taken a great control for me not to attempt to find you. I never hear of you, and I don't know where you are, for all I know you may be wandering in Europe again.[1] I am not hysterical, nor suffering from any illness, I know only that I love you with undying and undefeated love. I am waiting to see your work, how much you have gained by your freedom from our separation.

I am your faithful and loving friend. Aline

1. On 1 August 1932, Wolfe had moved to 101 Columbia Heights, Brooklyn.

1933–1934: One-Sided Love

Although she had not received a single letter from him in 1932, Mrs. Bernstein continued writing to Wolfe in 1933, vowing her undying love. She implored him not to waste his talents on magazine pieces, intimating that, if they could be together once more, she could help him produce his new book as she had helped with Look Homeward, Angel. *The year 1933 proved important for Wolfe. In April he changed the title of his huge manuscript from "The October Fair" to "Of Time and the River," and by December he had delivered the massive, incomplete manuscript into Perkins's hands. Meanwhile Mrs. Bernstein's first book,* Three Blue Suits, *had been published in November.*

Although she continued busily with both her writing and her theatrical work, 1934 proved to be a harrowing year for Mrs. Bernstein. She was well into writing sketches for An Actor's Daughter, *one small portion of which she sent to Wolfe, and was also recording scenes depicting their love affair, which she would later publish as* The Journey Down. *Her daughter Edla, to whom she was devoted, was married in the spring. The excitement of the past several months was more than she could bear, and in the summer, after having been ill for some weeks, she attempted suicide by taking an overdose of sleeping pills. It is doubtful that Wolfe even knew at the time of this attempt. In November, shortly after she had left for the West Coast with her friend, Aline MacMahon, tragedy struck again when she received news that her daughter's young husband had died suddenly. Throughout these crises, Wolfe did not respond. He worked during the year on revisions of his forthcoming book. In addition, six more stories were published. By year's end, he was busily working on the concluding sections of his manuscript.*

153. Armonk, N.Y. / September 28, 1933

Dear Tom.—

I have lost track of how many years ago we met, and lunched together on your birthday, but I have not forgotten, and I will carry with me to my death the mark you left upon me, and my deep love for you. It will never lessen, I will never change. I do not know whether you have the slightest interest in me, but this time since we finally parted has been a terrible and wonderful time. I have conquered myself, my outer self, and still preserved the treasure of my love. I am not in constant pain, and I know now that I must never see you again, that my future companionship with you must be in my mind and heart. In spite of all the black and dreadful years I have spent, I realize the beautiful thing that happened to me, that you and the way I loved you has released such wonder in my whole being, I have seen through you, through your touch upon me, a world that was dormant before. Have you seen a boy release homing pigeons from a cage? One day coming to see you in Brooklyn I watched that on a roof, and thought then how like it was to my own state with you. I wish for your happiness and success. I wish that I understood better what came between to destroy whatever good I held for you. I think you can look down to the very centre of yourself, and find beneath the hate for me, just one drop left of pure love.—God bless you, God help you to use your genius. I thought once that I could. I have the utmost faith in your greatness, and I send you, on this birthday, my whole heart of love. Aline

I have no idea where you are, I hope this will reach you the right day.

Wolfe agonized over Mrs. Bernstein's letter. For days he worked on an answer to her, making three lengthy drafts in all. Finally, as before, he broke off, once more deciding not to respond. The letter he finally did write in December, in regard to the publication of her novella Three Blue Suits *was typewritten, formal, and tightly controlled.*

154. [New York] October, 1933[1]

Dear Aline:

I have tried to answer your birthday letter twice in the last few days, and I have failed to finish it each time, after writing many pages. There is something that I want to say to you now, but there is a great deal which, it seems to me, does not need to be said. It is two years since I have seen you or written to you, and I may never see you or write to you again, and it seems to me it is better now to try to say what is in my heart than to try to conceal it. You say you don't know how many years it is since we met. Well, I can tell you. It is eight. The day I met you in front of the library was my twenty fifth birthday and I am thirty three now. When I met you I was a boy with the faith, passion, pride, ignorance and good constitution of a boy. Now I am a man alone, first youth has gone, the boy's face and figure is gone, I am a gross, heavy figure of a man, and I am getting bald. When I met you I was lonely and obscure and penniless, and bitterly resolved to justify my life and make it prevail. Now, after eight years, I am in the same boat: I am lonely and obscure and penniless and

Thomas Wolfe with one of three boxes of manuscript for Of Time and the River *(From a copy in the North Carolina Collection, UNC Library, Chapel Hill)*

although I have lost the faith and hope of youth I have something left. I have despair—and men have managed to live by that before. —What I want to say to you especially is this: when I met you, you were the only person who had ever had faith in me, you were the only one who believed in me, and I think you were the only woman that ever loved me. My family did not think that I was any good or that I would ever amount to anything, and later out in the world I found that the work-shoppers, the Neighborhooders, the precious people put their faith in other precious people and had no word of comfort or belief for me. My life before I met you was lonely and full of bitter self doubt and agony. It was as solitary and desperate a youth as any man ever had. When I met you it was as if I had discovered a new world—although perhaps I didn't know it at the time. But for the first time in my life I found a world more fortunate and happy than any I had ever known and from another person I had love and warmth and joy.

It is this that I wanted to tell you now. I want you to know that now I know how to value it and that I will remember and treasure it as long as I live. I want to tell you also that, no matter what else you did, or what anguish, madness and despair I knew, that that woman who came to my room day after day for years was beyond every standard of comparison, the greatest, loveliest, and most beautiful woman I have ever known. And I also want to tell you that I now know I loved that woman with my life, that she is mixed into my blood, and that I shall love her forever. I want to tell you this because it seems there are some things that can now be said, and it would be shameful not to say them. Now you are an old woman and I am a middle aged man and what has happened was inevitable and right, but there are a thousand things I bitterly regret, and would undo them if I could. I did them when I was mad of mind and full of agony and desperation in my heart, and for all that was wrong and bad in what I did and said I would like you to know that I am sorry. And I hope you can find in your own heart now some charity to admit that there was wrong upon your side as well. I hope vanity and pride is not so strong in you that you can now see nothing but right in everything you did.—It was for this reason that I could not finish the two letters I began to you. Too many bitter thoughts and memories came back and I see no reason now for speaking them. It seems to me now that a stranger and an enemy [who] walked in the image of someone that I loved did these things. Aline, if you—I will not call her you but this stranger in your mask—could have known what my childhood and boyhood was like, how desperate and wretchedly lonely my life was, how I had to go on alone in a world whose people, even my own family, had no idea what I was or what I wished to do, and where I had noone to believe in me and no way of knowing whether I had any of the artist's power in me, or was just another of those wretched, yearning, impotent young people one sees everywhere, who try to make of art the basis of their life without talent, energy or creative power of any sort to see it through —if that stranger who looked like you could have known this I don't think even she could have found it in her to strike the coward traitor's blow at the heart of life as she did. At the very moment when after all that black and wretched time of self-doubt, groping, bewilderment, and despair I had for the first time won a position that promised me some sort of security, honor, dignity and esteem in life—some entrance into the world of brightness, warmth and fellowship other men have—that woman mad with vanity and pride treacherously and deliberately destroyed what I had gained.

But I think that even she would not have dared to do this thing had she known how much I needed that entrance into the warmth and fellowship of life, the artist's place of dignity and honor, the beautiful good life of work and certitude and high esteem. I do not think even that woman could have done as she did had she lived alone as I have, and known what loneliness and despair is like. It is all over now, but when I think of it the hideous viper thoughts and memories come back. I remember all the things that I would fight if I could—the memory of which is like weariness and hell—now, so that words do no good to tell about them. I remember all the cables, letters, threats of suicide, warnings of death, bitter reproaches, falsehoods, last words written from hospitals, taunts, jeers, and the constant purlings of a morbid, hounding, hideous and unwholesome hysteria—the attack that never let up when I was living abroad and trying to get something done and went on after I had got back here. Finally I remember the bitter letters I have had during the last two or three years here in Brooklyn—the letters telling me how bad and vile my life was, how none of my work was any good any more, and how people were talking and laughing at me behind my back, and how the reason for this decay in my life, my work, my fortunes, was because I had deserted the source of my inspiration, my guide, critic, and the one who was responsible for all good in me, and how nothing could come of my life and work now since I had done this.

—I am taking this letter up again after having carried it around for several days and I am resolved to finish it at this time and send it on to you.—During the last few days I have moved again—the tenth or eleventh place I have lived in since coming to New York ten years ago—but the best and happiest places were the garret on Eighth Street and the place on Eleventh Street.

—What is life and what is it for? Ten rooms, ten different places in ten years, in each of them all of the life, hunger, joy, magic, fury, pain and sorrow that the world can know. Ten years, ten rooms, ten thousand sheets of paper in each of them covered with ten million words that I have written. Waking, eating, sleeping, rushing out on the streets where a million people are swarming past, staring into their faces and listening to what they are saying, trying to find out where they are going with all this fury and what is driving them on forever and what it is they hope to find—and finding nothing but fury in the end. Is there nothing but fury in the world—fury uncoiling in the streets at morning, fury driving, mounting, savage, overwhelming fury in the streets at noon, fury in the driver's eyes and tortured faces of the people as they thrust, curse, jostle, jeer, threaten, call one another fools, liars, cheats, cowards, tricksters, thieves, fury in the lives of the poor, fury in the lives of millions of wretched, stinking, tempted, superstitious, ignorant and submissive people crowding into subways, running out again, swarming drearily at night towards the barren glitter of Broadway trying to regale their jaundiced lives on brutal and sterile pleasures that are lower than the pleasures of a dog, swarming around the place where there has been a brawl, a shooting, an accident, or a suicide, staring with their grey faces, and dead fascinated eyes at the blood of a young man out of work whose brains have exploded on the pavement after a 20 story jump as if you had shot his brains out of a compression hose, being thrust and forced back brutally by the police, shuffling, bustling, swarming around and then going on again to the brutal idiot repetitions of ten thousand days of fury.

And in the lives of the rich and fashionable is it not the same? Is it not even true that their lives instead of being better than the lives of the poor people since their lives do not know the ugly poverty and despair that give the lives of poor people a little tenacity and courage, and are empty, barren, and brutal as the lives of the poor without knowing grim reality? Look about you at the people that you know Aline, and tell me if this is not true? How many of them are better, wiser, greater people than they were ten years ago? Year in, year out, they drive furiously after a barren, feverish, and empty life which has all the glitter and shine of a thousand vanities, but which is really false, empty, sterile, and monotonous as hell. They go to see the latest plays and talk about them later round the dinner table. They read the latest books that have been praised by critics and rave about them, or say they "hate" them or "dislike" them, but really what they saw, read, heard that they loved, hated, or disliked they can not remember from one season to another. Now it is Joyce, now Proust, now Gertrude Stein, now D. H. Lawrence, Faulkner, Hemingway or someone else, now Picasso, Matisse, Rivera, Sert, or someone else, now plays

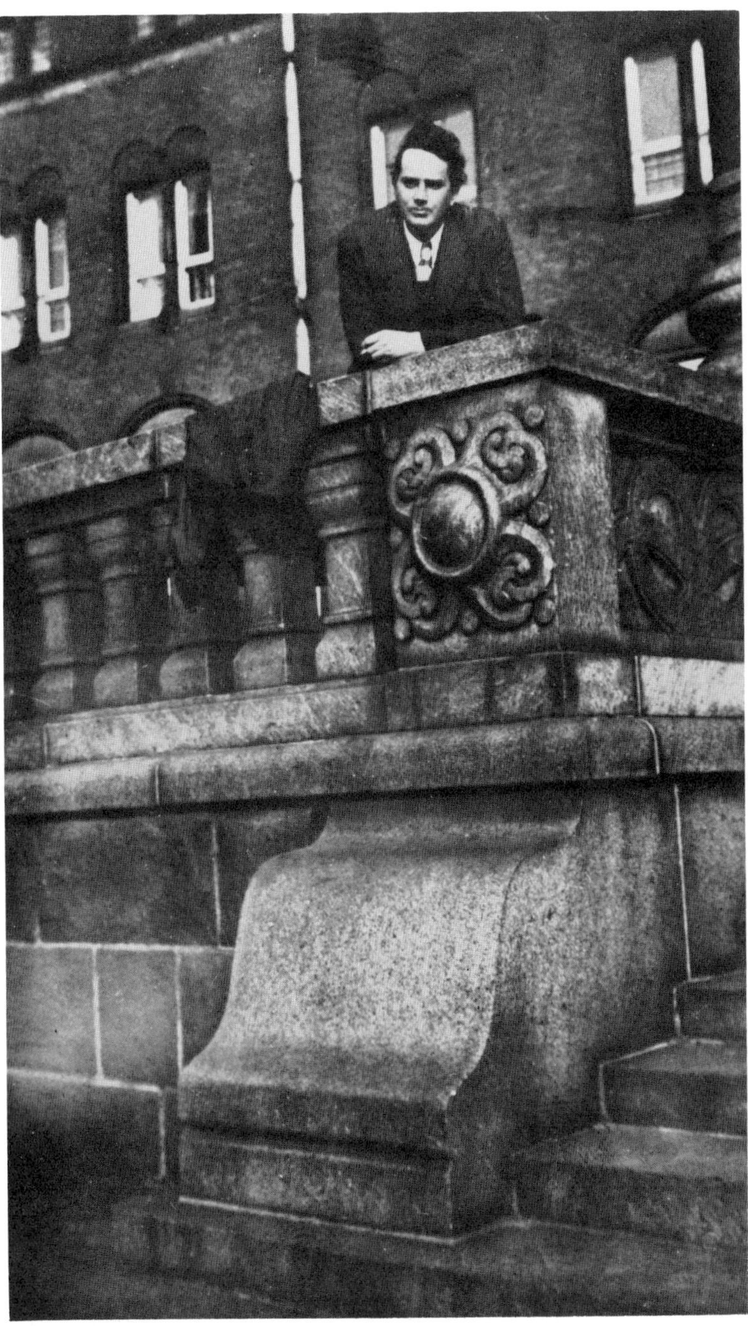

Thomas Wolfe traveling in Europe, June 1935 (From a copy in the North Carolina Collection, UNC Library, Chapel Hill)

about how gaily and lightly we frig in Vienna and now plays about we the people, now Alice in Wonderland, and now plays about lesbians and pederasts—

I will not answer this letter to you with bitter words, because it was not to revile you that I wrote it. I wrote it to tell you of the meaning of love and happiness I have when I think of the woman that I loved, who came to see me every day for years. I wrote it to tell you how much I now value her love and goodness, how bitterly I regret what I did that was wrong. But to get back to that woman that I loved I have to go around that ugly figure of that other woman—the stranger who came in and used every rotten and despicable means she knew to destroy me. Well, she got everything I had gained—reputation, security, the belief of people in my work—but she did not get me. I am 33 years old and I have nothing left, but I can begin again. My father, who was a stonecutter, began a new life when he was just my age, when it seemed to him that everything was lost: in that year he came up into the mountains, a stranger and an outcast, with nothing but ruin behind him—and he began a new life—the best part of his life—and his life was a strange and wonderful one. What he did I can do. There is just one person in the world today who believes I will ever come to anything. That person is Maxwell Perkins, but that man's belief means more to me now than anything on earth, and the knowledge that I have it far outweighs the disbelief of everyone else. In your letter you say you wish that you could help me, that you have faith in my "greatness" and my "genius" and that you pray for my success. If you do, you may have become again the great woman that I loved, but what you say belies everything you have said and done for four years, and men must live and prove themselves by deeds not works.—Aline the time for your helping me is past[.] There is nothing you have now that I want. It is not good to write me about the beautiful life you have achieved or about your flight of pigeons, threads of gold, and clear designs. It is no good for you to talk about "the great creature that lies dormant in me" and to hope that someday it will awaken and free itself from the chains that bind it. The woman who writes that [. . . .][2]

If I ever win release it will not be flights of pigeons or threads of gold or fine art theatre sentiments that do it. It will be because I am the son of a stonecutter and have known the same kind of fury, anguish, shame, drunkenness, regret, and suffering that my father knew. If there is any great creature dormant in me he will have to come out not because I am different from other men but because I am compounded of the same sweaty stinking clay of toil and agony as every mother's son of them—and the only difference is that I have more of that stinking sweaty clay [. . . .]

1. This is a final draft of a letter that apparently has not survived.
2. Page missing.

155. [New York] Gotham Hotel [November 1933]
Dear Tom.—

My stories, *Three Blue Suits*, have been published in a small book. I sent you the hand written manuscripts, so no doubt you have read them, and there is not much point in sending one of the books to you. Naturally, I have been much excited about the business, you know how deeply interested in life and character I am, and it seemed to me that I could never say my say with scenery and costumes alone. I trust that you will share my happiness in your mind, as I shared yours. Of course, my talent is slight, I will never be a writer, but this one small thing has been a triumph of self mastery.

I had your letter, and it moved me deeply as everything concerning you moves me, or anything associated with you, however small. When I see your name in print, a knife goes through me, and when I saw your handwriting, on the envelope, my heart leaped into my throat. You said good bye to me in the letter, but there is no goodbye between you and me. I love you forever, I know you and understand you, as no one in the world will ever do. Since we have separated, I have known loneliness, and I care literally about no other human being but my children.

You cried for love, you got it, and did not know what to do with it. It must have been something else you wanted, not love.—I still believe you are a great person, a great writer, and the only reason I care to live is to see you justify yourself. You must know by now that my feeling for you is not a matter of age, as you chose often to say, nor of the senses. If there is any thing divine, if there is God, my love for you comes from that great source. Do not understand by this that I will ever want to be with you again, I know it would be impossible. At times I long terribly to talk to you, and to hear you talk to me, and I hold imaginary conversations, with none of the anguish that was part of our real ones. I cook imaginary meals, and see you eating them. We live most of the year in the country, I can afford a cook only in the summer, and we do our own work. It is beautiful up there, and I hope we will be able to hold the house. I have grown to love the country, and only come down here when there is work to do. I have made a fine garden, and at last have my fill of flowers and I wish I could offer you a dish of my superb vegetables. I grow every thing, even ochra and brocoli. Brocoli is the most beautiful thing in the garden, far lovelier to look at than any flowers. This is a silly world, the silliest thing in it is that we cannot be friends, and another of the great silly things is that you will never admit the value of my dear love for you. But if you will not, you cannot. The tale of your family sounds unspeakably dreary, and I cannot see why they all should have such a frightful time of it. Is there not one of them who can take hold of life and live? You can, if you will. There is no need to be without some spark of delight, and you will never convince me that you need go without shirts and drawers and suits, if you want them. But you at least can enjoy life without, with your great gusto, so long as your belly is lined, and that I am sure you will always manage. I wish I could cook you one more of my marvelous meals. I have added to my repertory, and have plenty of time in Armonk to experiment. I make a dish with mushrooms, wild rice and cream that is as good as a Shakespeare sonnet.

I am writing a piece about the actor's daughter, which I will send you when it is finished. There is a great deal in it that I have told you about in those long lovely hours of our intimacy. I have not much time to write, as I have to earn my living. The theatre has been poor, but I am back designing on seventh Avenue again. There is not much money there either, but at least I can maintain my independence, and that means a great deal to me.—You are foolish, and what is more, you are untruthful when you say Maxwell Perkins is your only friend. I am your friend and always will be, and with your great qualities there is all the world for you to choose from—If you want my book, I will send you one, but I feel you hate every thing associated with me. Please do not, Tom, please love me in your soul, for I deserve it from you. I am not an old woman by a long sight, I look the same, my face is thinner, sharpened a little by these horrible years, but I am still nice looking, people even now tell me I am beautiful. You thought so, and would still, I am sure. And I still find wonderful things to look at, the daily pageant, buildings, sky, trees, people passing each other and moving together. I wish I could show it all to you. I love you forever— Aline

156. New York / 5 Montague Terrace / December 11, 1933

Thanks for your letter.[1] I have read your book and want to write you about it and congratulate you on its publication. I am sorry you did not send me a copy yourself or let me know that it was being published. Some news about its publication apparently came to Perkins some time ago, but he did not tell me about it for some reason, apparently because he thought it would worry me. I wish you or he had told me. The first news I had of it was last Sunday when I looked at the book columns of the New York Times and saw it listed there. I was tremendously excited about it and went out the first thing next day and bought a copy in Scribner's book-store, so you don't need to send me one now.

A party at the Costume Institute given by Irene Lewisohn, cutting cake; Aline MacMahon looking on; Aline Bernstein talking with Lee Simonson, circa 1935–36 (Courtesy of Edla Cusick)

I can understand your feeling of happiness and achievement in having published these stories and with all my heart I want to wish you the best and finest kind of success with them—the kind of success I believe you want yourself. As you know, I had the manuscript of two of your stories, the first and the last, which you sent to me a year and one-half ago, but I had never seen the second story, the one about Herbert Wilson, until I read the book.

I think that piece about Herbert Wilson is very fine. Of course, I know where the other two stories came from and whom you had in mind, but I will talk to you about them later. I don't know if Herbert Wilson has an actual counterpart in life as has Mr. Froelich or Eugene, or whether you got him from intuition and your observation of life, but I cannot tell you how moved I was by that story and how proud I am to know you could have done it. I am not a critic but a reader, and I believe in the reality of the character and the feeling in the story from beginning to end.

I think it is a very wonderful thing that a person who has never tried to write before can do something so true and good and full of pity. You made me live through the whole day with the man and understand all of his hope and expectancy in the morning when he saw that new and wonderful life opening up before him and then you made me feel how weariness and disappointment crept up on him as the day in the department store wore on; and finally, the cruel pity of his realization when he gets home at night and knows that his wife is dead and that there is no brave new world for him.

I thought all the other things in the story were fine: the cathedral and the shabby, dingy lives of the department store people and all the smells of food and sounds of people on the different landings of the tenement when he comes home. I think you can be proud of having written this story. As I say I am not a critic, but I do know that to get into the life of a little pavement cipher and make the reader feel and hope with him and understand him and finally feel that running pity at the loneliness and loss of life, is a rare and wonderful accomplishment and not often to be found in a piece of writing, even the writing of people with great reputations.

As you know, I was already familiar with your stories about Mr. Froelich and Eugene, because I read them over a year ago when you sent the manuscript to me. I didn't know then what you intended to do with this manuscript and thought you were sending it to me as a kind of letter to tell me something of yourself and the way you looked at life. The other night I took the book and compared the printed version of those two stories with the manuscript you had sent to me. I found that they were practically verbatim the same, with the exception of one or two minor changes. That also seems remarkable to me—that you could on your first attempt say what you wished to say so clearly and with so little revision. I wonder if you know what agony and heartbreak it costs many people when they write.

In your story about me, you picture me as a fellow who wants to look out the window dreamily, do a dozen things at once, and escape all the sweat and labor that goes into a piece of work—just to think his books out of his head, while he looks dreamily out of the window and have them magically appear on paper with no effort of his own. Is it not a strange and sorrowful fact in life that people can live together for years and love each other, and yet find out no more about each other than this? I wonder if you've ever understood what anguish writing contains and how hard I have worked. Didn't you ever see any of that during all the years you knew me? Well, it has been five times worse since then.

During the past four years, I have written over a million words and none of them, to my recollection[,] appeared magically on paper while I stared dreamily out of the window swilling down a drink of gin. Do you know how much writing a million words is? Well, it is a crate full of manuscript, six feet long and three feet deep, piled to the top, and it is more writing than most people ever do in the course of a life-time. Of those million words not over 150,000 have so far been published. A great deal more, and I hope and believe the best of it, may some day see the light of print, and there will be still more—how much I don't dare to think—which will be cut out, thrown away or destroyed.

I do not say that it is good—I only say that I have worked like hell, lived the life of a galley slave and done more hard work than anyone you know. And yet you picture me as a dreaming loafer. It seems to me that what people think and say of one another and the estimate the world puts on you and your life is usually just about as wrong as it can be—so wrong that if you stated just the opposite, you would usually come closer to the truth. You always said that you were the worker and that I had the inspiration without your capacity for work. Wouldn't it be funny if just the opposite were true?

I have never in my life been able to do a piece of writing that was so free from revision and the necessity to change, cut and rewrite as your own pages are. I don't know if you have ever seen one of my pages when I get through with it, or after I get through with the proofs—but it looks like a map of no man's land in Flanders. So again, you have done an extraordinary thing and shown at the beginning a clearness and certainty of purpose for which many of us would give our right eye.

But maybe, with all this talent and cleverness with which you have been so richly endowed by nature, you can still learn something from me—the final necessity of sweat and grinding effort. I think you have done some very fine writing in your stories about Mr. Froelich and Eugene, but I think you could have done better if you had worked harder. By work in an artist's life, I do not mean eight hours a day or fourteen hours a day, or all the different things you get accomplished, but I mean an integrity of purpose, a spiritual intensity, and a final expenditure of energy that most people in the world have no conception of.

I don't believe that you really think of your husband and me as you have portrayed us in these stories. I am sorry that you said some of the things you did, and that you have been willing to give out to the world these portraits as representing your own estimates of us. Perhaps it is false for the artist to picture people as being better than they are, but I think it is even more false to picture them as being worse and I do think that in your stories about Mr. Froelich and Eugene, you have sometimes been uncharitable and unjust, and that you could have shown them as better people than you make them without injuring the truth or quality of your writing.

I never got to know your husband very well and I don't suppose there was much love lost between us, but you did tell me many times that he had many fine and generous qualities—a generous devotion to his family and children and great liberality and affection for friends of the family and some of your own friends who were down on their luck, which he demonstrated time and time again by helping them. Don't you think since this is true, you could have this element in his character plain without injuring your story? You made him a leathery-hearted broker with hardly a spark of generous human affection left in him, and I think you were unfair in doing this.

I think you were also unfair in your story about me, and I want you to believe the truth of this, that I am sorry about this for your sake more than for my own. I hope and believe that through what you have done I can myself learn a valuable lesson. As you know, I have sometimes written pretty directly from my own experience—as directly as you did in your story about me—and now I admit, I want to be very careful in the future to be as fair and comprehensive in my understanding of people as I can be. I don't think that I have ever willfully and maliciously distorted what I believed and knew to be true about people, in order to satisfy a personal grudge. I think I have generally said what was true about people I put in books, and what everyone knew to be true, and have even understated facts about people which were discreditable to them, but even in doing this I am now conscious that I have sometimes been thoughtless of the distress and worry that something I have written may have caused certain people.

I don't believe that anything that is good and shows the integrity of the artist's spirit can do anyone any damage in the end, and of course, as I have found out in the last four years, the trouble and confusion comes from the difference between the artist's point of view, which is concerned with the general truth drawn from his personal experience, and the point of view of people which is, particularly if they are in your book, concerned with making personal identifications from something which is intended as a general truth.

That I am trying to tell you now I tell you not to criticize or condemn you for what you have done, but simply in the hope that it may help you when you next write something. I have learned things very slowly in my life, and I think you learn them very rapidly. But what I am going to tell you now I have learned in my whole life and know that it is true: it is right to have a passionate bias in everything you create. It is right to feel the indignation, the conviction, the certitude, the sense of conflict, with which it seems to me everyone who creates something must have, but I don't think you can stack the cards against someone in order to justify yourself without being yourself the loser for it. The temptation to do this carries with it its own punishment and if you try to set up dummy figures of your own instead of real people just for the satisfaction it gives you to knock the dummy figures down, your work will suffer for it in the end.

I think that what you did wrong in the story you wrote about me was to identify a living person so exactly, even to giving a kind of paraphrase for my name, describing habits of disorder and confusion in my life and giving other information about me which was so unmistakable that no one who knew me could fail to identify me, and then from this basis of fact, you proceeded to create a situation and a conflict which was false. You gave some of the facts, but the other facts which were vital to an understanding of the situation you suppressed, and in doing this, I think you have been the loser.

In your story, you make the man desert the woman and all the self-sacrificing love and devotion she has given him because someone suddenly suggested to him that he could get the Guggenheim fellowship and this sudden spur-of-the moment decision had nothing to do with the real situation. It gives you a false and easy means of justifying yourself in putting another person in a discreditable position, but of the real trouble which had already happened long [before] this thing you speak of, you say nothing. You say nothing of the bitter and complicated struggle which had been going on between two people for two years. You do not even mention the fact that at the time you write about the woman in the story is almost fifty years old and the man less than thirty. Perhaps you would say that this is a trifling and unimportant fact and has nothing to do with the truth of what you want to say, but I think few impartial and fair-minded people would agree with you on this score and I doubt very much if you yourself believe it in your own heart. You do not even mention the fact that the woman in the story is a woman of wealth and fashion, a married woman and the mother of grown children, and that she has never for a moment had any intention of leaving any of these things for the sake of this man who, she says, is now basely deserting her.

You do not mention the fact that the man has no money of his own, must live on what he can earn by teaching school and that such a thing as a Guggenheim fellowship with the chance it would give him to do the work he wants to do would be a God-send to him. Neither do you mention countless other vital and fundamental facts about the relations between these two people, and I think so long as you were going to write the story you should have done so,—that would have been a vastly more difficult thing to do, both as an artist and as a human being. It might even have been more painful for both of us, but you would have done a better, a more powerful piece of work.

I showed that story to only one person, Mr. Wheelock at Scribner's. He spoke warmly of the many fine things in it, of the skill and talent with which the appearance of the room, the meeting between the two people, etc. were presented, but in the end, he doubted the sincerity of the emotion. The situation described, the picture of self-abnegating love which the woman draws of herself, the declarations of incurable grief and intolerable suffering and the vows of eternal faithfulness, did not seem convincing to him, and I think the reason they were not convincing to him was because you shirked your task and stacked the cards against one of your two people in favor of the other one.

I have told you all this, not in the way of condemnation, but because I honestly want to give you what help I can, if it is worth anything to you and if you will take it. In all your stories you show the remarkably sharp accurate and cynical observation of your race—a quality which I must confess I never knew you had to such a degree, but which may be a most characteristic thing about you. I think, moreover, it is a quality which you can make use of with great asset to you if you use it in the right way. But you cannot use it upon other people and become a romantic sentimentalist when you think about yourself, so remember that all these fine gifts, valuable as they are, carry in them an explosive and destructive power against the person who uses them if he does not use them in the right way.

I agree with you that these stories are a triumph of self-mastery on your part and I assure you I am genuinely proud of you for some of the things you have done. I doubt if your own excitement about getting them published could have been any greater than my own. You say you hope I can share in your happiness about it. I assure you that I do with all my heart and in the best way, otherwise I could not have written you as I have. I want you to have from these stories and everything you do only the best and finest kind of success, the only kind worth having, the respect of fine people for fine work.

As for the other kind of success, the ugly, cheap and rotten kind, I hope and believe you have it in you to loathe and despise it with every atom of your life. What I am trying to tell you is that if these stories get pawed over and whispered about by wretched, verminous little people who want to poke around, pick out identities and gloat over whatever scandalous morsels they think they can pick out of them, I only hope for your sake that you won't allow yourself to be touched by it, and I can't believe you would be gratified at having the center of such attention, on account of the glamour you think it might give to you. If you would, I am sorry for you.

I don't know the names of all the people who have been associated with you in this enterprise, I only know the names of two of them which were told to me the other day for the first time at Scribner's; and I can only tell you plainly that I am sorry you achieved publication with the help of such people.

On the terrace of the house at Armonk; Alfred Knopf, left, Jules Romain, and Aline Bernstein, circa 1935–36 (Courtesy of Edla Cusick)

In your story, you call the people at Scribner's and Mr. Perkins a set of snobs. I have not found them so. I have found them thus far to be true friends of mine and among the best people I ever knew, although there are some very shabby, small people who might agree with you in your estimate. But if that kind of injury is in your mind, I don't believe it can do any real harm to any of us.

I think you will find people who would be glad to hear of any discreditable or malicious thing concerning me or of my failure, but even that does not bother me very much any more, and I still cannot believe you really had it in your heart to do me injury, even though other people that you know might want it.

I have just written you all this to hope that you will get the best from your success and happiness and not what is cheap and dirty and I hope I have made myself plain. I think you let resentment toward me get into your story and that it made you unfair, but I cannot and will not believe you were actively malicious. Finally, after saying all this I do want to tell you again how genuinely proud I am for all the fine and real and extraordinary writing you were able to do in this, your first piece of work. Noone will hope for your success more than I do, and noone will speak more warmly about it when I have the opportunity, although, because of its personal reference to me, with the chance of misunderstanding it, I will not speak about it as often and in the way I would like to, and I know that this is also right.

But I congratulate you again with all my heart and know you will believe me when I tell you I was as happy about your fine work as you are.

1. This is the only typewritten letter that Thomas Wolfe wrote to Aline Bernstein.

157. [New York] Gotham Hotel 12/12/33

Dear Tom—

Your letter is here, and I hardly need to say again how every word from you is like nothing else in life. I must at once correct a false impression, Mr. Froelich is not Theo, not by a long sight, but a combination of various men of the German Jewish banking circles I have known[,] not any one in particular, as much out of my own mind as Herbert Wilson. Theo is an entirely different character, a sweet fine good man, plenty of faults but at heart a warm and knowing person. Bert Wilson is a man I have seen for years at Altman's, the only knowledge I had of him is occasionally buying some silk there, his weary face always interested me.—I sent you the manuscript of that, but it must have got lost, as well as some others.—

Tom, I did not mean to picture you a dreamer, I know how terribly you work, I know your greatness of soul, I love you above and beyond anything in the world. No matter what you or Mr. Wheelock may say, about my words not being convincing, he knows nothing. Neither do you, I carry my love and grief with me like an incurable affliction[;] if you or Wheelock do not believe it, that is not my fault. The fact remains that it is here, in every cell of my mind and body. I have never asked another person whether he or she thought you loved me. The fact remains that my love is the same, never ending, and yours has ended and you deserted me and failed me. I am not resentful, I know that is the way life goes, but I never have [forgotten you], you are my constant companion, the glorious magnificent Tom I adore. I am sorry if what I said about the publishing seems wrong to you, but that is the impression you gave me yourself, or it is the impression my mind received from you. Every thing is so complicated, there are such infinite differences in impressions and feelings, and the way we say them. A few great poets can speak, Shakespeare and Keats and the wonderful early ones you used to read to me. I have tried to be true, *you* can speak but you, too, speak falsely, otherwise you could not write of me as you do. I will never be a writer, I work as hard at it as anyone else, only I sit and do the sentences in my mind before I put them down. I sit sometimes nearly an hour until I can get a sentence that looks right to me before I put it on paper, a page of handwriting sometimes will take me a day to do. So the work is awful for me, too. I don't want any cheap success, I've had enough. I hate my work in the theatre now, I'm awfully tired and I don't want any more. I hope no papers will notice these stories; but I hope some people will find some enjoyment in my sense of character. When you wrote of me in your story last summer,[1] I was hurt and excited, but I know you could not do other wise. What can I do, how can I say what I see? I have failed so terribly in the one burning wish of my soul, to keep your love and friendship. I have failed even in being able to serve you, any more. How can I find words good enough, pure enough to put together into some sense.

Your letter was good and generous, although mistaken in some things, I thank you for it. One more thing I want to say. The stories were sold through an agent, not personally; a magazine bought them first and published the Wilson one.

I get so angry when I think of all the stuff you have, and the millions of words, the most wonderful writing there is today. I wish I could be an invisible man and come and get them in order for you. I wish I could cut out any part of me that would help you, work for you, and throw the rest away. But every day I get up, pass the hours and go to bed, and living, I must live. My eyes look out, my mind sees, my hands are active and need an occupation, and I have to earn. The only thing I really like to do any more is work in the garden, arrange flowers and cook, but that does not buy my shoes, nor pay the bills.

Tom, I know your worth, your greatness and power. I love you, and respect you.

God bless you, Aline

Let us be friends, never again to see nor speak to each other, but friends, with love for each other. I have it in me, please you too, love me a little.

1. Mrs. Bernstein is referring to Wolfe's portrayal of her in the story "No Door."

158. [New York] Feb. 19, 1934

One other discovery I made the following year, in surroundings not so pleasant as my cousin's beautiful drawing room.

It was my first visit to the dentist. I had an ache in one of my teeth and Nana decided I had better have it seen to, so one Saturday morning our current housemaid and nurse girl named Betty took me to Dr. Goldsmiths. I was trembling with fright, my tooth was throbbing, I had heard such awful tales about dentists. In the outer office, where we sat waiting our turn, I was nauseated by the smell of medicine and my own fears. I clutched Betty's hand, she said maybe it did not have to come out, only filled; but that was no comfort, and I went into the dentist's chair like a murderer about to pay the final penalty. My heart beat way up in my ears, and I wondered how Dr. Goldsmith had it in him to smile, and his hair was so gold and curly too. The very cleanliness of everything was appalling. He arranged exquisite instruments on a frigid white tray, and pried open my mouth with the cleanest pair of hands I ever saw. It seemed the big pain came from a small hole in a back tooth, the tooth was good for another two years, so it did not have to come out: he would set the hairfine drill into the machine, and I have never been so frightened in my life except the time when I first realized that I was pregnant.

The pain of the drilling was terrible, I squirmed and wriggled; a moustache of cold sweat formed on my lip and I dug my nails into Betty's hand that I was holding tight. Dr. Goldsmith said for God's sake keep still, I can't do my work, and suddenly I knew that the pain was hurting nobody but myself. Here was a man, so close that I could feel the human warmth exuding from him, and he could not feel my pain; the tissue of his hand touched the stuff of my tooth, touched the very pain itself, and he could not feel it. I was an entity, a body so complete and so perfectly made that no one need know what I felt or thought if I did not choose to show it. I felt godhead in me and at once the tenseness of my muscles relaxed. I loosened Betty's hand, the strength from my extremities ran to one nugget in my centre, pierced by my own private pain. We cannot feel our brother's anguish, we literally cannot know it. We can see in sight, our own imagination, feel in our imagination, but it is forever our own sight, our own feeling. I loathe pain, I hate it, but through that hair fine drill on the nerve of my tooth I learned to know myself, to love myself, to regaiment my powers and to take my place in relation to the world. That seems like a large order for a little girl, I was conscious of this not in these adult words I am using now, but the fact pervaded my being as the body sensed the light of day.[1]

Dear Tom—

I have copied this short piece from something I am writing, it is called *An Actor's Daughter*. That first year you went away and did not write to me. I wrote out the story of my young life and later in anger I destroyed it. I showed you a few pages that were left. Now, I am trying to do it again, and it is far more difficult than the first time. The reason I am sending it to you is this.—I have been working hard, just finished two very unpleasant jobs. During the time, a few weeks ago, I was walking through 48th St. towards the east, about six o'clock or so, when I found myself walking directly behind you.

You were walking with a man, I don't know who; I quickened my own walk until I was close beside you. I touched your sleeve very lightly with my fingers, you did not know I was there. I wanted to call you, but I was afraid, I was afraid of what you would do, I was afraid you would be cruel and revile me, and I could not bear it, my wound is still open and sore. You went into the bar of the Chatham Hotel, and as you hesitated in your turning my fingers left your arm. Aren't you glad I did not speak? To think that you did not know I was there. It scarcely seemed possible to me.—Possibly we could not live unless we are so insensitive. When I finish this piece of writing I am going to send it to you, as it is for you that I have written it; but I will see that it is delivered to Scribner's by a messenger, I do not want it lost, as the other ones were, or did you ever receive them. I am terribly tired from my work this year, and most of my passion for it is gone. I want to write, I want to put down what I have experienced and learned. It was for you that I wrote first, to show you; so when I told you in a letter about the flock of pigeons I saw loosed from a cage, that is what I meant.—Writing is a thousand times harder than scene designing, a million times harder. I have to get it set in my head before I put it down, sometimes I will do only two paragraphs in an afternoon, that is why there is so little revision to be seen in my pages. Last night I read your story in Scribner's.[2] It is beautiful, no one can write like you. There is no one in the world like you, and I love you as ever. I do not know why, for you have not been worthy of it, you are not made of the stuff of constancy. Whatever stuff you are made of, is the stuff that quickens my being.—

God bless you Tom,
Aline

I miss you terribly, but when we were together how did I ever stand it. I have written down some of the scenes we lived through, they were incredible. If you saw it in print, would you believe that last scene when your mother was there?

1. Mrs. Bernstein had promised Wolfe in her letter of 16 December 1933 that she would send him the notes from what was later to become *The Journey Down*. This sketch was one of the few typewritten pieces that she sent to Wolfe.

2. In February 1934, "The Four Lost Men" was published in *Scribner's Magazine*.

159. New York / The Gotham [October 1934]

Dear Tom.—

Some years ago, when you went abroad on your Guggenheim fellowship, you gave me the manuscript of "Look Homeward, Angel."

I think it no more than just to tell you that I am sending it to Mr. Perkins, for him alone, with the stipulation that it will under no circumstances be given to you or any member of your family. He has stood by you as a loyal friend, as I have always had it in my heart to do; and although on your part, the relation between us has come to an end, on my part it never has, and never will so long as I breathe.

I loved you and always will, in spite of your unjust repudiation of me. For many years I have clung to simple faith in the old fashioned words of loyalty and truthfulness, and now realize how foolish I have been.

I am sick, returned from hospital a week ago, and I am obliged to give up all of my work for at least a year, and doubt if I will ever be able to return to it. I am also dead broke, and going to California for part of the winter. My good friend Aline MacMahon is treating me to every thing, even such clothing as I need. It is not easy for me to accept but I have to. We do not know what is becoming of the house, trying to sell it or rent it. So I thought it best to send your book to Mr. Perkins not knowing what might happen to it. I do not in the least mind the loss of my comfortable living, but the turnabout of my faith in you has really done me more harm than any physical or objective thing.

I still have faith in you as a writer, but you will achieve the beautiful thing only if you look deep into your heart for the truth. You just can't go wandering on putting musical words to paper. Too many people are doing that.—I leave about Nov. 15 and wish you luck, but I know luck means nothing. I am old and wise enough to have found that out.—

As always, devotedly yours
Aline

1935–1936: Friendship

On 2 March 1935, shortly before Of Time and the River *was published, Wolfe left for Europe. Before leaving he sent Mrs. Bernstein a prepublication copy of the book and marked for her the passage at the end in which Eugene first sees Esther aboard ship: "He turned, and saw her then, and so finding her, was lost, and so losing self, was found, and so seeing her, saw for a fading moment only the pleasant image of the woman that perhaps she was, and that life saw. He never knew: he only knew that from that moment his spirit was impaled upon the knife of love. . . ." Next to this passage he wrote the words "my dear."*

On the basis of this communication, a casual relationship was established between the two when Wolfe returned home at the end of June. She once more helped him to furnish yet another apartment, at 865 First Avenue, to which he moved in September 1935. But time and Wolfe's unquenchable desire for the isolation that he needed as a creative artist had triumphed. Mrs. Bernstein was now fifty-six years old. Although the love affair would continue to live on in the pages of both their works, in reality it was over. Two more major works by Wolfe, From Death to Morning, *a collection of his short stories, and* The Story of a Novel, *were published in 1936. No one could have foreseen that in merely two years time, Thomas Wolfe would be gone.*

160. [New York] The Gotham / Jan 21, 1936
Dear Tom:—

This is to acknowledge your gift to me of the written manuscript of "Look Homeward Angel." When you gave it to me, you loved me, and I have always held it as a treasure, an inestimable memento of the great and deep love we had for each other. I assure you that I have never considered it's marketable value, and I never will, while I live.

And while I live, I will never stop loving you, and hoping for your happiness and your success, and hoping that you will have kindliness and friendship for me in your heart. Aline

161. New York / The Gotham / April 3 1936
Dear Tom.—

I have already written twice to Mr. Perkins about the fact that you gave me the manuscript of "Look Homeward Angel." I did that

Thomas Wolfe at the home of Mabel Wolfe Wheaton, Asheville, North Carolina, 1937 (From a copy in the North Carolina Collection, UNC Library, Chapel Hill)

Aline Bernstein at work, late 1930s or early 1940s (Courtesy of Edla Cusick)

some time ago. You now want me to write to him to say that you gave it to me in repayment of any money that passed from me to you. That is not the truth. I understood at the time you gave it to me that it came as a gift of love and friendship, a token of the feeling you had for me at the time. I cannot regard it in any other light. But I will write this to you now, if it will ease your mind, you are under no indebtedness in money to me, none whatsoever, and never have been. Whatever happened when we were lovers, whatever you needed from me, was yours by right of the love I bore you, and that you bore me. Money was of no importance to me then beyond the benefits it could give us, and I hope that as long as I live it will never be the cause of any pain and misunderstanding between us. I assure you that it makes no difference to me. I do not mean to say that it is totally unimportant, for I know how necessary it is to eat and keep warm and be clothed. What I want to make clear is that money will never be a matter of contention between us. Can you get that through your head? Sometimes you are so stupid I could beat you. Or maybe you just like to make me angry. I am a fool to let you, but I love you a lot.

Now I hope you will stop fussing about the manuscript.

Fondly yours, Aline

162. Armonk, N.Y. [May 1936]

Dear Tom—

Your book came,[1] I am so happy to have it, I read it again and enjoyed it. Thank you, it is a fine addition to your works, and a unique piece of writing.

I will be in New York Monday and I will telephone to you in the morning. If you are not engaged, maybe we could dine together and I can take the train home. If you are busy Monday evening, I have to come in once more and we can make it another time. I always miss you and I always wish I could talk to you. I go so long without conversation up here that my voice sounds strange in my ears.

I had a thrill this week, the Metropolitan Opera called me to do the Dybbuk next year, if they do it. The Diamond Horseshoe is a teentsy weentsy bit afraid of the tallees (the prayer shawl,) the paes (the Jewish side curls,) the kaftan, (the Jewish cloak) and the Star of David. In other words, the Jewish subject. I went to a meeting, with some of your buddies from the social register, they seemed pleased and surprised that I did not have horns and a tail, that I drank my tea quietly, that my finger nails were clean, that I smelt sweet, and spoke English with no accent.—

I want to get back to work again. You sounded fine on the telephone, strong and full of work. I hope that all your unpleasant business is over. I have not called Mr. Perkins, too bashful, I hate to disturb him.—

Affectionately
Aline

I hope you are enjoying the Grunewald, before I sent it I looked at it hard and think I remember it all.

1. *The Story of a Novel* was published by Scribner's on 21 April 1936.

Mrs. Bernstein continued to write to Thomas Wolfe until 15 November 1936.

Aline Bernstein at the time of publication of An Actor's Daughter
(Courtesy of Edla Cusick)

Bibliography

Berg, A. Scott, *Max Perkins, Editor of Genius*. New York: E. P. Dutton, 1978.

Bernstein, Aline. *An Actor's Daughter*. New York: Alfred A. Knopf, 1941.

———. *The Journey Down*. New York: Alfred A. Knopf, 1938.

———. *Three Blue Suits*. New York: Equinox House, 1933.

Crowley, Alice Lewisohn. *The Neighborhood Playhouse*. New York: Theatre Arts Books, 1959.

Helburn, Theresa. *A Wayward Quest*. Boston: Little, Brown & Co., 1960.

Holman, C. Hugh. "The Dark, Ruined Helen of His Blood: Thomas Wolfe and the South." In *Thomas Wolfe: Three Decades of Criticism*, edited by Leslie A. Field, pp. 17–36. New York: New York University Press, 1968.

Kennedy, Richard S. *The Window of Memory: The Literary Career of Thomas Wolfe*. Chapel Hill: The University of North Carolina Press, 1962.

Langner, Lawrence. *The Magic Curtain*. New York: E. P. Dutton & Co., Inc., 1951.

Le Gallienne, Eva. *At 33*. New York: Longman's, Green and Company, 1934.

Mantle, Burns, ed. *The Best Plays of 1925–1936*. New York: Dodd, Mead and Company, 1926–37.

New York Times Directory of the Theatre. New York: Arno Press, 1973.

New York Times Theatre Reviews: 1920–1970. Vols. 1–3. New York: Arno Press, 1971.

Nowell, Elizabeth. *Thomas Wolfe: A Biography*. New York: Doubleday & Company, 1960.

Perkins, Maxwell. *Editor to Author: The Letters of Maxwell E. Perkins*. Edited by John Hall Wheelock. New York: Charles Scribner's Sons, 1950.

Reeves, Paschal. "Esther Jack as Muse." In *Thomas Wolfe: Three Decades of Criticism*, edited by Leslie A. Field, pp. 221–27. New York: New York University Press, 1968.

Rigdon, Walter, ed. *The Biographical Encyclopaedia and Who's Who of the American Theatre*. New York: James H. Heineman, 1966.

Rubin, Louis D., Jr. *Faraway Country: Writers of the Modern South.* Seattle: University of Washington Press, 1963.

Turnbull, Andrew. *Thomas Wolfe.* Charles Scribner's Sons, 1967.

Wolfe, Thomas. *The Hills Beyond.* New York: New American Library, 1941 (1935).

———. *Letters.* Edited by Elizabeth Nowell. New York: Charles Scribner's Sons, 1956 (1946).

———. *From Death to Morning.* New York: Charles Scribner's Sons, 1963 (1935).

———. *Look Homeward, Angel.* New York: Charles Scribner's Sons, 1929.

———. *Of Time and the River.* Vols. I & II. New York: Charles Scribner's Sons, 1971 (1935).

———. *The Notebooks of Thomas Wolfe.* Vols. I & II. Edited by Richard S. Kennedy and Paschal Reeves. Chapel Hill: The University of North Carolina Press, 1971.

———. *The Web and the Rock.* New York: New American Library, 1966 (1938).

———. *You Can't Go Home Again.* New York: Dell Publishing Company, 1960 (1939).

Index